THE PURITAN GENTRY
BESIEGED, 1650–1700

The latter half of the seventeenth century saw the Puritan families of England struggle to preserve the old values in an era of political and religious upheaval. Even nonconformist ministers were inclined to be pessimistic about the endurance of 'godliness' – Puritan attitudes and practices – among the upper classes at a time when moral standards were generally considered to be in decline.

Based on a wide-ranging study of family papers and other primary sources, *The Puritan Gentry Besieged* reveals that in many cases, Puritan county families were playing a double game: outwardly in communion with the Church, they often employed nonconformist chaplains and tutors and attended nonconformist meetings. Trevor Cliffe's study covers both the established and the 'nouveau riche' Puritan families. The book considers internal family divisions, marriage alliances, uses of wealth and links with the nonconformist interest at election time. It reveals that the situation was a good deal more complex than it appeared.

Following *The Puritan Gentry* (1984) and *Puritans in Conflict* (1988), *The Puritan Gentry Besieged* concludes Dr Cliffe's trilogy on the Puritan county families of the seventeenth century.

THE PURITAN GENTRY BESIEGED, 1650–1700

J. T. Cliffe

London and New York

First published 1993
by Routledge
11 New Fetter Lane, London EC4P 4EE

Simultaneously published in the USA and Canada
by Routledge Inc.
29 West 35th Street, New York, NY 10001

Typeset in 10/12pt Bembo by
Ponting–Green Publishing Services,
Chesham, Buckinghamshire
Printed in Great Britain by
T. J. Press (Padstow) Ltd, Padstow, Cornwall

British Library Cataloguing in Publication Data

A catalogue record for this book is available from the British Library

Library of Congress Cataloging in Publication Data
Cliffe, J. T. (John Trevor)
The Puritan gentry besieged, 1650–1700 / John Trevor Cliffe
p. cm.
Includes bibliographical references and index.
1. England–Social life and customs–17th century.
2. Puritans–England–History–17th century.
3. Gentry–England–History–17th century.
4. England–Religious life and customs.
I. Title.
DA440.C58 1993
942.06'08825–dc20 92–40813

ISBN 0–415–06727–8

... when the Rich are indeed Religious, and overcome their Temptations, as they may be supposed better than others, because their Conquest is greater, so they may do more good than others, because their Talents are more. But such (comparatively) are always few.

Any man that was for a Spiritual serious way of Worship (though he were for moderate Episcopacy and Liturgy), and that lived according to his Profession, was called commonly a Presbyterian, as formerly he was called a Puritan, unless he joyned himself to Independents, Anabaptists, or some other sect which might afford him a more odious Name.

Richard Baxter, Reliquiae Baxterianae, pp. 94, 278

CONTENTS

PREFACE

This is the final volume of a trilogy on the Puritan county families of the seventeenth century. *The Puritan Gentry* (1984) destroyed the myth that godliness was exclusively the preserve of 'the middling sort', though it also highlighted the conflict between religious impulses and class values. Along with other works which appeared about the same time *Puritans in Conflict* (1988) restored religion to its rightful place as one of the most potent factors in the Civil War.

The last chapter of *Puritans in Conflict* was entitled 'The Twilight of Godliness'. This was not intended to be a personal judgment but simply a reflection of the pessimistic views expressed by such contemporary commentators as Lucy Hutchinson and Richard Baxter. One of the main reasons why I embarked on this further phase of the study was that I was anxious to know what happened to the Puritan county families of 1642 during the half-century following the execution of Charles I and the establishment of a republic. Was their commitment to the cause of 'true religion' a purely temporary phenomenon which failed to survive the political developments of the turbulent years between 1648 and 1660 or the intellectual or social climate of Restoration England? In addition, I wanted to assess the impact, in religious terms, made by the new families which were entering the ranks of the country gentry. In the event this volume is mainly concerned with the gentry who occupied a position in the religious spectrum between conventional Anglicans (i.e. Anglicans who were fully satisfied with the ecclesiastical settlement of 1662) and Protestant separatists (i.e. sectaries who would have nothing to do with the established Church). Puritans had always been regarded as dissidents who wished to purify the Church from within and it had been the practice to draw a clear distinction between them and the separatists. In the latter part of the seventeenth century, however, there was a major new dimension which owed much to the purge of Puritan ministers in the early years of Charles II's reign. This was the tendency of persons of quality with godly inclinations to maintain close ties with nonconformist divines while remaining in communion with the Church of England.

ACKNOWLEDGEMENTS

I should like to record my grateful thanks to the following for permitting me to make use of material in manuscript collections: the Earl of Verulam (the Verulam (Gorhambury) MSS in the Hertfordshire County Record Office); Lord Cobbold (the Lytton MSS in the same record office); Lord Hazlerigg (the Hazlerigg MSS in the Leicestershire Record Office); Lord Lucas of Crudwell (the Lucas MSS in the Bedfordshire County Record Office); Sir Ralph Verney, Bart., KBE and the Claydon House Trustees (the Claydon House MSS (Letters) on microfilm in the Buckinghamshire Record Office); Mr J. T. L. Jervoise (the Jervoise of Herriard Park MSS in the Hampshire Record Office); the Trustees of the Firle Estate Settlement (the Knightley MSS in the Northamptonshire Record Office); the Trustees of the late Mrs C. Dryden (the Dryden (Canons Ashby) MSS in the same record office); the Director of Libraries and Information Services, Sheffield Central Libraries and Olive Countess Fitzwilliam's Wentworth Settlement Trustees (Wentworth Woodhouse Muniments, Bright Papers); the Trustees of Dr Williams's Library; the Bodleian Library; the City of Bristol Record Office; the Devon Record Office; the Guildhall Library, London; and the Lambeth Palace Library.

I should also like to express my appreciation of the help which I have received from the staffs of all libraries and record offices listed in the Bibliography.

Finally, the completion of this three-volume study is an appropriate occasion for me to acknowledge my indebtedness to Mr Andrew Wheatcroft of Routledge for his continuing support and encouragement over the last decade or so.

ABBREVIATIONS USED IN REFERENCES

A & O	Sir Charles Firth and R. S. Rait (eds), *The Acts and Ordinances of the Interregnum, 1642–1660*, 3 vols (1911)
Al.Cant.	Venn, J. and J. A. (eds), *Alumni Cantabrigienses. A Biographical List of all Known Students, Graduates and Holders of Office at the University of Cambridge, from the Earliest Times to 1751*, 4 vols (1922–7)
Al.Oxon.	J. Foster (ed.), *Alumni Oxonienses: the Members of the University of Oxford, 1500–1714*, 4 vols (1892)
BL	British Library
CJ	*Commons Journals*
Clarendon	*The History of the Rebellion and Civil Wars in England . . . by Edward, Earl of Clarendon*, ed. W. D. Macray, 6 vols (1888)
CR	A. G. Matthews, *Calamy Revised* (1934)
CSPDom.	*Calendar of State Papers Domestic*, Public Record Office
Clarendon State Papers	*Calendar of the Clarendon State Papers in the Bodleian Library*, ed. O. Ogle, W. H. Bliss, W. D. Macray and F. J. Routledge, 5 vols (1892–1970)
DNB	*Dictionary of National Biography*
Gordon	Alexander Gordon (ed.), *Freedom After Ejection* (1917)
HMC	Historical Manuscripts Commission
LJ	*Lords Journals*
Lyon Turner	G. Lyon Turner (ed.), *Original Records of Early Nonconformity under Persecution and Indulgence*, 3 vols (1911–14)
NM	Edmund Calamy, *The Nonconformist's Memorial*, ed. Samuel Palmer, 2 vols (1775)
PRO	Public Record Office
SPDom.	State Papers Domestic, Public Record Office
Thurloe State Papers	John Thurloe, *A Collection of the State Papers of John Thurloe*, 7 vols (1725)
VCH	*Victoria County History*

1

THE GODLY DIVIDED

During the summer of 1642, when the country was drifting into a civil war, most of the leading Puritan gentry decided to throw in their lot with Parliament, though with varying degrees of enthusiasm. Since they were generally men of conservative outlook it was not unlikely that their attachment to the cause of Parliament would be put under severe strain if it assumed a more radical character or if they felt that their own social and economic interests were threatened. When the Civil War was at its height Richard Knightley, a Puritan squire who was seated in Northamptonshire, complained in a letter to Sir John Dryden, who was one of the knights of the shire for that county, about the taxes he was having to pay for the support of parliamentary garrisons in the neighbourhood and expressed the hope that the war would soon be over:

> god send us peace or else we shalbe all in the same condition
> ... it is a mercie that we have here a very subsistence left us,
> and god knowes how longe we shall thus doe, without it
> please god to put an end to these differences we may expect
> worser times.

For Knightley the issues at stake, which were often succinctly described by well-to-do parliamentarians as 'liberty and religion', had ceased to be matters of prime importance.[1] As time went on more and more of these wealthy squires came round to the view that the paramount need was to conclude a treaty with the king which (they hoped) would bring about the restoration of order and stability. By December 1648 many Puritan MPs were so desperately anxious to secure his agreement to a constitutional settlement that they were prepared to forgo the kind of religious

1

safeguards which they would formerly have considered essential.[2] Unfortunately for them the New Model Army had different ideas.

Among the Puritan county families with their mansions and extensive landed possessions there were relatively few political radicals. Sir John Bourchier, who signed the king's death-warrant, was convinced that the act of regicide had been in accordance with God's will, though his involvement may not have been solely the product of religious fervour. Strafford had written of him that

> he Comes of a madd kindred, his father haveing many yeares lived and dyed a lunitick. This Gentleman generally observed to inherit a frenzy Constitution from his parent And to be more then halfe madd allready.

Before the time of the Civil War Sir John had been one of the king's most refractory subjects and his unruly conduct had cost him a substantial fine and a term of imprisonment.[3] John Hutchinson's political views were much more extreme than those of his father, Sir Thomas, who had been a cautious and inactive parliamentarian. According to his wife, he concluded, after seeking God's guidance, that it was his duty to sign the king's death-warrant since he could not refuse to do so without betraying 'the people of God' who had taken up arms for Parliament. In 1659 a royalist observed that he would oppose anything tending to monarchy.[4] There were other republican MPs who either chose to distance themselves from the proceedings against the king or withdrew before the final verdict was pronounced. Sir Henry Vane recounted in the course of a parliamentary speech delivered in 1659 that he had absented himself during the king's trial 'out of a tenderness of blood' but went on to say that 'all power being thus in the people originally, I myself was afterward in the business'.[5] Sir James Harrington shared Vane's belief in the imminence of the millenium when Jesus Christ would personally reign over his saints on earth. Viewed from this perspective the abolition of the Stuart monarchy may well have appeared not only necessary but inevitable. On the other hand, Harrington subsequently claimed that he had initially refused to sit in judgement on the king and that he had only changed his mind when threatened with a heavy fine.[6] In retrospect Sir Arthur Hesilrige saw the king's execution and the other revolutionary events which had taken place as the working of God's will. The Long Parliament, he maintained, had been 'a glorious Parliament for pulling down'; and in his opinion 'whatever we pulled down was good and necessary to be pulled down'.[7] Sir Gilbert Pickering was described by a contemporary as 'a knight of the old stamp' who had played an important part 'in the change of the government from kingly to that of a commonwealth'.[8] Sir Thomas Wroth told his fellow MPs in January 1648 that any form of government was preferable to a monarchy. As late as 1659 he was arguing that 'If we find kings destructive to the nation, we may lay them aside'.[9] Another Somerset landowner, John Pyne, helped to organise a county petition calling for the king to be brought to justice and would later emerge as a committed republican.[10]

Alongside the radicals in the Rump Parliament there were a considerable number of MPs of more moderate outlook. Lucy Hutchinson, the wife of John Hutchinson, writes that the members consisted of men who were either of the Independent faction 'or of none at all, but look'd upon themselves as call'd out to manage a publick trust for their country'.[11] Some moderates like Sir William Armyne and Sir William Masham sat on the republican Council of State; others remained more politically detached.[12] Alexander Popham, who was one of the wealthiest landowners in England, was gradually won over to the royalist cause, though he was reluctant to become too deeply committed.[13] Sir Thomas Jervoise's decision to stay on at Westminster may have owed much to his hopes of obtaining compensation for the losses which he had sustained during the Civil War. In July 1649, a petition which he had submitted was referred to a committee for further consideration; and in September it was agreed that he should receive the sum of £9,000 out of the sequestered estate of the Marquess of Worcester.[14] Bulstrode Whitelocke, who thought it expedient to retire to his country seat during the trial of the king, continued to serve as one of the Lords Commissioners of the Great Seal until 1655 when he was made a Treasury Commissioner. When taking up the first of these appointments (he tells us) he suffered an immediate loss of income: the profits did not amount to above £1,500 a year whereas his legal practice (which he had been forced to abandon) had brought in nearly £2,000 a year. Whitelocke prided himself on acting in accordance with his own judgement and conscience rather than the dictates of a party or faction. His contemporaries, however, were inclined to take a more cynical view of his conduct: among other things, he was described as a man who 'complyes for his own interest' and who was 'guided more by policy than by conscience'.[15]

3

In the course of time a number of MPs who had stayed away after Pride's Purge sought permission to return. Sir Thomas Wodehouse and Richard Norton were readmitted towards the end of 1651 and Sir John Dryden in April 1652.[16] According to a verse chronicle relating to the Wodehouse family, Sir Thomas had been so shocked by the execution of the king that it shortened his life. This 'hellish act', we are told,

> So smote his soul, that he ne'er joyed good day
> Here-hence.[17]

Neither Wodehouse nor Dryden was particularly active in public affairs during the Interregnum but Norton became a member of the Council of State in November 1652. Colonel Norton, as he was usually styled, had once been branded by a royalist newspaper as 'the great incendiary' of Hampshire where he had large estates. He was on close terms with Cromwell who referred to him affectionately as 'idle Dick Norton'. He appears, however, to have viewed the political infighting at Westminster with a certain degree of detachment: in March 1648, for example, he was writing to a friend that 'you cannot be ignorant of the parties and divisions that are amongst them'. In May 1651 he had been questioned by the Council of State following an allegation that he was ready to take up arms on behalf of the king, but nothing had been proved against him.[18]

Whether radicals or moderates, the Puritan squires who sat in the Rump had remained firmly committed to the cause of Parliament throughout the Civil War. In matters of religion there was less than complete unanimity. At one extreme, Sir Henry Vane held views of an intensely personal nature which many of his contemporaries regarded as bizarre and even dangerous. In Richard Baxter's view he was one of those who were primarily responsible for the break-up of the godly party since he had argued strongly for a universal liberty of conscience and had taught his adherents 'to revile the Ministry, calling them ordinarily Blackcoats, Priests and other Names which then savoured of Reproach'.[19] At the other extreme there was John Gurdon who favoured a Presbyterian system of church government.[20] In the main, however, the Rumper MPs were well disposed towards the cause of Independency, preferring at least some measure of toleration to what they regarded as the oppressive uniformity of Presbyterianism. Yet this liberal attitude had its limits: the wealthier members in particular were alarmed by the activities of sects which not only promoted novelty in religion but challenged the existing social order. In the first Parliament of the Protectorate Sir Gilbert Pickering, Sir William Strickland, Sir Thomas Wroth and Bulstrode Whitelocke all expressed concern about the subversive ideas which the Quakers were said to be propagating. 'Quakerism', lamented Pickering, 'is as infectious as the plague' while Wroth declared that the Quakers were 'a very numerous party and ought to be taken a course withal speedily'.[21]

The Presbyterians, in the sense that the term was commonly used in the 1650s, primarily consisted of noblemen, gentry, ministers and members of the urban middle classes who had appeared on the side of Parliament during the Civil War but had subsequently become disenchanted. Clarendon was in no doubt that there was a Presbyterian cast of mind which was inherently cautious and conservative; indeed he even went so far as to portray Thomas Lord Fairfax as a man who was possessed of a 'drowsy, dull, presbyterian humour'.[22] Many of the Puritan squires who were regarded as Presbyterians had been secluded from the Commons as a result of Pride's Purge or had chosen to absent themselves in a show of solidarity.[23] The military coup of December 1648 had abruptly ended an increasingly bitter conflict within the Long Parliament in which the Presbyterian MPs had been pursuing three main goals: a political settlement which preserved the monarchy while laying down constitutional safeguards; the disbandment of the New Model Army; and a godly religious settlement which was firmly based on the principle of uniformity in matters of doctrine, worship and organisation.[24] This did not mean, however, that the Presbyterians were a spent force in the country at large. Writing from his Somerset manorhouse in December 1649, John Pyne observed that 'the old deceitful interest under the notion of the Presbyterian party begins to rejoice and practise their old designs'.[25]

For the Presbyterians the execution of the king and the establishment of a republic fully vindicated their belief that the radicals or Independents, as they sometimes called them, had perverted the cause of Parliament. A declaration condemning 'the horrible and detestable murder' of the king which was published shortly after his death bore the names of many of the Presbyterian ministers of London, among them William Gouge, Edmund Calamy, Jeremy Whitaker, Simeon Ashe, Thomas Case, James Nalton, Thomas

Cawton and Christopher Love.[26] Besides their political grievances the Presbyterians were deeply concerned about the state of religion and more particularly the widespread anarchy which prevailed. In a letter dispatched from London in May 1653 it was reported that 'noe sett forme of governement more then of praier' would satisfy the sectaries who were so numerous in the army and that 'nothing is yet resolved towards a settlement'.[27] As Clarendon noted, the antipathy which the sectaries aroused was not wholly a product of religious susceptibilities. The Presbyterian party, he writes, 'exceedingly inveighed against the licence that was practised in religion by the several factions of Independents, Anabaptists, Quakers, and the several species of these, who contemned all the magistrates and the laws established'.[28] The Presbyterians looked upon themselves as moderates who, unlike their adversaries, had remained faithful to the Solemn League and Covenant whose provisions included the maintenance of the rights and privileges of Parliament, the preservation and defence of the king's person and authority, and a reformation of religion 'according to the word of God, and the example of the best reformed Churches'. In the opinion of Sir William Waller, who had been one of the leading Presbyterians in the Commons, many of the members of the two Houses who like him had felt obliged to dissociate themselves from the extremists were persons 'of eminent reputation for piety and integrity'.[29] On the other hand, the radicals were inclined to view the Presbyterians as men who had put self-interest before principle, abandoned the cause to which they had pledged themselves and sought to destroy all freedom of conscience in promoting their own religious designs. John Pyne claimed that when the Presbyterians were the dominant party in the Commons they 'acted nothinge of Justice, right or freedome' and that if the army had not carried out its purge 'ruine must have befallen honest Men'.[30] Others went so far as to argue that many of them had always been of doubtful loyalty but had thought it prudent to conceal their royalist sympathies.[31]

Some Presbyterian gentry such as Sir William Waller and Sir John Gell had served as military commanders during the Civil War. There were others, however, who had appeared to be lukewarm or even worse. Sir John Holland had sought to ensure that Norfolk remained at peace while arguing that Parliament should come to terms with the king. Following criticism in the Commons over his conspicuous lack of commitment he had completely distanced himself from the conflict by joining his wife in the Dutch Netherlands.[32] Sir Thomas Pelham had been relatively inactive both as an MP and as a member of the Sussex parliamentary committee. His feelings about the Civil War were probably fully in tune with those of his sister-in-law Lady Elizabeth Wilbraham who in July 1644 had told him that:

> I doubt not but if it pleas god to settle the times wee shall eassilye reconcile all thinges . . . I harttily wish that you may be freed from what we dalye sufer, and enioye the unestimable blessing of peace.[33]

Sir Francis Drake, whose estate had been seized by the enemy, had rejected the offer of a royal pardon but his brother Thomas had gone over to the king.[34] Sir Richard Onslow, Sir John Northcote and Sir Robert Pye and the heirs of Sir Gilbert Gerard and Sir John Horner had been suspected of harbouring royalist sympathies.[35] Sir Ambrose Browne's son Adam had been in arms for the king and he himself came under pressure when allegations were made during the early years of the Commonwealth that he had secretly provided the king with a troop of horse and given protection to a number of delinquents.[36] In some of these cases the evidence had been inconclusive but even when it had been clearcut the Commons had usually taken a lenient view. Referring to the case of Sir Robert Pye, who had managed to escape punishment after the interception of an incriminating letter, Sir Simonds D'Ewes remarks that the 'moderate honest' members who wanted a safe and honourable peace were always inclined to show mercy and pity when such matters were debated.[37]

In the main, the Presbyterian gentry viewed the issue of church government from an Erastian perspective which many of the clerical members of the Westminster Assembly had found deeply repugnant. Sir Robert Harley had been anxious to establish a thoroughgoing Presbyterian system on the Scottish model but most MPs with the same political outlook had been unwilling to go so far, largely because they feared that it would put too much power in the hands of the ministry. For such men the church settlement which the Long Parliament had painfully worked out had considerable attractions since it embodied the concept of a national Church with a parochial organisation, ordained ministers and lay patronage; satisfied their aspirations in matters of doctrine and worship; imposed strict limits on the powers of the clergy; and denied any measure of freedom to the sectaries. The classical presbyteries which figured in this settlement were made responsible for examining and ordaining candidates for the ministry; and among the qualifications prescribed for such candidates were a university education, a knowledge of Hebrew, Greek and Latin, and the ability both to preach and defend 'the orthodox doctrine'.[38] Few counties had functioning presbyteries but the Presbyterian ministers of London and Lancashire (where the new system had firmly taken root) ordained many candidates who subsequently served as parish clergy in other parts of the country. A Cromwellian ordinance of 1654 which laid down arrangements for the appointment of beneficed ministers and lecturers was completely silent on such matters as the ceremony of ordination and the possession of educational qualifications; on the other hand, it specifically acknowledged the right of lay patrons to make presentations to the livings in their gift. The ordinance named a number of godly divines as commissioners for the approbation of ministers. Although most of these were Independents Richard Baxter testifies that the commissioners 'did abundance of good to the Church' and saved many congregations from 'ignorant, ungodly, drunken Teachers'.[39]

Most Puritan squires who had occasion to exercise their patronage rights during the Interregnum revealed a marked preference for candidates with a university background. In August 1656 Sir John Dryden decided to present John Pasmore, an Oxford graduate, to the parsonage of Chesterton in Huntingdonshire. Accordingly he asked his friend Sir John Trevor to recommend his candidate to Philip Nye (a prominent Independent divine) or one of the other commissioners for the approbation of ministers and offered the assurance that 'hee is on my knowledg a very learned and an Orthodox Divine'. Later that year it became necessary for Sir John to recruit a new minister for his own parish, Canons Abbey in Northamptonshire, which the Drydens had always maintained was a peculiar and as such exempt from any kind of diocesan control. In October one of his ministers told him that Josias Bunne had intimated that he

> earnestly desired to know your thoughts, whether you would approve of him to bee your Minister at Ashby, for hee is earnestly sollicited by the people of Ashby to accept of that livinge and must give them answer on the next Lord's day.

Since Bunne was another Oxford graduate Sir John may not have hesitated for too long before deciding to fall in with the wishes of his tenantry.[40]

Richard Baxter draws a distinction between those 'grave, orthodox, godly Ministers' who were convinced Presbyterians and other godly ministers 'who had addicted themselves to no Party or Sect at all, though the Vulgar called them by the Name of Presbyterians'. He, for his part, disliked many aspects of Independency but he also had strong reservations about the more extreme Presbyterians who in his view were 'too much against liberty'.[41] In practice the Presbyterian gentry appear to have attached little importance to this distinction even if it had any meaning for them. Their main concern as the patrons of church livings was that they should be filled by able preaching ministers who had been ordained either episcopally or under the arrangements laid down by the Long Parliament. In 1654 Sir Walter Erle offered his Dorset living of East Morden with Charborough to Edward Bennet, an 'awakening preacher' who had entered into holy orders on the eve of the Civil War and had more recently found himself in trouble for refusing to take the engagement to be true and faithful to the Commonwealth. Bennet accepted the invitation and was duly admitted. In his judgement, we are told, he was 'a Presbyterian, but of known moderation towards those of other sentiments'. That same year Sir Walter presented Christopher Lawrence, another Puritan minister who had been episcopally ordained, to the living of Langton Matravers in the Isle of Purbeck.[42] When the Sussex living of Burwash Weald fell vacant in 1658 Sir John Pelham put in Thomas Goldham, a Presbyterian divine who had been ordained by the fourth London *classis* in 1649. Goldham would later be described as a 'man of good polite learning, and an acceptable preacher'.[43]

Sometimes the Presbyterian ceremony of ordination was performed immediately before the new incumbent took on responsibility for the cure of souls. This procedure was followed at Lytchett Matravers in May 1658 when Thomas Rowe, a young man whose preaching was 'very methodical and exact', was presented to one of the Dorset benefices belonging to the Trenchard family.[44]

Writing to his kinsman Edward Harley (the eldest son of Sir Robert Harley) in October 1651, Sir William Waller made a passing reference to 'our ministers, and all the zealants of our party'.[45] By associating with Presbyterian ministers, and more particularly with the London ministers who had publicly condemned the act of regicide, a Puritan squire ran the risk of being branded as an enemy of the Commonwealth. When Thomas Cawton preached a sermon before the lord mayor and aldermen of London in February 1649 he had the temerity to pray for the new king and his family and as a punishment was imprisoned for a time in the Gatehouse. After the Restoration his son published an account of his life and in dedicating it to Sir Anthony Irby and his wife took the opportunity to thank them for the love which they had shown him while he was in prison. At the time of his seclusion from the Long Parliament Sir Anthony had been described as 'one that was ever closed with that party in the House that most endeavoured reformation of things amisse, both in the Church and the Commonwealth'. What is certainly true is that he had strongly held opinions which his clerical associates would have found congenial. As a member of the Commons he had been in favour of taking punitive action against those of his colleagues who refused to subscribe to the Solemn League and Covenant; of providing in the Directory of Worship for a form of communion which accorded with the practice of the Presbyterian Church of Scotland; and of prohibiting anyone who had not been ordained from preaching or expounding the scriptures in churches and other public places.[46] Sir Harbottle Grimston was an 'exceeding good friend' of Cawton and may also have been on close terms with Thomas Case, another of the Presbyterian ministers who were based in London. Following the death of Grimston's heir in 1655, Case wrote of him that he was 'a Gentleman of great eminency, both for parts and piety, the honour and hopes of his father's house'.[47] In April 1651 it was claimed that Sir Richard Onslow, who was a powerful figure in Surrey, was anxious to further the political objectives of the Presbyterian party and that he was 'totally guided by the Presbyterian Ministers'. Although he was ill disposed towards the republican regime he was not the kind of man to put himself in jeopardy: in the words of one of his descendants he had 'a sort of art and cunning about him'.[48] Shortly afterwards some of the London ministers, among them Christopher Love and Thomas Case, were arrested for allegedly plotting to overthrow the government; and in August the 'holy Mr Love', as Edward Harley called him, was executed on Tower Hill. Two other Presbyterian ministers, Thomas Cawton and

James Nalton, fled to Holland where they became joint pastors of the English church at Rotterdam. After this episode, Richard Baxter tells us, 'the most of the Ministers and good People of the Land did look upon the New Commonwealth as Tyranny, and were more alienated from them than before'. In his commonplace book, Thomas Wilbraham, the son of a Cheshire baronet, inserted a poem about the death of Christopher Love which contained some striking rhetoric:

> me thought I heard beheaded saints above
> call to each other, Sirs make roome for Love . . .
> Spectators in his looke such life did see
> that they appeare more like to dye than hee.

Some years later Wilbraham was said to be a Presbyterian who was heavily under the influence of John Swinfen, one of the secluded members and a friend of Sir Robert Harley.[49]

In January 1653 the minister of the New Chapel in Tothill Fields, Westminster, informed Sir Robert Harley, who had formerly been a member of his congregation, that in a pamphlet which had recently appeared he had been severely criticised 'for countenancing the presbyterian ministers'. Sir Robert's friends among the Presbyterian divines included Edmund Calamy, Stanley Gower, Jeremy Whitaker and James Nalton. Nalton, who was known as the 'weeping prophet', did not remain long at Rotterdam and was soon officiating again at St Leonard's church in Foster Lane. Writing from London in February 1654, Edward Harley told his father that 'This day the monthly fast was kept at Mr Nalton's church very sweetly, where you were affectionatly remembered.' Gower had once enjoyed Sir Robert's patronage in Herefordshire but was now the minister of Trinity church in Dorchester. According to a report received by the Council of State in 1650 he had been striving, by his preaching and praying, to stir up the people against the government.[50] As one of the most prominent of the London ministers Calamy had many influential connections among the Presbyterian nobility and gentry. In 1658 he delivered the sermon at the funeral of Robert Earl of Warwick, a major figure in the Presbyterian party and a great patron of godly divines. When his son Edmund was put into the Essex living of Moreton in 1659 it was a truly Presbyterian occasion since he was presented by feoffees of the late Earl of Warwick who consisted of Edward Earl of Manchester, John Lord Robartes, Sir Gilbert

Gerard and three of their clerical associates, Anthony Tuckney, Simeon Ashe and the elder Calamy.[51] Calamy was also a friend of Sir William Waller who invited him to preach at the funeral of his third wife, Lady Anne, in 1661. Fittingly, the funeral was held in the New Chapel in Tothill Fields which had become one of the principal centres of Presbyterian worship in Westminster.[52]

2

DISAFFECTION

During the Interregnum some of the Presbyterian gentry seemed anxious to live as retired a life as possible, immersing themselves completely in their own private affairs and avoiding any political entanglements. After all the vicissitudes he had experienced Sir Samuel Luke must have concluded that this was the only sensible course to follow. In July 1642 he had been wounded by a royalist squire whom he had been seeking to apprehend and subsequently his estate in Bedfordshire had been plundered. Although he had distinguished himself as a military commander he had antagonised the Independents, mainly because of his open hostility towards the sectaries and, as a result, had been forced to relinquish the governorship of Newport Pagnell following the passage of the Self Denying Ordinance. In 1647 he had been seized by parliamentary soldiers at his house, Wood End, but in a letter to the Speaker had declared, in typically robust fashion, that 'no force shall make me change my duty to the parliament, nor my affection to my country'. The following year he had been taken into custody when the army carried out its purge of the Commons and had been held prisoner for several weeks.[1] For Sir Samuel this was something of a watershed: after the Restoration the king was informed that he had refused all public employment between Pride's Purge and the return of the secluded MPs to Westminster in February 1660. During the early 1650s he was heavily involved in family business, primarily because of the death of his father, Sir Oliver, from whom he inherited substantial property, and the growing financial problems which he seemed unable to overcome.[2] Writing to William Temple in May 1653 Dorothy Osborne describes a chance encounter with members of the Luke family who were near neighbours. Since the wars, she observes, 'wee

13

have had noe commerce with that famely, but have kept at great distance, as having upon severall occasions bin disobliged by them'. Recently, however, Sir Samuel had asked for some plants from her garden

> and withall made the offer of what was in his, which I had reason to take for a high favor, for hee is a nice florist, and since this wee are insensibly come to as good degrees of Civility for one another, as can bee expected from People that never meet.[3]

No doubt Sir Samuel considered it dangerous to be seen openly consorting with a family which had supported the royalist cause. In June 1652 he obtained permission to travel abroad and may possibly have undertaken his journey in the company of Sir Roger Burgoyne, another of the secluded Bedfordshire MPs, who arrived in Brussels later that month.[4]

Although the Presbyterian gentry often met and dined together when in London,[5] few of them appear to have been willing to risk their lives and fortunes by actively engaging in plots and conspiracies. Nevertheless the authorities were understandably wary of them and did not hesitate to take action when they judged it necessary. In March 1650 it was reported that the Presbyterians in Lancashire were planning to make common cause with the Scots and that one of the ringleaders was Ralph Assheton of Middleton, a wealthy landowner who had formerly commanded the parliamentary forces in the county. The Council of State decided that Assheton and other Lancashire Presbyterians, among them Sir Richard Hoghton and Richard Shuttleworth, should be deprived of their militia appointments; and some time later Assheton was required to enter into a bond in the sum of £1,000 as a guarantee of good behaviour. When Shuttleworth sought permission to visit London the request was granted with the proviso that he should report to the Council of State within three days after his arrival and give an undertaking to do nothing which was prejudicial to the Commonwealth.[6] In Herefordshire, Edward Harley was arrested but released after questioning. This led him to express his gratitude to God for delivering him 'from restraint ... unexpectedly, and without any prejudice to the peace of my Conscience'. His brothers Robert and Thomas were not, however, so fortunate. Their father was dismayed to hear that they had been imprisoned at Bristol but sought to encourage them with the thought that God would 'in his good Time Cleere your Innocency'.[7] Shortly after this Sir John Gell, who had been the leading parliamentarian in Derbyshire, was found guilty of misprision of treason. Imprisoned in the Tower of London, he was eventually allowed to spend some time in Bath 'for recovery of his health'.[8]

In March 1651 the governor of Stafford was ordered to take into custody all such persons as he considered to be dangerous and disaffected. Among those apprehended were two of the secluded Staffordshire MPs, Colonel John Bowyer and John Swinfen. Bowyer was taken to London for questioning but on 5 April the Council of State gave order that Swinfen should be released on entering into a bond in the sum of £1,000.[9]

Following Cromwell's victory at Worcester in September 1651 the republican government began to feel less beleaguered. In October Sir William Waller, who had been held prisoner since Pride's Purge, asked his kinsman Edward Harley to approach Sir Arthur Hesilrige (who had been making enquiries about him) to see whether he would be prepared to intercede on his behalf since it was possible that 'he may venture to be freer then he durst when things were more doubtfull'. Sir William regained his freedom at the beginning of 1652; and in April the government went further and ordered the release of Sir John Gell.[10]

When the Rump Parliament was dissolved in April 1653, Sir Henry Vane immediately left London and took up residence on his newly acquired estate in Lincolnshire. Since Pride's Purge he had been growing increasingly disillusioned. Writing to Cromwell in 1651 he had offered the opinion that

> we are like the children of Israel in former times, rather hardned and made worse, for the most of us, by God's appearances and deliverances then brought nearer to him, which if it continues with us will be bitterness in the latter ende.

Vane's model commonwealth was one in which an elected assembly governed a godly nation which enjoyed a wide measure of religious and political freedom. Godliness, however, appeared to be in decline; and with the demise of the Rump Parliament there could be little doubt that a military dictatorship was about to be established. At his trial in 1662 he would declare that he had opposed Cromwell's usurpation from beginning to end; and Edmund Ludlow testifies that since he looked upon Cromwell 'as

15

having betrayed the cause of God, and sacrificed it to his lust, he would never cast in his lot with him ... but bore a constant witness against his usurpation'.[11] Some of Vane's colleagues in the Rump Parliament were equally incensed by Cromwell's political aggrandisement, among them Sir Arthur Hesilrige who considered that after the dissolution 'the power was then in the people' and John Hutchinson who, according to his wife, was convinced that the surest guarantee of the people's freedom was a republic which was no longer in thrall to the army.[12]

The Parliament of Saints, which first met on 4 July 1653, consisted of men who had been selected by Cromwell and his Council of Officers from lists of nominees sent in by the Independent congregations in the various counties. A hostile observer described them uncharitably as 'empty pated things yet anabaptisticall and of the fanatique party'. Not surprisingly, given the method of selection, there were comparatively few Puritan squires of real substance in the new assembly. Of those who were chosen, the most important politically were Sir Gilbert Pickering and Richard Norton who were both elected to the reconstituted Council of State.[13]

A royalist informant would later claim that about this time 'most of the Presbyterian nobility, and divers of the ould Parliament-men' were planning to stage an uprising on behalf of the king; and that what primarily motivated them was their fear that the tyrant Cromwell intended to destroy the nobility and gentry. Among the noblemen engaged in this plot, it was alleged, were the Earls of Warwick, Salisbury, Manchester and Northumberland, Lord Robartes and Lord Grey of Warke. Sir William Waller was to have commanded troops in London and Middlesex. Others said to have been involved in the conspiracy included Sir Robert Pye and Sir Gilbert Gerard in Middlesex, the Harleys in Herefordshire, Sir Richard Onslow and Sir Ambrose Browne in Surrey, Sir Thomas Pelham and Herbert Morley in Sussex and Sir Thomas Alston and his brothers in Bedfordshire. Although there is no clear evidence to support this story it may have contained a kernel of truth. Some of the Presbyterian gentry who were named had already fallen under suspicion while in 1660 Sir Thomas Alston was depicted as a man who had 'allwayes professed himselfe readie for his Majesties service at an howres warninge'. The Presbyterian party, however, lacked the will and determination to stage an armed revolt.[14]

Whatever their private thoughts on the political issues of the day the Presbyterian gentry were often willing to hold public office in the counties where they were seated. Some of them had been removed from the commission of the peace but there were others who continued to serve as magistrates, among them Sir Francis Drake, Sir John Barrington, Sir Thomas Barnardiston, Sir Thomas Alston, Sir Richard Onslow and Sir Roger Burgoyne. Sir George Booth acted both as a justice of the peace and one of the Cheshire commissioners for the militia; as Clarendon testifies he was 'a person of the best fortune and interest in Cheshire, and, for the memory of his grandfather, of absolute power with the Presbyterians'.[15] Such men may have taken the view that in exercising authority within the local community they were doing no more than performing a function which had traditionally belonged to the gentry; or they may simply have thought it prudent to retain as much local power as they could at a time when the social fabric appeared to be crumbling. More unusually, Sir John Barrington was appointed high sheriff of Essex in 1654. As a kinsman of Cromwell he may actually have welcomed the establishment of the Protectorate; and it is perhaps significant that he had recently become very friendly with Cromwell's brother-in-law, Major General Desborough. In 1661 an informer alleged that he had embezzled large sums of money which his father had collected on behalf of Parliament. In the response which was drafted it was stressed that the only occasion on which Sir John had received money for public purposes was when he had served as sheriff under 'Oliver the Protector' and that he could if necessary produce his *quietus est* to show that he had faithfully discharged his trust.[16]

The first Protectorate Parliament, which assembled on 3 September 1654, included many Puritan gentry, both radicals and others. Among the successful Presbyterian candidates Sir John Northcote and Sir John Yonge were returned for Devon, Sir Walter Erle for Dorset, John Crewe for Northamptonshire and Sir Richard Onslow for Surrey. In the event the new Parliament proved to be too independent-minded to suit Cromwell's purposes and on 22 January 1655 it was suddenly dissolved.[17]

The elections for the next Parliament, which was summoned to meet on 17 September 1656, were much more hotly contested: 'every faction', declared Secretary Thurloe, 'hath bestirred themselves with all their might'.[18] The major generals who had been appointed as provincial governors did everything they could to ensure that the new assembly would be more compliant. Bulstrode Whitelocke, who as an office-holder had a vested interest in the future of the Protectorate, writes that his 'friends' staged an impressive demonstration of military force at the Buckinghamshire election and that as a result he was 'first and unanimously' elected along with Colonel Francis Ingoldsby, Sir Richard Pigott, Richard Hampden and Richard Grenville. Politically, Hampden was rather an unknown quantity (though he had Presbyterian connections) but the reputation of his father as a martyred patriot clearly stood him in good stead.[19] In Northamptonshire Major General Boteler nominated six candidates, including himself, Sir Gilbert Pickering and Thomas Crewe (the only son of John Crewe) and forced the sheriff to declare them all elected. There was a large body of electors who supported the candidature of Richard Knightley, one of the secluded members, and 'other considerable gentlemen of the county' but they were denied any opportunity to cast their votes.[20] At the Herefordshire election Edward Harley and other representatives of the local gentry found themselves opposed by three army officers who included Major General Berry. Earlier in the year Harley had been informed that some men were saying that he was 'the cause of all the troubles in this county'; that it was important that the county 'should not alwayes be under the servitude of one family'; and that he was a rigid Presbyterian who was incapable of moderation. Nevertheless he was returned as one of the Herefordshire members.[21]

In Hampshire Major General Goffe discovered that a list of recommended candidates was in circulation and that the names of men like Richard Norton who were known associates of the Protector had been deliberately excluded. Sir William Waller's name appeared on the list but he was not elected; Norton, on the other hand, was one of the successful candidates.[22] Sir William Brereton's defeat in the Cheshire election was a consequence of his political isolation: his autocratic behaviour as commander-in-chief of the parliamentary forces in Cheshire had made him unpopular and for some years he had been settled in Surrey where he had obtained a grant of the Archbishop of Canterbury's palace at Croydon. Shortly before the election Major General Bridge told the Protector that Sir William was endeavouring 'by himself and agents to procure voices; but I find his interest amongst the gentlemen very little; only some of the rigid clergy cry him up'.[23]

Writing from Nottingham, Major General Whalley informed Cromwell that much to his surprise the 'honest partie of the countie' had put forward the name of John Hutchinson as a candidate, 'he having satisfied some of them concerning his judgment of the present government'. He hoped, however, that the hints which he had dropped would persuade them to choose someone else. And for good measure he added that Sir Arthur Hesilrige, if nominated, 'will most blemish theyr choice in Leicestershire'. About the same time Major General Desborough was assuring the Protector that although the 'honest people' in the western counties were likely to meet with great opposition, they were determined that only men of 'known integrity to the present government' would be elected. Despite all the efforts of 'the old dissatisfied party', he went on, 'I shall make it my business to encourage the honest sober people, and strengthen their hands, as much as in me lyes'.[24]

Hesilrige was returned for Leicestershire but Whalley managed to prevent Hutchinson's election. Another prominent radical, Sir Henry Vane, found himself in trouble with the government over his book *A Healing Question*: on 26 August Thurloe was writing to Henry Cromwell that it 'strikes at the foundation of this government, and offers another to the people'. In September Vane was imprisoned in Carisbrooke Castle in the Isle of Wight where he remained for several months.[25]

On 14 September Richard Baxter observed in a letter to Edward Harley that the sooner the government was re-established in its ancient form, with the Crown, Lords and Commons, 'the sooner we may have quiettness, and some litle ease of our present burdens'.[26] It was a sentiment which Harley would readily have endorsed but at that time such a major turn of events must have seemed a remote possibility. The most immediate political development was Cromwell's decision to purge the new Parliament of men who had opposed him in the Parliament of 1654 or were otherwise regarded as hostile to his government. Many were denied admission, among them Sir Arthur Hesilrige, Alexander Popham, who had been a fellow member of the Rump Parliament, and Presbyterians such as Sir Harbottle Grimston, Sir Anthony Irby and Edward Harley. It is significant, however, that some Presbyterian MPs were allowed to take their seats. Possibly

Cromwell was hoping to secure the support of men like Sir Thomas Barnardiston, Sir Richard Onslow and Sir John Pelham who were extremely wealthy and of considerable standing in their counties.[27]

On the evidence of his accounts Sir John Pelham, who was seated in Sussex, waited until 2 October before travelling up to London and spent little time there while Parliament was sitting. When a roll-call was conducted at the end of the year he was one of a number of MPs who were recorded as absent. Sir Richard Onslow was described as 'not well' while his son Arthur, it was said, 'had smallpox in his family so dare not come up to sit here'. The Onslows, however, were immediately excused. Sir Richard soon took his seat again and was even prepared to argue in favour of a new land tax.[28]

When Parliament was informed in January 1657 that the authorities had discovered a plot to assassinate the Protector, Sir William Strickland, who was a man of strong conservative instincts, showed where his sympathies lay by expressing his profound relief at the failure of this undertaking:

> We are obliged to give thanks to God for this and all other deliverances, without whose providence a hair cannot fall from our heads. It is not improbable that the Levellers and the Cavaliers may join together in this assassination, or any other wicked thing, to overthrow the Government. We cannot be too thankful for such a mercy.[29]

Strickland was alarmed by the spectre of anarchy and believed that for the foreseeable future Cromwell represented the surest guarantee of order and stability. Nor was he alone in taking this view of the situation. Most of the wealthy Puritan MPs who still participated in the proceedings of Parliament came out in favour of the proposition that Cromwell should assume the style and title of king. Some like Bulstrode Whitelocke (who had been knighted by Cromwell) and Sir William Roberts held lucrative offices; others like Edmund Dunch and Richard Hampden were kinsmen of the Protector. Whitelocke was a member of a parliamentary delegation which sought to persuade Cromwell to accept the Crown. Among his associates on this occasion was Sir Richard Onslow who told the Protector that every office ought to have a name appropriate to it; and no other name than king 'could be suitable and comprehensive enough to contain in it the Common

Good to all Intents and Purposes'. In support of his arguments he drew on the Scriptures and even managed to work in a reference to the book with seven seals which had an important role in apocalyptic prophecies. According to the author of a contemporary tract, Sir Richard was 'fully for Kingship, and was never otherwise ... and, seeing he cannot have young Charles, old Oliver will serve his turn, so he have one'.[30]

Cromwell decided in the end to decline the offer of the Crown but was more receptive to the idea of setting up a second chamber. In December 1657 writs of summons were issued to the men whom he had selected for his House of Peers; in the main they were known or likely supporters of his regime though they also included some political opponents whom he may have been hoping to win over through the blandishments of a title of nobility. Sir Arthur Hesilrige, however, believed that God had decreed the abolition of the House of Lords as well as the monarchy and insisted on taking his seat in the Lower House. Some of Cromwell's other nominees also failed to respond to the summons: Sir Gilbert Gerard who claimed to be ill; John Crewe and Alexander Popham; and, more surprisingly, Sir Gilbert Pickering who had recently been appointed Lord Chamberlain of the Protector's household. Among those who sat as peers in the Upper House were Sir Richard Onslow, Sir John Hobart, Sir William Strickland, Bulstrode Whitelocke, Edmund Dunch and Richard Hampden.[31] Hobart had inherited Blickling Hall in Norfolk, together with large estates, from his uncle and namesake, and in 1656 had married Hampden's sister Mary. At the time of the Norfolk election of 1656 the government had been informed that he was 'the darling of this country, and chooseth whom he please' but a later report had conveyed the warning that he was faced with some opposition because of his marriage which had brought him into Cromwell's circle of kinsmen. His nomination as a member of the Upper House attracted the acid comment that 'His principles being so right for Kingship and tyranny, he is in great favour at court'. Similarly, Sir William Strickland was described as 'of good compliance ... with the new Court, and settling the Protector a-new in all those things for which the King was cut off'. Hampden may have been included on the recommendation of Colonel Richard Ingoldsby, another of Cromwell's relatives who sat in the Upper House. The object, it was alleged, was 'to settle and secure him to the interest of the new Court, and wholly take him off from the thoughts of ever following his father's steps or inheriting his noble virtues'.[32]

While the new constitutional changes were being introduced the royalists were seeking to gain the support of some of the leading parliamentarians for an uprising on behalf of the king in exile. As an inducement the Marquess of Ormonde made it known that although it was the intention to re-establish episcopal government there would be toleration for Presbyterians and others.[33] During the autumn John Stapley, who was one of the Sussex commissioners for securing the peace of the Common-wealth, received a commission signed by the king for raising a regiment of 500 horses. Clarendon writes that as the son of a regicide, Anthony Stapley, he hoped that his switch of loyalty would enable him 'to enjoy that estate which the treason of his father had forfeited'.[34] According to a royalist intelligence report there was a good prospect of persuading Robert Rolle, MP for Devon and 'a very popular man amongst the Presbyterians', to play a full part in the enterprise and it was likely that he could raise a force of over 3,000 men. Other letters received by the king's ministers conveyed assurances that Sir William Waller could be relied upon and that in the north Sir George Booth would not remain idle. More ambitiously, attempts were made to win over Alexander Popham and Richard Norton, both of whom had sat in the Rump and served as members of the republican Council of State. Popham, who resided at Littlecote House in Wiltshire, was an important figure in that county and the adjoining county of Somerset while Norton was governor of Portsmouth and one of the most substantial landowners in Hampshire. In March 1658 they were the recipients of personal letters from the king. Not long before this the Protector had declared in a letter to Norton that 'All that I have to say is to tell you that I love you'; now the king was telling him that he relied much on his 'discretion and interest'.[35]

In a letter written on 8 March, Norton, who was then at Portsmouth, informed his friend Secretary Thurloe that he be-lieved that

there is some intention of trobles to come upon us. I shall not troble you with the particulars of my reasons for my appre-hensions ... only in general I thought good to lett you know my feares; the Lord divert them. And to lett you know that ... there shall be noe care wanting in me for this place.

Probably he feared that the plot was about to be discovered and was taking out insurance against the possibility that he might be accused of conspiring against the Protector.[36] Before the end of March the authorities had apprehended many suspects, among them Sir William Waller and his kinsman Robert Harley, a younger brother of Edward Harley. Waller was soon released but Harley remained in custody for some months.[37]

John Stapley was summoned to London where he was questioned by the Protector. At this stage he gave little away but when subsequently examined under oath he was much more forthcoming. In a petition addressed to Cromwell he apologised for his earlier reticence and promised him that for the future he would 'not only live peaceably, but with the uttmost of my indeavours stand by your highnes with life and fortune'. Stapley was treated leniently, apparently out of regard for his father. During the formal investigation which the authorities carried out they collected the names of many persons of standing, among them Lord Fairfax, Sir William Waller, Sir John Pelham, Alexander Popham and Edward Harley. Often, however, there was a lack of hard evidence. On 20 April Secretary Thurloe was writing to Henry Cromwell that the plotters, who included Sir William Waller, had been hoping to draw in Lord Fairfax, 'whom I cannot say they had engaged, but promised themselves much from his discontents'. Sir John Pelham's name had been inserted in one of the blank commissions which had been sent over in bulk from the Court in exile, but this seems to have been done without his knowledge or consent; indeed it was said that Stapley, who was a kinsman of his, had decided not to approach him because of some personal quarrel. The same man who volunteered this information also testified that about the beginning of March he had been told that 'Mr Popham, a great man in the west, was engaged' and that he 'had three thousand arms, and had promised to bring some thousands into the field'. The government, however, made no attempt to arrest Popham and in October it was reported through royalist channels that his affection for the king was as strong as ever.[38]

The death of Cromwell in September failed to raise the hopes of the royalist party since the succession of his son Richard as Protector could hardly have gone more smoothly. 'Contrary to all expectation', writes Clarendon, 'this earthquake was attended with no signal alteration . . . the King's condition never appeared

so hopeless, so desperate.'[39] Towards the end of the year, however, it was becoming clear that a power struggle was developing
between the Protector's party which included relatives and office-
holders and the Commonwealthsmen who as ardent republicans
preferred a parliamentary form of government to any political
system in which executive power was concentrated in the hands
of a single individual. In November a royalist writing from
London commented that the Commonwealthsmen, who were
headed by Sir Henry Vane and Sir Arthur Hesilrige, were gaining
ground and that Sir Gilbert Pickering had decided to join them.[40]

For a time it looked as though the Commonwealthsmen had
triumphed. In May 1659 the military forced Richard Cromwell to
'retire as a private gentleman' and recalled the members of the
Rump Parliament. According to a royalist intelligence report
some 50 MPs assembled, all of them sworn enemies to kingship.
Sir George Booth, Sir William Waller, Richard Knightley and
others who had been secluded in 1648 attempted to take their
seats but were refused admission.[41] The Council of State which
was established mainly consisted of thoroughgoing republicans,
among them Sir Henry Vane, Sir Arthur Hesilrige and Sir James
Harrington, though it also included Lord Fairfax who in
Clarendon's estimation was 'a perfect Presbyterian in judgment'
and Sir Horatio Townshend who had received a commission from
the king.[42]

One of the most immediate consequences of this political
upheaval was the replacement of Richard Norton as governor of
Portsmouth following a report that he was discontented. Shortly
before this a royalist had described him as looking for security
and it is perhaps significant that he had obtained a pass for his son
Daniel to journey into France. According to Edmund Ludlow he
was a man of autocratic temper who could not bear to be crossed,
but on this occasion he proved to be a model of forbearance:
although he was 'much disturbed' by his sacking he assured
Ludlow (with his tongue firmly in his cheek) that he would be
very well satisfied if Parliament went ahead with 'the settlement
of an equal commonwealth'.[43]

3

BRINGING BACK THE KING

During the early months of 1659 the royalists were attempting to organise an uprising of national dimensions. While recognising the need to involve the Presbyterians they found it difficult to judge the strength of their commitment and were not inclined to be too sanguine. Many Presbyterians, wrote John Mordaunt, who was one of the key figures in the plot, were well disposed towards the king but 'their ease and their guilt' made them fainthearted. Although Sir William Waller was said to have received the king's instructions with a display of enthusiasm it was feared that he 'will not hazard much'. Sir George Booth was described in a letter to the king as 'very considerable in his county, a Presbyterian, but entirely reliable'. Later Mordaunt reported that Booth and Waller were in contact with other leading Presbyterians, Hugh Boscawen in Cornwall and Sir John Northcote and Robert Rolle in Devon.[1]

In April another of the royalist conspirators, Major General Massey, informed Sir Edward Nicholas, the king's Secretary of State, that he had spoken to Alexander Popham, emphasising that he was doing so at the command of the king. Popham had appeared to be very glad to see him and had responded to his approach in terms which were 'full of zeale for the King' but had been unwilling to enter into any specific commitment. When Massey asked him whether the king would be able to count on his assistance in the event of some design being put in hand he had replied, rather circumspectly, that 'if he saw any that his judgement could see likely he would imploy all hee was able therein'. Popham had probably been heavily influenced by Waller who had told him that he favoured a waiting game since he believed that the internal divisions at Westminster would open the way for the restoration of the monarchy.[2]

In July the Presbyterian lords were reported to have asked their royalist contacts to wait until they had completed their preparations by which time they would be able to ensure the success of the enterprise and establish the throne upon 'the true basis, Liberty and Property'.[3] The government, however, received intelligence of the plot and proceeded to round up a number of suspects. Bulstrode Whitelocke, who was then President of the Council of State, ordered an immediate search of Alexander Popham's Somerset mansion, Hunstrete House, on being told that a large quantity of arms had been assembled there. Popham was summoned before the Council for questioning but was soon released.[4] The rebellion of Sir George Booth, who was said to be inflamed with zeal for Presbyterianism and a free parliament, was too modest in scale to present a serious threat to the republican government. Before the end of August he found himself in the Tower where Sir William Waller, who had been taken into custody as a suspected person, was already a prisoner. Waller was eventually set at liberty on 31 October: 'the Lord', he relates, 'delivered me by my habeas corpus in an open cleare way, notwithstanding all opposition'.[5]

Alexander Popham was a trimmer before that term had acquired a political meaning. In contrast, John Pyne (with whom he had once been closely associated) was an ideologue who held tenaciously to his republican principles. In November he was in a deeply pessimistic mood, partly because the army had recently seized power and partly because he feared that the king would take advantage of 'the divisions of Reuben'. The true interest and constitution of a Commonwealth, he wrote,

> I doe dearely Love, And when I finde that foundation Layd, derived from good People and to them to be dulye conveyed, with that I cann willinglye and readylye engadge the small remainder of my old age . . . Oh my soule panteth for the Appeareinge and Preserveinge of the true good Old Cause, Whereof I can discerne Lettle Appeerence but rather a departure from it.[6]

Other Commonwealthsmen such as Sir Arthur Hesilrige held similar views. Sir Arthur, together with two of his associates, Herbert Morley and Valentine Walton, threw down a challenge to the Committee of Safety which had been established by taking over control of the key garrison town of Portsmouth. Writing to

General Charles Fleetwood, the new supreme commander, on 14 December they emphasised their commitment to parliamentary authority, the rights, liberties and properties of the people and true religion 'which is the good old cause so much owned by God, and valued by all good men'. And they went on to express the wish that the differences which had arisen could be resolved and the Commonwealth 'settled upon righteous and lasting foundations'.[7]

While political events in England were raising serious doubts about the future of the republic, General Monck was making preparations in Scotland for a military expedition, apparently with the object of asserting 'the liberty and authority of Parliament'.[8] According to his own account Bulstrode Whitelocke told Fleetwood that he was convinced that Monck intended to bring in the king without insisting on any terms, 'wherby all their lives and fortunes would be att the mercy of the King and his party'; that the Presbyterians and many others, including a great part of the soldiery, would support this objective; and that in these circumstances the coming in of the king was inevitable. He therefore proposed that Fleetwood should immediately enter into negotiations with the king but his advice was rejected.[9]

With the government seemingly paralysed many of Fleetwood's regiments came out in favour of the Rump Parliament and on 26 December its members reassembled once again. The following day Sir Gilbert Gerard, Sir William Waller, Sir Anthony Irby, John Crewe, Nathaniel Stephens, Richard Knightley and others who had been secluded in 1648 sought to take their seats but were prevented from doing so. The Rump proceeded to establish a new Council of State which included Sir James Harrington (who before long was made Lord President of the Council), Sir Arthur Hesilrige and Lord Fairfax.[10] The conduct of Sir Henry Vane and Bulstrode Whitelocke, who had served as members of the Committee of Safety during the 'late interruption', was regarded as too serious a matter to be overlooked. Fearing that he might be committed to the Tower, Whitelocke thought it prudent to retire to a friend's house in the country while his wife helped to cover his tracks by burning many of his papers relating to public affairs. Vane, for his part, was first interrogated and then banished to one of his country houses, Belleau Abbey in Lincolnshire.[11]

On 1 January 1660 Lord Fairfax took possession of York on behalf of Parliament and the following day General Monck, who had been in contact with him, crossed into England at the head of a sizeable army. From the early part of January onwards there were meetings of the gentry in a number of counties, and letters and declarations were dispatched both to Monck and to the Speaker, William Lenthall. In some cases they called for the return of the secluded MPs, in others for a freely elected parliament. The first county petition to be submitted to Monck was drawn up at a meeting of the Devonshire gentry which was held in Exeter. It was agreed that they should press for the restoration of the secluded members, some of whom, including Sir Francis Drake and Sir John Northcote, signed the petition. In response Monck expressed strong reservations about the proposal on the grounds that this would imply a return to monarchical government and episcopacy and in his opinion provoke a new war. In a letter addressed to Monck on 28 January the Devonshire gentry, among them Robert Rolle who appears to have emerged as one of their leaders, offered him their thoughts on the events of the previous decade. 'Since the Death of the late King', they told him, 'we have been Govern'd by Tumult; Bandy'd from one Faction to the Other: This Party up to day, That to Morrow, but still the Nation under, and a Prey to the Strongest.' Rejecting the proposition that England must necessarily remain a republic they maintained that it was not the form of government but the consent of the people which must 'settle the Nation'.[12] In Yorkshire, which had few secluded members, the gentry seemed reluctant to take up any public stance until the situation became clearer and it was not until 10 February, a week after Monck's arrival in London, that a declaration on behalf of the county was forwarded to him by Lord Fairfax and some of his associates. This proposed two alternative courses which perhaps reflected differences of view: either the secluded members should be allowed back or a new parliament should be called without any insistence on oaths or engagements. Among the signatories there were a number of Puritan gentry, including Sir Francis Boynton, Sir Thomas Remington, Thomas Hutton (a nephew of Lord Fairfax) and George Marwood.[13]

In London some of the secluded members entered into negotiations with Monck over their possible return. At this juncture John Crewe's town-house became a kind of party headquarters: in his diary Samuel Pepys, who was a friend of Crewe, noted that on 15 February at least 40 gentlemen had visited him and that on 19 February many of the secluded members had arrived after dinner. By this time it had been agreed that the secluded members should be readmitted on 21 February, subject to certain conditions which Crewe touched on when he told Pepys that it was the intention 'to do nothing more then to issue writs and settle a foundation for a free parliament'.[14] As an immediate consequence there was now a solid majority of Presbyterian MPs who were able to secure political control. On 23 February the House elected a new Council of State which included Lord Fairfax, Alexander Popham and Richard Norton but mainly consisted of Presbyterians, among them John Crewe, Richard Knightley, Sir Gilbert Gerard, Sir William Waller, Sir Richard Onslow, Edward Harley, Sir Harbottle Grimston and John Swinfen.[15]

On 25 February Edward Viscount Conway wrote to his kinsman Edward Harley to congratulate him on his return to Parliament and added that he was confident that 'you will favor all things which relate to the highest principles of honor and pietie'.[16] One of the conditions laid down by Monck was that the newly enlarged assembly should establish a national Church on Presbyterian lines before dissolving itself, and responsibility for preparing the necessary legislation was assigned to a Committee for Religion under Harley's chairmanship. For Harley and his fellow Presbyterians on the committee this was not an unwelcome task, though it is significant that they were unwilling to consult their clerical associates except over one relatively minor issue. In the legislation which was rushed through, it was decreed that ministers must perform their duties in accordance with the Directory of Worship which had been introduced in January 1645; that the ordinance of 29 August 1648, which embodied the ecclesiastical settlement of the Long Parliament, should be put in execution; and that justices of the peace, with the assistance of ministers and others, should consider how their counties might be divided into classical presbyteries. In addition, a number of commissioners were appointed, most of them Presbyterian divines, for the purpose of examining ministers who were put forward as candidates for benefices and lectureships and formally approving their admission.[17]

After the Long Parliament dissolved itself on 16 March a Presbyterian member, Sir Roger Burgoyne, wrote to a friend that

we are now at liberty though much against some of our wills: after many sad pangs and groanes at last we did expire, and are now in another world . . . theise were the last passages of that so long lived Parliament, which is not dead before, I question whether it lives not now.[18]

The demise of the Long Parliament did not necessarily mean that the restoration of the monarchy was a foregone conclusion; indeed Sir Henry Mildmay was said to be confident that the king would never return. The royalists, however, were generally optimistic, not least because they believed that the secluded members were prepared to enter into negotiations with the king. On 5 March the Long Parliament had decided that the Solemn League and Covenant should be published and read annually in every parish church. During the course of that debate (the Court was informed) Nathaniel Stephens, a Presbyterian MP who represented Gloucestershire, had declared that the Covenant 'included King, Lords, and Commons, and that was the pointe desired by all the nation, and to which they must come at last, and the sooner they went about it the better'. And on hearing this plain speaking the House had responded with cries of 'Well moved.'[19] Through their contacts the royalists felt able to count on the support of a number of former parliamentarians, among them Lord Fairfax, Alexander Popham, Sir William Waller, Sir Harbottle Grimston and Sir John Northcote. At the same time they drew a distinction between the moderate Presbyterians who would not insist on unreasonable conditions and the more rigid sort who were determined to exact a high price for their co-operation. On 19 March it was reported that some members of the Council of State, namely Sir Gilbert Gerard, John Crewe and 'that gang', were in favour of a restoration settlement based on the Newport articles of 1648 which the Presbyterian party had been ready to accept. Subsequently it emerged that there was a plan to secure the king's agreement to a settlement before the new Parliament assembled and that for this purpose a set of propositions was being extracted from the abortive treaties of Oxford, Uxbridge and Newport. According to one royalist correspondent, those who were 'most violent in this design' included the Earls of Bedford and Manchester, William Pierrepont, Alexander Popham, Sir William Waller and Oliver St John. In the event, however, it came to nothing.[20]

Although it had been decided that Cavaliers and their sons should be debarred from standing as candidates in the new parliamentary elections it proved impossible to enforce this restriction and in royalist circles there was considerable satisfaction over the outcome. The Presbyterian party, wrote one royalist, had been impotent in the county elections except where it had received the backing of the king's party, while another royalist declared that the Presbyterians were angry because they had fared badly and the king was likely to be restored without their assistance.[21] Nevertheless there was a significant minority of MPs from wealthy Puritan families which had supported the cause of Parliament in the Civil War. Among them were a number of county representatives, most of whom were Presbyterians with royalist sympathies: they included, for example, Sir George Booth (Cheshire), Hugh Boscawen (Cornwall), Sir John Northcote (Devon), Edward Harley (Herefordshire) and Sir William Waller (Middlesex). In the Middlesex election the voters rejected Waller's partner, Sir Gilbert Gerard, and two Commonwealthsmen, Sir William Roberts and Sir James Harrington. As a member of the Council of State Sir Richard Onslow was strongly in favour of inviting the king to return but he failed to secure enough votes in the Surrey election, partly because it was well known that he had been one of Cromwell's peers and partly because he was insistent that his son Arthur should stand with him. 'Sir Richard Onsloe', wrote Denzil Holles on 5 April, 'hath had ill luck about his knightship for Surrey, his nephew in law my Lord Angier and one Mr Harvey have carried it from him; and much by his owne fault, for he was offered one place but he desired them both, for himself and his sonne, and so hath lost both.' Another leading Presbyterian, Sir Harbottle Grimston, was defeated in the Essex county election despite his close association with the royalist party and the influence which the Earl of Warwick sought to exert on his behalf. Some of these men, however, were still able to gain admission to the Commons as borough representatives: Gerard was returned for Lancaster, the Onslows for Guildford and Grimston for Colchester.[22]

Besides this sizeable group of Presbyterian MPs, whom Clarendon describes as 'rather troublesome than powerful', there were former members of the Rump such as Sir Thomas Wroth, Alexander Popham, Richard Norton and John Gurdon. Norton was elected for both Hampshire and Portsmouth and decided that he would represent his county. On meeting Edmund Ludlow, who had been involved in a disputed election, he exclaimed with some feeling 'You see into what a condition you have brought us.'[23]

By the time of the elections many of the Commonwealthsmen

were in a state of despair. Sir Arthur Hesilrige told Monck that it now seemed certain that the king would be restored and he feared that this would mean ruin for himself, his family and his fortune. Monck, who saw him as a potential threat because of his military resources, advised him to live quietly at home and promised him that in return he would do all he could to save both his life and estate. Writing to Monck on 30 April Sir Arthur asked him to inform the Council of State of his loyalty to the government as it was then constituted and assured him that

> I have always acted with the authority of parliament and never against it and hold it my duty to submitt to the authority of the Nation and Not to oppose it. And have Hazarded my all to bringe the military power under the Civill authority.[24]

At the beginning of May the Commons considered the terms of the Declaration of Breda and voted for the return of the king. Not all MPs, however, viewed this prospect with enthusiasm: some, writes Edmund Ludlow, thought it prudent 'to swim with the streame ... others, by complying for the present, judged it the most probable way to be serviceable to honest men and their interest for the future'.[25] Although the Declaration of Breda appeared to offer a wide measure of religious toleration the Presbyterian MPs were anxious to ensure that the powers of the bishops were severely curtailed. When the terms of the formal response to the king were being debated they pressed for the inclusion of a passage which was intended, as Clarendon put it, 'to discountenance the bishops' but they were unable to carry the House with them.[26]

In the Declaration of Breda the king had also undertaken to grant a free and general pardon to all his subjects except for any persons whom Parliament might decide to single out for punishment. For the regicides and others who had been members of the Rump it was a desperate situation since it soon became clear that some men would be denied the benefits of the general pardon. In their own defence Sir Arthur Hesilrige and Bulstrode Whitelocke maintained that they had played no part in the death of Charles I (which was certainly true) or in the establishment of the Commonwealth. Hesilrige also stressed that he had been implacably opposed to Cromwell's usurpation but Whitelocke was more vulnerable in this respect and was obliged to resort to special pleading: 'his principle', he claimed, 'was not to disturbe the publicke peace, but to submit to what it pleased God to permit and was not in his power to alter'.[27] In a parliamentary speech John Hutchinson, who was the only regicide to be elected, told his colleagues that if he had erred 'it was the inexperience of his age and the defect of his judgement, and not the mallice of his heart . . . and if the sacrifice of him might conduce to the publick peace and settlement, he should freely submitt his life and fortunes to their dispose'. His wife, who was convinced that he was 'ambitious of being a publick sacrifice', persuaded him to go and stay with a friend and sought to ensure that he came off lightly by sending the Speaker a letter couched in appropriately contrite terms. This required the forging of his signature, but Lucy Hutchinson considered that in the circumstances the end justified the means.[28]

In June the Commons set about the business of selecting those men who were to be named as excepted persons in the forthcoming Act of Indemnity and Oblivion.[29] John Hutchinson was expelled from the House and declared incapable of holding any office or place of public trust; in comparison with other regicides he was treated very leniently. The Commons further agreed that Sir Henry Mildmay, Sir James Harrington and Sir Gilbert Pickering (all of whom had taken part in the trial of the king, though not to the extent of signing the death-warrant) and Sir Henry Vane, Sir Arthur Hesilrige and John Pyne (who had not been involved in any way) should be treated as excepted persons with the proviso that their lives should be spared. On 14 June it was proposed that Bulstrode Whitelocke should also be excepted but the motion was rejected by 175 votes to 134. According to Whitelocke's own account this narrow escape 'cost him a great deale of money in gratifications, and buying out of ennemies from their designs of destroying him'.[30]

The Bill of Indemnity and Oblivion did not become law until the end of August and in the meantime a considerable amount of lobbying went on. Samuel Pepys recorded in his diary that on 19 June Lady Pickering discussed her husband's case with him and gave him £5 in silver as an inducement to use his good offices; and that later that day they had a meeting with her brother Edward Lord Montagu (who would shortly be created Earl of Sandwich).[31] In an appeal to Parliament John Pyne contended, in a carefully worded document, that the Commons had made a mistake in deciding that he should be named as an excepted person since he had played no part in the trial of the late king, had refused to take on responsibility for levying the decimation tax and had held no salaried office or place of profit. 'The Righteous Judge of all the World', he declared, 'direct your spiritts to doe equall justice, and not soe without hearinge or prooffe destroy him and his ffamilye . . . and to strike his name out of the Act from beinge an excepted person'.[32] In the end it was decided that Pickering and Pyne should merely be disqualified from holding any public office.[33]

On 1 July the Commons agreed that Sir James Harrington (who was still at liberty) should be imprisoned for life; that he should be deprived of his estates together with his knighthood and baronetcy; and that on the anniversary of the king's execution he should be drawn on a sledge with a rope around his neck to the gallows at Tyburn. In December he was discovered in a house at Newington Butts, Middlesex but managed to escape to the Continent. In March 1661 he sent his wife a particular of his estate for the purpose of a projected approach to the king. According to this particular the gross revenue was £1,240 a year but the estate was heavily encumbered and he had debts amounting to £8,113. In his accompanying letter he wrote that

I Humbly spreade my sad Condition therein before his Maiesty for his gracious mercy and Compassion towards an antient Famyly, and numerous Issue; soe prayinge God for a blessinge on thy endeavours; and for his Maiesties temporall and eternall Hapinesse.

Recovery of the estates proved difficult while Harrington's exile dragged on for year after year. In one of his published writings he made a passing reference to 'my above Twenty removes to several Residencies, and more than seven years Exile, and separation from my Books, dearest Friends, and Relations'. Despite all his vicissitudes he remained strongly attached to his religious principles with their pronounced millenarian flavour. Convinced that he was a member of God's elect, he observed that this honour meant far more to him than any earthly titles.[34]

On 7 November 1660 a Bill of Attainder was introduced in the Commons and referred to a committee which contained a number of Presbyterian MPs. The primary object of the bill was to enable the Crown to take possession of the estates of the regicides and this immediately led to requests for exemption from some of their heirs, including Barrington Bourchier, the son of Sir John Bourchier whose death had been reported to the Commons in August, and Sir John Stapley, the son of Anthony Stapley who had died during the time of the Protectorate.[35] Shortly afterwards Sir John Barrington received a letter from a parliamentary colleague who urged him to attend the House in order to do what he could to further the interests of his kinsman Bourchier and others whom he numbered among his friends. In the event Bourchier and Stapley were allowed to keep the estates which they had inherited, though in Bourchier's case this was subject to the payment of a fine of £1,000.[36]

Some Puritan squires who had sat in the Rump Parliament were able to enjoy the full benefits of the general pardon. In view of their dalliance with the royalist party it was always likely that Richard Norton and Alexander Popham would escape any kind of punishment; and indeed Norton was once more entrusted with the military government of Portsmouth.[37] Sir William Strickland, Sir Thomas Wroth and John Gurdon, who were more vulnerable, also emerged unscathed from the events of 1660. In August, when the Bill of Indemnity and Oblivion was still under consideration, Gurdon thought it prudent to obtain a special pardon which cost him £48 19s 6d in fees and gratuities.[38] Others such as Sir Arthur Hesilrige and Sir Henry Vane were less fortunate. Hesilrige died of a fever in January 1661 while imprisoned in the Tower and left his family a legacy of unpaid debts amounting to £14,000. In July his estates were confiscated after he had been declared guilty of high treason and it was only with the greatest difficulty that his sons managed to regain possession of them.[39] Writing to his wife on 14 June 1662 Sir Edward Harley informed her, in a brief postscript, that Sir Henry Vane 'was this day beheaded on Tower Hil'. In a speech which he had prepared for the occasion Vane had written that the coming of Jesus Christ to secure 'a speedy and sudden Revival of his Cause, and spreading his Kingdom over the face of the whole Earth, is most clear to the eye of my Faith'.[40]

In his autobiography Sir John Bramston relates that the king had been persuaded that he could only be restored with the assistance of the Presbyterians who accordingly 'truckd for imployments and honors'.[41] In the main the Presbyterian gentry were rewarded by the conferring of titles. Sir George Booth and John Crewe were both ennobled at the time of the coronation;

John Bowyer, Sir Edmund Fowell, Sir John Yonge and Sir Thomas Barnardiston, who like Booth and Crewe had all been excluded in 1648, were granted baronetcies; and many others received knighthoods.[42] At the same time the Presbyterian gentry could not afford to be too complacent in view of the smouldering resentment in royalist circles. In June 1660 an attempt was made to secure the inclusion of Sir Richard Onslow's name in the list of excepted persons. Characteristically, Sir Richard succeeded in extricating himself from this potentially dangerous situation. On 25 November he obtained a special pardon for himself, possibly because he feared that the next Parliament would decline to confirm the Act of Indemnity and Oblivion, and shortly afterwards John Swinfen followed his example.[43] In Lancashire Sir Richard Hoghton's fitness to serve as a justice of the peace was challenged on the grounds that he was a person of doubtful loyalty. In October 1660, however, the Earl of Derby appointed him a deputy lieutenant while in May 1661 he was nominated as one of the Gentlemen of the Privy Chamber.[44]

During the early years of Charles II's reign there were frequent reports (which were often highly imaginative) about the seditious inclinations of both Presbyterians and sectaries. In official circles it was generally assumed that conventicles had more of a political than a religious purpose and in January 1661 they were prohibited by a royal proclamation which empowered magistrates to take action against those who attended them.[45] In this atmosphere of near hysteria there was an ideal opportunity for disgruntled Cavaliers to settle old scores. In September 1661 two Somerset gentlemen, John Pyne and William Strode of Barrington Court, were arrested on the grounds that they had refused to bear the military charges which had been laid on them and had openly declared their hostility to the Church of England. There was a mutual antipathy of long standing between Pyne the political radical and Strode, who had fallen victim to Pride's Purge, which effectively rules out any possibility of collusion. Strode was released on bond, protested about his treatment in a petition to the king and eventually made a humble submission for disobeying the deputy lieutenants. In July 1662 Pyne was arrested again and taken to London for questioning. According to a neighbour he had made some disparaging remarks about the king, claiming that he was seeking to restore popery. If the allegation could be proved, wrote John Ashburnham in a letter to his son-in-law Sir

Hugh Smyth, 'he will infallably be hanged'. Pyne was committed to prison but in October was allowed to return to his house at Curry Mallet.[46] While John Hutchinson was living a retired life at his Nottinghamshire seat, Owthorpe Hall, he applied himself to a more diligent reading of the Scriptures 'which every day gave him new glorious discoveries of the misteries of Christ and Antichrist, and made him rejoyce in all he had done in the Lord's cause'. His wife suggested that he should go abroad for his own safety but he told her that 'this was the place where God had sett him and protected him hitherto, and it would be in him an ungratefull distrust of God to forsake it'. In October 1663 he was apprehended on the pretext that he was involved in a plot against the Crown; and in September 1664 he died in suspicious circumstances while imprisoned in Sandown Castle in Kent.[47]

Sir John Curzon, who was Receiver General for the Duchy of Lancaster, had been serving as one of the knights of the shire for Derbyshire when secluded in 1648. Writing to his friend Lord Mansfield in March 1664 he expressed his concern that persons whose identity was unknown to him were alleging that he always obstructed the king's service, particularly in the matter of the subsidies. These accusations were completely false: 'There is non readyer then my selfe, upon all occasions, wherein I have a capacity as Justice or otherwise, to doe any thinge that may really conduce to the advanceinge of his Majesty's Revenue, Service and Intrest in the Affections of his People'. And he went on to stress, in an attempt to forestall the danger of guilt by association, that 'I have not a presbiterian nor sectary in my ffamily, nor in the Parrish and Towne I live in, beinge all my own Inheritance'. On the other hand, it was reported in 1669 that although Sir John was a magistrate he had made no attempt to suppress a Presbyterian conventicle which was held every Sunday within a mile of his house.[48]

Thomas Viscount Fanshawe, who had received a commission from the king for the raising of forces in Hertfordshire, had a hatred of former parliamentarians which must have owed much to the fact that his father had sustained heavy losses as a result of his loyalty to the Crown during the Civil War. In August 1666 Sir Harbottle Grimston, who was Master of the Rolls, and Sir Henry Caesar interceded on behalf of Sir John Wittewronge, once a member of the county committee for Hertfordshire, who according to Fanshawe had never shown any sign of repentance since the return of the king. As Sir Harbottle explained to Clarendon they had told Fanshawe that Sir John had only appeared in arms for a short time in 1643 and had then laid down his commission. They also testified that 'he constantly keeps his parish church, attending there diligently from the beginning of divine service to the end'; that he had never entertained any dangerous ill-principled persons in his house; and that there was no evidence that he had been present at any 'unlawful schismatical meeting'. Fanshawe, for his part, did his best to denigrate the Master of the Rolls by declaring that he had been as deeply involved in the 'late horridd and bloody rebellion' as any man.[49]

4

BARTHOLOMEW DAY

While he was a prisoner of the republican government Sir William Waller set down his thoughts on the major religious issues of the day. A moderate Presbyterian, he was repelled by the notion of 'a promiscuous toleration of all sects' but considered that there was a need for a church settlement which accommodated the main parties. 'Some', he observed, 'may be entitled Episcopians, some Presbyterians, and some Independents; and yet all be Israelites indeed, belonging to the same election of grace.' In his view it was inconceivable that there should be any question of making concessions to the sectaries whose beliefs were in direct conflict with the fundamentals of religion but 'as to those who are divided from us only in things indifferent, in matters only ceremonial and ritual . . . there should be much tenderness and condescension used towards them'.[1] His general approach was not dissimilar to that of Richard Baxter who prided himself on not belonging to any particular faction. In February 1657 Baxter told his friend John Swinfen, who was then serving as an MP, that 'The Gospel and Godlyness are in exceeding danger of ruine in England at this time' and expressed the hope that the Presbyterians, Independents and all honest Christians would be able to agree on a settled discipline which would apply throughout the land. He personally was in favour of a reconciliation of 'all the sober godly people' so far as this was possible and of legislation guaranteeing religious toleration which should include the episcopal party. As he explained in his autobiography, he thought that the guiding principle should be unity in things necessary and liberty in things unnecessary; and indeed this was the principle which he had followed in establishing the Worcestershire association of ministers.[2]

Edward Harley had a considerable regard for the works of

Edward Stillingfleet, including his *Irenicum* which was completed in 1660.[3] Stillingfleet was one of those divines whom Gilbert Burnet describes as 'men of latitude' and his professed aim in embarking upon this treatise, which bears the subtitle *A Weapon-Salve for the Churches Wounds*, was 'to lay a foundation for a happy union'. In the hope that the Presbyterians at least could be persuaded to remain within the national Church he raised the possibility of introducing the kind of ecclesiastical settlement which restricted the powers of the bishops and prescribed relatively few ceremonial requirements; religion, he stressed, should not be clogged with ceremonies. Like some of the leading Presbyterian divines he was attracted to the proposals put forward by Archbishop Usher in 1641 which, as Baxter put it, involved the reduction of episcopacy into a form of synodical government which reflected the practice of the ancient Church. During the years 1657 to 1665 Stillingfleet was the rector of Sutton in Bedfordshire and may well have exchanged views on these matters with his patron, Sir Roger Burgoyne, whose respect for him was fully reciprocated. In dedicating another of his works to Burgoyne in 1662 he told him that in view of their close acquaintance he was well aware how little 'You need such discourses which tend to settle the Foundations of Religion, which you have raised so happy a Superstructure upon'. Another of the secluded members who thought highly of Stillingfleet was Sir Harbottle Grimston, the Master of the Rolls, who chose him for the office of preacher at the Rolls chapel. According to Gilbert Burnet (who subsequently held this appointment) Grimston 'had always a tenderness to the dissenters, though he himself continued still in the communion of the church'.[4]

In April 1660 Dr George Morley reported to Hyde, who was employing him as an intermediary, that the leaders of the Presbyterian party were prepared to accept the name of bishops but wished to limit their powers. In his discussions with them he had emphasised that the canons, the ecclesiastical laws and a 'free synod' would prevent episcopal government from taking on an arbitrary character.[5] Following the king's return, and in advance of any permanent ecclesiastical settlement, many new bishops were consecrated and ministers who had been put into sequestered livings began to come under heavy pressure. In June 1660 the Presbyterian ministers of Hereford informed Edward Harley, whom they regarded as their chief patron, that 'We are dayly threatened that wee shalbe removed hence' and that if it was decided to reintroduce a dean and chapter their situation would become even more desperate.[6] Sir John Bramston writes that at an early stage in the proceedings of the Convention Parliament he declared himself in favour of episcopal government and that this led a Presbyterian MP, Sir Anthony Irby, to remark that he 'spake desperately for episcopacie'. One of the most hotly debated issues during the short life of the Convention Parliament was the question of how the Church was to be governed. Some Presbyterian MPs seemed anxious to make it abundantly clear that they were not opposed to episcopacy, though this was usually subject to qualifications. Sir John Northcote roundly condemned the deans and chapters who, he claimed, 'did nothing but eat and drink and rise up to play' and when a fellow MP reproved him for his outburst Sir Walter Erle immediately sprang to his defence. Walter Yonge (a grandson of the Puritan diarist of the same name) told the House that he was for episcopacy but not to the extent of treating it as an article of faith. John Swinfen and others argued for a limited form of episcopacy. Sir Gilbert Gerard felt unable to take a view on this proposition until he had considered whether it was in conflict with the terms of the Solemn League and Covenant.[7]

Richard Baxter relates that at the Savoy Conference in which he was involved no attempt was made to challenge the doctrine of the Church since it was accepted that the Articles of Religion were 'sound and moderate'.[8] Among the Presbyterian MPs, however, there were differences of opinion about the merits of the Thirty Nine Articles. Sir John Northcote and Sir John Bowyer had no reservations about them; William Prynne vehemently attacked them; and John Swinfen drew a distinction between the doctrinal provisions which for him were unexceptionable and the provisions concerned with discipline which in his view were 'too grating to the conscience'.[9] Discussion of the Thirty Nine Articles was largely a product of the House's consideration of a legislative measure which finally emerged as the Act for the Confirming and Restoring of Ministers. The primary object of this measure was the reinstatement of ministers who had been ejected since the beginning of the Civil War but in addition it granted security of tenure to ministers who had been presented to livings which had fallen vacant in the normal course of events. Significantly, it was decided that this latter provision should apply to ministers who before 25 December 1659 had been ordained by 'any ecclesiastical persons', a formulation which was intended to cover Presbyterian divines as well as bishops. There was also a caveat that men who had come out in favour of the trial and execution of Charles I should be turned out of their livings but for most Presbyterian incumbents this presented no problem.[10]

During the autumn recess the king issued a proclamation which held out the prospect of a national Church in which the powers of the bishops would be severely constrained and some freedom would be allowed over the ceremonial aspects of public worship.[11] On 6 November Sir Anthony Irby moved in the House that the king should be warmly thanked for his enlightened approach to the issue of church government and that the provisions of the declaration should be embodied in a parliamentary statute. In the committee which was set up for the purpose of preparing a bill the Presbyterian interest was represented by Sir Walter Erle, Sir Anthony Irby, Sir John Northcote, Walter Yonge and Hugh Boscawen. On 28 November several Presbyterian MPs spoke in favour of giving the bill a second reading. In the course of his speech Walter Yonge argued that the ceremonies of the Church were not of so great importance 'as to embroil us again in a new War' and pleaded for some indulgence to be shown to 'such as had ventured their lives for the Good of all'. John Swinfen claimed, not altogether convincingly, that nothing was more eagerly awaited by the people than the passage of the bill and that it was unlikely that the bishops would take exception to it since they had been associated with the framing of the declaration. When the House divided over the question of whether there should be a second reading Sir Anthony Irby and Sir George Booth acted as tellers for the ayes but their opponents won the day by 183 votes to 157. In a work published some years later John Collinges, a Presbyterian minister who had been serving as chaplain to the Hobart family, suggested that this had proved to be a disastrous decision:

> Whether the wisdom of his Majesty, or that party of the House of Commons who then opposed the passing of it into an Act, were greater let the experience now of Twenty years more determine, which for the most part have been years of confusion and disorder as to matters of Religion.[12]

Any lingering hopes that the policy of comprehension might still prevail were soon dispelled by the failure of the Savoy

Conference and the election of a new Parliament in which at the outset there were comparatively few Puritan MPs. On 3 July 1661 a Bill of Uniformity was given a first and second reading in the Commons and assigned to a committee for further processing. Sir Gilbert Gerard, Sir Anthony Irby and John Swinfen were nominated as members of this committee but they were heavily outnumbered and on 9 July the House approved the bill without a division.[13] Under the provisions of the Act of Uniformity, as it became in May 1662, ministers were required to declare their 'unfeigned assent and consent' to everything contained in the Book of Common Prayer (which had been slightly revised); to take the oath of obedience with its emphasis on the sovereignty of the diocesan authorities; and to acknowledge that the Solemn League and Covenant was an unlawful oath. For those who had been ordained under Presbyterian auspices there was the further condition that they must submit to episcopal ordination if they wished to retain their livings. This presented them with a particularly difficult decision since, as Richard Baxter observes, there was good reason to think that 'by submitting to be Re-ordained, Men do interpretatively confess the nullity of their former Ordination'.[14]

Generally the requirement that ministers should make a declaration of their conformity before 24 August, the Feast of St Bartholomew, allowed them little time to debate the matter among themselves. Writing to his friend Sir Edward Harley on 1 August Thomas Doughty, the vicar of Legsby in Lincolnshire, stressed that he had been unable to consult any of his fellow clergy and asked what the beleaguered ministers should do:

> do they petition . . . or do they only prepare and resolve to leave their employments and office? or do they any of them comply or conforme? is there no mitigation or Dispensation to be hoped for? Surely the hand of God is heavy upon many of his people.

In the end Doughty decided to conform, though with 'some inward regret and uneasynes'.[15] On 4 August Thomas Gilbert, who held one of Lord Wharton's livings in Buckinghamshire, was writing that along with many others he was certain to be ejected and that those patrons who had 'any thing of Religion' would have to pick up the best conformists they could.[16] In Northamptonshire Richard Knightley's ministers, John Wilson of Fawsley, John

Tompson of Preston Capes and Thomas Knightley of Byfield, all opted for conformity, no doubt following a conference at the house of their patron.[17] At Charminster in Dorset the minister, Samuel Hardy, managed to hold on to his curacy through a combination of factors: the church was a peculiar and therefore was exempt from normal diocesan jurisdiction;[18] his patron, Thomas Trenchard, ensured that he remained undisturbed by neighbouring magistrates; and he conformed to a limited extent by reading 'the scripture-sentences, the creed, commandments, lessons, prayer for the king'. During his time at Charminster he also acted as chaplain to the Trenchards and, we are told, exerted great influence over Thomas Trenchard and his brother John, the future Whig politician. In 1669 he moved to Poole where there was a chapel which, like its mother church at Canford Magna, was a royal peculiar. When Thomas Trenchard drew up his will in April 1671 he bequeathed £100 towards the cost of establishing a grammar school at Poole and a further sum of £100 as a personal gift to his former minister.[19]

For a substantial minority of beneficed ministers the conditions laid down in the Act of Uniformity were too high a price to pay for the security of tenure which they would have gained by complying with them. The resulting upheaval led one minister who refused to conform to express the hope that the cries of many thousands of souls for the bread of life would 'pierce the heavens (there being neere 2000 ejected ministers) and that God who hath now hid his face will not contend for ever, but will repent him of the evill'.[20] Unlike the intruding ministers who had been deprived of their benefices as a result of the earlier legislation[21] many of those who fell victim to the Act of Uniformity were forced out of livings in the gift of wealthy Puritan patrons, men such as Sir Edward Harley in Herefordshire, Sir Thomas Barnardiston and John Gurdon in Suffolk, Sir Walter Erle in Dorset and Richard Norton in Hampshire.[22] One of the most famous of the ejected ministers was Samuel Fairclough who had been presented by Sir Nathaniel Barnardiston to the living of Kedington in 1630 and had 'joined hand in hand' with his patron 'to promote both the form and the power of Godliness in that Town and County'. Fairclough had no objection to episcopacy as a human institution provided it was subject to constraints but he felt unable to declare his 'assent and consent' to the Book of Common Prayer. During the Laudian era he had frustrated the attempts of the diocesan authorities to bring him to book for his nonconformity; this time, however, there was no escape and as the day of reckoning approached Fairclough and his patron, Sir Thomas Barnardiston, had a special prayer session at which they asked God to further their aim of finding a worthy successor.[23]

In some cases an ejected minister was immediately taken into his patron's household and assigned the role of domestic chaplain. This happened at Cottesbrooke in Northamptonshire where the patron was Sir John Langham, a man whose 'plentiful Table was seldom without Divines of Note'. Sir John was a rich London merchant who had purchased the Cottesbrooke estate and made it his country seat. In his will, which was drawn up in November 1670, he left the sum of £100 to his chaplain Thomas Burroughs, the former rector of Cottesbrooke. Burroughs was the author of two published works: a sermon which he had preached at the funeral of his patron's grandson John Langham in 1657 and a work entitled *Directions About Preparing for Death* which first appeared in 1669. These directions, he explained in the second edition, had been produced in 1663 at the request and for the private use of Sir John Langham, 'a person of very Eminent worth' who would not soon be forgotten in the city of London.[24] Following the ejection of Burroughs Sir John presented Edward Pierce who subsequently married his niece Elizabeth Langham. Pierce was well regarded among the godly, as may be judged by the fact that Sir Edward Harley had offered him a living shortly after the Restoration; and in 1681 he revealed his liberal credentials in a work which was published under the self-explanatory title *The Conformist's Plea for the Non-Conformist*.[25] At Hickleton in Yorkshire Sir John Jackson employed the ejected minister, Hugh Everard, as his chaplain and Everard's wife as his housekeeper. Everard was a person of some standing: a younger son of an Essex squire, Sir Richard Everard, he had been appointed to a fellowship at Cambridge in 1658. In his will he left Sir John a legacy of £20 (which was an unusual gesture for a domestic chaplain) and put it on record that he had deposited the sum of £500 with him on good security.[26]

Hugh Boscawen, who was one of the leading magnates in Cornwall, was seated at Tregothnan in the secluded parish of St Michael Penkevil. His minister, Joseph Halsey, had been acting as his household chaplain as well as discharging his responsibilities as the rector of the parish. Many years after Halsey's removal by the ecclesiastical authorities Boscawen could write with feeling of 'the great change' which had been made 'to our very greate loss'. As his resident chaplain he brought in another nonconformist, John Cowbridge, who had been deprived of the living of St Anthony. Halsey, however, continued to enjoy Boscawen's patronage and regularly preached in his mansion-house on Saturday evenings and Sunday mornings.[27]

The domiciliary restrictions imposed on nonconformist ministers by the Five Mile Act of 1665 applied not only to cities, corporate towns and boroughs but to any parish where such a minister had been performing the functions of a parson, curate or lecturer or had preached in a conventicle or other unlawful assembly since the passage of the Act of Indemnity and Oblivion.[28] An ejected minister could free himself from these restrictions by taking the oath prescribed in this statute but many were unwilling to do so because it would have meant subscribing to the proposition that the government of the Church was unalterable and not infrequently they moved elsewhere to escape the penalties. Some Puritan patrons, however, were clearly in favour of defying the law. In 1665 the Bishop of Exeter reported that Joseph Halsey was living in the parsonage house of St Michael Penkevil 'which he renteth of the present Incumbent and is peaceable and Quiet'. Not long afterwards the Five Mile Act led Halsey to take up residence at Philleigh on the other side of the River Fal but Boscawen and his wife thought it inconvenient that he should be so far away from Tregothnan and persuaded him to settle in a neighbouring parish.[29]

In all, some 80 nonconformist divines who had been forced to relinquish their livings or fellowships were employed as chaplains in the houses of the Puritan nobility and gentry.[30] At the same time there was considerable support at this level of society for those men who aimed to secure a means of livelihood for themselves as schoolmasters. Some were taken on as private tutors, others provided tuition for the sons of major landowners in the schools which they established.[31] Richard Kennet, who had been a fellow of Corpus Christi, Cambridge for many years, set up a school in the Bedfordshire parish of Sutton with the generous assistance of the minister, Edward Stillingfleet. At first he entrusted the teaching work to a conformist but after a while he 'took the care of the school upon himself, and was connived at, the neighbouring gentry having a great esteem for him'. The most prominent of these gentlemen was Sir Roger Burgoyne, the squire and patron of the living, whose support for this undertaking was crucial. When his son John was admitted to St John's College, Cambridge in 1667 it was noted in the register that he had received his schooling at Sutton.[32] After forfeiting his Derbyshire benefice Samuel Ogden kept a school first at Mackworth where he had been the incumbent and then in Derby where the master of the public grammar school eventually began legal proceedings against him. When the Court of Arches ruled that his school should be closed down the future must have seemed bleak, but in 1686 he was appointed master of the free school at Wirksworth through the influence of Sir John Gell who was one of the governors and a grandson of the founder.[33]

Ministers in need of financial assistance to keep body and soul together were largely dependent on individual acts of charity. One of the most generous benefactors was Lady Mary Armyne, the widow of Sir William Armyne who had been a member of the republican Council of State. Following her death in 1675 Richard Baxter wrote that 'When she first heard of eighteen hundred Ministers ejected and silenced 1662 she gave a considerable summe towards the relief of some of them.' According to another account she asked Edmund Calamy, who had himself been deprived of his living, to distribute the sum of £500 on her behalf to those ministers whose financial problems were particularly severe. During her widowhood Lady Armyne lived mainly in Westminster and in a codicil to her will she left £20 to Gabriel Sangar, a nonconformist divine 'under whose ministery I some-time lyved' when he was rector of St Martin in the Fields. In a further codicil she settled a rent-charge of £40 a year on a number of trustees who consisted of her nephew William Pierrepont, once a leading member of the Long Parliament; two of the most prominent nonconformist ministers in London, Dr Thomas Manton and Dr Thomas Jacombe; her physician, Dr John Micklethwaite, who was the son of a nonconformist minister; and John Dan her Presbyterian chaplain. The purpose of the trust (which Lady Armyne specified in private directions) was to provide financial assistance to ejected ministers in Derbyshire, Huntingdonshire and Yorkshire and payments were still being made as late as 1694.[34]

Although Richard Knightley's own ministers conformed he was not slow to respond to the needs of other ministers who had felt unable to submit. In September 1662, shortly after the Feast of St Bartholomew, he made provision in his will for the distribution of £200 'to 20 such poore Ministers as my Executor shall think fit, or such persons who lately exercised the office of Ministers, equally to be divided amongst them'. The executor was his uncle Richard Hampden who employed ejected ministers as his chaplains and gave help to others.[35] William Strode of Somerset, who died in 1666, preferred a more targeted approach. In his will he left an annuity of £24 which was to be paid to twelve ejected ministers, all of whom were named, for a term of seven years after his death. For the most part these were men who had formerly held livings in Somerset. They included John Bush who had at one time served as Strode's domestic chaplain and considered his family to be the most 'regular' or orderly he had ever seen and Edward Bennet who had been deprived of the living of East Morden in Dorset which was in the gift of Sir Walter Erle.[36] In 1667 Strode's daughter Joanna eloped with Henry Hickman who had been forced to relinquish his fellowship at Magdalen College, Oxford and had more recently been employed by her uncle John Strode as a tutor for his son. The following year they began legal proceedings over a portion of £2,500 which Joanna Hickman was due to receive under the terms of her father's will. During the course of a long-running dispute her brother William, who had inherited the estate, claimed that Hickman had secretly married her in order to gain possession of her fortune and that the two of them had stolen some of his property.[37]

Samuel Dunch, a Hampshire squire with an income of £2,500 a year, was 'a great friend to all the suffering ministers whom he knew'. In his will, which was drawn up in November 1667, he granted life annuities amounting to some £68 to six nonconformist ministers, among them Robert Lancaster the former minister of North Baddesley where he was seated and Samuel Blower his chaplain who had 'taken great paines for the spirituall good of both me and my ffamily'. In addition, there were gifts of money for four other ejected ministers, including Simon Pole who, as he noted, was then a prisoner at Ilminster in Somerset.[38]

Although Sir John Wittewronge was portrayed in the early part of Charles II's reign as a man who was fully conformable in matters of religion[39] he was by no means out of sympathy with the plight of ministers who were suffering hardship because of their refusal to compromise. This is not altogether surprising in view of the fact that he had once been a member of William Bridge's Independent congregation in London. In his will, which in its final form bears the date 7 June 1688, he gave £100 to his son James, whom he appointed as executor, with the request that he should distribute it to 'such poore Ministers of the Gospell or the widows of such poore Ministers of the Gospell as shall bee by him judged fitt Objects of Charity'. Since Sir John lived on until 1693 there was a certain lack of urgency about his charitable instincts; nevertheless there were still many potential recipients even in the last decade of the century.[40]

On 24 December 1662 Samuel Pepys had dinner with John Lord Crewe and recorded in his diary that 'He pities the poor Ministers that are put out, to whom he says the King is beholden for his coming in; and that if any such thing had been foreseen, he had never come in.'[41] Crewe and the other Presbyterian leaders had contributed to this débâcle by their failure to insist on prior conditions for the return of the king but it was the poor showing of their party in the parliamentary elections of 1661 which had been the crucial factor. Among the Puritan county families there were some men who seemed ready to acquiesce in and even welcome a conservative religious settlement, perhaps because they had taken fright at the activities of the sectaries. When Sir William Lytton drew up his will in June 1660 he was anxious to make it clear that it was his 'earnest desire to bee buried by the booke of Common prayer privately without ffunerall pompe and not to have any Sermon for avoyding of fflattery'.[42] Others, however, were deeply concerned about the implications of the Act of Uniformity and more particularly the threat which it presented to 'soul-saving preaching'. The ministry of the Gospel, Sir Edward Harley would later declare, 'is the Necessary means of salvation'.[43] This was an aspect which was highlighted by Edmund Calamy when he delivered his final sermon to the congregation of St Mary Aldermanbury on 28 December 1662:

> where God is in a Nation, and where the Gospel is preserved in purity in a Nation, that Nation cannot but stand; but when God is gone, and the Gospel gone, then comes the misery of a Nation . . . When the Ark of God is taken, then the Souls of many are in danger; when the Gospel is gone, your Souls are in hazard.[44]

49

Similar fears had been expressed during the Laudian era but the situation was now much worse. For the future the survival of 'true religion' as men like Baxter and Calamy understood the term would depend to a very great extent on the commitment of members of the nobility and gentry both as patrons and politicians.

5

CHANGE AND DECAY

Shortly before the death of John Hampden in 1643 a royalist newspaper reported with evident delight that he had experienced many great misfortunes since the outbreak of the Civil War. His eldest son John, two of his daughters and a grandchild had all died; and of his remaining sons one was a cripple and the other a lunatic.[1] Richard Hampden, who inherited his father's estate, did not enjoy good health: in October 1677, for example, he was writing to a friend that 'The frequent returnes of my Distemper and my crazy condition makes it seasonable to thinke of a Change of affaires in my poore family.' Nevertheless he lived on until 1695 and although his heir committed suicide a year later after a period of depression it was not until 1754 that the family expired in the male line.[2] There were some Puritan county families, however, which lacked the durability of the Hampdens. One of the most prominent of these was the Armyne family whose principal residence was Osgodby Hall in Lincolnshire. Sir William Armyne, who was a leading member of the Long Parliament, had three sons, William, Theophilus and Michael. Theophilus Armyne, who served as a parliamentary colonel, died in battle in 1645 while Sir William, the second baronet, left only daughters. At the funeral of the second baronet in 1658 the preacher, Christopher Shute, dwelt at some length on the sins of the deceased but assured the congregation that he had been genuinely penitent. When the sermon was published he dedicated it to Sir Michael, the new baronet, and expressed the hope that he would inherit his brother's piety and humility. Not long afterwards the widow, Lady Anne, married John Lord Belasyse, a Yorkshire Catholic who had been a royalist general during the Civil War. Sir Michael, who was in serious financial difficulties, died unmarried in 1668 when the baronetcy became extinct and the estates were divided up among his kindred. 'I suppose', wrote Dr John Worthington of Jesus College, Cambridge to one of his academic colleagues, that 'you have heard of Sir Michael Armyn's death at London, the last of Sir William's sonns. Now is none living but Sir William's brother . . . about 70 years old, who hath no sons'. For many years the Puritan tradition in the family was maintained by Lady Mary Armyne, the widow of the first baronet, who survived until 1675. God, it was said, had confirmed her 'not only in the Protestant Religion, but also in the true love of practice and seriousness in that Religion which she profest'. During her widowhood she kept a chaplain in her household and provided financial support for ministers who had been forced out of their livings as a consequence of the Act of Uniformity.[3].

Another Lincolnshire family, the Wrays of Glentworth, also expired in the direct male line during the course of Charles II's reign, though there was a cadet branch which inherited their baronetcy. Sir John Wray, who died in 1655, had a number of children but his sons, who were described as 'almost all mad', left no male issue. The eldest son, Sir John, married twice. His first wife was Lady Elizabeth D'Ewes, the widow of Sir Simonds D'Ewes, who brought with her lands worth £1,000 a year which had once belonged to her father. There was a certain irony about this since D'Ewes had quarrelled with Wray's father in the Commons and had entered the scathing comment in his parliamentary journal that 'his wisdome was but small'. Wray and his brother Sir Christopher died in 1664 within a month of each other. The last brother, Sir Bethell, was formally declared a lunatic and his lands were managed on his behalf under arrangements which required the sum of £400 a year to be set aside for his maintenance. At his death in 1672 Glentworth Hall and the estates, which were worth £3,500 a year, were inherited by the only daughter of Sir John the younger who married Nicholas Saunderson, the eldest son of George Viscount Castleton.[4]

In the main the Puritan county families of Charles I's reign were still flourishing, in the sense that the male line remained unbroken, at the end of the seventeenth century; and with few exceptions they were still seated in the same localities. Among them were such families as the Barringtons, Barnardistons, Knightleys and Harleys which before the time of the Civil War had been particularly zealous in seeking to promote the cause of godliness. In some cases, however, there had been a good deal of turbulence as one premature death followed another in rapid succession. A high mortality rate (which is reflected in the church monuments at Fawsley in Northamptonshire) took a heavy toll of the Knightleys but fortunately for them there was a sufficient supply of younger sons to ensure their survival. Richard Knightley, who had sat in the Long Parliament, died in June 1661 shortly after he had been created a Knight of the Bath. Edmund Ludlow claims that these two events were not unconnected since Knightley's involvement in the 'popish and superstitious ceremonyes' associated with the making of Knights of the Bath had caused him severe anguish. Knightley, he writes,

> having some remaynder of conscience, scrupled for a while the bowing at the altar, and, being prevayled with to doe it, was so troubled for having done it that (as it was supposed) it was a meanes to shorten his dayes.

Sir Richard had two sons, Richard and Essex, who succeeded in turn to the family estates. On the death of Essex Knightley in 1670 his inheritance was divided up: the Northamptonshire estates came into the possession of his uncle Devereux Knightley while the unentailed estates in Warwickshire, Staffordshire and Worcestershire were reserved for his infant daughter, Anne, who eventually carried them out of the family. Devereux Knightley's son and namesake died in 1695 at the age of nineteen: according to a monumental inscription at Tarporley in Cheshire (where his mother's family was seated) he was 'a youth of great hopes and rare endowments both of body and mind (as his father was), highly valued in his country'. The Northamptonshire estates then passed to Lucy Knightley, a male cousin, whose father had been a merchant living in Hackney. Despite the loss of their outlying property the Knightleys were still major landowners but it is hardly surprising, given this lack of stability, that in the latter part of the seventeenth century they were far less prominent in either a political or a religious sense than they had formerly been. So far as religion is concerned there were two factors which provided at least some measure of continuity: in the first place, Lady Anne Knightley, the widow of Sir Richard Knightley, lived on at Fawsley for many years after her husband's death and, second, the patronage rights belonging to the Knightley livings of Fawsley and Preston Capes had been assigned in 1668 to trustees who included Sir Edward Harley and Richard Hampden.[5]

Another cause of instability was the domestic quarrel, usually between father and son or husband and wife. In October 1661 Sir William Waller informed his kinsman Sir Edward Harley, who was then governor of Dunkirk, that his younger son, Thomas Waller, would shortly be with him. 'You will finde him', he wrote, 'to be of a flexible, ductile disposition'; if he had a fault it was his love of gambling 'which hath putt him upon borrowing and shifting to his great disadvantage'. This poor youth, he went on, was now his whole stock since his elder son William had left home in a rebellious manner, though without the slightest provocation on his part. Shortly afterwards Edmund Calamy was preaching the sermon at the funeral of Lady Waller and thought it appropriate to give the matter a public airing. On her deathbed, he related, she had told some of her friends that she had been most unjustly accused of fomenting the differences between her husband and stepson; and when she had challenged her husband about this he had acknowledged that she had often sought to mediate between them and 'never had done him any ill Office'. From the evidence of his will, which was drawn up in 1668, it is clear that Sir William was determined to leave his sons as little as possible. Strict instructions were given to the friends whom he appointed as executors of his will that they should sell all his Middlesex property, including the Elizabethan mansion at Osterley where he was living; that after discharging his debts they should purchase other lands for the benefit of his descendants, subject to the proviso that neither son should be allowed to take possession of them; and that they should pay his sons only such amounts of money as they 'shall from time to time thinke fit'. In the event Sir William Waller the younger emerged as a fervent anti-Catholic while in 1676 it was reported that he and his wife attended Presbyterian meetings in London.[6]

In Somerset the Pyne family, which was seated at Curry Mallet, underwent a similar experience. For a man who had acquired a reputation as a Puritan of the most rigid sort, John Pyne had a surprisingly eventful private life. With Bulstrode Whitelocke's assistance he had eloped with a wealthy heiress, Eleanor Hanham, in defiance of her uncle who (according to Whitelocke) had been anxious to secure her estate for himself and his children.[7] Later on he was involved in a long-running quarrel with his eldest son which grew more bitter as it became clear that he intended to disinherit him. In 1668 John Pyne the younger brought a suit in

54

the Court of Chancery in an attempt to establish his right of inheritance and claimed (without justification) that his father regarded him as 'respectfull, dutifull and observant unto him in whatsoever he required'. In the event this suit failed in its purpose and Pyne and his son remained at loggerheads. In April 1669 Sir Edmund Wyndham, a kinsman, asked Pyne whether there was any prospect that after such a long period of disobedience his son would eventually return 'to pay you that dutye which god and nature requires of him, of which I should be very glad to heare bycause that it would redound to his good and I hope to your satisfaction to receive him as the father did the prodigall in the Gospell'. Later that month we find his cousin Alexander Popham commiserating with him over his son's disgraceful conduct. Such an affliction, he observed, 'brings us more earnestly to look after our great and happy eternity; sure we can never be truly happy until we come thear'. At the Taunton assizes his son had made several attempts to speak to him but he had told him plainly that he would have nothing to do with him.[8] Although there was some further litigation after Pyne's death in 1679 the bulk of his landed property came into the possession of a younger son, Charles, under the terms of a settlement which he had made three years earlier. Despite the differences with his father the eldest son appears to have been heavily influenced by his dissenting views on ecclesiastical matters. In his will, which was drawn up in 1696, he expressed the wish that he should be buried 'without Common Prayers' in his father's aisle in the parish church of Curry Mallet and that John Bush, a nonconformist minister, should preach the sermon.[9]

The Lyttons, who were one of the wealthiest families in Hertford-shire, were also faced with a major domestic crisis though in their case it was the product of a disastrous marriage. Sir Rowland Lytton had an only son, William, who like him had been an undergraduate at Sidney Sussex, Cambridge. In February 1666 he married Mary Harrison, a daughter of Sir John Harrison of Balls Park near Hertford who had built up a considerable estate with the profits of his business activities. Under the terms of the marriage settlement she was to have a jointure of £700 a year in return for a portion of £6,000. Almost immediately, however, a dispute arose which boded ill for the future. According to a letter written by Sir Rowland to the bride's father in July 1666, Lady Harrison had been pressing his son to meet some of the expenditure incurred when the marriage settlement was drawn up. In forwarding the money Sir Rowland stressed that he was doing so out of respect for Sir John and not because of his wife's importunity 'for I looke upon her as a person . . . resolved to disoblige me, and my whole family'. Even at this stage he was beginning to wonder whether the marriage had been a mistake:

> I am very much perplext at thes early differences, I know not what they portend . . . I know my sonn is good natured, free from vice . . . and though he is not so quick in his speech as others, yet he is not so wanting in judgement as some would make him, which is the ready way to make his wife dispise him, and he not love her.

He could not understand why Lady Harrison should talk so much about the size of the marriage portion since it was far from unusual. His main reason for concluding the match with the Harrisons rather than a greater family was that his son 'might have the more respect and kindnes, and besides you having raysed your estate by your owne industry and parts, he being naturally thrifty, you would the better like it'. He was so troubled that he could take no pleasure in anything and now regretted that he had done so much to beautify the family seat and improve the estate. Sir John, he hoped, would join him in seeking to promote the well being of the young couple for if they were separated they would both be ruined.[10] In July 1674, not long before his father's death, William Lytton granted a lease of property to trustees, including Sir John's widow, for the maintenance of his wife so long as she lived apart from him. This was subject to the caveat that the lease would be void if he were to pay her an allowance of £230 a year. Lady Lytton, as she became when her husband was knighted, died in 1685 and was buried at Hertford rather than in the Lytton family vault at Knebworth. Sir William married again but left no children. On his death in 1705 the estates passed to his nephew Lytton Strode who in accordance with his wishes assumed the name Lytton Lytton.[11]

The Barringtons, who were related to the Lyttons, met with similar problems. Sir John Barrington was involved in litigation with a number of his relatives, including his formidable step-mother, Lady Judith, and in December 1653 had to endure an enforced sojourn in the Fleet prison. Writing to his uncle Sir Gilbert Gerard he complained that 'I must first suffer an harsh imprisonment when I could not make good an Annuitie where it was pretended to be graunted.' His eldest son Thomas was the heir not only to a plentiful estate but a set of religious principles and values which had been nurtured by a succession of Puritan chaplains. He was reminded of his obligation to follow in the footsteps of generations of his godly family in a letter which he received from a kinsman: 'You are descended from Ancestors holy, honest and honourable', he was told, 'Grace with Industry makes you heire apparent to holiness and their vertuous manners ... I pray you to become a Theophilus.' In November 1664 he married Lady Anne Rich, the eldest daughter of Robert Earl of Warwick who had been the leading patron of Puritan divines in Essex. Although the two families had been on close terms for many years Sir John was soon engaged in a dispute with Charles Earl of Warwick, who was Lady Anne's uncle, over the implementation of the marriage settlement. At the Earl's request Sir Gilbert Gerard attempted to mediate. In a letter which he dispatched to his nephew in June 1667 he first observed that he had been extremely pleased by

that match of your sonne with that noble ladie now his wife ... not onelie as it was an honor to your familie, but as this union of your two families was very acceptable unto all your friendes and allies in these parts, and that which much reioices, all the godlie ministers and people about you.

He was concerned, however, about the differences which had arisen and he hoped that Sir John would accept the Earl's proposal that the matter should be resolved by arbitration. If he was disposed to reject it he should consider how prejudicial this might be to all the 'good endes' which could be expected from the alliance and particularly so far as his own family was concerned. In conclusion he expressed the wish that God would direct him 'to doe what may be most for his glory and the hapines and prosperity of your noble family, and the good of his Church'.[12]

The dispute dragged on and it was not until 1676 that the two families came to an agreement over the settlement of a jointure. Nor was that the end of the matter; indeed there were more serious developments ahead. Lady Anne preferred the social whirl of London to the rural solitude of Essex and was said to have acquired a particular aversion to Hatfield Broad Oak where the Barringtons were seated. For some years she and her husband lived in London where she bore him three sons and two daughters. Eventually, however, she deserted him, not because of any ill treatment but because of fundamental differences in outlook and temperament. At the same time she had financial grievances which brought her into conflict with her father-in-law. Writing to Tobias Hewitt, the family steward, in June 1680 a relative of hers acknowledged that she had acted rashly in leaving her husband, but proceeded to accuse Sir John of failing to provide his son with sufficient funds to cover his necessary expenses. In Lady Anne's view, he stressed, their household had been managed with thrift and economy; nevertheless she had been obliged to contribute £7,000 from her own inheritance for the payment of debts which had been unavoidably contracted. There was a danger, he went on, that Sir John 'will perfect and Compleat the ruine of his family, which this unhappy seperation most fatally portends'. In reply Hewitt told him that he had not yet shown his letter to Sir John, adding that 'I know his temper to be passionate and his condition at present weake.'[13]

In these circumstances Thomas Barrington sat down to compose a letter to his estranged wife in which his pent-up emotions found full expression. For fifteen years, he wrote, he had submitted to her wishes but he would never again consent to her living in London. He now expected her to conform to his will and in particular to settle the estate which she had inherited on their children, to give him a solemn undertaking that she would live a more sober life and to dwell with him 'as a wife ought to doe, wheare I shall thinke most convenient for us both'. 'These', he declared, 'are the resolutions which I have taken up and am (with God allmighty's assistance) resolved to follow.' Probably there was never any serious possibility that they would live together again. Barrington died in January 1682 and Lady Anne soon remarried; in November 1683 we find her new husband, Richard Franklin, writing to Tobias Hewitt to inquire about some East India Company stock which had been purchased on behalf of his wife and her late husband.[14]

In her diary, Mary Countess of Warwick, a woman of great piety, refers not only to the shortcomings of her niece Lady Anne Rich but to the internal dissensions of two other Essex families with a Puritan background, the Barringtons of Little Baddow and the Everards of Langleys in Much Waltham. In August 1672 she sought to persuade Sir Gobert Barrington 'to be reconciled to his eldest son whom he had cast off but prevailed not'. Later she attempted to mediate between Sir Richard Everard and his eldest son, Sir Richard the younger, and in August 1677 she noted that it had pleased God to crown her endeavours with good success 'and to inable me to reconcile all the many differences that were betwene them and to make an agreement betwene the father and the Sonn and the Gransone which gave me much satisfaction'. Unfortunately her efforts at peacemaking were not completely successful: the grandson, Richard, is said to have died young 'of a consumption (his heart being broke) contracted through his father's unkindness'.[15]

In September 1677 Lady Elizabeth Alston, the wife of Sir Thomas Alston, was buried in their parish church of Odell in Bedfordshire. In his sermon the minister, William Dillingham, related that God had made use of her in 'the seasoning of others with Religion, and the holding forth the power of Godliness in the midst of a crooked and perverse Generation'. More particularly, she had been careful to ensure that the duties of religion were kept up in her family and had given her children a thorough grounding in spiritual matters.[16] At the time of her death there was only one surviving son, Rowland, who had married Temperance Crewe, a daughter of Thomas Crewe (later Lord Crewe). On the face of it this was a perfect union between two families which had a common Puritan heritage. In 1679, however, Sir John Pickering claimed in a Chancery lawsuit that Sir Thomas (his father-in-law) had 'taken very great distaste' against his son 'for many yeares before his death'. When drawing up his will in 1686 Sir Rowland bequeathed to his 'dear and loving wife' all his jewels and plate and his best coach and four horses and gave direction that she should take on responsibility for the tuition and education of his daughters and younger sons if she survived him. In October 1691 Sir John Wittewronge was informed by his son James that he had recently met Lady Alston and her husband who seemed to him to be a very fond couple; and that 'she looks exceeding well but he has been ill and lookes porely'.[17] Within a few years, however, the marriage had completely broken down.

In July 1697 Lady Alston wrote despairingly to Sir Edward Harley, who was a distant kinsman, about the domestic strife which had compelled her to seek refuge at her sister's house. Her husband, she told him, had alleged that some of her children were not his, 'this after his pretended reformation upon his sicknes at

London', and that she had made several attempts to poison him and was still determined to do so. She went on to describe how he had abused her with foul language, physically assaulted her and denied her any money. He had also declined to provide any material support for the children yet at the same time he was living well beyond his means and it was generally believed he would ruin his estate. Lord Crewe found it difficult to accept his daughter's account of the situation and adamantly refused to intervene when approached by Harley on her behalf (though it is perhaps significant that in 1696 he had stipulated in his will that a legacy of £500 which he was leaving her must on no account be subject to the power or control of her husband). In a further letter to Harley she asked him to obtain the services of an able lawyer, 'otherwise I must goe home with greate reproch and perhaps in daunger of my life unlesse I consent to be an absolute slave'. Sir Edward hoped that through the mercy of God it might be possible to bring about a reconciliation. On 13 August he sent Sir Rowland a diplomatically worded letter in which he begged him to resolve the differences which had arisen. In his reply Sir Rowland put all the blame on his wife. She had left home without his consent and for no obvious reason. Through Christian patience he had submitted to many things for the good of the family 'which neither the laws of God or man hath required'. Lady Alston's sister, however, viewed the matter very differently. In correspondence with Harley she claimed that on one occasion, when Sir Rowland had been in a penitent frame of mind, he had told her father 'how bad a husband he had been, and cleared my sister'. In her estimation he was a violent man whose passions were laced with jealousy and ill will; and she was doubtful whether it would ever be possible for them to live together again 'unlesse it pleases God to work a great change in him which at present there is not the least sign of'. The death of Sir Rowland in September 1697 brought a sudden end to the quarrel but his widow was still faced with family problems. In March 1698 her sister was writing to Harley that 'shee is full of care and trouble in disposing of hir sons grown up ... I pray god make them Comforts to hir'. At present they were very stubborn but God 'that made the heart' could change it when he saw fit.[18]

When Thomas Manton the Presbyterian divine published a scriptural commentary in 1658 he prefaced it with a dedication to Letitia Popham, the wife of Alexander Popham, in which he expressed grave doubts about the durability of godliness among the wealthy gentry:

> never is the Lord more neglected and dishonoured then in great men's Houses, in the very face of all his bounty; if Religion chance to get in there, it is soon worn out again; though vices live long in a family, and run in a blood from father to son, yet 'tis a rare case to see strictness of Religion carried on for three or four descents . . . where is there such a succession to be found in the houses of our Gentry? The Father perchance professeth godliness . . . and a carnal son cometh and turneth all out of doors, as if he were ashamed of his Father's God.

Manton attributed this situation, as he perceived it, to wealth 'ill-governed' which bred vice and sin; the conviction of 'brave spirits' that strictness was inglorious and the power of religion a base thing; and the marriage of children into 'carnal families'.[19] After the Restoration there were a number of new factors which presented a serious threat to the survival of godliness at the upper levels of society: the identification in the public mind of Puritan fervour with political extremism; a more pronounced materialistic ethos which offered no encouragement to those who believed in the necessity of self-denial; and the potential implications of ecclesiastical legislation which was aimed at imposing uniformity.

From time to time Philip Lord Wharton received reports from his clerical associates on the personal qualities and religious sympathies of young men with a Puritan background who were regarded as possible husbands for his daughters. In April 1663 Thomas Gilbert forwarded his comments on Hungerford Dunch, the son of Edmund Dunch the parliamentarian, who was the heir to estates worth £5,000 a year. 'For the Power of Godlines', he wrote,

> your Honour know'th how hard it is to judge but his Inclinations are very virtuous, his aversion very great both as to debauchery and Superstition; his affection great to the best, both men and things; much of his time and delight taken up in his Gardens and Orchards.

Hungerford Dunch died in 1680 and left an only son, Edmund, who was to acquire a reputation as a bon vivant and gamester.[20] In January 1668 another nonconformist minister, John Stalham, supplied some detailed information about Thomas Honywood, the son of Sir Thomas Honywood the Essex parliamentarian, which he had obtained from friends of his mother, the pious Lady Hester Honywood. While they had much to say in his favour they did not feel able to describe him as truly religious:

> for his naturall temper, he is of a mild, affable, courteous disposition, peaceably minded, loves no squables at the Table, raised sometimes by the minister of the place, who is also Chaplain of the ffamily. As to his naturall parts they judg him to exceed his ffather, but as to a spirituall, godly principle, there he comes short, and for giving any account of a work of grace, there they desire to be spared . . . He is no wayes debaucht, or profane (not an oath of the lowest degree ever heard to proceed from his mouth) but inclined to the superstition of the times, and wonders why good men cannot conform to the orders of the Kirk.

The young man died unmarried in 1672 and was succeeded by his brother John Lemot whose own religious views remain more obscure, though he had connections with at least one non-conformist divine, Lewis Calandrine. In January 1694 John Lemot hanged himself for reasons which were not readily identifiable and since he left no issue the bulk of his estates passed to a kinsman, Robert Honywood of Charing in Kent.[21]

Sometimes the succession from father to son proved to be a major watershed in matters of religion. This was the case with two of the leading families in Northamptonshire, the Pickerings of Titchmarsh and the Yelvertons of Easton Mauduit. Sir Gilbert Pickering, who died in 1668, and his wife, Lady Elizabeth, who survived him, both maintained close contact with nonconformist divines in the aftermath of the Act of Uniformity. Sir Gilbert was succeeded by his son John who appears to have been a man of a very different character. In November 1660 Pepys noted in his diary that he 'doth continue a foole, as he ever was since I knew him'. After his father's death Sir John was involved in a dispute with his mother over the right of presentation to the living of Titchmarsh when it next fell vacant. In a Chancery bill, which she brought in 1675, Lady Elizabeth argued that under the terms of a trusteeship arrangement she was entitled to nominate a successor to the present incumbent. Following these legal proceedings she surrendered her interest in return for a payment of £200 but, as she was probably well aware, Sir John had no intention of performing the role of godly patron. In August 1677 he granted the next presentation to Sir Charles Caesar, a Hertfordshire landowner; and in January 1678 he secured an undertaking from the new incumbent, Henry Lee, that he would inform him if he obtained another living or decided to relinquish the living of Titchmarsh and that in the meantime he would employ a curate and pay him £40 a year. Subsequently, in 1693, the rector purchased the next presentation from him with a view to including it in a financial settlement for the benefit of his wife and children.[22]

The Yelvertons had the kind of Puritan lineage which few other gentry families could match. Sir Christopher Yelverton had set his family on the path of godliness in the reign of Elizabeth and his son Sir Henry and grandson Sir Christopher had followed in his footsteps. On the latter's death in 1654 his estates and baronetcy were inherited by his son Henry. In 1658 Edward Reynolds, a Puritan minister who would later become Bishop of Norwich, published the sermon which he had preached at the funeral of John Langley, the master of St Paul's School, and dedicated it to Sir Henry who had been one of his pupils. In the epistle dedicatory he took the opportunity to acknowledge his debt of honour to the Yelverton family, 'not onely for the favors received from your self but from your noble Father and Grandfather, now with God'. He went on to express the hope that Sir Henry would 'so tread in the steps of your worthy Progenitors (which I perswade my self you do) as not onely to keep up the life and power of Godliness in your own heart and Family' but to be a generous patron 'both of learned and godly Ministers and of others who love the Lord Jesus in sincerity'.[23] Henry was a man of scholarly accomplishments though he failed to impress Dorothy Osborne who considered that he spoke too much and to very little purpose. According to her account Lady Grey de Ruthin, who was about to become his wife, had grown tired of his foolishness yet she was pleased that he was due to inherit a great estate. In 1662 Sir Henry published a treatise in defence of Christianity but he had a much more conservative outlook than his father, primarily because of the influence of Bishop Thomas Morton who after his enforced departure from the see of Durham had been taken into the household at Easton Mauduit. In his will, which was drawn up not long before his death in 1670, he made a deliberate point of affirming his wholehearted loyalty to the Church of England:

and because it hath been my ffortune to be reviled by some
... who pretend greater piety than their neighbours of
Apostacy from the Truth because since I came to understanding I was unwilling to communicate with Schismatickes
I therefore doe declare that in the presence of God I doe live
and doe desire to dye a sonne of the Church of England,
believing the doctrine she teacheth and submitting my selfe
to her discipline. And this I doe because I judge it the most
pure of all Churches extant in the Christian world and most
conformable to the Apostolique Primitive Church.[24]

The failure of Sir Simonds D'Ewes to found a Puritan dynasty was
due to two factors in particular: a disastrously high rate of infant
mortality in his family and his death at the relatively early age of
48 which meant that he was able to play no part in the upbringing
of his only surviving son. Neither his son, Sir Willoughby, who
within a few years was left an orphan, nor his grandson, another
Sir Simonds, appears to have inherited any of his religious
fervour. According to Anthony Wood, Sir Willoughby was seen
entering a bawdy house in New Inn Lane when he was an
undergraduate at Oxford in 1664. In the reign of Queen Anne a
visitor wrote that Sir Simonds was 'a Gentleman very well
beloved in his neighbourhood, of great integrity and good humor
... Master of a plentifull Estate, and Keep's a very good Table'. At
his death in 1722, however, he was a prisoner for debt in the
King's Bench prison.[25]

For the most part the families which rejected their Puritan
heritage became indistinguishable, in terms of their religious
attitudes and practices, from the general body of the Church of
England laity. The Hampdens, however, went through a much
more traumatic experience, though one which apparently had no
permanent effects. Richard Hampden was described by his friend
Richard Baxter as 'the true heir of his famous Father's Sincerity,
Piety and Devotedness to God' while another nonconformist
divine, Francis Tallents, wrote at the time of his death that he was
'certainly a truly good Man'.[26] His son John received an education
which, in his own words, was very pious and religious but while
sojourning in Paris he fell under the influence of Father Richard
Simon who had challenged the authority of the Scriptures in a
treatise on the Old Testament. For some years he held and
propagated views on religion and social conduct which were

completely at variance with his father's convictions. In 1688 he felt obliged to write a 'confession' in which he begged God's forgiveness for the great sin which he had committed in repudiating the truths of the Christian religion and entreated all those who had been seduced by his misguided opinions to 'return to themselves and to god'. After this episode, which he attributed to intellectual vanity, he became very friendly with Sir Edward Harley who offered him spiritual guidance and comfort. In correspondence with Harley he told him that 'There is no man in England, nor in the world, that I esteem and honour more then your selfe, nor none that I desire more to be esteemed by'; and he acknowledged his indebtedness to him 'from whom I think it my honour to receive lessons of all Morall and Christian vertues'. In May 1693 he wrote to Francis Tallents, who had once been his mentor, to congratulate him on a book of his which had recently appeared and to commiserate with him over a libellous allegation that he had become a Jesuit while living in France. If, he observed, 'they see they can disturb you by saying you are a Jesuite it may be next time they will say you are a Mahometan or a Pagan'. He, for his part, had been depicted as 'a Papist, an Atheist, a Socinian, a Republican, a Madman' but he had chosen to ignore such false accusations.[27]

Tallents became increasingly concerned about Hampden's mental and bodily health and begged his friend Sir Edward Harley to do what he could to help him. In June 1696 he informed Harley that he had received a letter from Hampden's mother in which she complained that he had sold one of his most valuable manors and was cutting down his woods; that 'he casts off the seeming to own any thing or any body that looks to Religion'; and that he had visited her only once since his father's death.[28]

In December 1696 Sir Edward Harley gave his niece Sarah Foley a detailed account of Hampden's suicide and added that 'I beseech the Lord sanctifie this Providence not only to his friends and Relations but allso to all the pretenders to Reason as their miserable frail Idol, without the immediat support of Divine Power and Grace.' In a postscript he told her that on his deathbed Hampden had given direction that his son Richard should study and obey the Holy Scriptures. In February 1697 Sir Edward wrote in a letter to Richard Hampden, who had been educated at a nonconformist academy, that

> you are the fourth Generation of your Family to whom I desire to continue the best Expressions I am capable to make of most faithfull Service ... It is a bright but weighty Obligation upon your self to walk in the Course of Vertue. The late sad Cloud upon your Family ought in a special manner to be improved to walk with most humble Adoration before God, which is only Steerage to avoid the like Shipwreck.

The fear of God, he went on, was the foundation and beginning of true wisdom. This required a constant application to the Word of God together with fervent prayer for a divine blessing. On no account should he pay any regard to the destructive notion that young men must be allowed to sow their wild oats; for those who sowed must reap and the outcome could be utter ruin.[29]

6

A GODLY ELITE

When John Lord Crewe, who had once been a member of the Long Parliament, dictated his will in August 1678 he thought it worth recording that he was in his eightieth year 'and am of the same faith now that I am old wherein I was trained up in my youth'.[1] Despite all the strains and pressures to which they were subject in the later Stuart period many Puritan county families remained strongly attached to what they regarded as the fundamentals of 'true religion'. This is clear from such evidence as the religious attitudes revealed in their wills and private papers, the arrangements which they made for the education of their children and the maintenance of close links with nonconformist ministers, including their employment as domestic chaplains. Some Puritan squires who had been involved in the Civil War lived on until the 1680s or 1690s or even the beginning of the eighteenth century. Richard Norton died in 1691, Sir John Wittewronge in 1693, John Swinfen in 1694, Sir Edward Harley in 1700 and Hugh Boscawen in 1701. Generally such men clung to the old values and sought to ensure that their children followed their example. In February 1679 Mary Viscountess Massereene, whose husband had once been described as a rigid Presbyterian, told Swinfen that there were few in the world she more truly esteemed and loved than him 'whom god has kept in your Integrity in the degenerat and backslyding generation for which mercy thanks is due to the great provider who leads in paths of Righteousnes for his name's sake'.

Writing to Philip Lord Wharton in July 1668 Swinfen observed, in a reference to their children, that 'If God be soe good unto us as to lett us see them comfortably settled, for the service of God in theire generations after us, it is then a crowne to our old age.'[2] In 1688 it was reported that Hugh Boscawen had not only discharged some nonconformist ministers who for a long time had been 'very Acceptable to him' but had also forbidden them to come to his house, alleging that 'they had deceived him in their Constant opinions of the Bishops and Clergie of the Church of England who he now saw Acted more like protestants then [the] dissenters and the next Lord's day took the sacrament at his parish Church'. This story, however, needs to be treated with some caution since he remained on good terms with such nonconformist ministers as Francis Tallents, Joseph Halsey and Edward Lawrence. In his will, which was drawn up in July 1700, he left £100 to Halsey, £20 to John Howe the celebrated Presbyterian divine and £20 to another ejected minister, John Knight. Boscawen's last surviving son died of smallpox in 1680 and this drew the comment from Roger Morrice the nonconformist chronicler that 'he was a very serious prudent young Gentleman of very good parts'.[3]

One of the most important factors responsible for the continuing survival of godliness at this level of society was the intense piety of many of the womenfolk. Lady Margaret Hoghton, whose family was seated at Hoghton Tower in Lancashire, was said to have spent 'both her early and later houres in Communion with God'. Her house seemed like a college for the study of religion. In her library there were some books 'for contemplation, others for an Holy conversation, others for meditation, others for devotion' but the Bible was her favourite reading.[4] At the funeral of her son Sir Richard in 1678 the minister testified that 'he was free from those vices ... I meane intemperance, debaucheries, revellings, dissolute practises, profligate courses with which these evil times and daies of iniquity do so much abound'. Sir Richard, he assured the congregation, was 'a person of many moral virtues, and divine graces too'. On the other hand, Oliver Heywood the nonconformist divine was more restrained in his assessment. His wife, Lady Sarah, he noted in his journal, was 'accounted very eminent for Religion, and he was a favourer of good things, tho' no great zealot'. In the next generation Sir Charles Hoghton married Mary Skeffington, the daughter of John Viscount Massereene, who in 1699 was complimented by John Howe for bearing her part, 'with your like-minded consort, in supporting the interest of God and religion'. At the same time Howe expressed his delight at the way in which the Hoghtons had remained faithful to the cause of godliness from one generation to another:

through the singular favour and blessing of Heaven there has not been that visible degeneracy that might be so plainly observed, and sadly deplored, in divers great families . . . But, on the contrary, such as have succeeded have, by a laudable ambition and emulation, as it were, striven to outshine such as have gone before them, in piety and virtue.[5]

Oliver Heywood mainly carried on his pastoral activities in Yorkshire and among his acquaintances there was Dorothy Hutton, a sister of Thomas Lord Fairfax and the widow of Richard Hutton of Poppleton whose death in 1648 had left her with sole responsibility for bringing up their children. During the years 1662 to 1687 she and her eldest son Thomas employed an ejected minister, Thomas Birdsall, as their domestic chaplain at Poppleton Hall. Birdsall, we are told, 'was of great use in that honourable family, and to the neighbourhood, by his example, prayers, and preaching'.[6] In April 1663 Dorothy Hutton presented her son Charles with a set of instructions which she expected him to follow while he was living in London. In these last days, she told him, God was speaking through his Son in the written Word. He should, therefore, read the Scriptures 'diligently and daily' and attend the preaching of God's Word on the Sabbath 'and on other days if your Calling will permitt'. At the same time he should practise moderation in all worldly things. 'Let your moderation', she stressed, 'be knowne in avoyding inordinate eating and drinking . . . Avoyd such persons as may intangle your Affections unto any women.' He would be better able to keep clear of such snares if he applied himself with diligence to his calling since idleness was the nurse of all evil. Finally, she exhorted him to carry himself 'meekly, Humbly and wisely'. Whatever the effect of this austere document on its recipient it clearly impressed Thomas Hutton who made a copy of it, perhaps for the edification of his own family.[7]

In some cases there is a wealth of evidence about a family's standing among the godly during the second half of the seventeenth century. In Derbyshire the Elizabethan mansion of the Gell family was situated in the parish of Wirksworth which was one of the major centres of Presbyterianism in the north of England. Sir John Gell, the former parliamentary commander, was a patron of Puritan divines and for some years employed a domestic chaplain who had been ordained under Presbyterian auspices. At the beginning of the Civil War one of his servants had commended him as a singular Christian who was determined to do his best to defend God's 'true religion'; on the other hand, Lucy Hutchinson claimed that he was both lacking in piety and guilty of adultery.[8] His son John, who succeeded him in 1671, was described by Roger Morrice as a religious, wise and worthy gentleman. Katherine Gell, the wife of John Gell, was one of the daughters of John Packer of Berkshire, a zealous Puritan who had served as secretary to George Duke of Buckingham. During the years 1655 to 1658 she was in correspondence with Richard Baxter about her fits of depression which she eventually concluded might be due to a physical ailment which could not readily be cured. Baxter sent her books to read and an abundance of guidance. In November 1656 he was emphasising the need for patience and humility:

> doe you not set more by God, by Christ, by Heaven, than by all your Riches and Honors in the world? Are you not resolved against returninge to your former state of sin and negligence? . . . you must stay God's season, and looke not for perfection till you come to heaven; and expect not the highest place there neither.

Those who were advanced to the dignity of a saint should not cry and complain as though there was nothing more that God could grant them. To ward off melancholy she should busy herself in her 'necessary imployments in the world', mix with cheerful company and avoid spending too much time in secret meditations. In April 1657 she told him that she had 'willingly chosen . . . to live here farre from friends and in noe pleasant country because the plentifull inioyment of ordinances . . . and our good ministry' more than adequately compensated for these drawbacks. Though she was unable to serve God as well as she would like she would do as well as she could. With a great family and many children she could find business enough but, she confessed, 'I had rather locke my selfe up in a roome alone amongst my bookes for meditation.' Later that year Baxter was writing that he was very glad to hear that God had calmed and comforted her by means of a book written by William Gurnall (a Puritan minister who had obtained preferment from Sir Simonds D'Ewes). In response to a question about the practice of self-examination he observed that 'your Diary may well be used as your helpe' in remembering 'your most notable failings renewed since' but he would not advise her 'to spend so much time as the thoughtfull recounting and writinge downe of every infirmity would require'.[9]

After the passage of the Act of Uniformity the Gells were in regular contact with many nonconformist divines. Among these ministers was William Bagshaw who had been ejected from the living of Glossop. In an account of nonconformity in Derbyshire he wrote in glowing terms about the commitment of Sir John, as he became on his father's death, and his wife Katherine and described their house, Hopton Hall, as 'a Bethel, an house of God'. All who knew Sir John well, he declared, reverenced and loved him. Even when his house was full of company, 'and that of the Higher Rank', he still took care 'to observe his hours of Retirement, that he might maintain his Converse with God, in the Exercise of Closet Religion'. His wife, for her part, did much to promote God's work in Derbyshire. Like her husband it was her practice to engage in secret communion with God and on these occasions she read and meditated on the choicest books.[10]

Among the papers of the Gell family there are letters from a number of their clerical associates, including the nonconformist divines Francis Tallents and John Otefield. Tallents, who had been born in Derbyshire, resided for many years in Shrewsbury where he had been ejected but in 1669 he was serving as chaplain at Hopton Hall. There is an echo of this association in the will of Sir John Gell which was drawn up in 1687: among the bequests which he made was Tallents's large map of chronology, as he called it, which was clearly one of his prized possessions.[11] Otefield, like Tallents, had been ordained as a Presbyterian minister and during the 1650s had been a member of the Wirksworth *classis*. For a time he had enjoyed the patronage of the Gell family as the minister of a neighbouring church and may possibly have served as their chaplain, a function which was later performed by his son Joshua at the beginning of his ministry.[12] Following the death of Katherine Gell in 1671 he wrote in a letter to one of her daughters that 'such a Mother is a losse indeed . . . shee though dead yet speaketh, her instructions may yet live in your heart . . . and by following her steps you may hope to enjoy her again in a blessed eternity'. James Sutton, a minister who had recently been accused of holding conventicles, recalled in a letter addressed to her grieving husband that she had been deeply concerned about the future of the poor distressed Church of God. The godly, he went on, 'sayle from among us'; and there was good reason to fear the evil to come. In a postscript he suggested that Gell's chaplain and others of 'our brethren' in the ministry who visited him should join in prayer that 'we may make the Alsufficient, unchangeable and eternall God our portion in these hard times'.[13]

In 1674 Sir John had to come to terms with his deep sense of loss over the death of his eldest son John who was still only in his twenties. One of the young man's sisters, Elizabeth, received a letter of condolence from John Otefield who seemed anxious to satisfy himself that the deceased was numbered among the elect. Her brother, he told her, might have been 'a staffe in the hand of his aged Parent, an ornament to his family, a publick good in his station, a Countenancer of piety'. On the other hand, did she not have a father who was noted for his patience and submission, one who was accustomed to the yoke from his youth and well able to bear afflictions? And did he not have a Benjamin still left and others who might assuage his grief? Although it was many years since he had been intimately acquainted with her family he could recall her brother's early blossoming and his willingness to embrace 'the best things'. He was confident that her mother had never ceased to offer him guidance; nor was he in any doubt that in the last few years her father had advised and urged him to follow the way of practical godliness. He hoped that

> hee had not lost the savour of his Education, nor gave way to any of those debaucheries wherewith those of his Rank are in this age deeply tainted ... I have heard something, and I hope you know more, of his good inclinations, his Love to the word, his constancy in duty, his respect to them that feard the Lord, his desire to see the Liberty of the Gospell.

On the whole, he thought it safe to conclude that her brother's destiny was eternal happiness.[14]

In a letter dispatched from Shrewsbury in 1689 Francis Tallents told Elizabeth Gell and her sister Temperance that he was grateful that they counted him among their true friends and asked them to remember him in their prayers. God, he wrote, had been doing them good both by subjecting them to trials and freeing them; he would continue to do so and would (he hoped) give them many things even beyond their desires.[15] The following month their father died in London where he had been receiving medical treatment. When informing them of his death their brother Francis stressed that they must all submit to God's will and 'bee thank-full to allmighty god that hee hath continued him so long to us'. Some weeks later they received a further letter from Tallents in which he begged them to consider all their blessings. Their dear mother and father were now gone; but they had gone to a blessed life free from all sin and trouble and this was a good reason for rejoicing. Moreover

> you enjoied them a long time, and may think with joy of them, and your holy waies, and all the benefit you had by them. And now you are compassed with plenty of outward things, far above thousands and ten thousands of the people of God, and through grace delight to go in the path of God's commandments, and have a joyfull hope of that Blessed life before you.

At the same time he took the opportunity to offer them some spiritual guidance, exhorting them to walk humbly and thank-fully and to seek every day to please the Lord in heart and life.[16]

Sir John was succeeded by his son Philip who had been bred up as a merchant and had spent some time in captivity as a prisoner of the Tripoli corsairs. Almost immediately Sir Philip was elected to Parliament as one of the knights of the shire for Derbyshire, largely on the strength of his father's reputation. In June 1689 we find him writing from Westminster to his domestic chaplain, Timothy Manlove, a young man who had been ordained as a Presbyterian minister some months earlier. Sir Philip began by expressing his satisfaction that Manlove's efforts on behalf of his family were proving so successful. Manlove, however, had told him that he wished to leave his employment, perhaps because he was anxious to engage in more challenging pastoral work, and for Sir Philip this was clearly an unwelcome development. Stressing that he had always had 'a more than ordinary kindness for you, and for your advantage' he asked him to 'weigh all things well before you be too sudden in your resolutions and repent when it's too late'. But having said this he fully accepted that Manlove must be free to make up his own mind. The person whom he had recommended as his successor was completely unknown to him; consequently he could offer no opinion as to his suitability. He wanted to make it clear, however, that his next chaplain must not expect to have the same liberty which he had been allowed.[17]

The Gells continued to attach a high value to their association with nonconformist ministers during the more liberal era which was ushered in by the political events of 1688. In April 1692 William Bagshaw wrote in a letter to Elizabeth and Temperance Gell that he hoped that their latest renewal of covenant would be followed by 'an eminent shedding abroad of the love of God in Christ in both your hearts'. And he went on to say that 'We who rejoyce in the graces (and so society) of the meanest Christians bless God that anie of your quality will encourage us and them.' In his account of Sir John and his wife (which appeared in print in 1702) he offered an optimistic assessment of the spiritual qualities of the next generation: 'of which of the Children have we not cause to hope that the Root of the matter is in him or her; and O that others of their Rank evidenced such heights of Grace as divers of them do!'[18]

During the second half of the seventeenth century the decline in the number of established county families with the same kind of religious outlook as the Gells was partly made good by the emergence of new squirearchal families such as the Foleys of Worcestershire and the Langhams of Northamptonshire which built up large estates, usually with the profits of commercial or industrial activities. The Foleys mainly owed their wealth to the use of new technology in the manufacture of iron. Thomas Foley, who lived at Witley Court in Worcestershire, was one of the leading industrialists in England and a very substantial land-owner. His friend Richard Baxter writes that he had a reputation for great integrity and honesty in all his business dealings; that as a 'Religious, Faithful Man' he acquired the patronage rights in several parishes and exercised them to good effect; and that his sons were all 'Religious worthy Men'.[19] Following his death in 1677 the bulk of his estates, together with Witley Court, passed to his eldest son Thomas who a decade later commanded an income of over £7,000 a year. Generous provision was also made for his younger sons: Paul Foley, who settled at Stoke Edith in Hereford-shire, and Philip Foley, who was seated at Prestwood in Stafford-shire, each had an estate worth £2,000 a year. In Gilbert Burnet's opinion Paul Foley was 'a man of virtue and good principles, but morose and wilful'. Hitherto the Harleys had been the only Puritan family of real wealth in Herefordshire and it is hardly surprising therefore that they were soon on close terms with the Foleys. Sir Edward Harley and Paul Foley were frequently in correspondence about such matters as the recruitment of ministers either for the livings in Foley's gift or for the post of household chaplain at Stoke Court. In March 1685 Foley, who was a barrister, drew up the deed of settlement on the marriage of Sir Edward's heir, Robert Harley, and Elizabeth Foley, a daughter of Thomas Foley the younger of Witley Court. 'I desire allwaies to be very thankfull to God', wrote Elizabeth Harley to her father-in-law in October 1687, 'for his goodness to me in bringing me in to a Family not only where his fear is, but where I have found so much real kindness and tenderness.' Another daughter, Sarah Foley, lived for some time with the Harleys in the godly household at Brampton Bryan and eventually married Edward Harley, one of Sir Edward's younger sons.[20]

Both the Harleys and the Foleys figured in a network of closely knit families which had much in common in religious as well as social and economic terms and were very often active politically. Other families in this grouping included the Swinfens and Wilbrahams of Staffordshire, the Crewes and Knightleys of Northamptonshire, the Hampdens of Buckinghamshire, the Ashursts of Oxfordshire, the Hobarts of Norfolk and the Boscawens of Cornwall. In his will, which was drawn up in September 1662, Richard Knightley refers to a number of his relations and friends, among them Sir Thomas Crewe, the son of John Lord Crewe, Richard Hampden and his wife Letitia, and Lady Mary Hobart who was one of Hampden's sisters and the wife of Sir John Hobart. Knightley appointed Hampden, who was his uncle, as the sole executor of his will and left him the princely sum of £500 'as a token of my love'.[21] In 1669 his half-brother Essex Knightley, who had succeeded to his estates, married Sarah Foley, one of the daughters of Thomas Foley the elder of Witley Court. Within less than twelve months Sarah Knightley was left a widow but in 1674 she became the wife of John Hampden, the son and heir of Richard Hampden, and six years later we find them setting off for France along with Francis Tallents and her daughter Anne Knightley. When Richard Hampden made a settlement of his estates in advance of his son's marriage the parties to the indenture included Sir John Hobart, Thomas Foley the elder and his sons Thomas and Paul. Some years later Paul Foley's son Thomas married Anne Knightley who brought with her a substantial amount of landed property in various counties. The marriage aroused some controversy, perhaps because Paul Foley had been acting as her guardian: writing from London in July 1688 Robert

Harley told his father that 'The Town reflects too severely on Mr P. F.'s marriage of his son and conduct therein.'[22]

John Swinfen, who had a shrewd head for business, helped to manage the Midlands estates of the aristocratic Paget family whose principal seat was at West Drayton in Middlesex. William Lord Paget had been appointed by Parliament as lord lieutenant of Buckinghamshire in 1642 but had almost immediately joined the king at York. The Pagets were nevertheless a godly family (indeed Lady Paget was described as an 'eminent Saint')[23] and they had close ties with a number of Puritan gentry. Richard Hampden had married one of Lord Paget's daughters and others with Paget wives included Sir Anthony Irby, Sir William Waller, Sir Henry Ashurst and Philip Foley, the youngest son of Thomas Foley the elder. An account of the major landowners in Stafford-shire which was compiled shortly after the Restoration contains the cryptic observation that Lord Paget was a Presbyterian who was 'governed by Mr Swinfin'. When Swinfen was serving as an MP he was usually accommodated in the Paget family's Westminster residence which was situated in Old Palace Yard. In a letter addressed to Lord Paget in October 1673 he expressed his gratitude to him for providing him with a chamber in his house and added that 'It's a pallace (within a pallace) to me, and wants nothing that I stand in need of, being a private room and having a good bed.' This arrangement continued after the heir, William Paget, who was a personal friend of Swinfen, succeeded his father in 1678. In July 1679 Swinfen thanked him not only 'for the Noble favour I received in your family the last parliament but alsoe for your Lordshipp's free offer of the same in August next'. Many years later John Howe dedicated one of his works, *The Living Temple*, to Lord Paget and in doing so offered the comment that his family had long had

> great esteem and reverence for such a temple. And I doubt not but its having spread its branches into divers other worthy families of the Hampdens, Foleys, Ashursts, Hunts has given your Lordship much the more grateful and complacential view for the affinity to your own in this respect.[24]

Swinfen's circle of friends also included the Hampdens, Crewes, Harleys, Foleys and Wilbrahams. Sir Edward Harley and John Lord Crewe had been fellow members of the Long Parliament while his friendship with Richard Hampden may well have been a product of the Paget connection. In October 1677, when ill health prevented him from visiting Swinfen Hall, Hampden assured Swinfen that it was 'a place where I had rather have had 3 or 4 daies converse with you than any other you could name'. In August 1692 Sir Edward Harley was informed that Hampden, together with his wife and granddaughter, was travelling to Prestwood in Staffordshire where Philip Foley had his seat and that he also intended to spend some time with the Foleys of Witley Court. Subsequently Hampden told Swinfen how much he had enjoyed the pleasure of his company at Prestwood. In addition, there was a good deal of personal contact in London when Parliament was sitting. Writing to Swinfen in July 1679 Hampden intimated that he hoped to be in London in October as a member of the next Parliament and urged him to put himself forward as a candidate in the forthcoming election: 'Pray stand not upon your Termes, and think to indulge your selfe by your owne fireside this winter, but since his Majestie is resolved to give you the oppor-tunity to come up and see your friends, and serve your Countrey, do you resolve to accept it.'[25]

Another of Swinfen's correspondents was Letitia Hampden, the wife of Richard Hampden. Writing from Nocton in Lincolnshire in September 1691 she told him that her husband had been stricken by a violent attack of gout but she was hoping that they would be able to start their return journey within a few days, in which case they might visit him on their way home. Nocton Hall was a seat of Sir William Ellis who had married her daughter Isabella. In the reign of Charles II his father, Sir Thomas, had been characterised as 'a drunken sott' but he was a man of a very different temperament. During their visit the Hampdens would no doubt have benefited from the ministrations of his household chaplain, Joseph Farrow, a man who had been episcopally ordained but who for reasons of conscience was unwilling to accept a benefice. Farrow, it was said, was 'so pleased with that religious and regular family wherein God had placed him that . . . if he had lived never so long he would not have left it by his good will'. In 1701 the ties between the two families were further strengthened when Richard Hampden's grandson and namesake married Sir William's daughter Isabella.[26]

During the reign of Charles II John Lord Crewe was in regular correspondence with Swinfen and ofter sought his guidance on spiritual matters. 'You desire', wrote Crewe in July 1675, 'that whilest I live I may have greater foretaste of the life to come.' In practice, however, he had found it difficult to raise his spirits by meditating on 'the promises of this life and the world to come' when souls infused with the knowledge and love of God would experience 'ioyes supernaturall and endlesse'. What, he asked Swinfen, was the cure for this state of melancholy? 'I am to be humbled, I am to pray. These I know, yet I desire you to tell me, what is more to be done for the obtaining that which you say, and I beleeve, you heartily wish.'[27] Lord Crewe died in December 1679 and Roger Morrice noted in his journal that he 'had beene very eminent in his life for holinesse and charity, and at and in his death for usefull and suitable instructions to those about him, for well-grounded peace and solid comfort in himselfe'. Within a few months his son Thomas Lord Crewe was inviting Swinfen to spend some time with him at Steane, his country seat in Northamptonshire.[28]

Besides the Pagets and the Crewes there were other members of the nobility who were regarded as well disposed towards the godly, among them William Russell, Earl (and subsequently Duke) of Bedford, Gilbert Holles, Earl of Clare, Theophilus Clinton, Earl of Lincoln, and his daughter-in-law Lady Anne Clinton, John Skeffington, Viscount Massereene, Philip Lord Wharton, George Booth, Lord Delamere, Frances Cecil, Countess of Exeter, and Mary Rich, Countess of Warwick. Sir Edward Harley was on close terms with the Earl of Clare, Lord Wharton and Lady Clinton, who was a cousin, as well as with the Crewes. On the evidence of his surviving accounts he visited Lord Wharton at Wooburn, his Buckinghamshire seat, in 1677 and again in 1680.[29] Viscount Massereene was related by marriage to the Hoghtons of Lancashire and was also a friend of the Swinfens and Wilbrahams.[30] One of the Earl of Lincoln's daughters, Lady Margaret, was the wife of Hugh Boscawen, who was the wealthiest gentleman in Cornwall, while other daughters had married Sir George Booth, the future Lord Delamere, and Robert Rolle, the son of Sir Samuel Rolle of Devon.[31]

Among the Puritan nobility and gentry it was considered important that religion should be brought into the reckoning when marriage was being contemplated, though they were not inclined to disregard their financial interests. Nathaniel Stephens, a Gloucestershire squire who was one of the secluded members, told his daughter Katherine that he took it for granted that she would only wish to marry a man who in his religious outlook was 'every way Orthodox' by which he clearly meant Presbyterian. Some years later another of his daughters, Abigail, was married to Sir Edward Harley who had impeccable Presbyterian credentials. Sir Edward, for his part, was in no doubt that he had made a wise choice: in July 1664, for example, he was writing to his wife from Westminster that it was no small trouble to him 'to be from you whom God hath made so dear to mee, for without complement you are more to mee then all the world besides'.[32] In 1672 there was some discussion about the possibility of a match between Philip Lord Wharton's eldest son and a niece of Sir Edmund Fowell, one of the leading Puritans in Devon, who lived with her uncle. Lord Wharton was informed that Sir Edmund was very much in favour of the proposed match and that his niece was extremely gracious, sober and discreet and spent two hours in private prayer every day 'if there be never so much company'.[33] That same year Sir Ralph Verney sought the views of his friend Sir Roger Burgoyne on a kinswoman of his who had apparently been suggested as a possible wife for his son Thomas. Her father, Burgoyne assured him, 'hath very good parts, and I beleeve as good a purse; very sober and so is the whole family'. As for his 'Church principles' he thought that they were basically the same as Sir Ralph's while the mother 'differs not much from him, unless it be in what hir sex allows of, a greater volubility and readiness of speech'.[34]

In October 1677 Sir John Gell informed his son Philip (who was now his heir) that he would be content for him to marry

> provided that you act rationally, upon good grounds and to right ends. But . . . I shall deale plainely with you, I do veryly thinke that unles you be humbled for your former irregular proceeds that way, and repent of them, you will scarce obtain your desires, and before you begin afresh seeke to god to direct you as to your choyce, to such a one as may be instrumentall to promote god's glory, the welfare of the family, and be a meet consort for you.

The following year Philip Gell married one of the daughters of a Sussex Puritan, Sir John Fagg of Wiston.[35] About the same time John Swinfen heard from his friend Lady Elizabeth Wilbraham that a match had been proposed between Henry Hobart, the son and heir of Sir John Hobart, and her daughter Grace. The young man, she wrote, was excellently accomplished and qualified; and the Hobart estates were worth £5,000 a year. When visiting Richard Hampden (who was Sir John's brother-in-law) he might be able to obtain more information. In the event Henry Hobart married a daughter of Sir John Maynard the Puritan lawyer.[36]

Before his marriage in 1691 Thomas Jervoise, the grandson of Sir Thomas Jervoise the Hampshire parliamentarian, received a number of suggestions about possible matches. In June 1687 Lady Honor St Barbe told him that the relatives of an earl's daughter were anxious that he should become acquainted with her. The young woman, she assured him, had breeding and wit and had been brought up as soberly and prudently as any woman, 'I should saye religiously.' The portion on offer was £5,000 which was as much as he had in mind. Lady St Barbe had told her how sober and good he was and that there was nothing that any woman could take exception to apart from his lack of breeding. This deficiency, she had explained, was due to his unwillingness to go into 'the galant sort of company' to learn breeding because most persons of that kind were too lewd. Subsequently, in July 1688, she advised him not to marry a young country girl 'that knows nothing'; or the daughter of a rich city merchant who would be too full of pride; or a nobleman's daughter who had acquired only a knowledge of good behaviour and would despise him. The woman she wanted to recommend to him had been bred up 'with a religous sence of things' and had none of that pride and folly 'to sett her above a contrey gentle-man'. Her eldest brother was 'the most pyous best yong man' she had heard of, at least so far as persons of quality were con-cerned.[37] Possibly Lady St Barbe's unnamed candidate was a daughter of Thomas Foley who was seated at Great Witley in Worcestershire. In 1688 Foley wrote in a letter to Sir Edward Harley that he was being pressed to marry his daughter to Thomas Jervoise who was the heir to an estate worth £2,500 a year. Foley had received very good reports about him and was no doubt well aware of the family's Puritan lineage.[38]

Sometimes a clerical associate might try his hand at match-making. Ralph Strettell, who had been deprived of a London benefice, enjoyed the patronage of Sir James Langham and was also in contact with other Puritan notables who were all re-lated, George Lord Delamere, his son Henry (who had married

Langham's only surviving child), Theophilus Earl of Lincoln and his daughter-in-law Lady Anne Clinton. In a letter which was probably written in or about 1670 Strettell told Sir Edward Harley that Stephen Langham, a younger brother of his patron, had a daughter who would be a good match and offered the thought that she might be a suitable choice for Hugh Boscawen's son. In August 1674 he was reporting to Harley that he had recently become acquainted with a young Cornish gentleman, Humphrey Nichols, who had received a thorough grounding in Presbyterian principles and was a kinsman of Hugh Boscawen. Like Harley his father, Anthony Nichols, had been one of the eleven MPs who in 1647 had been faced with the threat of impeachment proceedings at the instigation of the New Model Army. The estate was worth £800 a year and was unencumbered except for payments due to relatives which amounted to £2,000. Nichols wanted to marry into 'a religious good family' of quality and Harley might therefore like to consider the possibility of a match.[39]

Writing in December 1696 another of Sir Edward's clerical correspondents, Erasmus Saunders, observed that few persons of quality approved and practised virtue and truth and he feared that this 'may be number'd among the sad occasions of the decay of Christian piety in our days'.[40] Upper-class families which were zealous in the cause of godliness were undoubtedly a small minority, as indeed they had always been. Yet they were an important minority because of their wealth and influence and there were many nonconformist divines and other ministers of the Word who had reason to be grateful to them for their patronage.

7

IN COMMUNION

Writing to the Bishop of London in January 1676 the Archbishop of Canterbury explained what would be involved in a forthcoming census of religious loyalties. For each parish it would be necessary to specify the number of popish recusants who lived there and also the number of other dissenters 'of which sect so ever which either obstinately refuse or wholly absent themselves from the Communion of the Church of England at such times as they are by law required'. On the evidence of the returns which have survived there was generally little or no Protestant nonconformity of this extreme kind in country parishes where Puritan squires had their residences and often owned the patronage rights.[1] As in the Laudian era it was comparatively rare for upper-class Protestants to abstain completely from attendance at Church of England services. Whatever reservations they might have had about the ecclesiastical settlement of 1662, few of the godly at this level of society considered it desirable, or perhaps even feasible, to adopt a thoroughgoing separatist stance; and indeed many of the Presbyterian ministers who had been deprived of their livings took the same view. In a contemporary account of the state of religion in the early years of Charles II's reign the anonymous author observed that the Presbyterian pastors 'and people of this sort ... generally frequent the Church and the service of it' and were 'true friends to the Civill Government'.[2]

When there was a sermon at the funeral of a Presbyterian of high social standing it was usually delivered by a beneficed clergyman who often considered it necessary to lay stress on the loyalty of the deceased to the Church of England. At Preston in Lancashire the incumbent, Seth Bushell, sought to demonstrate the conformity of his patron, Sir Richard Hoghton, by recalling how well he had comported himself at the communion service: 'his publick receiving the holy Sacrament of the Lord's Supper by my ministration in this place, and in this Congregation, according to the usage of the Church of England, as you can testifie, bear witness for him'.[3] At the funeral of Lady Elizabeth Alston, the wife of Sir Thomas Alston, in the parish church of Odell in Bedfordshire the minister, William Dillingham, related

> how diligent she was in her attendance upon the publick Preaching of the Word of God . . . and how desirous she was that all others should do the like. And it is well known to some how much she bewail'd the withdrawing of others from the publick Ordinance, the means of their Salvation, endeavouring to reclaim them.

Significantly, it had been reported a year earlier, when the 1676 census was undertaken, that there was only one nonconformist in the parish of Odell, as compared with a total of 218 conformists.[4] When George Booth, Lord Delamere, the leading Presbyterian in Cheshire, was interred in his parish church of Bowdon the preacher, Zachary Cawdrey, declared that, as his health permitted, he had constantly attended 'the Publick Service of God, according to the Order of the Church of England, by Law established, of which Church he lived and died a pious Member'. The family usually spent the winter in London and here 'he received the Communion Monthly, at Covent Garden-Church, if he was able to go thither; humbly kneeling at the Rails before the Altar, or Communion-Table'. Cawdrey, who was the rector of Barthomley, was highly regarded in Presbyterian circles and it is ironic that two years earlier, in 1682, he had been obliged to defend himself against a charge of nonconformity.[5] At Great Bardfield in Essex similar testimony was offered on behalf of Lady Anne Lumley, the wife of Sir Martin Lumley. Thomas Pritchard, who served as the family chaplain while holding a church living, emphasised that she had 'staid not from Church except Sickness or some unavoidable Accident prevented, whither she went not out of Custom, but Sence of Duty'; and that 'she did frequently partake of the Sacrament of Christ's Body and Blood'.[6]

In December 1665 Sir Edward Harley told Clarendon, the Lord Chancellor, that he understood that he had received reports alleging that he was not well affected either to the Church or to the State and that he 'countenanced factious persons'. These reports, he assured him, were entirely without foundation. So far as his religious loyalties were concerned he held no opinion which was not consistent with the Catholic faith[7] and the doctrines of the Church of England; and there was ample evidence of his 'constant and reverend attendance upon divine service'. At the same time he could truthfully say that 'I have not countenanced any factious persons, nor have such persons resorted to me, nor hath there been in my family any factious or unlawful meeting'.[8] Many years later one of his sons wrote of him that

> Though he was a favourer of such as dissented from the Church for conscience' sake, and though sometimes he went to hear Mr Baxter and others in London, yet he constantly attended the Church, having by the grace of God and a constant reading of the Scriptures attained to a very Christian temper, and therefore never engaged in the narrow principles with which the several parties in the Church had embroiled themselves and the nation.[9]

From the evidence of his private papers it is clear that Sir Edward and his family regularly attended services at their parish church; that one of his main concerns as a patron of ecclesiastical livings was to recruit ministers who were effective preachers of the Word; and that he was also in close touch with many non-conformist divines besides Richard Baxter.[10]

Occasionally the records of diocesan visitations reveal cases of nonconformity involving upper-class Protestants. In 1664 the vicar of Heston in Middlesex presented Sir William Waller 'for a continuall neglect of publick Service by absenting himself, with his whole Family, from the Church for three yeares together'. Sir William, who was then living at Osterley Park, no doubt preferred the ministrations of his Presbyterian chaplain. In September 1673 the churchwardens of another Middlesex parish, Stoke Newington, presented Sir John Hartopp and his father-in-law Charles Fleetwood and their wives 'for not comeing to theire said parish Church nor receiving the sacrament at Easter last past nor since to this day'.[11] Such cases are comparatively rare yet it is clear that there were other gentry (though not usually Presbyterians) who found it difficult to come to terms with the ecclesiastical changes which had taken place. At Titchmarsh in Northamptonshire Sir Gilbert Pickering and his wife were at loggerheads with the rector, Dr Henry Deane, who had been put into the living on the insistence of the Crown despite the fact that it was in the gift of the Pickering family. Shortly after the Restoration Deane was complaining in a letter to one of his official contacts that Sir Gilbert had refused to hand over the key to the church at the time of his induction and that his wife, 'with an Amazonian courage', had been laying siege to his parsonage house. The inhabitants of Titchmarsh, he went on, had hitherto 'knowne no other God and Goddesse' but Sir Gilbert and his wife; they were mainly Anabaptists and Independents, 'And I have an Herculean labour, an Augiean stable to purge.' Deane eventually entered into some kind of agreement with Pickering but a few years later he was reporting to the Bishop of Peterborough that the people of his parish had been set a bad example by his patron and that a relative, Christopher Pickering, had absented himself from church on Sundays and fast days for no less than six months. Perhaps because he had grown tired of all the turmoil he obtained a licence of non-residence and left the church in the hands of a curate.[12]

In 1663 Bulstrode Whitelocke purchased an estate at Chilton Foliot in Wiltshire and settled there with his family. On the evidence of his diary the Whitelockes sometimes went to Chilton church but clearly attached more importance to their own domestic worship. Whitelocke was not impressed by the rector's sermons and succeeded in making an enemy of him by inviting James Hounsel, who had been ejected from the living, to preach in his house. Some of the diary entries are particularly revealing. On 21 April 1667 Whitelocke thought it worth recording the fact that he had received the sacrament in Chilton church as though this was a comparatively rare event for him. On 18 July 1669 he heard a sermon by a new curate and gained the impression that he was being subjected to some veiled criticism 'for not comming to Church'. On 5 November 1671 he wrote that 'The Lord's day there was no sermon att Chilton Church' and that he made up for this by preaching to his family both in the morning and the evening.[13]

In Somerset Sir Thomas Wroth and John Pyne had been prepared to serve as Presbyterian elders but this appears to have been more a matter of expediency than principle. In September 1661 the lord lieutenant was informed that on the previous Sunday Pyne had held a private conventicle in his own house with some of his neighbours and 'doth openly declare that he cannot conforme to the discipline of the Church of England'. In February 1669 a clergyman of his acquaintance wrote to congratulate him on his recent marriage and expressed his delight that 'the solemnity was performed accordinge to the Rites of the Church, it being by this means soe firme that the sharpest tooth of your bitterest Enemies can by noe means dissolve this tye'. When Pyne drew up his will in August 1676 he indicated, as a final act of defiance, that he wished to be buried 'in the night time without any outward pompe or usuall Ceremony'. To the minister of his parish he left 20s for the expenses arising and asked him to ensure that the funeral was 'without sound of Bells or any speech or words . . . att the Grave in any formall, Customary or usuall manner'.[14] The Book of Common Prayer was also implicitly rejected when Sir Thomas Wroth, who died in 1672, made testamentary provision for his interment in the chapel which he had built at Newton Placey before the time of the Civil War. Although he requested a neighbouring clergyman to officiate he was emphatic that there should be no service or ceremony of any kind. His coffin was to be draped with a decent black cloth but on no account with velvet. Recognising that these arrangements might seem unusual for a person of his quality he felt it necessary to explain that he had been influenced by two factors in particular: the 'Condition of theise tymes' (which clearly appalled him) and the great losses which he had suffered in the last thirty years.[15]

Sir Richard Strode, who lived at Chalmington in Dorset, had long been regarded as a religious extremist of the most factious kind. In 1634 he had been described as 'a schismaticall person' and 'a man ill affected to the State and governement Ecclesiasticall and the orthodox true Religion' as established by law. His will, which was drawn up in July 1669, was typically idiosyncratic. By this time he had become a Baptist and was fired with all the enthusiasm of the newly converted. It was his wish, he declared, that his body should be buried on the north side of his garden at Chalmington in a place which he had appointed as a sepulchre for himself and those of his family 'that are baptized with the baptisme of repentance for remission of their sinnes'; and in an attempt to vindicate his beliefs he offered a list of scriptural references. Having fallen out with his elder son, Sir William, many years before, he studiously ignored his existence and left a substantial amount of landed property to his second son Joseph 'whome my wife doth wrongfully call John Strode'. To his daughter Susan he bequeathed a portion of £500 on condition that she married a merchant and a further sum of

£1,000 if her husband was baptised with the baptism of repentance 'That he may shew and persuade her the right way to heaven which Infant Baptisme which is without repentance can never doe.' In the event he was buried at Plympton St Mary where his elder son was seated and his legacy of separatist principles went with him to the grave.[16]

A continuing association with the established Church did not necessarily denote satisfaction with all aspects of public worship. Writing to his son Robert in August 1680 Sir Edward Harley expressed the hope that the Church would not lack the strength 'to bring forth a blessed Reformation; and caus all the conceptions of Babilon to prove abortive'. The following year he published a work entitled *An Humble Essay Toward the Settlement of Peace and Truth in the Church* in which he condemned idolatry and ceremonies which in his judgement had not been divinely ordained. God had decreed that his Church should embrace the simplicity and liberty of Gospel worship with its key element of godly preaching. 'Baptism' he observed, 'hath been wretchedly abused by the additions of vile and nauseous or vain and insignificant signs.' Liturgical requirements should be limited to such as were 'necessary to Salvation'. In his view the Act of Uniformity of 1662 had introduced new and unacceptable conditions for defining conformity:

> since the Reformation (until the last Act of Uniformity) the only condition of Communion enjoyned by Law was Subscription and Assent, not to a Uniformity in Rites and Ceremonies, but to all the Articles of Religion which only concern the Confession of the True Christian Faith and the Doctrine of the Sacraments.

Harley jotted down further points of criticism in a manuscript which has survived among his private papers. The surplice, he wrote, was 'a proper massing garment' which ought not to be used by a Protestant minister. Nor was it right to insist that communicants should kneel when receiving the bread and wine; instead it should be lawful to receive them 'in any Gesture comonly practised in this or any other Reformed Church'.[17]

The requirement that communicants should kneel rather than sit or stand had occasioned a good deal of heartsearching before the time of the Civil War[18] and it continued to do so after the Restoration. On 23 May 1661 Philip Henry the nonconformist divine noted in his diary that it had been decided that MPs should 'receive the sacrament together at Margarets Westminster else not to sit in the house, according to the rules and ceremonyes of the church of England, at which many stumble'. Among those who found it difficult to comply with this order were Hugh Boscawen, Richard Hampden and Richard Norton, all of whom were the patrons of ministers who would shortly be ejected from their livings for nonconformity. Another MP, Sir Ralph Assheton of Whalley in Lancashire, was exceptionally freed from the obligation by what was termed 'the tacit Dispensation of this House'.[19] Under the provisions of the Test Act of 1673 persons holding offices of trust were faced with the need to receive communion publicly according to the usage of the Church of England. On 18 April Sir Edward Harley obtained a certificate from the minister of God's Word at the parish church of Great St Helens which put it on record that on Easter Sunday, following the sermon, he had received the sacrament of the Lord's Supper as prescribed by law. The choice of church for this act of conformity is significant: its congregation consisted largely of Presbyterians or 'halfe Conformists' who had been drawn there by the ministry of Dr Thomas Horton, a godly divine who had enjoyed the patronage of Sir John Langham, the owner of the tithes; and the minister who issued the certificate was Richard Kidder who, like Horton, was willing to administer communion to persons who remained standing. In addition, it is ironic that one of the witnesses who countersigned the certificate was Ralph Strettell, a nonconformist divine with whom Harley was on close terms. In his autobiography Kidder writes that his congregation was 'very great and wealthy'; that many strangers attended services at the church, 'I presume for the opinion they had of Dr Horton'; and that he found 'a great number that kneeled not at the Sacrament, but were otherwise very devout and regular'.[20]

In Derbyshire the Gells decided that, on balance, they were justified in continuing to attend public worship in their parish church but apparently suffered agonies of conscience over the extent of their conformity to the ceremonial requirements. In 1669 it was reported that although conventicles were held in the house of John Gell, Hopton Hall, he 'comes to Church to Divine service and sermon constantly' and that such conduct was highly unusual since no other conventicle in the county 'observes this Decorum'. Many years later a nonconformist minister, William Bagshaw, had more personal insights to offer. Sir John (as he became after his father's death) had a great respect for worthy ministers who had been ejected but since he also considered it important to ensure that 'the Sabbath and most publick Worship' were not deserted he went as far down the road with 'sober diligent Conformists' as he felt it possible for him to do. Although his wife Katherine had some scruples about the liturgy she 'managed' them modestly, took advice from the best ministers and rejected the way of rigid separation.[21] In her youth Lady Diana Ashurst, the wife of Sir Henry Ashurst, had often been present at the prayer meetings which were held in the house of Samuel Cradock, a Presbyterian divine who would later set up a dissenting academy in Suffolk. This experience made a lasting impression on her and she always had a great regard for a form of worship which was much plainer than the Prayer Book services. Nevertheless she 'would seriously attend upon the Publick Forms and had a respect to those in whom She saw any thing of Christ, tho' of different Persuasions'.[22]

In Yorkshire the Huttons of Poppleton attended church but appear to have made little attempt to conceal their disdain for the Prayer Book services. During the course of a visitation in 1680 the churchwardens of Nether Poppleton (who had been involved in a dispute over tithes with the Huttons) presented Dorothy Hutton 'for not repairing to the Church till divine service be ended' and for not receiving communion at Easter; her son Thomas for irreverent behaviour in church, namely 'in not kneeling at the Confession and Lord's prayer nor standing up when the beliefe is said' and also for holding conventicles in his house; and their chaplain, Thomas Birdsall, 'reputed a nonconformist Priest', for preaching in Poppleton Hall.[23]

Sir Roger Burgoyne, the patron of Edward Stillingfleet, lived sometimes at Sutton in Bedfordshire and at other times at Wroxall in Warwickshire. Following his death in 1677 (when he was described as 'a Saint') his widow, Lady Anne, took up permanent residence at Wroxall where there was a long tradition of militant nonconformity. The church adjoining the Elizabethan mansion had been acquired by the Burgoynes when they purchased the estate belonging to the former priory and since it was exempt from normal diocesan jurisdiction they were able to put in a stipendiary curate without having to seek institution from the Bishop of Worcester. Although they had freehold rights in the church it had parochial functions and in 1676 there was a congregation of 90 persons who included the tenantry as well as members of the Burgoyne household. For many years before the Civil War Wroxall had been a sanctuary for nonconformist ministers, among them Simeon Ashe and Ephraim Huitt who had found it impossible to comply with the Laudian concept of the beauty of holiness. After the passage of the Act of Uniformity Luke Milbourne, a minister who 'was highly esteemed by religious people in this parish and neighbourhood', had been forced to relinquish his curacy on refusing to conform even to the limited extent which might have earned him a reprieve. About the same time Sir Roger had allowed another ejected minister, Thomas Fownes, to take over the tenancy of one of his farms in Wroxall. Despite the fact that he was an obdurate nonconformist who declined to be episcopally ordained Fownes was employed for some years as curate and chaplain at Wroxall where a wall plaque was put up in his memory.[24]

In the sermon which was preached at the funeral of Lady Burgoyne in February 1694 the minister, Humphrey Whyle, revealed that her strict Puritan upbringing in Yorkshire had led her to take a jaundiced view of the Anglican liturgy but he quickly went on to stress that she had experienced a complete change of heart. The published version of the sermon which was dedicated to the Bishop of Worcester and Whyle, who had succeeded Fownes at Wroxall, seemed anxious to reassure him that despite its privileged status it was a parish in which good order prevailed. Lady Burgoyne, he related, was

> a great admirer of the publick Prayers of our Church which she justly esteemed as the most excellent and exact Form in the whole World. And, notwithstanding the prejudices of her Education, which might easily have created an unconquerable aversion to our Sacred Forms, yet the Follies and Indecencies of that bold Extempore way soon made her weary and ashamed of that; and her Wisdom and Judgment in the examination of Ours not only reconcil'd her to our Rational Service but inspired her with a great affection and delight in it, as most becoming the Solemnities of Publick Worship, and best fitted to exercise the Devotion of those who desir'd to worship God in the Beauty of Holiness.

Lady Burgoyne, he observed, was insistent that none of her

servants should fail to attend public worship without her express agreement and anyone breaking this rule was severely reprimanded. Even so, she was a kind mistress who treated them more like friends than servants. Finally, Whyle thought it worthy of notice that she saw it as her duty to be punctual when attending church services; indeed he could not recall one occasion 'for Nine Years together wherein the stated time of Publick Prayers was ever delay'd one quarter of an Hour upon her account'.[25]

According to Whyle's panegyric Lady Burgoyne built up an excellent collection of 'good and rational' books. In her surviving accounts which cover the years 1679 to 1687 there are references to a number of book purchases which offer at least some indication of an inquiring mind. These include the works of Joseph Mede who was best known for his millenarian scholarship; the collected sermons of John Tillotson and John Wilkins, both of whom were in favour of opening up the Church of England to moderate nonconformists; Thomas Comber's *A Companion to the Temple* which became the standard work on the Book of Common Prayer; and Lancelot Addison's *An Introduction to the Sacrament, or A Short, Plain and Safe Way to the Communion Table*. Dr Addison, who was the father of the essayist, was the Dean of Lichfield and a High Churchman who was opposed to the policy of comprehension. The fact that Lady Burgoyne bought a dozen copies of his book (probably for distribution to the servants) lends weight to Whyle's comment that she had a particular liking for the sacrament of the Lord's Supper (and it is also significant that in her will she bequeathed to the church of Wroxall 'one silver patten of the full value of five pounds for the more decent administering of the bread in the Celebration of the Lord's supper'). On the other hand, her Puritan mentality is reflected in an entry recording the purchase, in July 1681, of 'a book to write sermons in'. According to Anthony Wood the taking of sermon notes was a practice which had been held up to ridicule in the University of Oxford ever since the Restoration.[26]

In a considerable number of parishes there were beneficed clergy who were neither fully conformable themselves nor inclined to take too serious a view of acts of nonconformity on the part of the laity. In practice much depended on the attitude of the bishop of the diocese. Some like Thomas Barlow of Lincoln and John Wilkins of Chester were favourably disposed towards Presbyterians and Independents; others were merely negligent. Barlow was described by Anthony Wood as 'a thorow-pac'd Calvinist'; in 1689 he was said to have expressed the view that the Presbyterian form of ordination was good and sufficient in itself. Wilkins, writes Adam Martindale, was anxious to turn out drunken clergy or at least to suspend them 'and to fill the places with better men, and having a good opinion of some of us, that he took to be moderate Nonconformists, he proposed terms to us, to which we returned a thankful answer, showing our willingness to comply in any thing that would not cross our principles'. This initiative, however, was aborted when the Archbishop of York temporarily deprived him of his powers.[27] In July 1693 Sir Edward Harley told his son Robert that he had heard that the Bishop of Lichfield and Coventry 'hath given favourable Expressions in the Visitation concerning dissent from Ceremonyes' and that as a result children were being baptised in Shropshire without the sign of the cross or the nomination of godparents.[28] On occasion an attempt might be made to secure the appointment of a bishop who was a known friend of religious dissenters. In July 1689, following the death of the Bishop of Worcester, Thomas Foley and others sought to persuade the king to bestow the bishopric on Dr John Hall, the Master of Pembroke College, Oxford, who would later be described as 'a thorough-pac'd Calvinist, a defender of the Republican Doctrines, a stout and vigorous advocate for the Presbyterians, Dissenters, &c'. Although this proved unsuccessful they were probably not unduly disappointed on hearing that Dr Edward Stillingfleet was the preferred candidate. In April 1691, when the Bishop of Hereford was dying, the Harleys were fervently hoping that Hall would be chosen to succeed him. In the event he became Bishop of Bristol.[29]

Among the nonconforming clergy were James Ashurst, the vicar of Arlesey in Bedfordshire, and Isaac Archer, the vicar of Chippenham in Cambridgeshire. Ashurst was replaced in 1667 but took over the cure of souls again in 1672, though he was only prepared to read certain parts of the Book of Common Prayer. That he was able to retain his living in these circumstances was mainly due to the influence of his patron, Sir Samuel Browne, 'a person of great Piety, zeale and courage'.[30] When Richard Parr was ejected at Chippenham in 1662 the patron, Sir Francis Russell, appointed him as his domestic chaplain and offered the living to Isaac Archer who was duly presented in June 1663. In his autobiography Archer writes that there had been no sacrament in his church for over twenty years and that in order to gain the love of his parishioners, who were all nonconformists, he dispensed with the sign of the cross in baptism. Subsequently, in March 1665, he decided that it was no longer possible for him to conform to any significant extent.[31] In 1683 there was a report that Sir Charles Hoghton had put in a nonconformist minister, Thomas Birch, as vicar of Preston following the resignation of Seth Bushell who had preached his father's funeral sermon. Birch, it was claimed, did not baptise according to the custom of the Church and he also declined to preach a sermon either on the martyrdom of Charles I or the Restoration.[32]

Writing to the Archbishop of Canterbury in May 1671 Bishop Sparrow of Exeter told him that 'I press earnestly upon the Clergy to observe your Grace's directions for the due observance of the Liturgy and Catechising. I find too many of them averse from both, but yet I doubt not to have them conformable.'[33] In Northamptonshire, which had long been regarded as one of the most Puritan counties in England, there was a particularly wide gap between the provisions of the Act of Uniformity and the situation which actually existed at the parish level, at least in the first two decades of Charles II's reign. In 1683 Bishop Lloyd of Peterborough sent the Archbishop of Canterbury a report on the state of his diocese which in its description of the problems he had faced presented a very different picture from the bald statistics which had emerged from the 1676 census. On taking over the diocese in 1679 he had very soon discovered that the discipline of the Church had been 'much despised' and 'sett at nought'. At his primary visitation in 1680 the general response from the parishes had been *Omnia bene* but he had been deceived by 'the falseness and perjury' of the churchwardens. After this a more rigorous survey had revealed that there were some 30 clergymen who wore no surplice when officiating at services in their churches; that others 'mangl'd the Divine Offices and said the Prayers by halves and not as the Law Directs'; and that seditious meetings and conventicles were held in many towns and villages in Northamptonshire and Rutland. More recently it had become clear that the people in most parishes 'were strangely Averse to the Liturgy and Sacrament of the Lord's Supper'. Accordingly he had informed his parish clergy that at the next visitation it would be necessary to present all persons above the age of sixteen who neglected to take communion at Easter. The clergy had displayed this order in their churches, in compliance with his instructions, and he was glad to be able to report that it had 'brought in a vast number of persons throughout the whole Diocese to heare Divine Service and to receive the Blessed Sacrament of the Lord's Supper'.[34]

The combination of a wealthy Puritan patron and a church in the shadow of his manor-house which enjoyed a privileged status or at the least had only a small congregation virtually guaranteed that any irregularities in public worship, whether on the part of the minister or the laity, would go unreported in the normal course of events. As revealed in the 1676 census there were many parishes with comparatively few inhabitants over the age of sixteen. In some cases the congregation must have consisted largely, if not entirely, of members of the family and household of the squire and patron. For the Northamptonshire parishes of Steane and Fawsley the figures returned were 20 and 40 respectively, all of whom were described as conformists. The church adjoining the mansion of the Crewe family was a chapel with parochial functions which had been built by the father of John Lord Crewe, the patron, in 1620. At Fawsley, where the Knightleys had their principal seat, only seven households had been recorded in the hearth tax return of 1670. No census return was forwarded for the Northamptonshire parish of Canons Ashby where the church was a peculiar which belonged to Sir Robert Dryden. During the early seventeenth century Canons Ashby had been a hotbed of nonconformity and it was named by Bishop Lloyd as one of the places in his diocese where conventicles had been held.[35] In the course of a visitation of the Archdeaconry of Northampton which was begun in October 1682 it was noted that there were no churchwardens at Steane, Fawsley and Canons Ashby. At the same time it was established that Maurice Holden, the minister of Canons Ashby, had died and the decision was taken to cite Sir Robert Dryden to appear in the Consistory Court, presumably because he had neglected to put in a replacement.[36]

Other parishes with Puritan patrons and small congregations included Kedleston in Derbyshire, Markshall in Essex, Noseley in Leicestershire, Weston under Lizard in Staffordshire and Barmston in the East Riding of Yorkshire. At Barmston, where Sir Francis Boynton was the squire and his son Henry the rector, there were said to be 50 conformists and 10 nonconformists in 1676. Henry Boynton probably served as domestic chaplain at Barmston

Hall which Sir Francis preferred to the splendid Jacobeanmansion at Burton Agnes which he had inherited from his uncle Sir Henry Griffith. Two years earlier he had been presented at an episcopal visitation for failing to produce documentary evidence of his ordination.[37] At Noseley the Hesilrige mansion was one of the few houses in the parish. The precise status of the chapel there had been the subject of a well-publicised dispute between Sir Arthur Hesilrige who had argued that it was a donative cure and Archbishop Laud who had maintained that it was only a presentative living. The census return for Noseley conjures up a picture of a service attended by 20 adults, including Sir Thomas Hesilrige who was then a widower with two young children, and conducted by the household chaplain, Samuel Muston, who had been ejected from the Leicestershire living of Hungerton. In effect it was a domestic chapel with all that this could mean in terms of liturgical freedom.[38]

8

GOSPEL PREACHING

For godly patrons the recruitment of 'worthy conformists' for the livings in their gift could often be a difficult and time-consuming process. Essentially they wanted pious and learned preachers of the Word who were men of strict morals and equable temperament; and, most important of all, they considered it essential that their preaching should be solid and spiritually awakening. According to Richard Baxter who delivered the sermon at his funeral Henry Ashurst preferred the kind of preaching 'which made much and pertinent use of Scripture, by clear exposition and suitable application. He liked not that which worthy Dr Manton was wont to call Gentleman Preaching, set out with fine things, and laced and gilded, plainly speaking self-preaching, man-pleasing and pride.'[1] Sometimes a candidate was asked to preach a sermon in the presence of the congregation before the patron finally decided whether to accept him. This was clearly a sensible precaution from the patron's point of view and it can also be seen as a continuation of the practice which had begun to gain ground in the later 1640s of consulting the parish over the choice of a new minister.[2] If the patron had particularly stringent requirements or if the financial terms appeared unattractive there was the danger that he would be unable to make a presentation within six months after the living had fallen vacant, in which case the bishop would be entitled to put in his own nominee. Faced with the possibility of 'a lapse' the patron might resort to the expedient of bringing in a minister of his acquaintance on the understanding that he would resign the living once a suitable candidate had been found.

Some of the ministers who were presented by Puritan squires came direct from the universities; others had already been serving as parish clergy or had been employed as domestic chaplains.

When it became clear that Samuel Fairclough, the celebrated rector of Kedington in Suffolk, would be unable to hold on to his living after Bartholomew Day, his patron, Sir Thomas Barnardiston, mounted an intensive search 'in both the Universities, and in the City and Countrey' for a successor who would follow in his footsteps. Eventually he chose John Tillotson, the future Archbishop of Canterbury, who had been recommended to him as 'a person of great worth and abilities, a man of a moderate and candid Spirit, and of a large and generous temper'. According to Gilbert Burnet he was generally regarded as the best preacher of the age but unfortunately his style of preaching did not go down well with his Puritan parishioners. In 1664 he left Kedington and was succeeded by his curate, Charles Darby, who continued as rector until his death in 1709 and who, among other things, was the author of an elegy on the death of Queen Mary which was published in 1695.[3]

Although Kedington Hall was the principal seat of the Barnardistons they sometimes resided on their estate at Great Coates, near Grimsby in Lincolnshire. In March 1667 Thomas Doughty, who was then vicar of Legsby, a few miles to the south, told his friend Sir Edward Harley that he had recently been visited by 'a Religious and worthy knight', Sir Thomas Barnardiston, who he felt sure was not altogether unknown to him. Sir Thomas had offered him the rectory of Great Coates, a living of considerable value, and had pressed him to decline an invitation he had received from Harley to take over one of his Herefordshire livings. Doughty had some misgivings about this offer: since Great Coates was near the mouth of the Humber he feared for his health and there was the further consideration that the parsonage house was in a poor state of repair. But what weighed most heavily with him was the fact that Great Coates was a far better financial proposition than Leintwardine, even though Harley had promised him an augmentation out of his own estate. He therefore intimated as tactfully as possible that he had decided that it was in his best interests to serve the Barnardistons and the following month Sir Thomas presented him to the living. In the event the fears which he had expressed about his health proved to be well founded. In January 1670 he was writing to Harley that 'I think I must never be resident at Coates more, to live any time.' In fact the situation had now radically changed through 'the removall of my late dear Patron and his family in September last into

Suffolk and of himselfe within a moneth after to Heaven'.[4]

Exceptionally, Sir Thomas Wilbraham recruited a schoolmaster, Samuel Edwards of Newport, for his Staffordshire living of Weston under Lizard when the previous incumbent resigned in 1687. In a letter addressed to a relative he described him as 'a Worthy, grave, honest and learned man, and I beleive well studyed in devinity'. Since Weston was not a rich living and the Wilbrahams had a domestic chaplain there was probably little prospect of securing the services of an experienced minister.[5]

Godly patrons with livings to fill might seek advice from their contacts at the universities or from nonconformist divines such as Richard Baxter and Francis Tallents. In September 1693 Hugh Boscawen wrote in a letter to Tallents that if he knew of anyone who was 'well qualify'd for a publick liveing, and of a quiet temper, I wo'ld gladly be acquainted with him, wanting a good man for the parish I live in (when in Cornwall)'. The living (St Michael Penkevil) was a rectory worth £80 a year which had a good glebe together with a stone-built parsonage house. Joseph Halsey (who had been ejected from the benefice some 30 years before) was 'still desirous the place should be well supply'd'. Since he assumed that Tallents was acquainted with 'the best of those that conforme' he hoped that he would be able to provide assistance.[6] In Baxter's case there was the difficulty that he was strongly opposed to clerical conformity, as he made clear in correspondence with Edward Eccleston, a young man who had once sought his advice on the subject of ordination. Thomas Foley, the Worcestershire magnate, had appointed Eccleston as his domestic chaplain on Baxter's recommendation and had subsequently, in 1673, presented him to the living of Old Swinford. His decision to conform angered Baxter who told him that he considered conformity 'to be (materially) a very heynous sin, or rather a multitude of sins'. As the correspondence became increasingly acrimonious Eccleston accused Baxter of 'mighty self conceit'.[7]

Of all the Puritan patrons, few took their responsibilities more seriously than Sir Edward Harley who was warmly praised for the zeal he displayed in a contemporary account of his character:

> whenever he had power and Interest he was carefull to provide such helps and Guides as might be most useffull to the faith and salvation of all, for it is very well known in all places at his disposall he planted men of moderate principles, of

good reputation and sufficient abilities to preach the Gospell, and gave proportionable encouragement both for countenance and maintenance and the assurance people had of his severity against any known evill was of great use to render the labors of the faithfull ministers the more successfull.[8]

Harley owned the patronage rights in the parishes of Brampton Bryan, Wigmore and Leintwardine in Herefordshire and Bucknell in Shropshire. Alexander Clogie, a Scotsman, had been put into the living of Wigmore in 1648 and he remained there until his death in 1698. On the other hand, there was a considerable turnover of ministers at Brampton Bryan where the Harleys settled once more after building a new house for themselves. The first resident minister there after the Restoration was Thomas Cole who had been forced out of his appointment of Master of St Mary Hall, Oxford when the king's commissioners carried out a visitation of the university. In November 1660 Sir Edward, who was then governor of Dunkirk, was informed by his brother Thomas that Cole had preached at Brampton Bryan and 'the whole parish are wel satisfied in him'. Following the Act of Uniformity, however, he came to the conclusion that it would not be possible for him to conform, though he appears to have deferred his resignation in order to allow his patron sufficient time to find a successor. Probably at his suggestion Sir Edward approached John Martin, a minister who had found favour with the Westminster Assembly of Divines, to see whether he would be willing to take over the living but there was the complication that he had also received an offer of preferment from another leading patron, Philip Lord Wharton. In January 1663 Martin wrote in a letter to Lord Wharton that Sir Edward had been in touch with him 'and after some conference with so much importunity urged me for a visit, that I must have beene extremely uncivill had I not forced myself to make him a promise'. Shortly afterwards Cole reported to Harley that he had spoken to Martin at Oxford and that he was prepared to visit Brampton Bryan before letting him have a final answer. He went on to say that

I hope he will in some measure answer your expectacions in the discharge of his duty there and prove A successefull instrument in the hand of God for the good of that people. I have ever took him to be A sober consciencious person, desirous to act according to his present light.

99

On 13 June Sir Edward sent his wife the disappointing news that Martin had declined his offer. This, however, was not the end of the matter: on 30 June he was able to tell her that Martin had now decided to settle at Brampton Bryan and he added with obvious relief 'I beseech the Lord bring him to us in the fulnes of the blessing of the gospel, And mak us thankful for so great a mercy.'[9]

After serving at Brampton Bryan for fourteen years Martin gave notice that he wished to resign the living. This came as an unpleasant surprise to Harley who told his wife that 'I shal be extremely troubled to part with so good a man.' In April 1678 Sir Edward was writing to his son Robert that 'Mr Martin is gone, I have presented in his room one Mr Barton of Shropshire. He preaches wel and I trust the Lord wil graciously make him a blessing to us at Bramton.' Three years later Samuel Barton was dead and another capable preaching minister, Richard Roberts, was brought in from Leintwardine. For a time it looked as though this change of incumbency had ushered in a period of greater stability but in April 1685 Roberts 'was taken away by a Sudden and Sharp Disease'.[10]

Between April and September 1685 the Harleys were making frantic efforts to find a new minister with the right qualifications. Sir Edward put the value of the living at £80 a year which was relatively modest but indicated that he would be willing to augment it with the tithes of Walford which were let at a rent of £11 a year. A number of relations and friends offered the names of possible candidates. Some were ruled out for one reason or another; others preferred to remain where they were. Sir Edward's nephew Nathaniel Stephens, who was seated in Gloucestershire, was consulted about the merits of a neighbouring minister and sent back word that while he thought very highly of him he felt obliged to stress that if he left Horsley all the people there 'would goe into factions'. Nathaniel Harley, one of Sir Edward's younger sons, told his father that Richard Baxter had assured him that Daniel Burgess (who had been ordained under Presbyterian auspices at Dublin) was 'a verry able and pious man and thinks you can scarse finde such another so fitt for Bramton'. As the months slipped away there was growing anxiety about the lack of progress. On 22 August Robert Harley wrote in a letter to his father that he begged the Lord 'to have mercy on us in this mighty concern without which Bramton will be little better then a wilderness'.[11]

By the end of August Sir Edward had been given the names of

two other possible candidates, George Nelson who was currently serving as chaplain to Sir Roger Hill and Thomas Oulton of Newcastle under Lyme. Writing to his son Robert on 1 September he confessed to having mixed feelings about Oulton's ability. Oulton, he observed, was no doubt pious and he preached well but he was not as good as previous ministers of Brampton Bryan and, in addition, his hearing was much impaired. Daniel Burgess, he went on, 'I hear must be Ordained legally, his ministerial abilities are represented advantageously'. The situation was now becoming extremely serious: 'The time of lapse hastens, therefor speedily send your thoughts to mee about this great matter concerning which the Lord vouchsafe an answer of mercy.' At this stage Robert Harley was inclined to feel that Burgess would be the best choice. In his reply he suggested that Baxter's views on his piety, learning and preaching were 'such as may preponderate some other objections, specially considering none of the other Candidates but may have many things objected to them'. Sir Edward, however, stressed that he had 'a great objection against Mr Burgess in regard of Ordination', though without specifying the precise grounds of his concern. In the end he came down in favour of Thomas Oulton. On 1 October he informed his son that he had just received a good report about George Nelson but since 'the time of the lapse' was so close he had been obliged to present Mr Oulton to the living. Oulton had duly received institution and had since preached 'with satisfaction'. Despite his initial reservations Sir Edward was soon rejoicing over the restoration of godly preaching: 'Is it not very good', he asked rhetorically, 'when the Joyful Sound is once more come to poor Bramton?'[12]

On 5 April 1688 Sir Edward received a letter from the mayor and corporation of Newcastle under Lyme in which they begged him to allow Oulton to return to them. In his reply he told them that Oulton was very well liked by the congregation at Brampton Bryan for 'both his Doctrine and his Conversation' but he was nevertheless prepared to accede to their request. 'My humble supplications', he went on, 'are for the Lord's gracious direction and blessing concerning this affair which is of so great concernment both to you and to this place.'[13] Oulton formally resigned the living on 30 July but well before then the search had begun for a successor and Sir Edward's sons Robert and Edward were busy making inquiries. On 7 July Robert Harley was writing to his father that 'Our great concerne at Bramton as to the Ministry reqires ernest prayer and serious consideration'. He personally was far from optimistic: 'those are desirable will not remove, those wil remove not desirable, the best I can hear is scarce tolerable'. As regards the possible candidature of Maurice Lloyd (who had been ejected in Wales but was now the vicar of Bucknell) he had hardly an equal in London so far as preaching abilities were concerned 'and I suppose greatly acceptable to my good mother. His failings are known . . . I confess Doubts as to his removal, both as to himself and his people who have receiv'd great benefit by him.' Not long afterwards a young minister, John Swinfen, arrived at Brampton Bryan with a letter of commendation from his uncle John the well-known politician who was held in great esteem by the Harleys. Sir Edward's impression of him, as succintly recorded in a letter to his son Robert, was generally favourable: 'He prayed in the family wel, seemes ingenious, was of Emanuel College.' He was not disposed, however, to put him into the living of Brampton Bryan, though he thought that he might be a suitable choice for one of Thomas Foley's livings in Worcestershire when a vacancy occurred.[14]

Eventually Sir Edward decided, with his wife's encouragement, that the best course was to transfer Maurice Lloyd from Bucknell if he was willing to move. In a letter dispatched to Lloyd on 6 August he made him an offer in terms which suggest that he might have had lingering doubts:

> I trust yet the mercy of God will not take away the Gospel from this unworthy place, though we have in few years felt the removes of several worthy Pastors. I have not ceased humbly to implore the Lord to be gracious unto us; wherein I trust it is an answer, to direct to pitch upon your self, who as you are very acceptable unto the most considerable of this Parish so I hope God will incline your heart and bring you hither with the fulnes of the blessing of the Gospel.

Lloyd's response was not particularly enthusiastic. He was clearly convinced that the proposed move would have no financial benefits for him: the two livings, he suggested, were of more or less equal value. More significantly, he was not at all sure that he had the kind of attributes which the Harleys required of a minister of Brampton Bryan; and he was also concerned about the implications for the people of Bucknell. Nevertheless he would accept the offer.[15]

Although Lloyd was quick to respond it was not until December that Sir Edward presented him to the living, perhaps because of the difficulty he was experiencing in finding another minister for Bucknell.[16] The following autumn the new minister of Brampton Bryan contracted a serious illness and there were fears that the unhappy saga of events was not yet over: it was 'a great Alarm to this unworthy place', wrote Edward Harley to his father, 'that has buried and parted with so many excellent Ministers'. Lloyd, however, recovered and the Harleys were soon enthusing over the quality of his preaching. When Sir Edward's daughter Abigail was staying in London in August 1692 she delivered herself of the opinion that apart from James Beverley (a nonconformist preacher of growing reputation) Mr Lloyd had 'more in one sermon than any four I have heard here'.[17]

From time to time the Harleys were drawn in when the Foleys, who were also major patrons, had a vacant living to fill. Paul Foley, who was seated at Stoke Edith in Herefordshire, owned the patronage rights there and in the parishes of Dormington, Felton, Mordiford and Tarrington. In April 1684 he told Sir Edward Harley that following the death of Robert Scudamore, the rector of Stoke Edith, it was now incumbent on him as patron to make provision for the parish and the neighbourhood. This, however, was no easy task and he hoped that Harley would pray on his behalf for God's direction and blessing. 'I look on this affaire', he went on, ' as one of the greatest concern.' His aim was to recruit 'a pious and successfull Minister' and, as an additional bonus, the kind of person with whom he could 'heartily converse'. Mr Jackman,[18] who had been offered the living, had promised to let him have his final answer within a matter of days but he thought it likely that he would decline. He dare not press him to take the living 'with a scrupled Conscience . . . he raiseth many scruples to stay where he is'. The other principal candidate, John Wickens, was a very young man 'yet he is freest having noe Cure but a mere lecturer, of pious parents, orthodox and good life'. When Jackman turned down the offer Foley invited Wickens to come and see him at Stoke Edith; wrote to 'some good people in his neighbourhood for their opinion of him'; and also consulted Dr John Hall, the Master of Pembroke College at Oxford. In the light of his inquiries he concluded that Wickens had the necessary attributes and the new minister was duly instituted on 16 April. The following day Foley wrote exultantly to his friend Harley that 'I bless God Mr Wickins met with no opposition yesterday'.[19]

Thomas Foley, the elder brother of Paul Foley, lived at Witley Court in Worcestershire and was patron of the livings of Great Witley, Kidderminster (where Richard Baxter had once been minister), Oddingley, Old Swinford and Pedmore. In November 1685 his son-in-law Robert Harley suggested that George Nelson, who had recently been recommended for Brampton Bryan, would be a suitable choice for the vacant living of Oddingley. Writing to Harley on 7 November Foley asked him to send Nelson down to Witley Court with all possible speed, adding that 'I suppose he must be ordained, if he is not, before he Can have the living'. Nelson preached in the parish church of Great Witley on 15 November and Foley told his son-in-law that 'we like him very well, this morning I gave him his presentation, he is gone to Worcester'. At this point, however, difficulties began to arise. On 23 November Foley was writing, in a letter addressed to Sir Edward Harley, that 'our Bishop will not ordaine him, I am near lapsing but I hope it will not proove so'. A way out of this impasse had to be found quickly but Foley was equal to the challenge. Six days later he informed Sir Edward that Nelson was now settled at Oddingley after being ordained by Francis Turner, the Bishop of Ely, in London; that he had been instituted and inducted with 'foure days to spare of the six months'; and that 'we all like him and the parish are fond of him'.[20]

In September 1687 George Nelson preached once again in the church at Great Witley and Robert Harley, who was then at Witley Court, subsequently gave his father a graphic account of what was clearly regarded as a very special occasion:

he read the prayers with a great deal of devotion, as became prayers to God: his prayer in the Pulpit was very serious and pertinent, his text Acts 19.2 on which he preachd with a great deal of plainess, without affectation of Learning, yet those truths were pressd with ernestness, intelligible to the meanest, and suitable to the highest Capacity. The church was so full in the morning wee could hardly get to our seats and the afternoon many at the windows (tho' a rainy day). I have seldome seen an auditory so attentive and affected, specially young persons. After the first sermon, besides those that had friends or acquaintances to goe to, about a hundred went into the Church again to stay between the sermons, and one to repeat according to their Custome, but were sent for in

heer to dinner and repitition ... I pray God encrease his
graces, and continue him humble.[21]

Nelson's brand of preaching went down well with the godly, and
not least the Harleys, but he met with hostility from some of his
fellow clergy in the county as well as those of his parishioners
who had no wish to be reformed. In 1690 the ecclesiastical
authorities attempted to get rid of him by pressing him to accept a
military chaplaincy in Ireland but he declined to take up the offer.
When the Bishop of Worcester undertook a visitation in November
1696 several of the clergy alleged that he was 'a great ffanatick'
and an enemy to the Church, that he held conventicles and that he
disturbed the peace of churches in other counties. Bishop
Stillingfleet was at first inclined to suspend him but in the event
he merely admonished him in private.[22]

During the course of the 1690s Nelson became increasingly
depressed. In his darker moods he was highly critical of his patron
and desperately anxious to settle in another county. This was
partly because he found it difficult to subsist on the income from
his living which amounted to between £40 and £50 a year and
partly because he was convinced that Foley had turned against
him. Now and again the Harleys invited him to Brampton Bryan
and on one occasion he poured out his troubles to Sir Edward's
daughter Martha who was a sympathetic listener. Her father was
then serving in Parliament and she immediately sent him an
account of their conversation. Nelson had told her that he had it
on good authority that his patron had declared that 'Mr Nelson
was a burden to him and it were wel if he were removed'; and
with tears in his eyes he had recounted an episode in which Foley
had treated him very unkindly. He was also suffering financially;
indeed he had been obliged to spend £20 a year of his own money
to maintain himself. From another source she had heard that
Philip Foley (who was a leading patron of nonconformist divines)
was doing all he could 'to set his Brother Foley against him; and
not to alow him anything'. In September 1694 Nelson complained
in a letter to Sir Edward Harley that his patron had only been
prepared to see him once since returning into the country; that 'he
drives on an interest that I cannot well engage in'; and that 'he
gives but little countenance to Religion'. When Sir Henry Ashurst
offered him a living in Oxfordshire he was keen to seize the
opportunity but found too many obstacles in his way.[23]

Although Nelson's relations with his patron were sometimes strained Foley seems to have retained a high opinion of his abilities. In March 1697 he substantially increased his income by allowing him to hold the rectory of Pedmore, which was worth £80 a year, as well as his living of Oddingley. Subsequently, in June 1699, Robert Harley informed his father that Nelson had imprudently refused his patron's offer of the rectory of Old Swinford; and shortly afterwards Foley presented William Hallifax, a man of 'Puritanical stamp' who had been serving as chaplain to the English factory at Aleppo.[24]

In Northamptonshire the right of presentation to two of the Knightley livings, Fawsley and Preston Capes, was vested in a number of trustees under the provisions of a deed executed in February 1668. The Knightleys had always attached particular importance to these livings since their principal residence was at Fawsley and they had a secondary house at Preston Capes. The trust arrangements appear to have been a product of fears both about the effects of the Act of Uniformity and the durability of the male line.[25] The composition of this body of trustees changed over the years as some died and others were appointed in their stead but generally they were relatives and friends of the Knightleys who considered themselves to be sober and godly men. They included John Lord Crewe and his son Thomas, Richard Hampden, John Swinfen, Sir Edward Harley and his son Robert, Thomas Foley (the son of Paul Foley) and Sir John Crewe of Cheshire. On 3 February 1685 Thomas Lord Crewe, who was then in Paris, wrote to his friend John Swinfen about the choice of a minister for the vacant living of Fawsley. He had received a letter from his cousin Lady Anne Knightley, the widow of Sir Richard Knightley, in which she had suggested that the trustees should nominate Edward Richardson who had been serving as curate to Thomas Knightley, the venerable rector of Byfield. Lady Knightley wanted 'a good and a peaceable man' and in the light of what she had heard from the rector she believed that Richardson would fully meet her requirements. Lord Crewe expressed the hope that his fellow trustees would be willing to grant her request, bearing in mind that she would be living under his ministry. The other trustees appear to have raised no objections and on 25 February Richardson was duly instituted.[26]

Although the trustees occasionally had minor items of business to transact[27] it was not until a decade later that they were again called upon to fill a vacant living. By this time Fawsley had a new squire, Lucy Knightley, who had succeeded his cousin Devereux some three years earlier. In January 1699 Robert Harley told his father that he had just heard from Lady Knightley that William West, the vicar of Preston Capes, had died and she was hoping that the trustees would consider Edward Richardson as a possible candidate for the living. Sir Edward's response was to write to Lady Knightley to make it clear that he had strong objections to pluralism and to ask her to send Richardson to Brampton Bryan for an interview. Shortly afterwards Sir Edward received a letter from another of the trustees, Thomas Foley, who reported that the Knightleys were in agreement over Richardson's candidature and that Lady Knightley had said that he 'had no thoughts of keeping both Fawsley and Preston, that he should wait upon you at Bramton where she doubted not but he would give you satisfaction'. In conclusion he assured Harley that so far as he was concerned there could be no question of presenting anyone who did not have his full approval.[28]

Richardson was presented to the living in March and by that stage the Harleys had already made up their minds about the choice of a successor for Fawsley. In the event Lucy Knightley rejected their preferred candidate, Joseph Walferne, apparently on the grounds that he held unacceptable political views. Walferne told Robert Harley that the probable reason for Knightley's antipathy was that he had been given a false account of a sermon he had preached at Chester. In that sermon he had argued that the papists had been more deeply implicated in the Civil Wars than was commonly believed; but there had not been a single word reflecting on the person of the king. Others mentioned as possible candidates included John Wickens, the rector of Stoke Edith, who was not interested and Daniel Marks who was currently serving as domestic chaplain to Sir John Crewe. Walferne offered the suggestion that if the trustees resubmitted his own name together with that of Marks, for whom he had the highest regard, it would 'puzzle Mr Knightley to make a choice'. Before long, however, there was news of a surprise candidate, Thomas Danby, who was described, somewhat disparagingly, as a great friend of Richardson 'and much of the same principles'. The trustees finally put forward the names of two candidates, Thomas Danby and Robert Comyn the elder (the father of one of Sir Edward Harley's ministers), and after complaining about the short notice he had been given Lucy Knightley came down in favour of Danby.[29]

Although a considerable number of ministers who had godly patrons had decided to conform in 1662 it proved much more difficult to persuade a hardened nonconformist to accept the offer of a living however attractive the inducements. After Thomas More's ejection from the Dorset living of Hammoon he and his family found themselves in a situation where they had no assured means of support. The Trenchards 'had such a value for him that as there were three vacancies at that place from Bartholomew-day during his life they made a free offer of the parsonage to him every time; but he still refused it because unsatisfied with the terms of conformity'.[30] Despite the problems of recruitment the Puritan gentry appear, on the whole, to have been well satisfied with the kind of ministers they were able to secure for livings in their gift. In October 1698 Paul Foley wrote approvingly of three of his ministers, John Wickens of Stoke Edith, William Crowther of Tarrington and John Nash of Dormington, who in his estimation were 'all orthodox and preaching very piously'. By 'orthodox' he no doubt meant that their preaching was deeply rooted in Calvinist doctrine. Perhaps significantly, he had used some of his impropriate tithes in Herefordshire to augment the income of both Crowther and Nash.[31] A number of conforming ministers, among them Nathaniel Parkhurst of Yoxford in Suffolk and William Stevens of Sutton in Bedfordshire, were on good terms with nonconformist divines and earned such complimentary epithets as 'worthy' and 'moderate'. Parkhurst was also domestic chaplain to his patroness, Lady Elizabeth Brooke, and testified in an account of her life that she had relieved many sober non-conformists.[32] At the same time there are some indications of a decline of religious fervour even among the clergy who occupied livings in the gift of Puritan patrons. Before the time of the Civil War the Barringtons had been deluged with spiritual advice by Ezekiel Rogers and William Chantrell, the ministers whom they had presented to their Yorkshire livings of Rowley and Walkington. In contrast, the letters which Sir John Barrington received from John Burnett, who was rector of Walkington during the years 1667 to 1698, were largely concerned with the manage-ment of the family's northern estates.[33]

9

CONVENTICLES AND MEETING HOUSES

In a memorandum which was apparently written in the latter part of Charles II's reign it was argued that there were too many dissenters holding offices of honour and profit under the Crown. By dissenters, explained the anonymous author, he meant not only persons who never came to church but occasional conformists who regularly attended conventicles. In his view church attendance which was motivated by a desire to secure the necessary legal qualifications for office was no true indication of loyalty or love to the Church.[1] Although the Puritan nobility and gentry almost invariably remained in communion with the Church of England they were also in close contact with nonconformist, and particularly Presbyterian, ministers. Besides providing financial assistance they employed nonconformist divines as their domestic chaplains or entertained them in their houses; and not infrequently they went to hear them preach at private meetings in London and elsewhere. Samuel Pepys records in his diary that on 20 January 1668 he dined at the house of his friend John Lord Crewe and that another of the guests was Thomas Case, the well-known Presbyterian minister, who, he observes, 'doth talk just as I remember he used to preach'. From the discussion which they had about the state of religion he learned that some form of toleration was expected, 'so that the presbyters do hold up their heads, but they will hardly trust the King or the Parliament where to yield to them – though most of the sober party be for some kind of allowance to be given them'.[2] In September 1682 Sir Leoline Jenkins, one of the Principal Secretaries of State, was informed that there were several gentlemen in Cheshire and Staffordshire who attended church services but consorted with and mainly employed 'fanatics'. Later, in July 1683, it was reported that Sir

John Bowyer, who was seated in Staffordshire, had always been a very factious man and a great favourer of the dissenters. His house, Knypersley Hall, was situated in the parish of Biddulph where he owned the patronage rights and the minister also acted as his household chaplain. This part of the county, it was alleged, was an 'odd nook' where he and his neighbours were all brutish beasts and cursed 'fanatics'.[3]

In September 1661 a proclamation was issued which prohibited all meetings for religious worship except in parochial churches or chapels or in private houses where only the residents took part.[4] This, however, proved ineffective. In London, where many of the most celebrated nonconformist ministers were living, the number of conventicles went on increasing. 'The presbyterian party', claimed an informer, 'hold their conventicles dayly, and have their Fasts every weeke once or twice, and have their frequent conferences and collections of money whereby to hold their party together, and to bee in a readynes for an opportunity to Resoume the Church and the Court'. It was the practice, he went on, to admit none to their meetings without a ticket and the great ones were asked to leave their coaches at home and come privately. Richard Baxter often preached at the house of his friend Richard Hampden near St John's in Clerkenwell which was 'fitted for the purpose'; and conventicles were also held at the house of Frances Cecil the Dowager Countess of Exeter where the preachers were her chaplain Dr Thomas Jacombe and two other ejected ministers, William Whitaker and Matthew Poole.[5] In February 1664 it was alleged that an all-day fast had been observed at a house in Whitefriars; that Matthew Poole had conducted prayers and Dr Thomas Manton and Dr William Bates had preached; and that the lay participants had included the Countess of Exeter, Lord Wharton, Sir William Waller, Lady Mary Armyne and Richard Hampden and his wife. Later that year there was a report that a conventicle in Covent Garden had been attended by many persons of quality, among them the Countesses of Peterborough and Anglesey, Lady Mary Armyne and her daughter-in-law Lady Anne Armyne and four or five knights whose names could not be discovered.[6]

In the West Country conventicles were frequently held in such places as Exeter, Taunton, Bridgwater and Dorchester.[7] Bishop Ward of Exeter was concerned not only about the activities of the ejected ministers who were seeking to promote the growth of nonconformity but the extent to which they were benefiting from the connivance and protection of the magistracy. In Devon, he told the Archbishop of Canterbury, there were at least fourteen justices of the peace 'who are accounted arrant Presbyterians'. These included Sir John Davie, whose house at Sandford was 'the chief place of resort' for the Presbyterians, Sir Walter Yonge, Sir Edmund Fowell and two other major landowners, Matthew Hele and William Walrond. He had heard of some conventicles in Cornwall but he had assumed that they had been suppressed by the magistrates in the neighbourhood. In fact, he lamented, they were still flourishing 'and when I complaine to the same Justices I find them very coole and shifting'. The Presbyterian party was headed by such men as Hugh Boscawen and Francis Buller, both of whom were in the House of Commons, and most of their fellow justices were prepared to go along with them, either from conviction or for other reasons.[8]

Lady Frances Hobart, who lived at Chapelfield House in Norwich, was a nonconformist 'as to some Modes of Worship' and disliked set forms of prayer. According to her Presbyterian chaplain, John Collinges, she converted some of the lower rooms of her house into a chapel which could accommodate 200 persons and here he regularly preached to 'a very full Auditory'. For two or three years before her death in 1664 she 'restrained her self to those exercises of Religion which were performed within her own walls, or in some other places not so publick'. Eventually the authorities carried out a search of her house in the hope of finding incriminating evidence. This caused a considerable stir and Horatio Lord Townshend, the lord lieutenant of Norfolk, hastened to apologise to her for the distress she had suffered. 'I dare say', he wrote, that the officers concerned 'may plead ignorance as not understanding theyr duty, nor how to demeane themselves with that due respect becomes them to a person of your quality'. For the future he would ensure that she remained undisturbed since he felt able to rely on her prudence 'in not suffering any scandalous number to meet'. In reply Lady Frances thanked him for the assurance he had offered her and added that she hoped 'to walke with such future caution that your Lordship shall have no cause to think that you have herein shewed too much civility and favour'.[9]

When the first Conventicle Act came into force in the summer of 1664 Lady Hobart told Collinges that it was of no consequence to her: she was now so ill that she would never again be able to come downstairs.[10] Under the provisions of this statute anyone aged sixteen or over who attended a conventicle could be fined £5 or, failing payment, sentenced to a term of imprisonment not exceeding three months. For this purpose a conventicle was defined as a private meeting held 'under colour or pretence' of a religious exercise at which five or more persons were present in addition to members of the household.[11] In Richard Baxter's opinion this definition involved particular difficulties for wealthy landowners:

> In a Gentleman's House it is ordinary for more than four, of Visitors, Neighbours, Messengers, or one sort or other, to be most or many days at Dinner with them: and then many durst not go to Prayer, and some durst scarce crave a Blessing on their Meat, or give God thanks for it.[12]

The act may have deterred some godly squires from allowing their houses to be used for conventicles but its impact was not as great as had been hoped. Bulstrode Whitelocke, who was regarded as a major patron of the Independent divines, often held conventicles at his country house, Chilton Lodge in Wiltshire. In September 1665 he noted in his diary that a friend had informed him that she had 'heard much discourse touching Conventicles' at Chilton Lodge 'and wished him to be Cautious'. Despite this warning, however, he continued to receive visits from nonconformist ministers such as James Hounsel and George Cokayne and also employed a domestic chaplain, James Pearson, who was regularly called upon to deliver a sermon. In June 1666 Whitelocke wrote that Hounsel had preached at the Lodge and that the rector of Chilton Foliat had sent a spy, while in September 1667 he inserted the revealing entry that 'Mr Cokaine preached, and many strangers heard him.' When visiting London he and his wife attended Cokayne's meetings and also those of Dr John Owen who had many friends among the nobility and gentry. On 20 December 1668 Owen preached to a large gathering which had assembled in Whitelocke's lodgings.[13]

A more detailed and comprehensive account of conventicles emerged from a special survey conducted by the diocesan authorities in 1669. Among the gentry named in the returns were Edmund Prideaux of Forde Abbey in the parish of Thorncombe which was then in a detached part of Devon, Major Dunch of Pusey in Berkshire and Lady Mary Rodes, the widow of Sir Edward Rodes, of Great Houghton in the West Riding of Yorkshire.[14] Forde Abbey had been a centre of nonconformity before the time of the Civil War and in 1639 Sir Henry Rosewell, who was then the owner, had been arraigned in the Court of High Commission following allegations that the chapel had been used for conventicles. Prideaux was the son of one of the leading campaigners for a Presbyterian church settlement in the Long Parliament and it is therefore not surprising that those attending the conventicles under his patronage were described as Presbyterians. The ministers who preached at these meetings, when 'about 100, oftentimes more' were present, were identified as Nicholas Wakeley, formerly the vicar of Thorncombe, and John Hodder who had been ejected from the living of Hawkchurch in Dorset.[15] Major Dunch, who at this time was only sixteen years old, had inherited the family estates in 1668 when his father and grandfather had died within a week or so of each other. In a letter addressed to Lord Wharton a nonconformist divine had written of him that in every respect he was 'one of the hopefullest young Gentlemen I know in all these parts'. When his father, John Dunch, was on his deathbed he had instructed him to take his kinsman Humphrey Gunter 'for your father and to consult with him and bee ordered by him in all things'. Gunter, who had been deprived of an Oxford fellowship, was acting as his guardian, tutor and chaplain and it was clearly through his influence that the Dunch mansion had become a major centre for Presbyterian worship in north Berkshire. In July 1669 Bulstrode Whitelocke received a visit from Dunch and Gunter who were accompanied by several persons from Marlborough and Ramsbury. The object of the visit, as Whitelocke noted in his diary, was to seek his advice on what they should do in a situation where they were faced with proceedings in the ecclesiastical court for staying away from church and frequenting conventicles.[16]

The conventicles at Great Houghton (which was situated in the extensive parish of Darfield) were said to have been attended by about 60 Presbyterians and Independents. The chapel adjoining the Elizabethan manor-house had been built by Sir Edward Rodes in 1650 for the use of his household and tenantry and had been fitted out in a manner which accorded with his Puritan convictions. The patronage of the chapel was entirely in the hands of the family and the minister performed the functions of a domestic chaplain. After the passage of the Act of Uniformity there were also frequent visits by nonconformist preachers, men such as

William Benton of Barnsley, Luke Clayton of Rotherham, Jonathan Grant of Thurnscoe, Oliver Heywood of Northowram and Joshua Kirby of Wakefield. Heywood relates that on 3 November 1668 he travelled to the house of Lady Rodes (who by that time was a widow) and that on the following day a solemn fast was observed:

> Mr Clayton of Rotherham and I preacht and prayed and Mr Kerby closed the work with prayer, the day after being the 5th of November my lady prevailed with us to stay and spend some time in thankfulnes, Mr Graunt begun and I preacht and prayed and Mr Kerby concluded, they were two precious days.[17]

The first Conventicle Act expired in May 1668 and a bill for its continuance made slow progress. In March 1668 the Commons decided to ask the king to issue a proclamation for enforcing the laws against conventicles and this duly appeared. In the debate on this proposal John Swinfen, Hugh Boscawen and Sir Walter Yonge expressed their misgivings. Swinfen declared that although he was not in favour of any general toleration 'as to parties' he considered that some freedom should be allowed to those who dissented only in the matter of ceremonies. Boscawen argued that Protestant England ought to be prepared to adopt a more enlightened stance than Catholic Spain: 'Let us not compell people in point of conscience, as the Spaniards baptized, by driving thousands of Indians into the river at once.'[18] Subsequently, on 8 April, Sir Walter Yonge told the House that he hoped it might be possible to dispense with the requirement that ministers should signify their assent and consent to everything contained in the Book of Common Prayer. Swinfen, for his part, was anxious to expound his views on the suppression of conventicles. In the past, he maintained, it had never been thought that 'the Law for Conventicles extended to any other persons than such as were out of all communion with us in doctrine, and hold no salvation in our Church'. In his judgement it was entirely wrong to apply the term to meetings of dissenters who were 'with us in doctrine, though different in ceremonies'.[19] In July 1669 the Privy Council approved a further proclamation in which it was stressed that more conventicles than ever were being held and that this endangered the public peace. The following day Sir Edward Harley wrote in a letter to his wife that a severe proclamation against nonconformists was being issued and added

'The Lord glorifie his Name in bringing good out of this to poor England.'[20]

The second Conventicle Act, which came into effect in May 1670, introduced heavier penalties for the ministers involved and those who allowed their houses to be used for this purpose.[21] Bulstrode Whitelocke applied his lawyer's mind to the detailed implications of this new measure; discussed the subject of liberty of conscience with Lord Wharton; and continued to hold conventicles in his house. On 28 May George Cokayne and his wife arrived at Chilton Lodge 'and on the Lords dayes he preached twice in the house, very well, and divers neighbours came in to heare him'.[22]

When Sir Roger Burgoyne heard in February 1672 that the king had plans for a general toleration he wrote ecstatically that 'the good nature of our king is allmost to a miracle. God bless him from all such.' Following the issue of the Declaration of Indulgence on 15 March the authorities were bombarded with requests for licences both for nonconformist ministers and nonconformist places of worship. Among those named in the applications for the licensing of houses there was an impressive array of godly women of high social rank who were generally widows. Some like Frances Countess of Exeter, Lady Bridget Roberts of Glassenbury in Kent and Lady Mary Stanley of Bickerstaffe Hall in Lancashire favoured a Presbyterian form of worship; others such as Sophia Viscountess Wimbledon, Lady Eleanor Roberts of Willesden in Middlesex and Lady Frances Vane of Fairlawne in Kent, the widow of Sir Henry Vane the younger, revealed a preference for ministers of the Independent or Congregational persuasion.[23] Lady Mary Rodes secured a licence for the chapel at Great Houghton but there was some uncertainty about the denomination of the minister whom she had selected. Jeremiah Milner, who had been ejected from a Yorkshire living, was initially described in his licence as a Congregational minister but the authorities subsequently received a request that he should be shown as a Presbyterian.[24] At Titchmarsh in Northamptonshire there was a similar degree of confusion. Lady Elizabeth Pickering, the widow of Sir Gilbert Pickering, at first nominated a Presbyterian divine, Henry Searle, as her minister but he died shortly after his licence was granted and she then recruited Nathaniel Whiting, a Congregational minister who had been the pastor of a gathered church at Cranford. Probably her main concern was to acquire the services of an able preacher.[25]

Lady Bridget Roberts, who was the widow of Sir Howland Roberts, sought licences for both the private chapel adjoining the house and her Presbyterian chaplain, Thomas Brand, who was said to be 'one of the most fervent useful preachers the age hath afforded'. There was, however, some delay in dispatching the licences and on 29 April Brand was complaining to a friend that the situation was becoming serious. The Churchmen and the magistrates, he wrote, were determined to challenge the legality of a declaration which lacked any statutory cover and he feared that they would begin proceedings against Lady Roberts in the hope of deterring others. Eventually he became the pastor of a Presbyterian congregation in Staplehurst but not before he had found 'a worthy Successor, whose great Piety and ministerial Abilities' were above the ordinary.[26]

Bulstrode Whitelocke managed to obtain a licence for his chaplain, James Pearson, who was described as a minister of the Congregational persuasion. In his diary he wrote that on 26 May 'a licence came from London for Mr Pearson to preach in Chilton Lodge and to allow a roome there for preaching'. This was on a day when George Cokayne delivered two sermons at the Lodge in the presence of 'many strangers' from Hungerford and Ramsbury.[27] Other gentlemen who had their houses licensed for nonconformist worship included Sir John Holman, Sir John Stapley the regicide's son, Major Dunch, John Gurdon and Thomas Hutton of Poppleton in Yorkshire.[28] In 1635 Gurdon, who was one of the leading Presbyterians in Suffolk, had presented Thomas Walker to the living of Assington; in 1662 Walker had been ejected for refusing to declare his assent and consent to the Book of Common Prayer; and in 1672 he was authorised to preach to a Presbyterian congregation at Assington Hall. When Gurdon drew up his will in 1677 he left bequests to several Presbyterian ministers, including Walker and his domestic chaplain, John Hinde.[29]

The authorities may well have been surprised to see some of the names which appeared in the applications for the licensing of manor-houses. More striking, however, is the absence of names such as Harley, Foley, Boscawen, Hampden, Hoghton, Strickland and Irby; indeed there were many wealthy gentry with nonconformist chaplains who made no effort to take advantage of the Declaration of Indulgence. Some Puritan squires like Sir Edward Harley may have thought that there was no need for conventicles or licensed meeting houses when the livings in their gift were well supplied with godly preaching ministers; others may have considered it imprudent to advertise their association with nonconformists. A Cheshire squire, Sir John Crewe, had his house, Utkinton Hall, licensed for Congregational worship but was apparently anxious to ensure that his name was omitted from the application. In addition, a number of gentry, among them Sir John Davie and Sir Philip Harcourt, allowed their chaplains to take out general licences which enabled them to preach at any authorised meeting place.[30]

Under pressure from the House of Commons the king recalled the Declaration of Indulgence on 8 March 1673. A bill 'for the ease of dissenters' raised hopes of a more permanent accommodation but these were quickly dashed; when informing his wife of the outcome Sir Edward Harley expressed the hope that God would be gracious to 'those who find few friends in this world'.[31] In October Samuel Hieron, a nonconformist divine who lived at Honiton in Devon, was writing that 'Many people in our Country have suffer'd much for meetings, and the more upon occasion of his Majesties licences, for in the confidence of it, they set open their doors, and so gave informers opportunity to enter at pleasure.'[32] With the cancellation of the licences there was renewed persecution of nonconformist ministers, though in practice much depended on the willingness of local magistrates to execute the penal laws. In Lancashire some soldiers burst into the chapel at Bickerstaffe Hall while the minister, Nathaniel Heywood, was conducting a service. According to Sir Henry Ashurst's account of this episode, Lady Stanley came down from the gallery 'and placed herself near the Pulpit-door, hoping to over-aw their Spirits and obstruct their designs'. As Heywood was about to deliver his sermon they seized him and took him away. On hearing of his arrest 'abundance of People, and many considerable Gentlemen, and some that were no friends to his Cause, yet out of respect to his Person, mediated for him'. After a short period of imprisonment he was released on 28 January 1675 but was unable to continue his ministry at Bickerstaffe Hall. Heywood died in 1677 and not long afterwards his brother Oliver published some of his last sermons and dedicated the work to Lady Stanley and her second husband, Henry Hoghton (who was a younger brother of Sir Richard Hoghton) in recognition of the great kindness they had shown to him and his family. 'God Almighty', he told them, 'maintain you as choice instruments of his glory in the land of the living.'[33] In March 1675 a raid was mounted on a conventicle which was being held at Dr Thomas Manton's meeting house in Covent Garden. The intruders threatened Lord Wharton with imprisonment when he refused to give his name but thought better of it. The minister who was standing in for Manton had fines amounting to £60 imposed on him; these, however, were paid by Lord Wharton, the Countesses of Bedford, Manchester and Clare and other persons of substance who had been present.[34]

About this time Richard Baxter, who was now under continuing harassment, had a new chapel built for himself in Westminster. Among those who contributed to the cost were the Countesses of Clare, Tyrconnel and Warwick, Lady Mary Armyne, Lady Anne Clinton, Lady Eleanor Holles, Sir John Maynard, Sir James Langham, Sir Edward Harley, Richard Hampden and his son John and Alderman Henry Ashurst.[35] Lady Armyne was on her deathbed when she gave order for the payment of £60 and within a few months Baxter was supplying a preface for the printed version of the funeral sermon which was preached by her chaplain, John Dan. While acknowledging that she had never been a regular member of his congregation he nevertheless felt able to write of her that 'Though according to her rank she lived in the decency of a plentiful estate, it was with humility and lowliness of mind; Her Prudence, Sobriety and Gravity were very exemplary.'[36] He was on much closer terms with Henry Ashurst who, he tells us, was 'commonly taken for the most exemplary Saint that was of public notice in this City'. In 1680 he preached the sermon at Ashurst's funeral and in the dedication which appeared in the published version he exhorted his widow and eldest son to live as he did, 'and it will be a cure of melancholy, passions and discontents, and a constant tranquillity and delight'. Nine years later he dedicated his work *A Treatise of Knowledge and Love Compared* to the son, Sir Henry, and his wife Lady Diana and took the opportunity to express his gratitude for their friendship and kindness.[37]

As we learn from her diary Mary Countess of Warwick often went to hear Baxter delivering a sermon when she was staying in London. On 23 December 1675 she noted that he had urged his congregation 'to avoyd too much carnall mirth, which he sayde wold indispose us for the prayseing of God, and to indeavor to keape up a chearefull frame that we may be allwayes fitt to prayse

God'. Occasionally she visited Baxter at his lodgings where she had the benefit of his 'good edifying warmeing discourse'.[38]

Sir Edward Harley's friendship with Baxter was of long standing. As early as 1656 he had sought his advice on what he should do as an MP 'for the service of the distressed Church'.[39] According to some accounts which have survived among his papers he went to hear Baxter preach on 1 June 1677; and both he and his sons appear to have had regular contact with him when they were sojourning in London. In November 1680 Baxter offered him his latest thoughts on how the moderate nonconformists might be accommodated within the Church and no doubt found that his friend held similar views:

> The middle true way . . . is Parochial Reformation . . . let us have Christ's true Doctrine, Worship and Church-Communion, and let General Bishops over us keep their Baronies, Lordships, Wealth and Honour . . . But let them have no Power as Bishops, but of the Church-Keys . . . The Truth is, Civil and Church Government will be well done if we know how to get still good Men to use it.

In December 1691 Robert Harley, who was then in London, informed his father that Baxter had gone to 'his everlasting Rest which he hath so long panted for'; and in reply Sir Edward expressed his profound sorrow over the loss of 'incomparable Mr Baxter'. Another of his sons, Edward, was one of the executors of Baxter's will along with such men as Sir Henry Ashurst and Rowland Hunt.[40]

Despite all the efforts to root out nonconformity many of the Puritan nobility and gentry continued to attend conventicles. In July 1676 the Earl of Danby, the Lord Treasurer, received a report on London conventicles which showed that Baxter and Manton still had a considerable following among persons of high social rank. The membership of Manton's congregation in Covent Garden included Lord Wharton and his family, the Countesses of Clare, Manchester and Bedford and Lady Anne Clinton. The Countess of Bedford was also named as a member of Baxter's congregation, which then met in Holborn, along with a number of other notables, including the Countess of Exeter, Lady Ranelagh, Lady Holles, Sir James Langham and his wife and Martin Lumley, the youthful heir to an Essex baronetcy and Langham's nephew.[41] Manton enjoyed the patronage of the Earl of Bedford who owned

Covent Garden and was also allowed to hold meetings in Lord Wharton's town-house in the parish of St Giles. At his funeral in October 1677 the preacher, Dr Bates, recalled that the general aim of his sermons had been to open the eyes of his hearers 'that they might see their wretched condition as Sinners'.[42]

Besides attending Baxter's meetings, the Langhams had other links with the nonconformist world. A few years earlier the great hall of their Bishopsgate mansion, Crosby House, had been made available as a meeting place for a Presbyterian congregation which had Thomas Watson, a former minister of St Stephen's Walbrook, as its first pastor. The church prospered under Watson and his successors; and the Langhams took up residence in the more fashionable Lincoln's Inn Fields.[43]

At Great Houghton in Yorkshire the cancellation of Jeremiah Milner's licence appears to have had little effect. Milner continued to act as chaplain to the Rodes family and to preach two sermons every Sabbath day in his usual powerful style. One of the most attentive members of his congregation was Elizabeth Rodes, a daughter of Sir Edward Rodes, who made notes of his sermons and repeated them. For a time she suffered from some kind of affliction which made her reluctant to speak in normal day-to-day conversation. In April 1676 she wrote that 'I cannot now read in any book, but only in the bible, sermons or such books as I finde strength of desire to, and delight in, and in all such I can read up, with as strong a voyce as ever I did in my life.' Oliver Heywood, who describes her as a very kind friend, was still visiting 'that sweet ingenious family' from time to time and preaching in their chapel. In his diary he noted that when he was at Great Houghton in July 1679 'I prayed and preached 4 or 5 hours, a full assembly, god graciously helped, blessed be his name.'[44]

In 1681 Great Houghton was a place of mourning. Jeremiah Milner died on 7 March, Lady Mary Rodes on 22 April and her son Godfrey, who was the head of the family, on 26 April. The deaths of both mother and son within such a short space of time occasioned the writing of a funeral elegy which was singularly devoid of any literary merit:

> Now Houghton Hall's with double mourning clad
> the noble Lady and the Squire's dead . . .
> they wear their Crowns in Glory richly sett
> She hath her Crown and he his Coronett . . .

Let Houghton hall their memory revive
keep up Religion ye that do survive
Let's meet and pray and preach til we be fitt
as blissfull Peers with them in Heaven to sit.

In the event there was no break in continuity. Milner was succeeded by another ejected minister, Nathan Denton; and William Rodes, who inherited the estate from his brother, was clearly determined to ensure that 'true religion' was preserved. When Ralph Thoresby the antiquary called on his Puritan friends the Wordsworths of Swathe Hall in October 1681 he found that they had gone to hear a sermon at Houghton Hall.[45]

During the 1680s there was a more intensive campaign against Protestant nonconformity which was often equated with disloyalty to the Crown, particularly in the light of the Monmouth rebellion and the events leading up to it. In October 1682 proceedings were started against Richard Baxter, Dr John Owen, George Cokayne and other London ministers for holding conventicles; and in June 1683 Sir Edward Harley was told by his son Nathaniel, who was apprenticed to a London merchant, that the ecclesiastical court 'thunders out excommunications by the hundreds which hath made many Citizens quit the City'. Philippa Trenchard, the wife of John Trenchard the Dorset politician, was apprehended at a conventicle in Taunton, while a London magistrate, Sir William Langham, was fined £100 for declining to execute the laws against conventicles.[46] Gilbert Earl of Clare was prosecuted at the Middlesex sessions in October 1682 for 'wittingly and willingly permitting sixteen several unlawful conventicles' to be held in his house in the parish of St Clement Danes. As a result he was fined a total of £320 but a year later the warrants which had been issued for the levying of the fine were declared invalid.[47] In July 1683 some of the inhabitants of the Surrey parish of Worplesdon had fines of 5s each imposed on them for attending a conventicle held in the mansion house of Sir Nicholas Stoughton at Stoke next Guildford.[48] In April 1686 a band of informers broke into the house of Sir John Hartopp and his father-in-law Charles Fleetwood at Stoke Newington in Middlesex and sought to levy a distress on the grounds that they were guilty of holding conventicles. Hartopp and Fleetwood insisted that the matter should be brought to trial and claimed that there had been irregularities. In December it was reported that some of the money which they had deposited pending the outcome of their case had been returned to them.[49] Sir John had been a nonconformist for many years. When staying in London he attended meetings at the Independent church in Leadenhall Street which had been established by his friend Dr John Owen and at Stoke Newington he and his father-in-law employed a Congregational minister, Edward Terry, as their domestic chaplain. Following Sir John's death in 1722 Isaac Watts, who had spent five years in his family, preached the sermon at his funeral in Stoke Newington. Sir John, he stressed, had preferred to worship with the Protestant dissenters 'for he thought their practice more agreeable to the Rules of the Gospel'.[50]

10

KEEPING A CHAPLAIN

If the laws on the employment of domestic chaplains had been
rigorously applied very few Puritan gentlemen could have
claimed that they were legally qualified in this respect. Under the
provisions of certain statutes which had been enacted in Henry
VIII's reign it was a privilege limited to archbishops, bishops,
peers, knights of the garter, judges and senior officials of the
Crown. During the 1630s Archbishop Laud, with the backing of
the king, had sought to ensure that these statutes were properly
enforced but his efforts had met with little success, not least since
a chaplain could be passed off as a tutor or as a scholar who was
simply pursuing his studies.[1] In the latter part of the seventeenth
century no attempt was made to introduce new legislation on the
subject: there is, for example, no reference to chaplains in the Act
of Uniformity. Nor did the ecclesiastical or secular authorities
show much interest in the presence of chaplains in private
households except when they were suspected of holding conventicles or engaging in activities of a political nature. The squire
who wanted to take a chaplain into his household was under no
obligation to seek the prior approval of the bishop of the diocese;
in practice he had a complete freedom of choice just as he had in
the case of a steward or butler or any other employee. In these
circumstances many of the Puritan gentry (as well as the Puritan
nobility) had their domestic chaplains,[2] as indeed did some of the
gentry who had no pretensions to godliness.[3]

In 1671 it was reported that Dr Thomas Jacombe received a
salary of £120 a year as chaplain to the Dowager Countess of
Exeter.[4] Generally, however, the domestic chaplain was not well
paid, though he might possibly be remembered in his employer's
will. The accounts of Sir John Pelham, who was seated at Laughton

123

in Sussex, reveal that a salary of £20 a year was paid to Edmund Thorpe, an ejected minister who served as his chaplain during the years 1662 to 1665 and subsequently opened a private school.[5] Another ejected minister, John Fenwick, first became chaplain to Lady Elizabeth Brooke in Suffolk and was then taken into the household of Sir Thomas Alston at Odell in Bedfordshire. In Chancery proceedings which were begun in 1679 Sir Rowland Alston stated that following his father's death he had paid Fenwick his annual salary of £20, apparently before discharging him.[6] Adam Martindale, who acted as chaplain to George Lord Delamere during the years 1671 to 1684, writes that his predecessor, Robert Eaton, had received £40 a year. His own salary was also fixed at £40 a year, though he had an opportunity to earn £4 or £5 more by teaching mathematics to the children. In fact his emoluments were often significantly less since his services were not required when the family was wintering in London. Even so, he only took his leave of Dunham Massey when he had no choice: in 1684 he was lamenting 'the unspeakeable losse of my deare and faithfull friend, my noble Lord Delamer, together with all hopes of employment at Dunham'.[7]

Occasionally a chaplain might have another source of income. Arthur Onslow, a Surrey landowner who was noted for 'the plainness and sanctity of his life', not only employed Edward Vernon as his chaplain at his house at West Clandon but also appointed him, in May 1684, as rector of the neighbouring parish of Merrow. Vernon is said to have been a 'most serious and devout man, of the principles (somewhat moderated however) and the manners of those who in a former age had been called Church Puritans'. During his incumbency at Merrow 'the communion table stood in the middle of the Chancel, and he administered the Sacrament always in that particular place, and not at the east end'.[8] Richard Winwood, who was seated at Ditton Park in Buckinghamshire, had a domestic chaplain, Benjamin Archer, who managed to retain his fellowship at Exeter College, Oxford and also served as rector of Wexham, a living belonging to the Crown. In his will, which he drew up in January 1687, Winwood indicated that he would leave it to his wife to decide whether to have a preacher who would reside with her in the great capital messuage at Ditton and exercise the functions of a chaplain in the same way as Archer was currently performing them. Archer, for his part, was rewarded for his services with a legacy of £50.[9]

Not surprisingly, the nonconformist divines who had been forced out of their livings or fellowships in the years 1660 to 1662 represented the main source of supply for Puritan households during the reign of Charles II. Among those who gave them employment as domestic chaplains there were a number of gentry who had been members of the Long Parliament, men such as Sir William Waller the parliamentary general, Sir Anthony Irby, Sir William Strickland, Sir John Barrington, Sir John Fagg, Sir Richard Hoghton, Hugh Boscawen, John Gurdon and Richard Norton.[10] Sir Anthony Irby, whose principal residence was at Boston in Lincolnshire, had several chaplains who had been recruited from this source. After the resignation of Thomas Cawton in 1665 he was succeeded by Thomas Clark who remained with Sir Anthony for ten years. From time to time Lady Irby was visited by her nephew Sir Philip Harcourt who was so impressed with Clark that in 1675 he persuaded him to come and live with him at Stanton Harcourt in Oxfordshire, even though he already had a Presbyterian chaplain, Henry Cornish, who continued to enjoy his patronage. Whatever Sir Anthony's feelings might have been, he was soon able to make good his loss by the appointment of William Bruce, a Scotsman who had been ejected in Cheshire. On the other hand, Clark's removal to Oxfordshire had completely unexpected consequences for the Harcourt family. Sir Philip's heir, Simon, secretly married Clark's daughter, settled with his wife at Chipping Norton when this came to light and never returned to Stanton Harcourt.[11]

After his ejection from the living of Topcliffe, in the North Riding of Yorkshire, James Calvert lived privately in York and when the Declaration of Indulgence was published secured a licence to hold Presbyterian meetings in his house. Not long after this he was invited to join the Strickland household at Boynton Hall, the Elizabethan house which is situated a few miles inland from Bridlington. By this time Sir William Strickland was dead and the head of the family was his son Sir Thomas who was described by Roger Morrice as 'a serious person' who 'gave much Countenance to Religion and vigerously endeavoured a further Reformation'. Calvert acted both as chaplain and as tutor to the children. For some years he appears to have enjoyed a tranquil existence but in June 1683 there was a sudden flurry of excitement when Sir John Cochrane and his son, who were suspected of complicity in the Rye House Plot, arrived unexpectedly at Boynton

Hall. The Cochranes were related to the Stricklands and with their assistance were able to take ship at Bridlington and find sanctuary in the Dutch Netherlands. When it was discovered that they had escaped, the local magistrates exonerated Sir Thomas, dismissing him as 'a melancholy, distracted man'; Calvert, however, incriminated himself under oath and was imprisoned in York Castle, though not apparently for long. Significantly, when Sir Thomas drew up his will in August he made provision for the payment of a legacy of £20 to 'Mr James Calvert whoe at present resides in my house'.[12]

Richard Hampden's chaplains included two ejected ministers, George Swinnock and John Nott. Swinnock, who had been ordained under Presbyterian auspices, was a notable preacher and the author of a number of published works. In 1665 he dedicated a collection of his works to Hampden and his wife Letitia but perhaps considered it impolitic to explain why he was recording his gratitude to them.[13]

A Yorkshire minister, George Ewbank, was already serving as chaplain to Sir George Marwood of Little Busby when he was deprived of the living of Great Ayton which was in the gift of the Marwood family; indeed he styled himself as such when publishing a sermon shortly after the Restoration. In this sermon, which had been delivered at the funeral of Marwood's daughter-in-law Margaret, he testified that she had been 'eminently pious' and 'not at all given to foolish talking, unseemly jesting . . . but grave and sober'.[14]

Most of the ejected divines who became chaplains regarded themselves as Presbyterians or simply as ministers of the Gospel who belonged to no particular faction. There were some Puritan gentry, however, who had a clear preference for Independent or Congregational ministers. At Southwick in Hampshire, Richard Norton appointed as his chaplain the 'truly admirable' Urian Oakes who 'was of the Independent denomination, and discovered a very high opinion of the congregational discipline, as being by far more scriptural and rational, and attended with much greater advantages than any other'. Oakes had been educated at Harvard and had a considerable reputation both as a preacher and a scholar. Since Norton was not only the squire but the patron of the church, which was a donative cure, it was comparatively easy for him to impose his own religious views on the parish; and in this respect it is significant that in 1676 he was reported to have told the Earl of Shaftesbury that 'the Church of England is the greatest schismatical church in the world'. During the early years of Charles II's reign there were other Congregational ministers living at Southwick, among them Richard Symons who had been ejected there in 1662 and Walter Marshall who secured a licence to preach a decade later. In addition, another Congregational minister, Giles Say, sometimes delivered a sermon in Norton's house. On the evidence of the visitation records of the Diocese of Winchester it is clear that the churchwardens of Southwick were not inclined to say anything to the ecclesiastical authorities which might embarrass their landlord. In 1664 their presentments referred only to Quakers and Catholic recusants, while in 1668 they reported that the curate was 'sufficiently qualified and conformable' and that the inhabitants of the parish were 'generally conformable'. In 1673 they presented a papist and a Quaker but in 1687, 1692 and 1696 there were nil returns.[15] A more celebrated Independent minister, Henry Lukin, was employed for many years as chaplain to Elizabeth Masham, the mother of Sir Francis Masham, the Whig politician, at Matching in Essex. Strictly speaking, Lukin was a silenced rather than an ejected minister since he had been travelling abroad as tutor to her eldest son, Sir William, when the Act of Uniformity was passed. An accomplished author, he appears to have written one of his most popular works, *The Chief Interest of Man*, while he was sojourning in France, but presumably before the tragic death of the young baronet who had been entrusted to his care. In April 1672 he obtained a licence authorising him to act as minister of a Congregational flock in Matching, though not in the house where he was serving as chaplain.[16]

As time went on it became necessary for the Puritan nobility and gentry to rely more and more heavily on other sources of supply for meeting their domestic needs. In the main this meant recruiting young men who had recently graduated at the English or Scottish universities or who had been educated at the dissenting academies which were beginning to mount a serious intellectual challenge to the supremacy of Oxford and Cambridge.[17] Some of the university graduates who were taken on as chaplains in godly households may have suffered agonies of conscience at the thought of entering the ranks of the conforming clergy; others were certainly hoping that they would eventually be put into valuable livings, given the fact that a number of Puritan landowners had substantial resources of patronage at their disposal. In Derbyshire the Presbyterian chaplains employed by Sir John Gell included Francis Tallents who had been ejected in 1662; Joshua Oldfield who had studied at both Oxford and Cambridge during Charles II's reign but had come down in favour of nonconformity; and Benjamin Robinson who had received his education at Derby under a nonconformist divine, Samuel Ogden, and at John Woodhouse's dissenting academy at Sheriff Hales in Stafford-shire.[18] During the 1690s Philip Foley, a leading patron of non-conformists who was seated at Prestwood in Staffordshire, had three chaplains who were products of Woodhouse's academy, William Willets, John Warren and George Flower. In 1698 Flower became the first pastor of a nonconformist chapel at Stourbridge in Worcestershire where another branch of the Foley family resided.[19] When Lady Katherine Irby, the widow of Sir Anthony Irby, drew up her will in June 1695 she left a number of legacies to nonconformist ministers, including £20 to Joseph Hill 'my present chaplain'. Like his predecessor, Samuel Lawrence, Hill had been educated at Charles Morton's academy at Newington Green in Middlesex where Daniel Defoe had once been a pupil.[20]

Despite the contribution made by the dissenting academies it was not necessarily an easy matter to obtain the services of someone with the right combination of qualities for household duties. As the century was drawing to its close the two wealthiest Puritan patrons in Herefordshire, Paul Foley and Sir Edward Harley, were corresponding about the difficulties involved in seeking to ensure that the Foley household continued to enjoy the benefits of a resident chaplain with appropriate preaching skills. Writing to his friend in October 1698 Foley reminded him that he had been able to count on his assistance when he had last been in need of a minister to officiate in his family and to take it in turns with John Wickens, the incumbent, to preach both at Stoke Edith and another village, Westhyde, in the general neighbourhood. On that occasion Harley had recommended a young Oxford graduate, Robert Comyn, whose preaching had 'greatly improved' since his arrival at Stoke Court. However, he had recently informed him that he was thinking of settling in Surrey where his father was a minister. In the event Robert Harley presented him to the living of Wigmore, though only after Sir Edward had cleared up a mis-understanding which had arisen over the ownership of the patronage rights. Comyn was instituted on 27 March 1699 and in

July of that year Foley was again requesting Sir Edward's help over the recruitment of a chaplain. Following Comyn's departure in April, he wrote, he had been forced to 'make bold' with his neighbours. He had then had a young man as his chaplain, 'such as I never met with his fellow; he was at last willing to be instructed, and after great paines taken with him was comeing about to do tollerably well'. Having heard that a chaplain's post had fallen vacant in Kent he had now left Stoke Court and a replacement would need to be found. His wife, Foley went on, had once seen a minister at Harley's house who was at present serving as chaplain to Lord Newport but was anxious to leave him. This man was 'much commended'; on the other hand, it might not be tactful to approach him, assuming he was fully suitable, while he was still living in Lord Newport's house. 'It is vain', he added, 'to tell you the difficulty of getting a good Supply, you have had Sufficient experience of these matters but I beg your prayers and your advice.' Sir Edward's response was to send him another Oxford graduate, Silvanus Woodhill, who may have been residing with him at Brampton Bryan. In acknowledging Harley's gesture Foley told him that so far he had heard Woodhill pray only once but he would be preaching a sermon on the following Saturday. At this stage he was inclined to be wary because of some private information he had received; he enclosed a note which Harley should burn after reading. Probably the doubts about Woodhill were resolved: in 1703 he was presented to the Foley living of Dormington.[21]

A domestic chaplain naturally lacked the security of tenure of a beneficed clergyman and if he was particularly unfortunate could be faced with the need to seek alternative employment on the death of the head of the family. On the other hand, he might decide to move on himself, perhaps for mainly financial reasons or, if he was a hardened nonconformist, because he wanted to have his own congregation. Some nonconformist ministers acted as chaplain or tutor in several prominent families. James Small, who was ejected from an Essex living, had been born at Sandford in Devon and he returned there to serve as chaplain to Sir John Davie of Creedy who was regarded as one of the leading Presbyterians in the county. When Sir John drew up his will in January 1678 he left a legacy of £10 to Small whom he described as 'my present Chaplin'. Sir John was succeeded later that year by a nephew and Small entered the household of Viscount Massereene in Ireland, though before long he was back in Essex as chaplain to Sir John Barrington at Hatfield Broad Oak. The Barringtons do not appear to have been unduly concerned about the denomination of their clerical associates: the parish minister resided with them at Hatfield Priory and John Warren, the Congregational minister who had been deprived of the living, continued to enjoy their patronage, sometimes accompanying Sir John's wife, Lady Dorothy, when she visited the Countess of Warwick at Leez Priory. In August 1680 we find Small writing from Hatfield Broad Oak to Philip Lord Wharton in response to an offer of preferment. Thanking him for his great favour and condescension, he wrote that

> by reason of the distance of the place of the Lady's constant residence (my most materiall exception against the undertaking) I am not willing to undertake the service, but shall rather waite for and accept of an employ neerer at hand, tho upon the encouragement of a better salary.

Sir John died in 1683 but his widow was anxious to retain him as her chaplain and he was still living with her in 1690, though at that time he was also regularly preaching at Bishops Stortford.[22] Elias Travers, who was the son of an ejected minister, served as chaplain to John Lord Robartes, Sir Thomas Barnardiston, the second baronet, and Viscount Massereene. Among the surviving papers of the Barnardiston family there is a manuscript diary of his, written in Latin, which covers the years 1678 to 1680.[23] Joshua Oldfield, who was first employed by Sir John Gell, is said to have been appointed as tutor to a son of Paul Foley and to have declined the offer of a Foley living worth £200 a year. After this he became chaplain to Lady Susan Lort, a daughter of John Earl of Clare, in Pembrokeshire. A few years later his brother Nathaniel, who was also a nonconformist divine, was taken into Sir Edward Harley's household at Brampton Bryan. In May 1685 Sir Edward wrote in a letter to his wife, who was then about to go on a journey, that 'I desire Mr Oldfield may take care of the worship of God in our family and that you will before you goe charge them to be Observant therein.' Oldfield was still at Brampton Bryan in January 1687 when we find him writing to a fellow nonconformist, Chewning Blackmore, about the Church's ceremonial requirements. It was said, he observed, 'to be the mystery of puritanism that theye allowed nothing in the worship of God but what is commanded in the Word of God'. Was this not in fact part of the mystery of godliness? In his view it was necessary to take into account the opinions of the primitive Churches and bishops as well as the Scriptures. Subsequently he became chaplain to Thomas Foley at Witley Court in Worcestershire. In a letter addressed to his son Robert, who was staying at Witley Court with his wife, in August 1687 Sir Edward commented that he was sorry to hear that Mr Oldfield 'is not satisfied where he is. Speak to him that he give not any disgust nor forget the prudence and gentlenes which are the braceletts of pietie.' In November Foley told Robert Harley, his son-in-law, that Oldfield was 'more and more a Comfort to us' but he did not remain long at Witley Court: in March 1688 Foley was writing that he had received an invitation to settle at Derby 'which he thinks is providentiall and so inclines to goe which is a disapoyntment to me'; and two years later Chewning Blackmore reported that he was being prosecuted for preaching without a licence in Essex.[24]

In the case of some families such as the Hoghtons and the Wilbrahams the practice of employing domestic chaplains is particularly well documented. Sir Richard Hoghton of Hoghton Tower in Lancashire, who was represented as a loyal and orthodox member of the Church of England at his funeral in 1678,[25] was more at home in the clandestine world of nonconformist preachers, chaplains and tutors. John Howe, the celebrated Presbyterian divine, described Hoghton Tower as a seat of religion and of the worship of God, the resort of his servants and a house of patronage to the sober and virtuous and of good example to all those who lived in the neighbourhood.[26] Adam Martindale, who was tutor to Sir Richard's children during the years 1665 to 1671, tells us that 'for libertie to preach there was more than I desired, for they had an able and godly chaplaine of their owne, that I delighted to heare, besides many eminent men that came occasionally'. The chaplain who so impressed Martindale with his preaching can be identified as Josiah Holdsworth who had been brought in following his ejection from a Yorkshire living, though other nonconformist ministers like Thomas Key and John Harvey were also given shelter. Holdsworth was succeeded by a young man, Timothy Hill, who had studied at Cambridge and had been awarded an MA at Glasgow University: Hill, writes Martindale, had given himself up to 'plaine country preaching, being Sir Richard Hoghton's chaplaine'.[27] According to Oliver Heywood, who was acquainted with the Hoghton family, Sir Richard moved at some stage to a secondary house, Walton Hall, where his chaplain, Mr Ainsworth, Thomas Key and Charles Sagar (who had been turned out of Blackburn grammar school) preached on the Lord's Day in rotation. Sir Richard appears in fact to have fallen out with his wife, Lady Sarah, who was herself a major patron of nonconformity: we learn, for example, from another source that John Bayley, who received Presbyterian ordination in 1670, forfeited the friendship of Lady Hoghton after admonishing her for leaving her husband.[28] Lady Hoghton held two days of prayer each month over a long period and among those who were frequently present was Thomas Jolly, the pastor of a nonconformist congregation whose preaching was 'plain, practical, and very pathetic'. During her widowhood she had a number of chaplains, including Thomas Cotton and John Ashe who had both been educated at the dissenting academy of Richard Frankland. Cotton stayed with her about a year 'and was forced from thence by a very severe fit of sickness'.[29]

The Wilbrahams, who were even richer than the Hoghtons, had two mansion houses, one at Weston under Lizard in Staffordshire where Sir Thomas and his family lived and the other at Woodhay in Cheshire which had been assigned to his mother, Lady Elizabeth, as part of her jointure. When Lady Elizabeth drew up her will in December 1673 she left a legacy of £20 to John Cartwright, an ejected minister who had been serving for some years as her chaplain.[30] In the spring of 1683 Sir Thomas was in need of a chaplain for his own household and Sir Edward Harley, acting on his behalf, sought the assistance of Dr Gilbert Burnet who was able to make use of his connections with the Presbyterians in Scotland. Burnet was Sir Harbottle Grimston's minister at the Rolls chapel and had no doubt been responsible for recruiting his domestic chaplain, James Blair, who was a graduate of the University of Edinburgh. In June he informed Harley that he had interviewed a possible candidate and had found him to be 'a truly mortified and serious as well as an able man'. He hoped that within a month 'he will have so shaken off the rudeness of his dialect that his pronunciation shall not be at all offensive'. The candidate was dispatched in a coach towards the end of July but as late as December Burnet was still anxiously inquiring whether Sir Thomas was fully satisfied.[31]

By 1686 Sir Thomas had a new chaplain, James Illingworth, who had been deprived of a fellowship at Emmanuel College,

Cambridge after the Restoration and had subsequently been taken on as Philip Foley's chaplain at Prestwood Hall. In October Illingworth gave his friend Ralph Thoresby a graphic account of the situation at Weston under Lizard as he had found it:

> I live in a great and good family (so Providence hath ordered it) where at present I want nothing, to the content and satisfaction of soul and body, in the best seat, and as good air, as I believe is in the county, where we have all things pleasant, convenient, and plentiful; but we have no abiding city here, but must seek for one to come. Sir Thomas is . . . as good-natured, bountiful to the poor, free to his friends, respectful to all good men, as heart can wish, but grievously exercised with the stone, which hath tried his patience . . . now above six years and, as he grows in years, is more painful and troublesome.

Sir Thomas had received the best medical advice but he was not expected to live long,

> then how things may alter in the family, I leave you to judge. My lady is a person of wonderful parts and discretion, able to manage greater matters than so great a family requires, but it is her unhappiness that she hath been many years (as we say) hard of hearing, yet quick of apprehension, sober, pious, faithful to the interests that are really good.

Sir Thomas died in 1692 leaving no male heir but his wife lived on until 1705. When Illingworth died in August 1693, Ralph Thoresby was anxious to ensure that his manuscript collections were preserved and Francis Tallents promised to take up the matter with Lady Wilbraham 'whom I know very well'. Another non-conformist divine, Henry Newcome, told Thoresby that 'Sir Thomas being dead, and the lady intending to give over house', Illingworth had been obliged to seek employment elsewhere and had received several offers 'but it pleased God to save him that trouble, and to take him to his rest'. Oliver Heywood, however, had been given a rather different account. Lady Wilbraham, he related, had informed Illingworth that she intended to take another nonconformist divine and his wife into her house; that she had no need for two chaplains; and that he should therefore take steps 'to provide for himself, which some think he laid so to heart that it shortened his days'.[32]

Illingworth's successor was Samuel Beresford, once the vicar of St Warburgh in Derby who had settled at Shrewsbury after his ejection. Beresford had been a regular visitor for many years: in 1673, for example, a Presbyterian minister, Philip Henry, noted in his diary that he had heard a sermon preached by Beresford at Weston under Lizard which was based on a text from the Epistle of St Paul to the Philippians, 'Holding forth the word of life; that I may rejoice in the day of Christ, that I have not run in vain, neither laboured in vain'.[33] During her widowhood Lady Wilbraham demonstrated the truth of a general judgement which was passed on her that she adopted an even-handed approach to all good ministers, whether conformists or nonconformists. Among other things, she built the present church at Weston which was formally opened with a sermon on 30 November 1701; augmented the income of the rector, Samuel Garret, by granting him a rent-charge of £10 a year; and erected a chapel at Woodhay and settled an annuity of £25 on Sir John Crewe and other trustees as a stipend for the preaching minister there.[34]

Besides the Hoghtons and the Wilbrahams there were many other gentry who received visits from nonconformist ministers, in some cases on a regular basis. John Maidwell was highly regarded by Sir Thomas Alston and his wife and often preached in their house at Odell in Bedfordshire.[35] Oliver Heywood recorded in his diary that in 1666, following the passage of the Five Mile Act, he travelled with his father-in-law John Angier, who like him was a nonconformist divine, to Sir Thomas Stanley's house at Alderley in Cheshire. On the first night of their stay Heywood was called upon to conduct the family prayers and was tempted

> to study and speak handsome words, from respect to that company; but reflecting to whom I prayed, and that it was no trifling matter, I set myself to the exercise in serious earnestness, and God helped me to speak to Him devoutly, with respect to the state of their souls and the good of their family.

A few days later, 'upon a call to keep a private fast', they visited John Crewe at Utkinton Hall 'where we had a very sweet day'. According to Heywood's biography of Angier his father-in-law was on very close terms with Crewe who 'had an entire love for him'. During a further visit Crewe showed his friend a portrait of Dr John Wilkins who was about to be consecrated as Bishop of

Chester but declared that 'Mr Angier is my Bishop.'[36] Although Richard Winwood appears to have had a preference for chaplains who were conformists he was certainly not averse (as his friend Bulstrode Whitelocke testifies) to entertaining nonconformist ministers in his Buckinghamshire mansion. Among those who visited Ditton Park was John Batchelor, formerly Vice Provost of Eton and vicar in the neighbouring parish of Datchet. On one occasion he preached in Mrs Winwood's chamber 'uppon the want of children'; but in the event Winwood died childless.[37] When Richard Hampden visited John Swinfen at his Staffordshire seat in September 1687 he was accompanied by John Howe who had many friends among the Puritan nobility and gentry. Subsequently, in a letter dispatched from Great Hampden, Howe expressed his gratitude to Swinfen and his wife 'for the most friendly reception we found with you'. And he added, with a veiled reference to the political discussions which had taken place, that he prayed to God that the remainder of Swinfen's life 'may be proportionatly serviceable to him, as the present state of things requires, and as your former life hath been; wherein it will certainly be most comfortable to yourself'.[38]

11

THE GODLY HOUSEHOLD

One of the highest accolades a godly divine could confer on a Puritan squire was that he had a 'well ordered family'. In December 1678 Samuel Hieron wrote in a letter to Philip Lord Wharton that Sir Walter Yonge, who was seated at Colyton in Devon, was a young man of sober conversation 'and by the other party counted a Fanatick. His family wel order'd, himself praying in it morning and evening.' When Philip Henry visited his friend Philip Foley at Prestwood Hall in Staffordshire in June 1682 he noted in his diary that he had a 'good and great Family wel order'd' and added 'would there were more such'.[1] Besides the maintenance of strict moral standards the hallmarks of a godly household were a daily routine of corporate worship, private prayer and meditation, and religious instruction which might be provided for the servants as well as the children. While serving as an MP Sir Edward Harley frequently urged his wife or children to ensure that religious duties were properly observed during his absence. Writing to his daughter Brilliana in June 1670 he laid down his requirements in some detail:

> You must be Careful to keep the family in good Order, and that all come to prayers constantly night and morning and that prayers be in sesonable Time. Be you very watchful over yourself that not any thing divert you from your morning and Evening worship of God in secret and Constant reading the scripture and some other good book. Warn your sisters from mee to doe the like. Tel your brothers that I hope they will be careful in learning theyr book, praying and saying their Catechisme every day.[2]

It was the kind of letter which his father, or indeed any other

Puritan squire, might have written in similar circumstances before the time of the Civil War.

On 15 January 1691 Thomas Pritchard, who was Sir Martin Lumley's chaplain, delivered a funeral sermon in the parish church of Great Bardfield in Essex. The deceased, Mary Dawes, was the sister-in-law of Martin Lumley, the heir to the estate, and had lived with the Lumleys for some time. In the course of his sermon Pritchard expressed his regret that too many families of substance were unwilling to follow the example of the Lumleys in the performance of religious duties. 'And well were it', he declared,

> if all Persons of Quality, the Plentifulness of whose Estates freeing them from those mean Employments which Persons of Lower Rank are busied in, and so having more leisure and time to spare, would devote a greater share of their time to God and their Souls.

Mary Dawes, he stressed, had regularly been present at family prayers; indeed he could hardly recall an occasion when she had been absent.[3] In September 1692 he preached the sermon at the funeral of Sir Martin's wife Lady Anne, describing how assiduous she had been in her private devotions, her reading of the scriptures 'from whence all saving Knowledg is to be learnt' and her attendance at family prayers. A woman of exemplary piety and strict virtue, she would often say what a great care and concern she had for the salvation of her soul.[4] Sir Martin died in 1702, having indicated that he wished to be buried privately 'with as little expence as may be', while his daughter-in-law, Lady Elizabeth, was laid to rest two years later. At the request of her husband the funeral sermon was preached by Henry Cooke, a fellow of Christ's College, Cambridge who confessed that he had little personal knowledge of her and was clearly relying to a large extent on the testimony of others for his account of her religious zeal. In reminding the congregation in Great Bardfield church of the need for diligence in making their calling and election sure Cooke put his finger on the motivation of upper-class Puritans who devoted much of their time to spiritual matters: above all they were anxious to obtain assurance that they were numbered among the elect. 'I desire in all humility', wrote Sir Edward Harley, 'to resigne my self to the good pleasur of the Lord, And to be assured of and fitted for blessed Eternity.'[5]

Anthony Wood retails a story about the form of domestic

worship at Sir Philip Harcourt's Oxfordshire mansion where he
had a Presbyterian chaplain, Henry Cornish, who lived with him
for over twenty years. When James Parkinson, a fellow of Lincoln
College, Oxford, who was regarded as a political radical, was told
by Cornish's son that the Book of Common Prayer was used in the
household at Stanton Harcourt he exclaimed 'What! does Sir
Philip begin now to use the common prayer when every body is
going to lay it aside?'[6] Generally, however, the Anglican liturgy
does not appear to have figured much in the kind of worship
which was practised in the houses of the Puritan nobility and
gentry. Writing of his time as chaplain to George Lord Delamere
at Dunham Massey in Cheshire, Adam Martindale tells us that
'Mine employment there (besides accompanying my Lord abroad)
was family duty twice a day; which, before dinner, was a short
prayer, a chapter, and a more solemn prayer; and, before supper,
the like, only a psalme, or part of one, after the chapter.'[7]
According to a contemporary account of Sir Edward Harley he
was

> most precisely regular in the religious conduct of his family,
> particularly in the worshipping of God in his family, Joshua
> like . . . How amiable and lovely a sight to see morning and
> evening his whole family from the meanest servant to the
> Eldest child worshipping God with great seriousness and
> sobriety, with good order and decency; his constant method
> was, he read a chapter . . . both in the old and new Testament,
> sung a psalm and pray'd; and each servant had a bible, and
> were instructed in what was read, and in the principles of
> the Christian faith from the poor postboy to the waiting
> Gentleman.[8]

When Thomas Brand was serving as chaplain to the Roberts
family at Glassenbury in Kent the household met twice a day for
prayers which were accompanied by scripture readings, catechising or the singing of psalms; and psalm singing was also a
regular feature of domestic worship at Hopton Hall in Derbyshire
where Sir John Gell's wife was a wholehearted participant.[9]

Although the influence of Sabbatarian doctrine was declining
during the later Stuart period it still commanded the loyalty of
wealthy Puritans. When a work by George Hughes in defence of
the doctrine was published by his son Obadiah in 1670 it was dedicated to Lady Margaret Boscawen, the wife of Hugh Boscawen,

who had befriended the author. In the epistle dedicatory Obadiah Hughes (who like his father was a nonconformist divine) explained how fitting it was to involve her 'who so well understand and as justly value the blessing of a Sabbath as you Faithfully improve it'. And he knew that it would be a matter of concern to her that the Sabbath was 'visibly expiring . . . in many men's judgments, and more in men's practise'[10]. In June 1685, when he was under house arrest at Hereford, Sir Edward Harley took the opportunity to set down his thoughts on the sanctification of the Lord's Day. It was God's command, he maintained, that on the Sabbath all mankind should

> rest from all the avocations of Labour and Sport, And Employ the whole day in both private and public solemn acts of worship to God . . . The profanation and polluting of the Sabbath is the dangerous inlet to the Contempt of Religion and the power of Godlines.

Harley refused to allow his servants to undertake journeys on the Sabbath and in December 1690 asked his son Robert, who was then serving at Westminster, to do what he could to ensure that a bill for the licensing of hackney coaches contained no provision which granted authority 'for any to ply or stand in the streets on the Lord's day'.[11] According to one of his friends, John Hoghton, the eldest son of Sir Charles Hoghton, spent his Saturday afternoons in reading divinity and preparing himself for the Sabbath. So strict was he in his observation of the Lord's Day that 'if he happened to lie longer than ordinary in the morning he would continue the later in duties in the evening'.[12]

Household worship on Sundays often involved the preaching of sermons, in some cases by visiting ministers, and the repetition of sermons which had been delivered in the parish church or elsewhere. In February 1673 Sir Edward Harley, who was then at Westminster, was informed by his wife, Lady Abigail, that the household at Brampton Bryan was in good order and family duties were being fully observed. On the last Sabbath day she had repeated the main heads of the morning sermon for the benefit of the maids and in the evening John Martin, the rector, had performed this function, presumably after preaching in the parish church.[13] On Sunday 8 June 1684 Ralph Thoresby the antiquarian visited Denton Hall, the seat of Henry Lord Fairfax who was regarded as the head of the Presbyterian party in

Yorkshire. In his diary Thoresby noted that the chaplain, Thomas Clapham,

> preached exceedingly well, both forenoon and after. Was much pleased . . . with the good order observed in my Lord's religious family, all called in and Mr Clapham read three or four psalms and a chapter or two out of the Old Testament, and as many out of the New, and then, after a psalm sung, prayed very seriously.[14]

Some men like Sir John Hartopp and Bulstrode Whitelocke who favoured the Independent or Congregational approach to religious worship regularly delivered sermons or lectures in the privacy of their own homes, usually when the household was assembled for prayers on a Sunday evening. Whitelocke appears to have begun this practice on 7 October 1666 when he expatiated on the lessons to be drawn from the Great Fire of London.[15]

Given the concept of the godly household it is hardly surprising that wealthy Puritans should consider that they had a duty to promote the spiritual and moral well-being of their servants. Lady Elizabeth Langham, the second wife of Sir James Langham, often told her husband that she fully subscribed to the precept that 'Governors of families are to be accountable to God for the souls of the meanest under their inspection.' Among other things, she required her maids to give her an account in writing (if they could write) of the sermons they had heard and made up any deficiencies by consulting 'her own more exact Notes'.[16] Lady Anne Lumley frequently called upon her servants to attend family prayers, 'thinking it not enough to be present herself unless she endeavoured at least to have them there too, that so not she only but her House might serve the Lord'. Similarly, Lady Anne Burgoyne would not allow any member of her household to be absent from family prayers without a reasonable excuse; and if she discovered any kind of immorality the guilty person was sharply reproved and warned that there must be no repetition in the future.[17] Sir Thomas Roberts, who was seated at Glassenbury in Kent, also saw a need 'to engage his Tenants . . . more effectually to the study and practice of Religion'; accordingly he called together their servants and children every Sunday, following the afternoon sermon, 'and himself Catechiz'd them'. At the same time the services which his chaplain and brother-in-law, Edmund Trench, conducted in the private chapel were attended not only by the Roberts family and their servants but by others from the general neighbourhood who found the form of worship to their taste.[18]

Corporate religious worship in a Puritan household might include regular fast days or alternatively special days of prayer might be arranged when there was some issue, either public or private, on which the family felt a need for God's guidance.[19] In addition, considerable importance was attached to 'Christian conference' with or without the involvement of ministers. In a book of occasional meditations Mary Countess of Warwick wrote that she was convinced of

> the necessity and usefullnes of the Communion of Saintes, who while they are kepte togeather ... are discourseing of the matters of Religion and relateing to one another the mercyes of God towardes them, and telling their own experiences of the inward workeing of God upon their Soules, and declareing, as David did, what God had done for their Soules, and how sweet and pleasant a thing it was to walke Closely with God, and by their mutuall discourses Considering one another to provoke unto love and to good workes.[20]

Her diary, which covers the years 1666 to 1677, contains many references to visitors she received at Leez Priory and visits which she made to her Essex friends and neighbours. Following a visit to the Bramston family at Roxwell she inserted the comment that the discussion had been 'vain and frothy' but she generally used such terms as 'good and Christian conference' or 'profitable discourse' in describing her meetings with well-to-do Puritans such as Lady Dorothy Barrington, Sir Gobert Barrington and his wife, Lady Hester Honywood, Sir Richard Everard and his wife, Lady Essex Cheke and Lady Mary Lumley. When Lady Warwick and her sister Lady Ranelagh called on Lady Honywood at Markshall on 2 July 1674 Ralph Josselin, the vicar of Earl's Colne, was present and noted in his diary that it was 'A choice day of civil concourse mixt with religious ... goodnes and greatnes sweetly met in them.' Lady Warwick, however, was not without her troubles. On one occasion a servant drank too much and swore in public 'to the disgrace of my famely'; on another occasion she had to remonstrate with Robert Earl of Manchester over his 'ill and irreligious' discourse. More seriously, she was appalled by her husband's cursing and swearing when he chose to vent his spleen on her. On

6 February 1667 they had a lengthy discussion 'wherein I did with great earnestness beg of him to watch against his swearing, and did with great plainness tell him of the danger of it and how he provoked God by it'. In the event her prayers and entreaties proved ineffective but he made amends for his behaviour by leaving her the bulk of his landed property.[21]

One of the most common characteristics of upper-class Puritans was the diligence they displayed in their private or secret religious activities. A typical account of such activities was provided in the sermon which a Devonshire minister, Joseph Rowe, a man of Puritan sympathies, delivered at the funeral of Lady Dorothy Drake, the wife of Sir Francis Drake, in the parish church of Buckland Monachorum on 9 February 1679. Lady Drake, he related, 'spent much tyme, day by day, in her closet devotions. Praying, reading of the Scriptures and other good bookes tooke up some houres of her tyme every day ... She knew closet prayer is as much a duty as Church prayer'.[22] Every day Sir Harbottle Grimston spent at least an hour in the morning and as much again at night in prayer and meditation. George Lord Delamere 'visited his Closet frequently every day for his private Devotions, and withdrew for that good work even in the greatest throng of Business'.[23] Lady Anne Burgoyne read the Old Testament once and the New Testament three times in the course of a year.[24] Many of the Puritan gentry had large collections of religious works which were not merely for display. In his will, which was drawn up in June 1665, William Strode of Barrington in Somerset left a number of books as legacies to his sons: these included John Foxe's *Book of Martyrs* and works by Arthur Hildersham, John Cotton, Samuel Clark, Archbishop Usher and Bishop Joseph Hall as well as Sir Walter Raleigh's *History of the World* and William Camden's account of the reign of Queen Elizabeth.[25] In October 1662 Sir Edward Harley's library contained works on a variety of subjects, including science and experimental philosophy. Among the many religious works which were catalogued were pamphlets on such current issues as the toleration of nonconformity and the provision relating to reordination in the Act of Uniformity. In June 1675 he bought a pamphlet by Thomas Tomkins, a critic of Richard Baxter, which challenged the case for toleration. Subsequently we find him asking his son Robert, who was then in London, to purchase copies of that edition of William Gouge's book *Of Domesticall Duties* 'wherein were the principles of Religion and famely prayers, allso these smale Books, memorialls of godlines, a guide to heaven, Pink's sinceare Love to Christ, Baxter's now or never, and call to the uncommitted'.[26] Sometimes a religious work provoked strong feelings. Writing to Harley in November 1680 Paul Foley condemned Henry Hammond's *Paraphrase and Annotations on all the Books of the New Testament* on the grounds that he had expressed views which were in conflict with the conventional wisdom about Christ's Second Coming. 'I am in great admiration', he declared

> how his Annotations have gotten so great an Esteeme as I find they have with our clergy and thinke if any account is to be given thereof it must be the desire they and their predecessors of the last age have had of laying aside the Revelations of St John and all notions that create any expectation of a change in the world.[27]

A favourite technique which was employed during the hours of study and meditation was to copy out passages from the Bible and other edifying books, usually under various subject headings, as a means of increasing knowledge and understanding. When John Lord Crewe informed his friend John Swinfen in December 1671 that his granddaughter Jemima Cartwright had died in child-birth he added that 'my comfort is, I have great reason to think she is in heaven. She was constant in privat and publique duties, and as one told me who since her death hath seene them, had fild forty sheets of paper with collections out of scripture under heads well chosen.'[28] A Lancashire baronet, Sir Ralph Assheton of Whalley, observed in his will that he had taken great pains during the course of his life in transcribing divinity notes out of 'severall bookes and Authors as I have happily mett with in my Readeing'. He was anxious that some knowledgeable and diligent scholar should examine these notes, which were in three folio volumes, and that (if he thought they were worth printing) steps should be taken to publish them. In the event they remained unpublished.[29]

In the 'well ordered' family it was usual for the parents, and in particular the mother, to be personally involved in the religious upbringing of the children even though there was often a resident chaplain. In a funeral sermon which was republished in 1675 Thomas Burroughs, who had served as chaplain to Sir John Langham, stressed how important it was that parents should be 'dropping principles of Religion into their little ones, and to be

doing it betimes ... We know not how soon God may be pleased
to work upon the hearts of our children, even the youngest of
them.'[30] Lady Anne Lumley, the wife of Sir Martin Lumley, 'took
great care to have her Son in his younger Years instructed in
Religion, whom she herself taught the most necessary and fundamental Points thereof; and the like Care and Pains she did
likewise take of her Grandchildren'.[31]. Lady Mary Langham, the
first wife of Sir James Langham, ensured that her children applied
themselves to 'the reading and committing to Memory both
Scripture and Catechism' and through her diligence they made
exceptional progress. His second wife, Lady Elizabeth, had no
children of her own but displayed the same kind of zeal as her
predecessor in carrying forward the religious education of her
stepchildren. On her deathbed she exhorted her husband 'to
breed them up in the Exercises of severe Godliness; And to see
them taught such Evidences of Salvation as might support them
one Day in their Dying Agonies'. The only surviving child, Mary,
who had been required to repeat and to analyse the sermons she
had heard, eventually married Henry Earl of Warrington, the son
of George Lord Delamere, who had 'a true Value for Religion'.
According to the minister who preached at her funeral she had
instilled into her own children 'the early Instructions of Piety, and
solid Grounds of Religion, which even Children are Capable of
remembring, and which if duely Cultivated, they never forget all
their life after'.[32]

Edward Harley, one of Sir Edward's younger sons, described his
mother, Lady Abigail, as a person of most exemplary piety who
'took all fitting occasions from our youth to instruct us in principles of religion, virtue and honour'. Sir Edward himself devoted
a great deal of time and effort to the religious instruction of his
children and grandchildren, though it appears from the account
of his contemporary biographer that some backsliding was in
evidence after his death in December 1700:

O how did he follow them, with godly exhortations, intreaties
and prayers, longing to see Christ formed in them, and there
were promising hopes of all of them that his labour was not
in vain in the Lord, for some of them especially must
remember what zeal for Christ and his kingdom they once
had and shewed, and now I wish their zeal be not for the
kingdom of this world ... and fear least what the Apostle

says of beginning in the spirit and ending in the flesh be not too much verifyed in them.[33]

Robert Harley's first wife died in 1691, leaving a son and two daughters. In May 1696 Sir Edward wrote in a letter addressed to his granddaughter Elizabeth that she must remember that her life had been given to her to glorify God. It was therefore a sin to misemploy her time and do anything that might be unfit for the service of God. He hoped that she and the other children were 'Carefull every day in reading and praying not only as a taske but as the spetiall exceling of life, in every act of worship drawing neer to God with reverence and Godly fear'.[34] Harley's old friend John Swinfen held similar views on the upbringing of children as can be seen from a letter which he dispatched to one of his granddaughters in September 1687 when she was living with the Wilbrahams at Weston under Lizard. Through Lady Wilbraham's favour, he told her, she had been able to observe 'much of the highest splendor that almost att any time appeares in the Country'. There were, however, temptations which accompanied such great-ness; and they were too strong for 'our frayl natures' without the support of God's grace. He went on:

> Is not a private condition that imploys us in soe much diligence as prevents idlenes (the mother of sin), that wants nothing necessary for a comfortable life, that allows us time to search the scriptures and our own hearts, that hath few temptations and much opportunity for comunion with our god and for serving him and enioying him, Is not this an happy condition? Observe what may make you walk the more humbly with your God, and retire into yourselfe and prevent the vain shewes of this world from being a temp-tation or snare to you.

In his will, which was drawn up shortly before his death in 1694, Swinfen expressed the hope that all his children and grand-children would live in the fear of God and die in his favour.[35]

When Paul Foley's son Thomas fell ill in 1684 he seized the opportunity to remonstrate with him over his failure to profit from the religious upbringing which he had received. As he explained in a letter to Sir Edward Harley there were signs that his warning had been taken to heart: 'I thanke God', he wrote,

> I find him more and more serious and sensible how ignorant

he hath beene of himselfe and of his duty and he seemeth at present with concerne to hearken to good advice and gives franke promises that he wil make Religion his study, care and practise.

He was now of the opinion that plain speaking was the best policy.[36]

In February 1683 Dr Gilbert Burnet told Sir Edward Harley that his son Robert showed such great promise that he lived in hope that he was born to be a blessing to the rising generation and that he would inherit his qualities as well as his estates. Writing to his son in November 1685 Sir Edward stressed that he regarded him as his heir not only in a material but in a religious sense: 'I have Long prayed to the God of all grace that I might committ that service of the Gospel to you and that you might therein be faithful as I have been through help obtained from God, in the trust received from my Father.' Accordingly he continued to offer him spiritual and moral guidance and even to admonish him if he considered this to be necessary. In June 1691 Robert Harley, who was then in London, received a disturbing letter from his father. Sir Edward informed him that there were reports that he had 'not walked Circumspectly nor Temperately, specially in the Hours of Night and darknes. If this be the Guilt, make hast in unfeigned Repentance for that which otherwise wil burden the Heart to depart from God unto utter Ruine of Body and Soul and the whole Family.' In his reply Robert sought to reassure his father. He began by soliciting God's mercy 'that this rebuke may bring forth in my soul a joyful Harvest of humble strict walking, with al circumspect holyness, in faith and obedience'. But as to the accusation which had been levelled against him he could most humbly declare that 'I have not been in any public House (excepting just the time of dining) since I came out of the country'; nor was he guilty of consorting with bad company. This appears to have satisfied his father who was writing a year later that 'in this World my Joy and Crown are your Holy and Righteous Conversation, And Service by the wil of God to your own Generation'.[37]

12

EDUCATION IN AN
UNGODLY WORLD

In his autobiography Adam Martindale relates that shortly after the passage of the Act of Uniformity he came to the conclusion that his schooling of young gentlemen was likely to be short-lived. At Chester the assize judge Sir Job Charlton 'gave a severe charge against Non-conformists being entertained as tutors in great families, or teaching private schools; which our severe justices highly approved'.[1] One of the major consequences of the Restoration church settlement was a profusion of nonconformist teachers who either had their own schools and academies or were employed as tutors in private households. Despite the requirements of the Act of Uniformity which applied to all kinds of schooling, many of them appear to have been unlicensed even though the penalties for such an offence included a term of imprisonment. If they were reluctant to seek licences from the diocesan authorities this is not altogether surprising given the need to make a formal declaration acknowledging that they were fully content with the liturgy of the Church of England.[2] Some schoolmasters were subjected to periodic harassment, not least because of the further restrictions imposed by the Five Mile Act of 1665,[3] but relatively few were forced to abandon their activities altogether. At the same time it was often not easy for upper-class Puritans to decide what was best for their sons when considering the arrangements for their formal education: on the one hand, there was a natural concern that they should receive a sound academic education to fit them for their station in life; on the other hand, they were afraid that the religious and moral principles which had been instilled in them might be put at risk by outside influences. 'Parents', observed John Lord Crewe in 1673, 'find difficulties in the education of youth.'[4]

147

Some Puritan landowners sent their sons to public grammar schools. Felsted School in Essex had come to be regarded as a Puritan seminary during the 1630s when Martin Holbeach was the headmaster and John Seaton his assistant.[5] Christopher Glascock, who was the headmaster in the years 1650 to 1689, had been appointed by Robert Earl of Warwick and as noted in the diary of Mary Countess of Warwick he frequently preached in the family's private chapel at Leez Priory. According to the minister who delivered the sermon at his funeral he had 'a Compassion for Dissenters, and such as by some might be interpreted as favouring of their way; But his Charity was more to their Persons than their Cause'. A moderate in matters of controversy 'that were of less necessity', he valued religion above learning 'or any other Accomplishments of this Life'.[6] The accounts of the Barrington family reveal that Sir John Barrington's son William and his grandsons John and Charles Barrington were all pupils at Felsted School. An entry dated 11 May 1683 records that Sir John (who had recently inherited both the baronetcy and the estate) returned to Hatfield Broad Oak 'feareing the small pox to be in the house where he boarded'. Others who were admitted to the school while Glascock was headmaster included Richard Everard, the son and heir of Sir Richard Everard; John Lemot Honywood whose father, Sir Thomas, had been one of the leading parliamentarians in Essex; and Edward Jocelyn, a younger son of Sir Robert Jocelyn of Hertfordshire.[7] On the evidence of his accounts Sir John Pelham the Sussex magnate favoured a more flexible approach to the education of his sons. In May 1663 he sent his eldest son Thomas to Tonbridge School in Kent, no doubt because of the growing reputation of the headmaster, Christopher Wase, who was highly skilled in Latin, Greek and the oriental languages. Four years later he was transferred to a private school in Chelsea which was run by another distinguished scholar, Adam Littleton, who had been an assistant master at Westminster School. In contrast, his brother John was initially entrusted to the care of a nonconformist schoolmaster, Thomas Goldham of Burwash in Sussex. Goldham had been ejected from the living of Burwash Weald, which was in the gift of the Pelham family, but he continued to reside there in defiance of the Five Mile Act. Subsequently, in 1672, we find John Pelham at Bicester in Oxfordshire where another nonconformist, John Troughton, had opened a school after being deprived of his fellowship at St John's College, Oxford.[8]

Despite his forebodings Adam Martindale obtained employment as a tutor with two Lancashire Puritan families, the Hoghtons of Hoghton Tower and the Asshetons of Middleton, during the period 1664 to 1671. At Hoghton Tower, where he spent about a year, his pupils included Sir Richard Hoghton's sons Charles and Benjamin, while at Middleton Hall he taught Richard Assheton and his cousin Peter Bold who had inherited a considerable estate. Although Martindale's sojourn at Middleton was relatively short he found it highly rewarding in more than one sense: 'besides the spiritual libertie I had in the neighbourhood', he writes, 'I never had a more profitable time of employment in all my life' since he was earning about 30s a week. Martindale had a particular expertise in all aspects of mathematics which he had acquired with the help and encouragement of George Lord Delamere who, among other things, had given him 'many excellent bookes and instruments' and lent him some of his choicest manuscripts.[9]

John Thornton, the nonconformist chaplain who lived for many years in the household of William Earl of Bedford, taught mathematics to his son Lord Russell who was executed in July 1683 as one of the alleged participants in the Rye House Plot. In his speech on the scaffold Russell declared that 'I was born of worthy good Parents, and had the Advantages of a Religious Education, which I have often thank'd God very heartily for, and look'd upon as an invaluable Blessing.' In addition, Thornton educated his son Wriothesley, who eventually became the second Duke of Bedford, and his daughters in 'piety and useful knowledge'.[10] Bulstrode Whitelocke employed a private tutor, Ichabod Chauncy, who was the son of a nonconforming minister who had emigrated to New England during the Laudian era. In August 1661, however, Whitelocke decided to dispense with his services, noting in his diary that he had dealt too harshly with his sons and 'strucke one of them with a great booke uppon his head, wherof he was ill'. He was succeeded by James Pearson who served both as tutor and chaplain.[11]

'Fanaticks', writes Anthony Wood, 'keep their children at home or breed them in privat schooles under fanaticks or send them beyond sea.'[12] During this period a number of young Puritan noblemen and gentlemen were accompanied on their travels abroad by nonconformist divines who acted as their governors or tutors: these included two sons of Philip Lord Wharton, Thomas and Goodwin, Sir William Masham, Samuel Rolle (the only son of

Robert Rolle), John Hampden, Theophilus Boscawen (one of the sons of Hugh Boscawen) and Samuel Barnardiston (the nephew and heir of Sir Samuel Barnardiston).[13] In February 1671 John Swinfen informed Lord Paget that his daughter Mrs Letitia Hampden would shortly be coming to London with her son John 'who within a fortnight or lesse begins upon his travails'. A few days later a licence to travel was obtained in the names of John Hampden and Theophilus Boscawen. They were joined by Francis Tallents and embarked on a journey through France which ended tragically when Boscawen died of smallpox at Strasbourg. After returning home Tallents remained on close terms with the Hampdens. In October 1680 he again travelled to France with his former pupil who went there for 'recovery of his health' while in June 1686 he was said to be leaving London for Great Hampden 'whither hee was importunately invited, and where hee intends to stay some weeks or months'.[14] Sir Samuel Barnardiston arranged for his nephew to go on the Grand Tour in the company of John Shower, a Presbyterian minister, and Thomas Goodwin who like his more famous father was an Independent divine. The party left for the Continent in the early part of 1683 and spent the summer in Geneva and the following winter in Rome. From Italy they travelled back through Switzerland and Germany and eventually arrived in Holland where Barnardiston was persuaded to throw in his lot with the Duke of Monmouth who was in the process of organising his ill-fated rebellion. In April 1686, when he and Shower were still sojourning in Amsterdam, the young man sought a pardon for taking up arms against the king and this was duly granted. Shower, who was anxious to play down his own involvement, explained in a letter to the British envoy at the Hague that they had entered Holland 'in that unhappy Juncture when a knot of such Company was here as we little expected to have met with, and inconsiderately falling into their Acquaintance were made believe many things which since we have found to be altogether fals'.[15]

While they were still very young Sir Edward Harley's sons received some tuition from a resident tutor, Thomas Blagrave, who had only recently left Oxford. In January 1671, however, Lady Harley told her husband that she felt it would be better if they were sent away to school. So long as they remained at home it was impossible to prevent them mixing with the servants and acquiring a strange clownish speech and behaviour 'which our boys have very much already'. Moreover, they were disinclined in these circumstances to pursue their studies, 'having nothing of emulation to spur them on'. Although Sir Edward had been thinking of securing the services of another tutor he was prepared to go along with this proposal and in the summer Robert and Edward were admitted to Samuel Birch's boarding school at Shilton in Oxfordshire where they were later joined by their brother Nathaniel.[16] Birch was a Presbyterian divine who had been ejected from the living of Bampton. Since opening his school in 1664 he had been molested by both the deputy lieutenants and the diocesan authorities and it was apparently with the aim of affording him some protection that Lord Wharton had appointed him as one of his chaplains.[17] While he was a pupil at Shilton Sir Edward's eldest son Robert frequently received paternal instructions and guidance. On one occasion Sir Edward wrote that 'I hope you improve in the Hebrew and Greek which wil bring you the comfort of understanding the Scriptures. But let your aim in all knowledg be to learn to Love God.' On another occasion he advised him to be very particular about what he read: 'Covet not to have or look upon many books, read thoroughly a few necessary Ones.' In February 1677 Lady Harley informed him that his father would like him to learn to fence and dance if he was so minded but added that she had heard that Mr Birch was not very proficient at teaching his pupils to dance. Robert Harley, for his part, was not unreceptive to his father's exhortations: in September 1677 he asked him to pray that he might be safeguarded 'from youthfull lusts, and the wickednesses of the nation wherein we live'.[18]

Birch's reputation was such that he was able to attract pupils from many wealthy Puritan families. Besides the Harley brothers and their cousin James Kyrle they included Henry Wharton, a younger son of his patron Lord Wharton; Sir William Ellis who had inherited his father's baronetcy and estates while still a minor; Simon Harcourt, the son and heir of an Oxfordshire landowner, Sir Philip Harcourt; and Thomas Foley who at the time of his admission was the only son of Paul Foley. In March 1674 Birch sent Lord Wharton a report on his son. Henry Wharton, he wrote, had done well at Latin but not so well at Greek. He had 'taken much paines with him in Geography and the grounds of Chronologie' which were 'necessary for a gentleman, and any person that would know history or would be able to do his countrey service'. However, he felt obliged to say that now he was grown up the vanities and lusts of youth had grown up with him. He had done all he could 'to give him a full sense what the excellencie and beautie of true Religion and real holines is' but when Henry looked abroad into the world 'he is on fire to try what he sees others Act'. In conclusion he suggested that Lord Wharton should instruct his son to show more diligence and submit to the discipline of the school since 'an irregular Libertie in him' was setting a dangerous example for others as well as harming himself.[19]

When Gilbert Earl of Clare made inquiries about the school he was told by Lord Wharton that it was 'very full'. Nevertheless he was still anxious to send his sons there and in January 1680 sought the help and advice of his kinsman Sir Edward Harley, emphasising that he considered it important that they should have their own private quarters. His mother, he added, was very much in favour of placing them with Mr Birch since she understood that it was his practice to instruct his pupils 'in the best things as well as in learning, by catechising, praying to them and hearing of them pray, to have them well grounded in all principles of religion'.[20] Birch, however, was already seriously ill and died shortly afterwards. He left behind him, writes Anthony Wood, 'the character of a good man among the precise people, but otherwise among the neighbouring royalists, who esteem'd him an instiller of evil Principles into youth'.[21] In February Sir Edward Harley heard from Lord Wharton that he was thinking of putting in William Taylor, his domestic chaplain, as Birch's successor. In his reply Harley warmly welcomed this proposal but went on to say that in view of the uncertainty about the future of the school he had already placed his sons under the tuition of 'a very worthy person neer mee'.[22]

Most of the Puritan squires of Charles II's reign had studied at Oxford or Cambridge either before or after the outbreak of the Civil War. Even in the Laudian era there had been a number of colleges which had enjoyed a very high reputation amongst the godly: in particular, Exeter, Magdalen Hall, Brasenose and Lincoln at Oxford and Emmanuel, Sidney Sussex, Christ's College and St Catharine Hall at Cambridge.[23] After the Restoration, however, there was an extensive purge of heads of colleges, fellows and scholars at both universities. In June 1660 William Lynsett, a fellow of Trinity College, Cambridge, told the Earl of Bedford's chaplain that as the result of a visitation which was being carried out 'the condition of our University hath been much alter'd to the worse: all our scholars are dismissed, we shall not have above a dozen of fellowes remaining in our College and we shall meet together again as God shall please'. In February 1661 the Senior Dean and many of the fellows of St John's College, Cambridge, submitted a petition to the king in which they complained that Anthony Tuckney, who was Master of the college and Regius Professor of Divinity, had declined to attend services in the chapel ever since the reintroduction of the Book of Common Prayer. When it became clear that he had incurred the king's displeasure Tuckney resigned both appointments and settled in London.[24] In August 1660 Sir Edward Harley was informed that there were many who had lost their places at Oxford, 'being most of them of your Acquaintance and Gospell friends here'. Those conducting the visitation were 'hostile to any one that regards not their Idolls, Comon prayer, Surplisses, Ceremonies, and Byshopps'. They intended to remove most of the fellows and scholars in the university and all the indications were that 'the Issue wilbe very Sad and obstructive to the power of Godlynes, and the propagation of the Gospel'.[25]

Although Anthony Wood had no liking for Puritans he was highly critical of developments at Oxford during the latter part of the century. Learning, he tells us, was in decline; preaching was 'foolish and florid' and was sometimes used as a vehicle for the propagation of Arminian doctrine; and praying tended to be lacking in both zeal and content. At the same time the authorities connived at Sabbath breaking, swearing, drunkenness and wenching. The scholars, for their part, did not live 'as students ought to do, viz temperat, abstemious, and plaine and grave in the apparell'; instead they sought to live like gentlemen, keeping dogs and horses, storing wine in their studies and coalholes, and wearing flamboyant clothes and long periwigs.[26]

According to Wood there was also a falling away of student numbers at Oxford which was due to the unwillingness of Presbyterians, Independents and 'other fanaticall people' to send their sons there 'for feare of orthodox principles'.[27] Among the Puritan nobility and gentry, however, there were differing views on the subject of university education. A number of major families such as the Boscawens, the Harleys and the Hoghtons were clearly convinced that their sons would be exposed to too many dangers at the English universities. In 1678 Sir Edward Harley was toying with the idea of sending his son Robert to Oxford but soon thought better of it: in June he told his wife that 'I am more then before discoraged from Oxford' while in a subsequent letter to her he stressed that 'I utterly dislike the universitie for any of mine.' After the children had been withdrawn from Shilton there was some talk of allowing Robert to travel on the Continent. In the event this came to nothing. Writing to his wife in July 1680 Sir Edward announced that he had changed his mind 'upon weighty reasons both as to the private and public, not so fit now to be expressed'. Instead he thought it best for him to spend some time at the French academy of Henri Foubert, a Huguenot refugee, in London where the curriculum included riding, fencing, dancing, handling arms and mathematics. Before the end of the month Robert was admitted to the academy, along with a manservant, and almost immediately received a letter from his father in which he was urged to ensure that bodily exercise 'hinder not your Endevors after Godlines which is profitable for all things'. Harley remained at the academy until December 1682 by which time it appears to have been in a state of considerable disorder. In January 1683 a friend wrote to him that 'The academy stands where it did, but seems only like a sodome that you have left for fear of a punisment on Your selfe.'[28]

If some families boycotted the universities others took a less critical view, at least of particular colleges or fellows. That the Barringtons continued to send their sons to Trinity College, Cambridge, is not altogether surprising given the special relationship which existed. The college owned the patronage rights in the parish of Hatfield Broad Oak and the Barringtons held a lease of the tithes from the college authorities. In addition, there were college exhibitions for which the family had the right of nomination. Sir John Barrington, who had been an undergraduate there in the reign of Charles I, placed his sons Thomas and John with James Duport, the Vice-Master, who had formerly acted as tutor to their uncle Sir Gobert Barrington.[29] In 1664 Sir John Wittewronge's son James was admitted to Magdalen College, Oxford where his elder brother had been a student during the late 1650s. Although many of the Puritan fellows had been ejected in the purge of 1660 he had no complaints about the choice of tutor: in January 1665 he remarked in a letter to his father that he would always be indebted to his tutor 'for his care and love towards me'.

An account of his expenses which has survived records the purchase of a Greek lexicon and books on logic, geography, antiquities and history.[30]

During Charles II's reign Christ Church, Oxford took in students from a number of major Puritan families, including three sons of Sir John Pelham. According to Anthony Wood the Dean, Dr John Fell, preferred 'Fanaticks and rogues' to 'true sons of the Church of England' as fellows of his college.[31] Another Oxford college, St Edmund Hall, had even greater attractions for godly parents, primarily because of the reputation of Thomas Tully who held the office of Principal during the years 1658 to 1676. Tully, writes Anthony Wood, was 'a Person of severe morals, puritanically inclin'd, and a strict Calvinist'.[32] In July 1666 John Gell told his son and namesake, who had just arrived at St Edmund Hall, that he had spoken to Dr Tully who had promised to be very civil to him and take care of him. He would continue to forward money for his support so long as he was 'constant and conscientious in duty, carefull to shun idlenes and ill company, and industryous to improve that time, and those parts and gifts god hath vouchsafed you'. Dr Tully and others had undertaken to keep him informed of his actions, the company he kept and the progress he made in his studies. In view of the great help he had received from Francis Tallents (who served for a time as chaplain to the Gell family) it would be appropriate to write to him. 'Let religion be your business', he stressed, 'be carefull to do your duty to god and man and the lord blesse you and make you usefull in church and state.'[33] Others who were admitted during Tully's period of office included Thomas Alston, the son and heir of Sir Thomas Alston, who died in 1668 while still at Oxford; two of Bulstrode Whitelocke's younger sons, Carleton and Samuel; Philip Wharton, the son of Sir Thomas Wharton and nephew of Philip Lord Wharton; and Richard Onslow (later Lord Onslow), the eldest son of Arthur Onslow.[34] In July 1669 Whitelocke noted in his diary that he had heard that his sons 'were not so studious and thrifty as they should be'. The admission of Philip Wharton was the subject of correspondence between his uncle and Thomas Gilbert who had continued to live in Oxford after being deprived of his fellowship at St Edmund Hall. In March 1670 Gilbert wrote that Dr Tully was 'absolutely the best Governor in Oxford' but it was unlikely that he could spare the time to act as the young man's tutor. Instead he suggested that he should be placed with John

March, the Vice-Principal, who was 'the best tutor by much I know, and a Man truly fearing God'. March, he added, had been tutor to 'Lord' Whitelocke's sons.[35] After Tully's death St Edmund Hall no longer attracted students from the Puritan nobility and gentry. Some years later White Kennet, who was then Vice-Principal, was reported to have said that it was 'a debauch'd college, that they were all given to loosness'.[36]

When Lord Wharton was thinking of sending his son William to Oxford in 1679 Gilbert expressed the hope that he would be able to 'come off hence with all the Advantages of a Universitie Breeding without any the now too usual Deboch either in Principles or Practice'. He was afraid, however, that when many of the current generation of undergraduates left Oxford they would lack any of the benefits of a university education and would merely be debauched.[37] At Cambridge there does not appear to have been a single college with anything like the appeal of St Edmund Hall under Dr Tully. Emmanuel and Sidney Sussex could no longer be regarded, in Laud's terminology, as nurseries of Puritanism; and when Sir Thomas Barnardiston decided in 1664 to place his eldest son at St Catharine Hall this was probably due largely to his recollections of the time when he was himself a student there during the Mastership of the celebrated Richard Sibbes.[38]

Some Puritan squires who considered it unwise to send their sons to the universities were more favourably disposed towards the Inns of Court, though even then they might have worries about the temptations awaiting them in London. From the late 1660s onwards, however, there was another option available, and one more directly relevant, in the form of the dissenting academies which were run by men of considerable scholastic ability who had been deprived of their livings or fellowships for nonconformity. Among the more important of these academies were those of John Woodhouse at Sheriff Hales in Staffordshire, Charles Morton at Newington Green in Middlesex, Richard Frankland at Rathmell in Yorkshire and other places, and Samuel Cradock at Wickhambrook in Suffolk.[39] Besides the guarantee of a sober and godly environment the academies offered the same kind of subjects as the universities and in some cases rather more. A major point of contention was whether such men were entitled to compete with the universities in this way, given the fact that Oxford and Cambridge graduates were required to take an oath by which they promised not to teach 'as in a University' unless they obtained prior approval. Morton and Cradock both produced tracts in which they defended the practice of establishing academies but the controversy dragged on for many years. In June 1692 Archbishop Tillotson told his fellow primate Archbishop Sharp of York that he was doubtful whether it would be in order to allow Richard Frankland a licence even though he was now conformable to the Church of England; and that one reason for this was the oath which was administered to university graduates.[40]

John Woodhouse's academy at Sheriff Hales was described as 'a Nursery for Heaven as well as a School for improved Learning'. His basic aim, it was said, was to save the souls of his pupils and he took care 'to adapt their Study and Labours to this End'.[41] As a general rule he had about 40 students in residence at a time. Not a few were drawn from the Puritan nobility and gentry: they included William and Henry Paget, the sons of William Lord Paget; Walgrave Crewe, a grandson of John Lord Crewe; Thomas and Edward Foley, two of the sons of Thomas Foley of Worcestershire; Henry Ashurst, the only son of Sir Henry Ashurst; Thomas Hunt, a son of Rowland Hunt of Shropshire; and Richard Hampden, a great-grandson of John Hampden the parliamentarian.[42] Woodhouse thought very highly of Walgrave Crewe. In February 1693 he wrote in a letter to Thomas Woodcock, an ejected minister who was the stepfather of Crewe's mother, that 'his fixed sobriety and disposition to religion and those that are religious give me reason to hope for good things from him'. During his time at the academy he had carried himself well, joining with 'a praying company, and praying with them in his turne'. Indeed, Woodhouse declared, he knew no young nobleman like him.[43]

In December 1687 Thomas Foley told Sir Edward Harley that he was thinking of sending his eldest son, Thomas, to Mr Woodhouse because he lived in the country and added that 'I am afraid to venture my son to London.' The young man was duly admitted to the academy, along with his brother Edward, but in February 1689 he suggested to his father that he could better pursue his studies in London:

I have read Logick, natural Philosophy, and some of the Mathematicks, which I think are necessary for the accomplishment of a gentleman ... Ethicks and Metaphysicks by what I can learn from those of the best iudgment here, who

157

have read it lately, will not be very necessary for me, especially Metaphysicks. I am now reading Anatomy, for which I should have better advantage at London, with seeing the most renowned books, and conversing with Physicians and such as have the greatest skill therein.

His cousin Thomas Hunt and Henry Ashurst would both be leaving at Easter and before long there would be no one he could converse with or 'get any improvement from'. The academy, he concluded, was very much altered for the worse. In the event Ashurst returned to Sheriff Hales after Easter and was joined by the Foley brothers whose father was strongly opposed to the idea that Thomas should remove to London. Before the end of the year, however, Thomas Foley was studying at the University of Utrecht with the aim (as he later explained to his brother-in-law Robert Harley) of making himself serviceable for his country.[44]

In November 1693 the Bishop of Lichfield and Coventry informed a fellow bishop that during the recent visitation of his diocese Mr Woodhouse of Sheriff Hales had been ordered to appear and show his licence to teach. Woodhouse, he went on to say, 'keeps not only a school but an academy for all sorts of learning and especially he pretends to breed up young men for the Ministery'. After completing their education these young men were immediately ordained by Presbyterian ministers or were sent forth to hold conventicles in his own and neighbouring dioceses. Woodhouse had claimed that following the Act of Toleration (which had been passed in 1689) it was no longer necessary for him to have a licence; and in response the Bishop had suggested that he should seek a legal opinion on this issue from the judges at the Stafford assizes. Since the Act of Toleration contains no specific reference to schools or schoolmasters his assertion lacked conviction; nevertheless the academy survived until 1697, three years before his death.[45]

Charles Morton's academy at Newington Green offered a wide range of subjects but as Samuel Wesley, who spent two years there, would later testify the main speciality was mathematics and particularly 'the Mechanic part thereof'. Among other things the academy had a laboratory with an air pump, a thermometer and all kinds of mathematical instruments. During the time that Wesley was a boarder there were 40 to 50 pupils and almost all of them 'entertain'd a mortal Aversion to the Episcopal Order'.

Some of his contemporaries were the sons of knights and baronets and there was also a nobleman's son; these, he observes, had been sent to the academy 'to avoid the Debaucheries of the Universities'.[46]

After satisfying himself that Morton's academy was suitable in all respects Sir Edward Harley decided that his son Edward should become a pupil there. In March 1682 he wrote in a letter to him that 'I bless God you are placed with a person in whom you find so much Encouragement in the way of holy Erudition. The Lord give you wisdome to redeem that Time.' Sir Edward had been worried by the poor spelling in letters which he had received from his sons and in a postscript he urged him to 'Forget not the first step in Liberal Science, Orthographie.'[47] Morton, for his part, appears to have had a very high regard for Harley's son. In a letter which he sent him in December 1683 he wrote that 'I know none of my Children (as I call them) that I more heartily rejoyce in.' While expressing the hope that he would shortly be returning he had some disturbing news to impart: he was being persecuted in the Bishop of London's court and it was not at all certain what the outcome would be; nevertheless, he assured him, 'we shall proceed as if there were noe danger'. Morton also had news about a number of his former pupils: some were now studying at the Universities of Leiden and Utrecht; Mr Waller had died at Amsterdam (where his father, Sir William Waller, was a political exile); and George Fagg (a younger son of Sir John Fagg) had also died, in his case when he was about to be married.[48] In August 1685 we find Robert Harley reporting to his father that Morton had been released on bail with the proviso that he should never teach again. Shortly afterwards he departed for New England, though his academy would remain in being for another twenty years or so.[49]

Following the letter which he received from Samuel Birch about the conduct of his son Lord Wharton decided to take him away from Shilton and in May 1674 he was admitted to Samuel Cradock's academy at Wickhambrook. In July Cradock told his father that Henry was displaying considerable diligence and could prove to be a good scholar. 'It will be a great mercy of God to him', he continued, 'if he be preserv'd from the evil genius and inclination of this age which is so wild and licentious . . . I shall endeavour (the Lord assisting me) to instill into him the principles of reall piety and vertue.' By December, however, Cradock was in a state of despair. Imploring Lord Wharton to remove his son as soon as possible, he declared that 'I am in perpetuall fear and unquietness of mind concerning him' and was afraid that he might do 'a great deale of hurt to those under my care'. Henry Wharton subsequently took up a military career and in 1686 it was reported that he had killed an Irish officer in the same regiment as himself.[50]

Despite this traumatic episode the academy went from strength to strength. According to the minister who preached the sermon at his funeral in 1706 Cradock's pupils included 'many serviceable Instruments in Church and State (both in and out of the present Establishment) at this Day'.[51] Edmund Calamy, who was at the academy during the years 1686 to 1688, names several persons of quality who had been educated there, among them Sir Francis Bickley, a Norfolk baronet, and William Ellis, the eldest son of Sir William Ellis who had been one of Samuel Birch's pupils.[52] In November 1687 James Wittewronge told his father that he had been dining with Sir William Ashurst who had spoken very highly of Mr Cradock and that he was so impressed by what he had heard that he had made up his mind to send his son Jacob to the academy if there was a place available.[53]

Richard Frankland's academy, which was opened in 1669 and continued to function until his death in 1698, was the foremost establishment of its kind in northern England and most of its pupils were drawn from that region. Although he had an estate at Rathmell he was so frequently put under pressure that he was obliged to change his place of residence from time to time. Possibly for this reason the academy attracted very few young men from Puritan county families. A comprehensive list of pupils which has survived contains the names of St Andrew Thornhagh, the son and heir of a Nottinghamshire squire and the grandson of a parliamentarian, Francis Thornhagh, who had been killed at the Battle of Preston in 1648; Charles Duckenfield, the eldest son of Sir Robert Duckenfield of Cheshire, and his half-brother Joseph; and Joseph Ashurst who may be identified as a brother of Sir Henry and Sir William Ashurst. In sending his sons to the academy Sir Robert Duckenfield was no doubt acting on the advice of a clerical associate, Samuel Angier, who had himself been a pupil of Frankland.[54]

In the main the Puritan gentry appear to have been well satisfied with the scope and quality of the education provided by the dissenting academies. Lord Paget's decision to send his sons to Sheriff Hales was almost certainly taken on the advice of John Swinfen who resided in the same county and was a friend of John Woodhouse. Thomas Foley's main criticism of Woodhouse as a teacher concerned his degree of proficiency in mathematics but the jaundiced views which he expressed in correspondence with his father probably owed much to his yearning to spend some time in London.[55] If, however, such establishments often built up a good reputation for academic learning there was no automatic progression from nonconformist schools to nonconformist academies. Some of Samuel Birch's pupils, among them Sir William Ellis, Simon Harcourt and Thomas Foley, the son of Paul Foley, subsequently went on to study at Oxford. The choice of a university education in these circumstances was sometimes due to special factors: for example, Simon Harcourt's admission to Pembroke College can be attributed to the influence of Edmund Hall, a Presbyterian fellow of the college who was on close terms with Sir Philip Harcourt, while another Presbyterian, Dr John Wallis, found a suitable tutor for Thomas Foley at the same college.[56] More generally, however, it seems likely that residual feelings of loyalty towards the universities were mixed with fears that in the face of official hostility the academies had a bleak and turbulent future ahead of them.

13

GETTING AND SPENDING

Although many Puritan squires who sided with Parliament during the Civil War suffered financial losses as a result[1] it was only rarely that these had any permanent consequences. Sir Henry Rosewell, a Devonshire landowner, disposed of his Forde Abbey estate in January 1650 and settled at Limington in Somerset where he had other property. The purchaser was Edmund Prideaux, one of the leading Presbyterian members of the Long Parliament, who had built up a vast fortune as Attorney General and Postmaster General.[2] In June 1650 another Devonshire squire, Sir Francis Drake of Buckland Abbey, sold his wife's jointure lands at Werrington for £4,750. Although he had been reduced to a state of penury during the war he attributed this enforced sale to the fact that he was faced with the need to raise portions for his brothers and sisters. After this the fortunes of the family began to improve: at his death in 1662 he left an estate worth over £1,000 a year and his nephew and heir, another Sir Francis, was able to purchase additional property.[3] The severe financial difficulties experienced by the Lukes of Bedfordshire may well have been due in part to their involvement in the Civil War but there were probably other factors of greater importance. In July 1666 Sir Samuel Luke and his son Oliver entered into an agreement with trustees acting on behalf of Sir George Carteret over the sale of the manors of Haynes and St Makes for the sum of £19,000. In a Chancery bill, however, the trustees claimed that after making an initial payment of £10,000 they had discovered that the manors were heavily encumbered with debts incurred by Sir Samuel and his father Sir Oliver who had once been described as 'decayed in his estate'. The Lukes, for their part, maintained that some of these debts had already been paid and that it had always been their intention to satisfy the remaining creditors by drawing on the purchase money. Eventually the dispute was resolved and the sale went ahead. Following Sir Samuel's death in 1670 his son Oliver inherited the residue of his estate but in 1686 was forced to sell the ancestral property at Wood End in Cople, though the family continued to reside there until the male line expired in 1732.[4]

According to his own computation Sir Robert Harley's losses in the Civil War amounted to £12,990. His houses at Brampton Bryan and Wigmore had been destroyed by the royalists and for some years the family had difficulty in making ends meet. In August 1653 there were principal debts totalling £5,490 but by then his annual income was rather more than £1,400 which was not far short of what it had been a decade or so earlier. At the time of his death in 1656 the process of recovery was well advanced and his son Edward was able to face the future with reasonable equanimity. When taking stock in August 1659 he noted that the outstanding debts of his father, himself and his wife came to £1,521 12s 0d and that he also had to pay out £1,250 in legacies. Shortly after this the Harleys embarked on a major building programme which heralded a long period of uninterrupted prosperity.[5] Sir Thomas Jervoise, who lived at Herriard in Hampshire, initially put a figure of £13,448 on his losses but later adjusted it to £15,000 'and upwards'. With the aid of the financial compensation paid by Parliament he and his son Thomas, who succeeded him in 1654, managed to keep the estate intact. While Sir Thomas had an income of £1,500 a year on the eve of the Civil War his grandson's estate revenue in 1696 amounted to some £2,500 a year. The latter, another Thomas Jervoise, improved the rents of the property settled on him in 1692 by at least £400 a year and rebuilt the house at a cost of £7,000; sadly, however, his only son 'had the misfortune to become disordered in his Senses'.[6]

Even before the restoration of the monarchy some Puritan squires were not simply holding their own but growing richer. Sir Richard Onslow, Sir Walter Erle and Edward Mainwaring enlarged their estates by purchase. Sir Thomas Cheke gave direction in his will that within a year of his death the sum of £8,000 should be spent on the acquisition of lands worth £400 a year for the benefit of his grandson Robert.[7] Sir Francis Boynton inherited an estate worth over £2,000 a year from his uncle Sir Henry Griffith who had supported the royalist cause in the Civil War; and Sir

John Dryden secured property worth at least £800 a year as his share of the estate of the Bevill family of Huntingdonshire after the expiry of the male line.[8]

The restitution of Church property which followed the return of the king[9] had particularly serious implications for the Hesilrige family. Sir Arthur Hesilrige and his son Thomas had laid out some £22,000 on the purchase of lands belonging to the Bishopric of Durham and in the process had apparently overstretched their resources. Although the Hesilriges were able to recover their lands of inheritance, which were worth over £1,500 a year, they were faced with the need to clear them of debts amounting to £14,000 and continued to struggle financially until the end of the century.[10] Following the execution of Sir Henry Vane in 1662 the Crown required his family to return the Lincolnshire estate which he had bought a decade earlier to its previous owner, Montague Earl of Lindsey, who had been one of Charles I's most loyal supporters. The Vanes, however, were soon in possession of their property in Kent and the county palatine of Durham which had been described in 1650 as 'well worth' £3,000 a year with the qualification that its potential value was nearer £5,000 than £4,000 a year. In 1673 Sir Henry's son Thomas, who was then the head of the family, sought the hand in marriage of Lady Essex Rich, one of the daughters of Robert Earl of Warwick. Her aunt, Mary Countess of Warwick, strongly advised her to choose 'so good and sober a person' but she declined to do so 'upon account of his Family'. In 1698, when the Whigs were in the ascendant, his brother Christopher was created Lord Barnard of Barnard Castle.[11]

Besides the Lukes and the Hesilriges there were other Puritan county families, among them the Hampdens and the Whitelockes,[12] which sold or mortgaged some parts of their estates during the years 1660 to 1700. Very few, however, suffered complete financial ruin; and there are indications that when this occurred the Puritan strain had already given out. Sir John Jackson, who was made a baronet in December 1660, was one of the leading Presbyterian patrons in the West Riding of Yorkshire. When he died in 1670 he left an encumbered estate but the decline and fall of the family was largely due to the extravagance of his son, another Sir John, who succeeded him while still a minor. In his will, which was drawn up in January 1680, he related that 'Whereas my debts are greate, And itt haveing all waies beene my desire that all my just debts should be duely paide', he had settled his lands on trustees for that purpose. In 1704 his half-brother Sir Bradwardine Jackson disposed of the remnants of the estate in return for annuities amounting to £120 a year and not long afterwards was imprisoned for debt.[13] In the case of the Hungerfords the financial crash was even more spectacular. Sir Edward Hungerford, who was a member of the Long Parliament, died childless in 1648 when the bulk of his estates passed to his half-brother Anthony. His widow, Lady Margaret, who had a jointure of £2,000 settled on her, was a woman of exceptional piety who subsequently employed a nonconformist divine, Thomas Rosewell, as her household chaplain. In her will, which was drawn up shortly before her death in 1673, she recorded her belief that 'God from all eternity hath chosen mee to salvation in the Number of those on whom hee hath sett his free Love.' More prosaically, she was very worried about the extravagance of Sir Edward Hungerford, the son and successor of Anthony Hungerford, who owed her money. In bequeathing to him a set of diamond buttons she took the opportunity to 'recommend to him that he doe not by Improvident Courses lessen the Estate of his Famuly, but leave it faire to him that shall come after him'. Lady Hungerford was clearly pinning her hopes on his son Edward who had received some tuition from Thomas Rosewell but in the event he died while still a young man. In 1679 Sir Edward was said to have had an income of £6,000 a year or more. Before long, however, he was busily engaged in selling off his inheritance: among other things, the Corsham estate in Wiltshire, along with the Elizabethan mansion, was lost to the family in 1684 while in March 1687 there was a report that he had received £56,000 from the sale of his Farleigh Hungerford estate in Somerset. Not surprisingly, he came to be known as 'the spendthrift'.[14]

For many of the Puritan gentry the later Stuart period was a time of increasing affluence. Families with estates worth £3,000 a year or more were relatively numerous: they included the Boscawens of Cornwall, the Barringtons of Essex, the Foleys of Herefordshire and Worcestershire, the Grimstons of Hertfordshire, the Hobarts of Norfolk, the Langhams of Northamptonshire, the Pelhams of Sussex, the Wilbrahams of Staffordshire and the Pophams of Wiltshire.[15] Some of these families were engaged in commercial or industrial activities; others advanced their fortunes through office-holding or marriage. According to one of his account books Sir John Pelham's income in 1660, which included receipts from the sale of iron, amounted to some £4,800.[16] Sir John Barrington's steward calculated that in 1678 his revenue had come to £4,104 8s 6½d and the total disbursements to £3,081 6s 2d. Among the items of expenditure were £415 for allowances payable to Sir John's wife and children, £124 19s 6d for the servants' wages and £44 6s 1d for taxes and poll money. In contrast, an analysis which had been undertaken of the family's ordinary expenses in the years 1669 to 1675 had revealed that they had averaged only £1,208 a year. Sir John had made some land purchases in Essex since the Restoration and as a result of the marriage between his son Thomas and Lady Anne Rich, one of the daughters of Robert Earl of Warwick, the Barringtons eventually acquired other property there worth £1,000 a year. When Sir John Barrington, the fourth baronet, died of smallpox in November 1691 he was described as a man of £5,000 a year.[17] Hugh Boscawen had inherited an estate worth £3,000 a year when his elder brother was killed in action in 1645. In 1661 he paid £10,000 for property at Poynton in Lincolnshire which he had been offered by his father-in-law Theophilus Earl of Lincoln, who was in considerable financial difficulty, while in 1676 he bought the manor of Fentongollan in Cornwall for £7,000. Boscawen was a major Cornish industrialist who owned tin mines and copper works. In September 1663 we find his wife, Lady Margaret, writing to her brother-in-law Edward Boscawen, who was a London merchant, that she was very willing to supply him with tin 'not douting but you will be pleased to give mee as Good a prise for it as any other'. Like the Barrington family Boscawen held East India Company stock: an entry in his accounts for December 1681 records the receipt of £79 6s 8d as interest on an investment of £3,500.[18]

Sir Harbottle Grimston had been left an estate worth £2,000 a year by his father. In 1651 he married a rich widow, Lady Anne Meautys, who had a life interest in the Gorhambury estate in Hertfordshire, and shortly afterwards purchased the reversion for £10,000. Following the marriage he abandoned the old family seat at Bradfield in Essex and settled with his wife at Gorhambury where her kinsman Francis Bacon had once lived in splendour. By the time of the Restoration he had an estate revenue of some £3,000 a year and his appointment as Master of the Rolls in November 1660 enabled him to continue the process of increasing his landed possessions. In January 1669, when he was involved in negotiations leading to the marriage of his son Samuel with

Elizabeth Finch, a daughter of Sir Heneage Finch, he put the value
of his estate at £4,000 a year and agreed to allow her a jointure
of £1,000 a year in return for a portion of £4,000 and an undertaking that she would settle her own lands on her husband for life
when she came of age. As a tailpiece to these financial propositions he wrote

> And then for a fineall conclusion of this kinde Treaty I shall
> humbly begg God Almighty who onely hath the power of
> hearts to dispose and inclyne the Affections of the younge
> persons to love each other intirely, and soe to bee helpefull
> to one another heare in this world, that they may obtaine
> through fayth in Christ a better portion in an other world.

Shortly after his death in 1685 (when Roger Morrice described
him as 'that great and good man') an examination of the rent-rolls
indicated that the estate revenue amounted to £4,885. Gilbert
Burnet, who considered him to be a very pious and devout man,
observes that 'I thought his only fault was that he was too rich:
and yet he gave yearly great sums in charity, discharging many
prisoners by paying their debts.'[19]

One of the more obvious manifestations of the wealth of the
Puritan gentry was the amount of housebuilding which went on.
This, however, was not always a matter of choice: sometimes it
was necessary to replace or rehabilitate a house which had suffered
damage during the Civil War. Charborough House in Dorset,
which had been built by Sir Walter Erle during the early part of
the century, had been burnt down by royalist troops. Towards the
end of the Commonwealth period Sir Walter erected a new house
which incorporated the remains of the previous house and subsequently found himself accused of using stone and timber taken
from Corfe Castle which had also been reduced to a ruin.[20] At
Brampton Bryan in Herefordshire the Harley mansion, Brampton
Castle, and the church had both been destroyed in the Civil War.
Characteristically, the Harleys decided that the rebuilding of the
church should have first priority. At the Restoration they were
living at Bucknell in Shropshire, a few miles to the north-west of
Brampton Bryan. In 1660 a start was made on the construction of
a new house on a site adjoining the ruined castle and from time to
time Sir Edward Harley, who was often absent, received reports
on the work from his steward, Samuel Shilton, as well as members
of his family. Progress was initially slow but in November 1661

Shilton was able to inform him that 'The New building is now brought up to the first floor, all except the kitchen chimney.' In June 1663 Sir Edward told his wife that he was very distressed to hear about the death of one of the workmen, adding that he 'would very contentedly live alwayes in a poor Cottage, Could that have saved his life'. Some provision (he went on) would need to be made for his next of kin and it would also be necessary to instruct the workmen 'to fasten and band theyr scaffold carefully'. Eventually the Harleys were back in residence at Brampton Bryan, twenty years after the destruction of the old house. In March 1667 a clerical friend, Thomas Doughty, expressed his pleasure over their return in a letter addressed to Harley: 'it is content to me', he wrote,

> to know that you have brought on your approaches so neere the poor dismantled Castle, and perfected that Worke, and do season it with your Presence and Prayers, not doubting but the same will promote (by more wayes then one) the Restauration of that ennobled seat, and lifting up the head therof in due time.[21]

By the later decades of the century some Elizabethan and Jacobean houses were in urgent need of renovation simply through the passage of time. Sir Roger Burgoyne frequently lamented in letters to his friend Sir Ralph Verney that his house at Sutton in Bedfordshire was in a very poor condition. In February 1675 he declared that 'something must be done before this ruined place be fitt for any gentleman's constant residence' while in May he was writing that 'We are now come to our most ruinous habitation wher we meet with nothing that is good besides the ayre.' Some work was put in hand that summer but since he frequently claimed to be short of money it was probably limited in scale.[22] Richard Hampden's house at Great Hampden in Buckinghamshire was perhaps even more dilapidated: in December 1676 he told John Swinfen that 'the house is decaying, and when it will drop downe, I know not'. No doubt it was primarily for this reason that a major rebuilding programme was carried out before the end of the century.[23]

Housebuilding sometimes reflected the social or territorial ambitions of newly emerging county families which often acquired baronetcies or knighthoods as a further means of enhancing status. Sir John Wittewronge, who built up an estate worth well over £1,000 a year, purchased the Buckinghamshire manor of Stantonbury in 1650 and erected a new house there after the Restoration. The house and the adjoining property were put into the possession of his eldest son while Sir John himself continued to live at Rothamsted in Hertfordshire.[24] Sir Henry Ashurst, who was a wealthy Turkey merchant, bought the Waterstock estate in Oxfordshire for £16,000, demolished the old house and built a new one of brick. In his will, which was drawn up in December 1710, he observed that the purchase of the estate had 'cost me the labour of my life'.[25] Paul Foley, who was the first of his family to settle in Herefordshire, began work on the rebuilding of his house at Stoke Edith in 1694. In a letter dispatched from Stoke Court in May 1694 he wrote that 'by being employed in pulling down all the things about this place I make it every day like a new one'. The new house was finally completed in 1699 but it very soon became a house of mourning: Foley died suddenly in November, leaving an estate worth £4,000 a year to his son Thomas.[26]

Among the more established gentry there were a number of families which took a similar delight in housebuilding and had the necessary resources to satisfy their aspirations. Hugh Boscawen the Cornish magnate rebuilt his ancestral home, Tregothnan; Richard Winwood 'delicately altered' his Buckinghamshire mansion, Ditton Park, which had been built by his father; and Sir John Crewe, who was seated in Cheshire, made substantial improvements to Utkinton Hall which was Elizabethan in origin.[27] In December 1678 a nonconformist divine, Samuel Hieron, informed Lord Wharton that Sir Walter Yonge, one of the leading Puritan squires in Devon, lived at Colyton where his house was 'but little, and indeed a good house is that he wants, which he did once design to build upon a great Barton . . . which he hath within 3 miles of Honyton, but I think that design is laid aside'. Not long afterwards, however, Sir Walter began to build a new mansion, Escot House, in the parish of Talaton. In May 1687 he commented in a letter to his friend John Locke that 'there is no end of charge in building . . . yet I love the building so well that I should be glad to find a meet help to finish it'. The work clearly took longer than he had anticipated, possibly because of the premature departure of the architect; a year later he was writing that there were still six rooms to be completed.[28] Sir William Ellis, a Lincolnshire squire with a rent-roll of at least

£3,000 a year, decided to take up residence at Nocton (in preference to Wyham) where an estate belonging to his great uncle had
come into his possession in 1680. The house which he built there
was no ordinary habitation: in 1693 it was described as a 'pallace'
in which Sir William 'lives like a prince'.[29]

The magnificent red-brick mansion at Weston under Lizard in
Staffordshire testifies to the wealth of Sir Thomas Wilbraham
who was said to have an income of £4,000 a year in 1664 and to be
'well monyed'. Construction began in 1671 and was closely
supervised by his wife, Lady Elizabeth, as may be judged by the
notes she made in her copy of Palladio's *First Book of Archi-
tecture*.[30] Some years later she confided to her friend John Swinfen
that she was concerned about the decay of the old house at
Woodhay in Cheshire where the Wilbrahams had formerly been
seated: 'if we Live to another somer', she wrote, it would be
necessary in her view 'to Lay out some money upon it, in respecte
to the paternall place of our family'. In April 1691 she noted in a
memorandum on the settlement of the estates that if Sir Thomas,
who was then in poor health, died before finishing his building
work at Woodhay it would be her intention to complete the
project by drawing on the rents of the Cheshire property which
were received during the year following his death. In a letter
addressed to Swinfen in April 1692 she told him that her husband
(who died shortly afterwards) was in financial difficulties because of his building 'and perhaps other more unprovitable
Expences'; that his personal estate was diminishing daily; and
that he had already cut down timber worth over £1,000 and was
talking of felling the remainder of his woods.[31]

During the early seventeenth century a country squire with an
income of £1,000 a year or more had usually owned a coach, often
no doubt because of the attractions which this type of conveyance
had for the womenfolk. One man who had stood out against the
general trend was Sir Robert Harley whose attitude probably
owed more to his austere Puritan temperament than to his
financial circumstances. In 1641 his wife, Lady Brilliana, had
commented in a letter to her son Edward that 'I should be very
glad if your father would be pleased to bye a coach . . . I thinke it
would not cost him much.' Sir Edward, for his part, was more
ready to conform. In April 1662 he told his wife that he had been
offered a 'likely' coachman; in December 1662 he expressed the
hope that she had arranged for the coach to be repaired, adding

that Charles was so lazy that he would do nothing without firm direction; and in February 1665 he was writing that 'I have bought a Coach, the cheapest I could', yet the price of the coach and harness had come to £38.[32] During the latter part of the century it was not uncommon for a well-to-do Puritan squire to own more than one coach. In their wills Richard Winwood and Hugh Boscawen bequeathed 'all' their coaches and coach horses to their wives while Sir Roger Burgoyne's wife received both his coaches and the four coach horses together with four other horses.[33] The expenditure on the purchase of a coach could be considerable: in June 1678 Edward Mainwaring, a Staffordshire landowner, paid £43 for a new coach, £12 for the fittings and harness, and £48 for a pair of horses.[34] At the same time there were other aspects which required attention: Sir Roger Burgoyne, for example, felt it necess-ary to ask his friend Sir Ralph Verney 'whether button, and hoop, hold still in fashion for Liveries and what is the usuall price of them by the dozen and how many serve for a footboy, a groom, a coachman'.[35] In view of the generally poor condition of the roads a journey by coach could sometimes be a hazardous undertaking. In his old age Sir John Pelham liked to take the air in his coach but this eventually ended in tragedy: on a journey in January 1703 the coach overturned and within a few days he died from the injuries which he had received.[36]

In the matter of dress there was a conflict between godly principles and social attitudes which had been exercising the minds of upper-class Puritans for several generations. Sir Harbottle Grimston had condemned the wearing of garments which were 'too gay' in a published work which had extolled the virtues of sobriety in all its forms but among the Puritan gentry as a whole practice had varied according to individual temperament and circumstances and may even have reflected regional differ-ences.[37] After the Restoration some of the womenfolk continued to dress plainly except perhaps on special occasions. According to her chaplain Lady Frances Hobart's expenses were 'great and noble, yet those upon herself were mean and inconsiderable: She cared not to be known by so plentifull a badge of Honour as Costly Apparel'.[38] Sir Harbottle Grimston's second wife, Lady Anne, was clearly in agreement with him on this subject. In a work which appeared in 1660 James Barker, a minister who held one of the Grimston livings, wrote in an epistle dedicatory which he addressed to her that

It is your Meeknesse, Madam, that gives a lustre to all your other vertues and Graces which beautifie your person, and Christian conversation, and render you an Ornament to your Sex: no plaiting of the Hair, wearing of Gold, putting on of Apparel do set forth a Lady in that high estimation with God and good men as her exemplary vertues do; those outward Adornings you do not use them, for you do not need them, God having abundantly stored you out of his own Treasury of nature and Grace.

Lady Grimston also earned the praise of Gilbert Burnet who, among other things, confirms that she was always very plain in her clothes.[39]

In June 1666 Lady Anne Burgoyne, the wife of Sir Roger Burgoyne, received a gift of rich lace from their friend Sir Ralph Verney. In thanking Verney for his kindness Sir Roger told him that his wife 'so much approves of the lace as to think it too good for her selfe to weare but I am apt to beleive all women will be soon weaned from such thoughts: only shee desires to know what it cost'. Although Lady Burgoyne usually bought her clothes in London the minister who preached the sermon at her funeral was at pains to stress that they counted for little in her scale of values. Her circumstances were such, he said, that she would have been able to indulge herself in many of the vanities which 'a loose and wanton Age might prompt her to'; in fact she had always looked upon them with the greatest indifference and contempt imaginable. 'Not', he went on,

> that she proudly set herself against the innocent Customs of her Countrey, or the indifferent fashions of her Age and Quality, which in modesty and civility she complied with, lest she should be too justly censur'd as more Proud and Conceited by her fond Opposition; but yet even her compliance seem'd to be with such indifference and unconcernedness, as to the manner of her Dress, and outward Ornament, as could not but discover that she never valued any the least respect or esteem upon such poor and pitiful accounts.[40]

It is significant that a woman with many Puritan characteristics who lived mainly in Warwickshire felt obliged to fall into line, at least to some extent, with the dictates of fashion even if she did so without genuine enthusiasm. But an interest in London fashion was not unknown in a more remote county such as Derbyshire which was described by Elizabeth Countess of Chesterfield as 'a dull place' which 'needs something to make it pleasant'.[41] In a letter which was probably written in 1669 Elizabeth Gell of Hopton Hall asked her brother John, who was then a student at Gray's Inn, to send her three pairs of gloves, 'not too big, the lesser size of women's gloves usually fit for me, and if ther be such a thing as a fashionable colour pray let me have that, otherwise I like brick and cream colour'. She also wanted to know whether laced shoes were 'out of the mode or noe': she had some lace but not enough for a pair and she would be reluctant to incur any expense 'to put my self out of fashion'. A further point on which she required information was the price of the 'pretty pendants' which were set in gold and enamelled; during a visit to London she had noted that these cost about 22s but she assumed that they would now be cheaper. Teasingly, she added that 'I suppose it's a part of your diversion now and then to observe the women's cloths and thén you might doe wel to inform your understandings for we live much in ignorance and you wil be apt to be ashamed to be seen with us when you come again into the countrey.'[42]

So far as the Puritan menfolk were concerned the most obvious concession to current fashion was the wearing of a periwig which would almost certainly have met with the disapproval of an earlier generation of godly divines. In December 1672 Sir John Hobart paid £7 for a periwig, 30s for the repair of a wig and 5s for two pounds of hair powder.[43] Sir John Pelham's accounts frequently record the purchase of wigs, many of them for his sons while they were at school and university.[44] Sir Edward Harley also adopted the practice, though this was apparently more for health reasons than out of any desire to keep abreast of fashion: not long after the Restoration his wife told him that her brother considered that he would be well advised to wear a periwig 'for he thincks most of your colds come from the thinnes of your haire upon your ears'.[45]

Visits to London could not only stimulate an interest in prevailing trends in dress but, more seriously, involve exposure to a social climate which was anathema to a zealous Puritan. Bulstrode Whitelocke noted in his diary that in December 1671 his son Samuel married Elizabeth Gough, the daughter of a Hampshire landowner, but within a few weeks he was beginning to have doubts about her willingness to comply 'with the wayes of his family, hearing her to plead much for blacke patches, and painting, and playes, and living in London'.[46] Mary Countess of Warwick had similar worries about her niece Lady Anne Barrington, the wife of Thomas Barrington, whose fondness for London reflected a taste for self-indulgence. As recorded in her diary Lady Warwick spent virtually a whole afternoon attempting to bring home to her the vanity of her life and begging her 'to repent, and live bettar' but failed to make any impression on her.[47]

Stage plays had always attracted Puritan hostility but early Restoration drama of the kind which appealed to a dissolute Court was capable of causing much greater offence than anything which had gone before. Writing to a kinsman of his in January 1668 Sir John Hobart asked him whether he thought it possible that wickedness could swell to such a monstrous size as to 'make poyson of the only salve and salvation' for men's souls. Some persons of quality, he went on, 'have put the passion of our blessed saviour in to Burlesques and, after the way of Hudebras, Inverted that sacred and soleme Tragedy into ridicule. This . . . I abhor'd to see, and trouble to think on.'[48] The attitude of Lady Elizabeth Langham, the second wife of Sir James Langham, to plays and recreational interests generally was probably not un-usual among the stricter sort of upper-class Puritans. While declining to be unduly critical of others who took a different view 'she never allowed herself to see any Masks, Interludes or Plays; or to play at Cards or the like Games'.[49]

On one occasion Sir Edward Harley told his son Robert that the first step to happiness lay in humble self-denial and the next in renouncing 'the Love of the world and the things thereof, as being Inconsistent with the Love of God'.[50] A capacity for self-denial was one of the attributes which Richard Baxter singled out in the sermon which he preached at the funeral of his friend Henry Ashurst who had made a fortune as a London merchant. Ashurst, he related, 'was a great disliker of proud vain attire, boasting speech and pomp, and inordinate worldly splendor, especially that which was chargeable, while so many thousands were in want . . . His Habit, his Furniture, his Provisions were all plain.'[51] Self-denial, however, is not a quality which can readily be associated with country squires who owned large mansions, gold and silver plate, pictures, tapestries, jewellery and coaches and employed considerable numbers of indoor and outdoor servants even if they often stipulated in their wills that they should be interred without pomp or vanity. This was a point which Puritan divines were not slow to appreciate. In an epistle dedicatory which prefaced one of his published works Thomas Manton told his godly patron, Alexander Popham, who would leave estates worth over £5,000 a year, that

> men of your rank and quality are liable to great Corruptions: they soon grow proud, sensual, oppressive, worldly, stubborn against the Word ... To a spiritual eye the condition is no way desirable but as it giveth fairer advantages of publique usefulness, and a more diffusive Charity.[52]

Some of the Puritan gentry were indeed generous benefactors by the standards of the time. Lady Dorothy Drake, it was said, 'visited the sicke, fed the hungry, clothed the naked'. Sir John Curzon charged his estate with a perpetual annuity of £20 for the binding of poor children as apprentices while Hungerford Dunch's bequests included the handsome sum of £600 for the relief of the poor in various parishes.[53] Lady Margaret Hungerford built a school and almshouses at Corsham in Wiltshire where the family had one of its principal seats and Lady Mary Armyne and Richard Winwood also provided funds for the erection and endowment of almshouses. When Thomas Foley the Worcestershire ironmaster drew up his will in January 1672 the school (or hospital as it was sometimes called) which he had built at Old Swinford already had 60 boys in its care and as a further act of charity he gave direction that £2,000 should be spent on the purchase of lands in order to ensure that it had adequate financial support. Sir John Langham established a school at Guilsborough in Northamptonshire, a few miles from his country seat at Cottesbrooke; and Sir John Yonge, Sir Richard Lucy, Sir John Davie and Thomas Trenchard all left money for the provision of schooling in their particular localities.[54] At the same time it was considered important that the wealthy Puritan should be neither proud nor supercilious. According to his anonymous biographer Sir Edward Harley's humility 'was conspicuous, for the poorest Christian had free access to him and a familiar conversation with him in his house and at his table, not insisting upon but declining those acknowledgments of respect and deference that were due to him.'[55]

14

PARLIAMENT AND THE NONCONFORMIST INTEREST

Some of those who were elected to the Long Parliament believed, and were encouraged in that belief by their clerical associates, that they had been called by God to do his work.[1] During the latter part of the century the concept of the godly MP (like that of the godly magistrate) still had its adherents, as did the conviction that divine providence was a potent factor in political affairs. Writing from London in December 1672 John Lord Crewe told his friend John Swinfen that a new session of Parliament was in prospect and added that 'Those who have abilities, calling and opportunity must to work. 'Tis for incouragement that those who serve God serve a Master who rewards good endeavours which have not good successe.'[2] In February 1674 Sir John Hobart, who was one of the knights of the shire for Norfolk, informed a kinsman of his that Parliament had been prorogued 'And with good (though sorrow-full) hearts we tooke leave of one another, with more feares then hope not to meet againe.' 'If', he went on, 'not a sparow falls to the ground without the immediate providence of god, Then cannot soe great a visitude as this happen but by his divine permission?'[3] When Robert Harley was elected for New Radnor in February 1690 his father wrote to him that 'This is from the Lord, therefor the intire Glory must be given unto God alone, not only in thankful Prays but in Ordering your Conversation aright.' Unfortunately the Herefordshire gentry had decided not to endorse Sir Edward's own candidature, much to his disgust, but in February 1693 he was successful in a by-election for one of the county seats and this led him to express his gratitude for 'the Holy Dispensation of the Lord in Causing the Election at Hereford . . . to pass' without any kind of opposition.[4]

After the Restoration some Puritan squires appeared reluctant to engage in political activities. In January 1661 Sir Roger Burgoyne observed in a letter to his friend Sir Ralph Verney that he might be urged to stand in the forthcoming elections but he feared that the expenditure involved would be very high 'which can not well be born by me in so low a Condition as I am in'. Although Burgoyne favoured some measure of toleration for Protestant dissenters he was content to leave such matters to others since he preferred the peace and security of a private life. In December 1674 he assured his friend that 'I shall not envy any so they will but let me live quietly at home.'[5] Sir Roger's attitude was not particularly common but in any event it was highly unlikely that men of Puritan outlook would ever again be a dominant force in the Commons. The choice of MPs, wrote Mary Foley, the wife of Paul Foley, in a letter addressed to Sir Edward Harley in May 1689, was a matter of concern to all the people of God and it was painful 'to see how many bad men gett in and how impossible it is to keep them out; the people are of such mercenary sperits that they will Choose none but those that bid most for it and take such methods that an honest man does not doe'.[6]

During the lifetime of the Cavalier Parliament, which was not finally dissolved until January 1679, the Presbyterian party in the Commons was always a relatively small grouping and the extent of its influence was therefore largely dependent on the parliamentary skills of its leaders and their ability to find common ground with the more moderate or uncommitted members of the Lower House.[7] Among those who had been returned in the general election of 1661 were John Swinfen, one of the most highly respected of the Presbyterian MPs, Hugh Boscawen and his brother Edward, Richard Hampden, Sir Edward Harley, Sir Anthony Irby, Sir John Barrington, Sir John Pelham, Sir John Fagg and Arthur Onslow. Significantly, they were all classified as 'worthy' in the political analysis of MPs which was undertaken by the Earl of Shaftesbury in 1677 while he was a prisoner in the Tower.[8] So far as religion was concerned the Presbyterian members wanted to put an end to the persecution of Protestant dissenters and to open up the Church of England to the kind of nonconformist ministers who served as their domestic chaplains and taught their children. Henry Booth, who was the son and heir of George Lord Delamere and the son-in-law of another Presbyterian, Sir James Langham, provides an insight into their thinking on this issue in some manuscript notes which were published after his death:

> though I can and do conform to what the Church enjoyns,
> yet I have so much charity as to believe that the Protestant
> Dissenters are in a direct way to Heaven, though they do not
> use the ceremonies commanded by the Church, provided
> that they worship God in fear, with a good Conscience, and
> live according to the Rule of his Word . . . I do acknowledge
> that Order and Unity are very necessary to be maintained;
> but surely that is not the right way to preserve Order and
> Unity in the Church by making things necessary that are
> indifferent . . . to keep Thousands out of the Church.

A man who was said to have love and charity for all Protestants,
Booth had nothing but contempt for those whom he termed
'Ceremony-Mongers' and considered that the ceremonies should
be treated as optional rather than mandatory.[9]

In the course of time more Puritan gentry were admitted to the
Cavalier Parliament as a result of by-elections, though this had
only a marginal impact in purely numerical terms. In October
1666 Sir Philip Harcourt, the leading Presbyterian in Oxfordshire,
was elected as one of the members for Boston in Lincolnshire, no
doubt through the influence of his uncle Sir Anthony Irby who
resided in the town and had been returned for the other seat at the
general election.[10] In January 1667 Sir Walter Yonge, who was
described as 'a very sober gentleman', emerged victorious from a
hotly contested by-election at Dartmouth in Devon. Sir Walter
was not only recommended by his friend Sir William Morice, who
was one of the Secretaries of State and a man of Puritan sympathies,
but enjoyed the support of most of the deputy lieutenants in the
eastern part of the county together with many of the 'fanatic
party'.[11] Thomas Trenchard's success in the by-election held at
Poole in Dorset in November 1670 owed much to the efforts of the
minister of the town, Samuel Hardy, who had once served as his
chaplain and was a legatee in the will which he had drawn up a
few months earlier. His parliamentary career, however, was
tragically cut short by his death in November 1671 when he was
still a young man.[12] In February 1673 there was a double victory
for the Presbyterians in East Anglia: Sir John Hobart was elected
for Norfolk and Sir Samuel Barnardiston for Suffolk, in both cases
with the backing of the nonconformist interest. According to one
account of the Suffolk by-election Sir Samuel was able to count on
the support of the dissenters, sectaries and factious persons of

every sort while the Court candidate, Lord Huntingtower, had the votes of the gentry and all 'the Church and loyal people'.[13]

In December 1675 a Herefordshire landowner, Herbert Aubrey, informed his brother-in-law Herbert Westfaling that, on the assumption that Parliament would shortly be dissolved, the 'close designing party' had met at Paul Foley's house at Stoke Edith in order to draw up plans for the next general election and had then sought endorsement of their choice of candidates from the Bishop of Hereford. The Bishop, however, had expressed strong reservations about the proposed candidates who included Viscount Scudamore and Sir Edward Harley for the county and Foley for Hereford. In Aubrey's view such men had no love for the Church nor, he suspected, were they well pleased with the State in its present form. It had been established, he went on, that Paul Foley's chaplain, Samuel Hopkins, had said that the bishops were a dead weight and that in parliamentary elections they usually exerted their influence on behalf of the Crown.[14]

In the first of the two general elections which were held in 1679 Paul Foley was duly returned for Hereford but Sir Edward Harley had to be content with a borough seat at New Radnor where he met with no opposition.[15] In February Philip Foley told his friend John Swinfen that at a meeting of the Worcestershire gentry his brother Thomas had refused to 'joine intrests' with Colonel Samuel Sandys as he considered him to be 'an ill man, a man in necessities and soe . . . under temptacions at Court' and had many other objections to him. In the end they had agreed that the two men should stand for the county on the basis that his brother would not oppose Sandys, 'tho' hee would not joine his Intrest, And that all the Gentlemen there and their Intrests should bee for them both'. Philip Foley was confident that his own candidature at Bewdley in Worcestershire would be successful since he had already had a promise of above 30 votes. In the two previous Parliaments of the reign Swinfen had represented the Staffordshire market town of Tamworth and his 'friends' there had decided once again to choose him as their candidate. 'I beseech you most passionately', wrote Foley, that 'you will suffer them to doe soe, God hath given you soe great abilities and soe proper for that worke that I am sure you cannot justyfie the hydeing them in a napkin.' In the event Thomas Foley, Philip Foley and Swinfen were all elected.[16]

Sir Walter Yonge, who had captured one of the Devon county

seats in 1667, had since died and his son and namesake was now in possession of both the estate and the baronetcy. The young man had also inherited his family's Puritan characteristics: according to Samuel Hieron, the nonconformist minister who lived at Honiton, he was a person of sober conversation who was regarded by 'the other party' as a fanatic. In February 1679 he was declared successful in the Honiton borough election along with a High Churchman, Sir Thomas Putt. Following the election Hieron reported the outcome to Philip Lord Wharton, referring to Putt as 'a neighboring persecutor'. Sir Walter, he wrote, had heard that John Hampden had been returned as a knight of the shire for Buckinghamshire 'and did mightily rejoyce at his election'. In a subsequent letter he told his aristocratic patron that Sir Walter 'is very kinde to me since that I was instrumental in his election' and added that he was even more convinced that he would make a good husband for one of Wharton's daughters.[17]

The new Parliament assembled on 6 March but was prorogued on 27 May and finally dissolved on 12 July. The announcement of the dissolution was accompanied by the news that another Parliament would be called for October and almost immediately Sir John Hobart, Sir John Holland and other Norfolk gentry attended a meeting at Lord Townshend's house, Raynham Hall, where they discussed the choice of candidates for the next general election. Horatio Lord Townshend, who had received some part of his education from a Puritan tutor, was a friend of Sir Edward Harley and employed a chaplain, William Michell, who had married Harley's sister Dorothy. His second wife, Mary Ashe, was described by his brother-in-law William Windham as 'a perfect pattern of great vertue and strict piety'. As lord lieutenant of Norfolk he had sought to maintain an even-handed approach in the face of an increasingly bitter conflict between the Court party and the Country party which was sometimes called Sir John Hobart's party. In 1676, however, he had been replaced as lord lieutenant by Robert Paston, Viscount Yarmouth, who headed the Court party and in December of that year we find Michell observing in a letter to Harley that his 'interest' was 'increasing by his clashing with the Court'. On 16 July Hobart informed one of his relatives that at the meeting which had been held William Windham, who had stood with him in the previous county election, had declined a similar offer 'with more obstinacy then reason' but stressed that 'as I never did yet refuse any occation to

serve my Countrey soe I shall not at this time'. In the end it was
agreed that Hobart should have Sir Peter Gleane, a 'new man', as
his partner in the county election. One of Hobart's main supporters
in Norwich was John Collinges, the Presbyterian divine who
served as chaplain to the Hobart family. Following Sir John's
death in 1683 he declared in a letter to his son Henry that 'I
beseech the God of Heaven that your Noble Father's and Lady
Mother's prayers may be answered unto your bosom and that
your country might repay to you all your father's merits of them.'
Hobart's enemies had not forgotten that he had once been a
member of Cromwell's Upper House and it was an obvious
political ploy to insinuate that he still had a high regard for the
Lord Protector and his cause. In August, however, Hobart and
Gleane were returned as knights of the shire.[18]

During the course of the summer John Swinfen received a
number of letters from his friends and associates about the
elections in various counties. John Lord Crewe urged him to stand
either at Lichfield or Tamworth 'that the Public may not want
your service . . . there being never more need of able and moderate
men since I was born'. Richard Hampden, who had joined in this
plea, subsequently gave him an account of the situation in
Buckinghamshire. 'This County', he wrote,

> have ever since the dissolution profess'd their willingness to
> adhere to their last choice, and to do it without charge to the
> persons to bee elected . . . My Borough of Wendover is very
> kind to mee, and I think there is like to be no change in the
> whole County unless Sir Richard Temple come in at Bucking-
> ham and a younger son of Mr Hoby's at Marlow.

At the same time he believed that there would be many changes in
other counties. Lady Elizabeth Wilbraham told her friend that at a
meeting of the Cheshire gentry it had been proposed that her
husband should partner Henry Booth, the son of Lord Delamere,
in the election for knights of the shire. Sir Thomas, however, had
made it clear that he would only stand for the county if he had the
general consent of the gentry; and although Booth had commended him he had felt obliged to decline the offer. Shortly
afterwards he appeared as a candidate in the Stafford borough
election after receiving an assurance that most of the burgesses
there were prepared to give him their support.[19]

On 13 August Swinfen informed Richard Hampden that he had

been very narrowly defeated in the Tamworth election, adding that 'I could hardly (my strength being decayed) beare such another dayes trouble.'[20] His friends, on the other hand, fared better: Hugh Boscawen was returned for the Cornish borough of Tregony, Sir Edward Harley for Herefordshire, Richard Hampden for Wendover and his son John for Buckinghamshire, Thomas Foley for Worcestershire, Paul Foley for Hereford, Philip Foley for Bewdley and Sir Thomas Wilbraham for Stafford. With the fear of popery acting as a powerful unifying agent there was every prospect of a solid Commons majority in favour of excluding the Duke of York from the succession to the throne. Faced with this threat the king prorogued the new Parliament and as a result was subjected to a major petitioning campaign in which the Earl of Shaftesbury had a key role.[21] The signatories of an Essex petition which was submitted in January 1680 included Sir Gobert Barrington and the two knights of the shire, Henry Mildmay and John Lemot Honywood. In his autobiography Sir John Bramston describes Honywood, who was the only surviving son of Sir Thomas Honywood the parliamentarian, as 'a chip of the old block' and attributes his success in the county election to Mildmay's influence and his 'stickinge to the factious partie'. When Mildmay, a zealous Puritan who was suspected of having republican sympathies, presented the petition the king remarked that he remembered 1640 and 1641; and Mildmay immediately riposted 'And I remember 59 and 60.' A few days later Parliament was again prorogued.[22]

Parliament finally assembled on 21 October 1680 but within three months it had been dissolved. If the policy of exclusion was the predominant issue there was also a substantial amount of ecclesiastical legislation concerned with the relief of Protestant dissenters, though in the event it came to nothing. The most important elements of this legislation were a comprehension bill whose object was to accommodate nonconformists of the Presbyterian persuasion within the Church of England and an indulgence bill which would have allowed some measure of freedom of worship to the Independents and other sects. Responsibility for the processing of these bills was assigned to a committee which included a significant number of Puritan MPs, among them Hugh Boscawen, John Hampden, Paul Foley, Sir John Hobart, Sir William Waller, Sir Roger Hill and Thomas Foley.[23] If the comprehension bill, or the bill for uniting the king's Protestant subjects as it was called, had reached the statute book it would have brought about a major relaxation of the requirements which had led to the mass exodus of ministers from the Church of England. Among other things, it would have been unnecessary for ministers to declare their assent and consent to the liturgy or to take the oath of canonical obedience; the surplice would have been worn only in cathedrals and royal chapels; and the sign of the cross in baptism and kneeling at communion would have been treated as optional ceremonies. In addition, ministers who had been ordained under Presbyterian auspices between 1642 and 1660 would have been able to hold church livings without having to submit to episcopal ordination.[24] Writing to his wife on 21 December Sir Edward Harley informed her, with obvious satisfaction, that the comprehension bill had just received a second reading in the Commons. Harley himself does not appear to have taken part in the second reading debate but Sir John Maynard, Hugh Boscawen, John Hampden and Paul Foley all spoke in favour of the bill. Presbyterian ministers, however, displayed little enthusiasm, not least since they had been attempting for some years to negotiate a form of union with the Independents. In March 1681 John Tillotson, who was then Dean of Canterbury, observed in a letter to a friend that 'There was litle progress made the last Parliament towards a reconciliation of Dissenters.' So far as he could establish neither the comprehension bill nor the indulgence bill had pleased any of the interested parties: 'The Bishops thought this too much, and the Dissenters too litle.'[25]

Shortly after Tillotson dispatched his letter a new Parliament met at Oxford following a general election in which the Country party had again achieved considerable success. On 26 March the Commons decided that another comprehension bill should be brought in but two days later the assembly was dissolved.[26] In September it was reported that in Sussex the local gentry had been meeting at Petworth to concert their plans for countering the Presbyterian campaign in the general election which was anticipated. The dissenting faction, for its part, had already drawn up a list of parliamentary candidates which included Sir John Fagg for the county, two of his sons for Steyning, his son-in-law Philip Gell (the heir of Sir John Gell the Derbyshire Presbyterian) for New Shoreham and Thomas Pelham (the eldest son of Sir John Pelham) for Lewes.[27] Contrary to general expectations the king declined to call another Parliament. The dissolution of the Oxford Parliament ushered in a period of extreme tension in which the non-conformists were savagely persecuted and the Whigs (as the king's political opponents were beginning to be called) found themselves coming under heavy pressure as men who were known to favour the policy of exclusion or suspected of conspiring against the Crown.[28]

Many of the Whig gentry had already been removed from the commission of the peace. In July 1678 the king had asked the Lord Chancellor to omit Sir John Hobart and Sir John Holland from the Norfolk commission of the peace, adding that 'ther is no objection against it but in disobligeing those sorte of people who will never be obliged'. From a list compiled in November 1680 it is clear that a substantial number of Puritan squires had been singled out in this way: they included, for example, Sir John Gell, Sir Philip Harcourt, Hugh Boscawen, Paul Foley and Thomas Jervoise. This meant, among other things, that there were fewer magistrates who were likely to take an indulgent view of the activities of Protestant nonconformists.[29]

One of the counties which were regarded as particularly dis-affected was Northamptonshire with its long-established reputa-tion for political and religious dissent. In 1682 a list was drawn up of the principal landowners in the county who in the event of another election could be expected to vote for exclusionist candi-dates who had sat in the Oxford Parliament. Headed by the Earl of Exeter who lived at Burghley House the list includes such wealthy Puritan gentry as Sir James Langham and his brother Sir William, Sir Edward Nichols the former parliamentarian and William Tate, the son of Zouch Tate.[30] In July 1682 the government was informed that some time after the dissolution of the Oxford Parliament Sir Edward Harley, Paul Foley and other political dissidents had attended a meeting at Hampton Court, the Herefordshire mansion of Thomas Coningsby, and that Harley had declared that the nation was suffering from slavery and injustice and that he believed that there was not a single lord lieutenant or militia officer in England who was not 'a damned papist'.[31] During the autumn a number of reports were received about the Duke of Monmouth's visit to north-west England where he was seeking to gather support. The Duke, it was said, had been entertained by Lord Delamere and his son Henry Booth and many other persons of quality had consorted with him, among them Sir John Bowyer, Sir Thomas Bellot, Sir Peter Stanley, Sir John Crewe and Sir

Thomas Wilbraham. At the end of September the king gave direction that some of these men, including Crewe and Booth, should be removed from the commission of the peace. Before the news came through of his dismissal Booth seized the opportunity, in his capacity as a Cheshire magistrate and *custos rotulorum*, to deliver a speech at the Knutsford sessions in which he claimed that it was well known that the Presbyterians had been responsible for restoring the king and expressed the view that the penal laws should no longer be put in execution against Protestant dissenters.[32]

The period between 1683 and 1688 was a time of gloom and anguish for men of property who were described by their enemies as Whigs, Presbyterians or dissenters or, more ominously, as 'the disaffected'. Stories of varying credibility about an assassination plot or plans for a general uprising led to the execution of Lord William Russell and Algernon Sidney, the suicide of the Earl of Essex and the imprisonment of Henry Booth, John Hampden, John Trenchard and Sir Samuel Barnardiston. Many other Presbyterian landowners, including relatives and friends of Hampden, fell under suspicion and had their houses searched for arms. In July 1683 the Earl of Lindsey told Sir Leoline Jenkins, one of the Principal Secretaries of State, that in his view it was likely that Sir William Ellis had been involved in the conspiracy which had been uncovered since he had voted for the exclusion of the Duke of York, had married Hampden's sister and had apparently been in frequent contact with the Duke of Monmouth. Sir William, he added, was the head of all the Presbyterians in Lincolnshire.[33] On the same day that the Earl dispatched his report some of the Surrey deputy lieutenants signed a warrant authorising the county militia to search for and take possession of arms in the house of Arthur Onslow who was considered to be 'dangerous to the Peace of this kingdome'. According to an account of his life and character Onslow was a man who sought to uphold 'the liberties of the people and the Protestant interest', and who generally voted against the Court.[34] In December Sir John Bowyer, who had been marked down as a factious person, took fright and submitted a grovelling letter of apology which the king directed should be kept as evidence that he had recanted. In this letter Sir John expressed his profound regret that he had voted for exclusion and offered a firm assurance that he would never do so again. Acknowledging that he had been too anxious to court popularity and secure the votes of the Staffordshire electorate he stressed that in future his primary concern would be to gain the favour and good opinion of the king. When Bowyer drew up his will in February 1688 he inserted the request that his wife should educate and train up his son

> in the Principles of Religion, I mean those of the Church of England as now by Law established, in the principles of true and unfeigned Loyalty towards the king but above all in the fear of God which will certainly teach him the other two.[35]

Sir Francis Drake, who had been removed from the Devonshire commission of the peace in 1675, was known to be strongly opposed to the persecution of Protestant nonconformists. In January 1684 it was alleged that some years earlier he had remarked that 'it would never be well with England till the Duke of York was excluded, and that he hoped to see him excluded'. When the Duke began proceedings against him he conveyed his estates to a relative and fled abroad and it was not until August 1687 that he was able to obtain a royal pardon.[36] In February 1684 John Hampden was tried in the Court of King's Bench on a charge of high misdemeanour. Gilbert Earl of Clare, Lord Paget, Thomas Pelham and Sir Henry Hobart appeared on his behalf and sought to demonstrate that it would have been completely out of character for him to have participated in any kind of conspiracy against the Crown. Lord Paget depicted him as 'an honest and a prudent man, a man of honour, and virtue, and integrity . . . a man that hath loved his study, and books, and a contemplative life'. Despite such testimony Hampden was found guilty, fined no less than £40,000 and committed to prison until payment had been made.[37] In contrast, John Trenchard was released from his imprisonment and allowed to return home to Somerset where, it was reported, he received a rapturous welcome from the Anabaptists, sectaries and other malcontents.[38]

The general election which followed hard on the heels of James II's accession in February 1685 resulted in a heavy defeat for the Whigs which was due not only to such measures as the issue of new borough charters but to the aggressive campaign tactics of the Court party. In the Surrey county election Arthur Onslow and his partner George Evelyn appeared to be heading for victory but were thwarted by the 'arbitrary and partial proceedings' of the sheriff and the physical intimidation of their supporters.[39] On 19

May, the day on which the new Parliament assembled, instructions were issued for the apprehension of a number of Whigs, among them Sir Walter Yonge, Sir William Courtenay and John Trenchard. Three weeks later the Duke of Monmouth launched his rebellion in the West Country but few persons of substance were disposed to join him. As a precautionary measure the government ordered the arrest of many of its political opponents, though as a general rule they were soon released. In a letter from the king the deputy lieutenants for the East Riding of Yorkshire were required to seize all disaffected and suspicious persons, including Sir William Strickland (whose grandfather had been a member of the Rump), Sir Francis Boynton and his son William; and in other counties such leading Presbyterians as Hugh Boscawen, Sir John Bowyer, John Swinfen, Sir Edward Harley, Thomas Foley and his brother Paul were all taken into custody. Harley, who spent some time under constraint in Hereford, asked his wife and family to 'Pray incessantly for the church and this poor sinful Nation.' In a memorandum recording his experience he wrote that during his confinement he had enjoyed inward peace and quietness of mind; that he had been treated with great civility, even to the extent of being allowed to go to church where he had heard several good sermons; and that on 15 July 'The goodnes of God brought mee in peace to my Family at Bramton.'[40] Richard Norton, whose survival instincts had stood him in good stead over the years, feared that he would also be arrested and asked the Earl of Middleton, who was one of the Principal Secretaries of State, to assure the king that 'I have ever had a love for his person since I had the honor to know him . . . and that since he came to the Throne I have been, Am, and ever will be as dutyfull a subject as he may Justly expect me to be.'[41]

Attempts to prove that John Hampden had played a key part in the Monmouth conspiracy led to fears that he would finish up on the block. In November Philip Henry the nonconformist divine was informed that Francis Tallents was proving to be a great comfort to Richard Hampden and his wife in their present troubles: their son was a close prisoner in the Tower and many were 'expecting the worst concerning him'. On the assumption that it was the only way of saving his life he pleaded guilty and threw himself on the mercy of the king; and in February 1686 he was granted a pardon which was 'ample and full as to fines, estate, life &c'.[42] Henry Booth, who had recently inherited the title of Lord Delamere, was accused of attempting to organise an uprising in Cheshire in support of the Duke. Thomas Jolly, an Independent minister who was himself imprisoned for a time, wrote that 'Prayer was made solemnly and generally, yea, incessantly for the Ld. Delamere and other worthies whose lives were industriously sought after and were in most apparent hazard.' When he was acquitted by the House of Lords on 14 January 1686 another nonconformist minister, Henry Newcome, noted in his diary that on hearing the news he 'could do little all day for the thoughts of the unexpected mercy' but felt that the drinking of Lord Delamere's health was 'a poor way of rejoicing'.[43]

In the latter part of 1687 there were strong rumours that the king would soon be calling a new Parliament. By the Declaration of Indulgence issued on 4 April he had granted freedom of worship to both Catholic and Protestant dissenters but he was now anxious to secure parliamentary approval for the repeal of the Test Acts and the penal laws. For this purpose he needed a submissive Parliament which would be ready to further his aims and regarded it as axiomatic that the Whigs with their nonconformist connections would be more amenable than the Tories who were identified with the Church interest. The Whigs, however, were understandably concerned about the implications of the king's pro-Catholic policy and the situation was further complicated by the fact that there was talk of a coalition between sober Anglicans and moderate dissenters in defence of the Church against the threat of popery and on the basis that concessions would be forthcoming for Protestant nonconformists.[44] John Swinfen was at pains to emphasise in discussions with Philip Foley and Robert Harley that it was important that the Whigs should make a good showing in the election; that there was a need for MPs who were staunch rather than compliant; and that Churchmen could not be trusted. Shortly after this Roger Morrice was writing in a memorandum book that the Dean and Chapter of Lichfield cathedral were agreed that Swinfen, who lived in the neighbourhood, was 'the fittest man to serve them for they now see they were mistaken in him, and understand by information hence that he was always against the king's death, That he has carryed in all Parliaments with great moderation and Temper'.[45] At the beginning of October there was a meeting of the Worcestershire gentry about the choice of candidates for the county election and this was the occasion for a special religious exercise at Witley

Court, the home of Thomas Foley. In a letter addressed to his father Robert Harley related that Foley's chaplain, Nathaniel Oldfield, had begun with a prayer, George Nelson (the minister of Oddingley) had preached and prayed and Edward Primrose (a nonconformist divine) had concluded with a sermon and prayer. And Harley added that 'I hope God will hear the supplications of his servants for his church, and for our selves.'[46]

Doubts about the dependability of the Whigs[47] led the king to hesitate over the calling of a new Parliament. In the meantime he embarked on the wholesale replacement of Tories by Whigs as deputy lieutenants and justices of the peace in the various counties. Sir John Bramston writes that Henry Mildmay, Sir Gobert Barrington and others 'of the same stamp and principles' were put into the Essex commission of the peace, 'the Kinge judgeinge that out of hatred to the Church of England, and out of desire to have the penal laws abrogated, they will also promote the takeing away the test too'. In February 1688 Edward Harley, another of Sir Edward's sons, told his father that the whole operation was managed by a private committee of dissenters and that those whom they employed 'to bring them in lists do it so impartially that they have put in for most counties the persons of the best estates and for the most part Churchmen' by which he clearly meant that sectaries had largely been excluded.[48] The second Declaration of Indulgence which was issued on 27 April indicated that it was still the king's intention to summon a new Parliament. But although the king's agents were reporting that some Presbyterian gentry such as Richard Hampden would be prepared to vote for the repeal of both the Test Acts and the penal laws it is unlikely that there would have been any significant support from the Whigs for Catholic emancipation.[49] In Derbyshire there was an electoral pact, or 'compromise' as it was called, between the Churchmen and the dissenters which covered all four parliamentary seats. One of the main architects of the pact was Sir John Gell, the leading Presbyterian in the county, who had not sat in any Parliament since the Restoration. In August he was informed that for the 'compromise' at Derby the Churchmen had put forward John Coke of Melbourne, 'a Modderate man and Steddy', as their candidate but that there was some disagreement between them and Sir John's 'friends' over the choice of candidate for the other borough seat. Accordingly his correspondent suggested that he should recommend to his 'friends' either his son Philip, his son-in-law William Eyre or Robert Wilmot, any of whom would probably be readily accepted by the Churchmen.[50]

Writs for an election were issued in September but they were never executed. On 5 November the Prince of Orange arrived in the West Country and shortly afterwards Lord Delamere delivered a speech to his Cheshire tenants in which he urged them to join him in supporting the Prince in an enterprise which would secure the restoration of 'religion and liberty'.[51] In Herefordshire Sir Edward Harley and his son Robert took up arms for 'the Gospel and our Countrey'. On 13 December Anne Pye was writing to her cousin Abigail Harley that she had read in public newsletters that they had gone to meet other gentlemen who had declared for the Prince: 'thank god', she added, 'there is like to be noe fighting, al people being of a mind'.[52]

15

FIN DE SIECLE

For the nonconformists the general election which took place in January 1689 was of crucial importance since the revolution had opened up the possibility of a new religious settlement which was sanctioned by parliamentary statute. Thomas Jolly, an Independent minister, hastened to Lancaster for the election of the knights of the shire and was overjoyed that his friend Sir Charles Hoghton 'was chosen as freely as possible'. Although some favoured a rival candidate, Lord Brandon, 'the dissenters were perswaded concerning him and soe did carry it'.[1] Other Presbyterians who were elected included Richard and John Hampden, Hugh Boscawen, Sir Edward Harley, Thomas and Paul Foley, Sir John Pelham and his son Thomas, Sir Henry Ashurst, Sir John Gell and Sir Walter Yonge. Gell died on 8 February, 'to the great loss of the kingdome' as Roger Morrice put it, and the Earl of Devonshire, who was the leading Whig magnate in Derbyshire, endorsed the nomination of his son Philip as a candidate in the resulting by-election while expressing the hope that there were no reservations about his principles and ability. A political associate of the Gells, Cornelius Clarke, told Sir Philip (who was duly elected) that he rejoiced that the county had chosen 'soe worthy a man, the sonn of such a father cannot vote amisse in Parliement ffollowing his example'.[2] In another by-election Robert Harley was returned for the Cornish borough of Tregony in place of Charles Boscawen. When informing his son that he had been elected unanimously (a result which was entirely due to the influence of the Boscawen family) Sir Edward added that he prayed to God that he would endow him 'with every good and perfect gift that you may with Godly Sincerity be faithful and serviceable in this great Occasion'.[3]

Although the Presbyterian candidates had done far better than in the 1685 election those MPs who had close ties with the nonconformists were still only a small minority and much would therefore depend on the attitude of moderate Anglicans, whether Whigs or Tories. In the event it was the House of Lords which took the initiative over the settlement of religion. On 11 March two ecclesiastical bills were introduced in the Upper House: a comprehension bill which had its origins in a meeting of senior clergy at the house of Dr Edward Stillingfleet, the Dean of St Paul's, and an indulgence bill on similar lines to that which had been drafted in 1680.[4] On 1 April the House of Commons decided to commission its own comprehension bill and entrusted its preparation to a committee which included John Hampden, who acted as chairman, Hugh Boscawen, Paul Foley, Sir Edward Harley and Thomas Foley.[5] The committee took the comprehension bill of 1680 as its model and produced a bill which was far more radical in nature than the Lords bill. On 9 April Charles Hatton wrote in a letter to his brother Lord Hatton that the Commons had 'brought in a Comprehension Bill of their owne, if possible, more favourable to the fanaticks then yours and more destructive' to the Church of England.[6] In fact most MPs were reluctant to accept any form of comprehension and in a deal which was struck between the Whig and Tory leaders it was agreed that this method of approach should be abandoned and that instead the aim should be to secure the passage of an act based on the indulgence bill which had begun life in the Lords. The Commons appointed a committee for processing the bill and among those chosen to serve on it were John Hampden, Hugh Boscawen, Sir Walter Yonge, Richard Hampden, Thomas Foley, Paul Foley, Sir William Ellis and Sir Thomas Barnardiston. Although the progress of the bill was far from smooth it finally received the royal assent on 24 May.[7]

The Toleration Act, as it was generally known, was regarded by many High Churchmen as an unmitigated disaster. Humphrey Prideaux, the Prebendary of Norwich, observed that 'as to the Toleration Act, unless there be some regulation in it, in a short time it will turn halfe the nation into downe right athiesme'.[8] For the most part, however, the Puritan gentry appear to have been reasonably well satisfied with the religious settlement which had emerged. While they would have preferred a settlement based on the principle of comprehension they had probably had few illusions about the strength of the opposition. On 16 May, the day after the Commons had given a second reading to the indulgence bill, James Wittewronge was reporting to his father, Sir John, that 'yesterday the Parliament was upon the bill about religion, and have voted what I have often heard you say, viz that those only shal be punished that doe not goe to Church or to some other publike meeting wher God is worshipped, and it shal be at every one's liberty wher they will goe'.[9] 'Thanks be to God', wrote Robert Harley on 25 May, 'the King yesterday passed the Bill of Indulgence'. One of his father's main regrets was that attempts to bring about the abolition of the sacramental test for office-holders had proved unsuccessful: in a note which bears the date 3 December 1692 he commented that 'It would be Hopeful if the Sacramental Test might not remain a Sad profanation of the Highest and most awful Spiritual Mysterie of Religion.'[10] In May 1692 John Hampden told his friend Francis Tallents that he would be very much in favour of a union of all Protestants in England if he felt that it could be achieved. However, he had laid aside all thoughts of comprehension once it had become clear to him that 'the design of some who drove it was only to destroy obliquely, and by a side-wind, what had been gain'd, at a favourable time, in the Act of Toleration'. Half a loaf was better than no bread and it would be prudent to settle for liberty of conscience.[11]

The Toleration Act provided relief from the penal laws for all Protestant dissenters who were willing to subscribe to the Thirty Nine Articles except for those relating to such matters as the ceremonies and ordination of priests which were specifically excluded from the requirement. By virtue of the Act non-conformist congregations were able to worship in their own way in meeting houses which were licensed for this purpose provided the doors were left unlocked while their meetings were in progress.[12] From 1689 onwards many requests for licences were received but in contrast with the kind of response which the Declaration of Indulgence of 1672 had generated[13] very few gentry families were prepared to have their houses or private chapels registered as nonconformist meeting-places. During the two decades following the passage of the Toleration Act only four county families, all seated in northern England, appear to have asked for licences: the Hoghtons of Hoghton Tower in Lancashire, the Crewes of Utkinton Hall, the Duckenfields of Duckenfield in Cheshire and the Rodes family of Great Houghton in the West Riding of Yorkshire.[14]

Lady Sarah Hoghton, the widow of Sir Richard Hoghton, was described by a dissenting minister as 'a great patroness of religion and non-conformity'. In January 1690 she obtained a licence for Dutton Hall, the house in Cheshire where she was then living, while in October 1693 a licence was issued for another house of hers in the same county. Her son, Sir Charles, secured licences for his houses in Lancashire, the first for Walton Hall, the ancient seat of the family, in July 1689 (though in this case the recipient of the licence was Thomas Key, a nonconformist minister who enjoyed his patronage) and the other for his fortified Elizabethan mansion, Hoghton Tower, in January 1703. It is perhaps indicative of his general attitude to the Church of England that as patron of the parish church in the neighbouring town of Preston he allowed the mayor to select a new minister when a vacancy occurred.[15]

The licence for Utkinton Hall, which was issued in January 1690, contained no reference to the owner, Sir John Crewe, who may possibly have asked for his name to be omitted. It was not the first occasion on which the hall had been registered as a place for nonconformist worship: as we have already seen, a licence had been procured when the Declaration of Indulgence was published in 1672. A domestic chapel had been consecrated by the Bishop of Chester in 1635 but it seems likely that a new building was erected since Crewe recorded in a manuscript journal that on 17 November 1700 the first sermon was preached in Utkinton chapel. The preacher on this occasion can be identified as Jonathan Harvie, a young Congregational minister whose father had been ejected from a Cheshire living. Sir John, who died childless in 1711, was buried in his parish church of Tarporley where his memorial proclaims that

> He was a lover of the constitution, both in Church and State, and consequently an enemy to popery and arbitrary government: steadfast to the establisht religion, but charitable to such as dissented from it, who he thought were to be won over rather by mildness than severity, by the force of reason than persecution. He was exemplary in his devotions, and carefull to have his family joyn with him twice a day therein . . . He strenuously maintain'd the Revolution principles.[16]

For a time the Duckenfields had given shelter to an Independent congregation but Sir Robert Duckenfield and his son Sir Charles preferred the Presbyterian form of worship. Samuel Angier, who began his ministry at Duckenfield in 1681, had been ordained at a ceremony in Manchester at which both Presbyterian and Congregational ministers had been present. A 'judicious and lively preacher', he proved so popular that from 1686 he held his meetings in a large barn which he fitted up for the purpose. In July 1689 he secured a licence for his house at Duckenfield while in October 1695 Sir Robert acquired two licences, one for Duckenfield Hall and the other for his domestic chapel where members of the family were baptised and buried. Some years later, in April 1707, Sir Robert granted a plot of land on which a new chapel was to be built for the use, as he put it, of 'a Protestant Presbyterian Minister of the Gospel of our Lord Jesus Christ, Dissenting from the Church of England'. A licence for the 'newly erected chapel' at Duckenfield was issued in January 1708 and on 19 August Samuel Angier, as its first minister, preached an inaugural sermon.[17]

At Great Houghton the domestic chapel built by Sir Edward Rodes in 1650 appears to have been capable of accommodating a congregation of at least 60 persons. Since it had been used for nonconformist worship for many years the grant of a licence in August 1689 for William Rodes's mansion house and chapel did little more than regularise existing practice. Rodes died five years later, confidently expecting that he would be saved so that he could praise and sing alleluia to 'God the Father, Son and holy Ghost, three Persons but one God, for ever and ever'. The nonconformist tradition, however, was maintained after his death and may even have survived the extinction of the male line of the family in 1740.[18]

In a report on nonconformist congregations which was compiled during the years 1715 to 1729 the chapel at Duckenfield was said to have 887 and Hoghton Tower 180 'hearers'. The report also reveals that two other gentry families with a Puritan lineage had taken advantage of the liberty of conscience provided by the Act of Toleration. At Sawbridgeworth in Hertfordshire Sir Strange Jocelyn of Hyde Hall was the patron of a Presbyterian congregation of 130 persons while at Belsay in Northumberland Sir John Middleton's chaplain, Cumberbach Leech, had an additional role as the pastor of a congregation numbering 300.[19]

While it would be tempting to regard the Toleration Act as a major watershed for the Puritan gentry the indications are that few of them drew the conclusion that they were now faced with a stark choice between orthodox Anglicanism and out-and-out

THE PURITAN GENTRY BESIEGED, 1650–1700

nonconformity. Generally, they remained faithful to the religious
practices which they had followed before the passage of the Act,
though in this new situation they no doubt felt more comfortable
about their association with dissenting ministers. At Glassenbury
in Kent the Roberts family continued to use their domestic chapel
for nonconformist worship without apparently considering it
necessary to go to the lengths of applying for a licence. When Dr
Samuel Annesley the Presbyterian divine published an account of
the life of Thomas Brand, who had once been their chaplain, in
1692 he dedicated it to Lady Bridget Roberts and referred
approvingly to their house as 'the Sanctuary for Divine Worship,
for the spreading of Religion' through the county.[20] In July 1690 a
Common Fund was established for the support of Presbyterian
and Congregational ministers and among the early subscribers
were Sir Henry Ashurst, Thomas Foley and Philip Foley. During
the years 1690 to 1692 the managers of the Fund compiled a report
on the financial circumstances of individual ministers which was
based on information received from correspondents in various
parts of the country. Although the report is far from exhaustive it
lists a considerable number of persons of quality who had
nonconformist chaplains, including Richard Hampden, Lady
Katherine Irby, Lady Essex Cheke, Sir William Ashurst, Sir Robert
Pye, Sir Francis Masham, Lady Dorothy Barrington and Sir
Thomas Wilbraham.[21] Lady Irby, who was the widow of Sir
Anthony Irby, lived in Westminster and was on close terms with
Dr Annesley, Vincent Alsop, Daniel Burgess, Richard Stretton and
other Presbyterian divines who exercised their ministry in the
capital. In 1705 her grandson Sir Edward Irby was described as a
nonconformist.[22]

For the Harleys, as for many of the Puritan gentry, the need to
remain in communion with the Church must have appeared self-
evident. At the same time they continued to maintain contact with
nonconformist divines, among them Francis Tallents who had a
meeting house in Shrewsbury, John Weaver of Hereford, William
Woodward of Leominster and Chewning Blackmore who had
been a student at John Woodhouse's academy at Sheriff Hales. Sir
Edward was in correspondence with Tallents over such matters as
the validity of Presbyterian orders and the relief of poor ministers
and their families. In December 1695 Tallents told his friend that
'we are very sensible of the pains and inconveniences You endure
in attending the House, but it's for God, and that sweetens all to

You'.[23] Writing to Blackmore in July 1692 Edward Harley referred to the loss of William Woodward, who had recently died, as a great wound which he feared would not easily be healed. It was a matter of major concern, he went on, that the congregation at Leominster should be provided with a person of ability and prudence. Some members of Woodward's flock had been to see him and had emphasised that a minister who had been suggested as his successor was not generally well liked and would be unable to keep the congregation together. Shortly afterwards the two men hastened to Leominster to discuss the situation. In October Sir Edward was seeking to persuade Blackmore to continue his ministry at Worcester: it was necessary, he stressed, to settle the Gospel, 'the Palladium of our Nation', and in his view there was no other place 'to which you are so much engag'd with a clear affectionat Cal from the People that much need you'.[24] Weaver and Blackmore sometimes participated in spiritual exercises at Brampton Castle and also contributed to the monthly lecture programme at Knighton in the adjoining county of Radnor. The Harleys took a close personal interest in the Knighton lectureship arrangements which had been formally approved by Bishop Croft of Hereford in 1665 on the clear understanding that only beneficed ministers would be included in the schedule of preachers. On one occasion Sir Edward's daughter Martha asked Blackmore to let her know whether he would be coming to preach in April or May so that she could give Mr Weaver reasonable notice and added that 'the Lord I trust will voutsafe his blessing and make them blessed days of newbirth'. Subsequently Blackmore was employed for a time as tutor to Paul Foley's grandson Thomas.[25]

In February 1690 an Anglican divine, Richard Burd, told his friend Thomas Jervoise, the son of a Hampshire squire, that 'I desire that no Tory Churchman nor any violent Whig may ever sit in the House again, but only such that fear God, honour the King, support the church and study an union between us and the dissenters.' This, however, proved to be wishful thinking. After the passage of the Toleration Act, writes Gilbert Burnet, the clergy began 'to show an implacable hatred to the nonconformists, and seemed to wish for an occasion to renew old severities against them'.[26] In parliamentary elections the religious divisions acquired a new intensity. Edward Harley's account of the elections which took place in the early months of 1690, as retailed in letters to his father, makes it clear that the days of electoral pacts between the

Churchmen and the dissenting interest were well and truly over. The clergy, he declared, were taking more pains in procuring votes than they had ever done over the saving of souls. It seemed very ominous to him that they had 'in a manner excommunicated from their church the greatest part of the unspotted gentry of the Nation'. In all places they were exerting 'their utmost vigour', especially against Sir John Maynard in Devon and Henry Mildmay in Essex. The Bishop of London had gone down to Essex to act as commander-in-chief against Mildmay while 'not above 4 parsons' had voted for Sir John. In Cornwall Hugh Boscawen was vigorously opposed by the Bishop of Exeter 'who has made a very considerable interest against him'.[27]

In the Essex election the Earl of Oxford, who was lord lieutenant of the county, the Earl of Manchester and Lord FitzWalter appeared on behalf of Henry Mildmay and his partner Sir Francis Masham while the other candidates, Sir Eliab Harvey and Sir Anthony Abdy, had the backing of the Bishop of London and the Earl of Dorset. On 11 March the voting went in favour of Mildmay and Masham who were also able to count on the support of what Sir John Bramston uncharitably called 'the fanatick and discontented partie'. One explanation which was offered for their success was that the clergy had been unable to travel to Chelmsford for the election as a special fast had been arranged for the following day. In addition, it was reported that some of the electors had talked of the severity which Abdy had shown towards Protestant dissenters and had therefore chosen to vote for Masham, a person of 'known candour and moderation'.[28]

Whig candidates were described by their political opponents as Commonwealth men, republicans and enemies of the Church. In November 1693 Humphrey Prideaux, the Prebendary of Norwich, observed in a letter to a friend that whenever there was a new Parliament the knights of the shire for Norfolk would be Sir Henry Hobart and Sir Roger Potts and those for Suffolk Sir Samuel Barnardiston and Sir Gervase Elwes, 'all stiffe Republicarians'.[29] Sometimes an attempt was made to damage a candidate's reputation by claiming that he attended nonconformist meetings. In October 1695 Thomas Foley, the son of Paul Foley, gave his kinsman Robert Harley an account of the tactics which he was having to contend with as a candidate for the Herefordshire borough of Weobley. One of his adversaries was saying that 'he will nail up the meeting house doors; that I constantly go to them

... and hopes they will not be for one so much against the church as I'. He was sure, however, that this had done him little harm and he was not disposed 'to deny anything I do'.[30]

If Churchmen and dissenters were ranged on opposite sides in parliamentary elections they were generally agreed thaat the country was faced with a spiritual and moral crisis, though they viewed the causes from rather different perspectives. When inaugurating his primary visitation in 1692 Bishop Kidder of Bath and Wells instructed his clergy to preach frequently 'against the reigning sins of the time, against drunkenness, common swearing, uncleanness, profanation of the Lord's day, neglect of the publick worship of God, of publick prayers and sacraments'. Among other things, the sacrament of the Lord's Supper was 'notoriously neglected by the People to the great decay of Christian Piety'.[31] In 1699 John Howe the Presbyterian divine published the sermon he had delivered at the funeral of Dr William Bates and in dedicating it to the Duke of Bedford, who had been the deceased's patron, took the opportunity to express his grave concern about the state of the nation. 'Serious Piety and Christianity', he complained, 'Languishes every-where ... Our Obduration and insensible Stupidity portends a deadly Darkness to be drawing on.' Atheism, scepticism, infidelity, worldliness and formality had 'quite swallowed up our Religion'.[32] Puritan-minded gentry were equally pessimistic. To Sir Henry Ashurst it was a degenerate and licentious age, though he acknowledged that there were some who were notable for their sincere piety in 'all the different Parties that we are so unhappily broken into'.[33] In their private correspondence Sir Edward Harley and his family frequently gave vent to their feelings about the evils of post-Restoration England:

> a deluge of Misery is following that flood of prophanes and Hatred of Religion which has now so long covered the Land ... profane Iniqity abounds and Daies appoynted for Imploring Mercy from God are contemned ... There are many Prognostics of God's displeasure, Sin being Every where an Augury against us ... We ought to pray that the mercy of the Lord may save a wretched and sinful Nation.[34]

In March 1695 Sir James Langham, who had no male issue, was delighted to hear that his nephew John Langham's wife had given birth to a son and so restored 'the Hopes of the Resurrection of our Name'. In a letter to her husband he told him that he had little doubt that the child would live and that he envisaged that 'by the Pious Formations of his many Relations, whose nigh and dear Care he will be, he is likely to be that Example of Vertue this depraved Age never more wanted than in these low Dregs of it'.[35] In a work which was eventually published in 1705 Lady Damaris Masham, the wife of Sir Francis Masham, wrote that 'this heretofore sober Nation has been debauch'd from Principles of Vertue and Religion to such an excess of Vice and Prophaneness that it has been Fashionable to have no shame of the grossest Immoralities; and Men have thought even to recommend themselves by avow'd Impiety'. In these circumstances it was necessary for the laws against immorality and profaneness to be vigorously executed and for proper care to be taken of education. Parents, she argued, had neglected to give their children any religious instruction or had instructed them very badly; and too many persons of quality permitted their daughters to indulge themselves in a 'Ridiculous Circle of Diversions'.[36]

One of the most striking developments during the 1690s was the growth of a moral reform movement which was the product both of religious zeal and concern about social disorder. Some of those involved were Puritan gentry, among them the Harleys, Hugh Boscawen and Sir Thomas Roberts, but many were Anglicans of the more conventional sort who had no connection with the nonconformist interest.[37] At the same time the Crown was seeking to promote a reformation of manners by means of proclamations and directions to the bishops and justices of the peace. In a series of letters to his father Edward Harley periodically reported from London on the efforts which were being made to improve the morals of the populace at large. The Queen, he wrote in July 1691, had sent a letter to the Middlesex justices requiring them to take all necessary steps for the suppression of profane swearing, the profanation of the Lord's Day and the sin of drunkenness; and later he expressed the hope that the Herefordshire magistrates would follow the example of Middlesex and other counties where action was already in hand. In January 1692 he informed his father that a proclamation against vice and debauchery was being issued while in December he had news of a parliamentary bill in which the penalties laid down for profane swearing varied according to the social rank of the offender. Sir Edward, for his part, considered that it would be unwise to meddle with the existing legislation relating to the Lord's Day and that the principal crimes for which new legislation was needed were profane swearing, whoring and drunkenness.[38]

From 1691 onwards a considerable number of voluntary societies for the reformation of manners were established, many of them in London and Middlesex. Edward Harley was a member of a London society formed in June 1693 for the purpose of promoting the execution of the laws against profaneness and debauchery. At the outset it was agreed that members of the society would meet once a week; that they would act as in the cause of Almighty God; and that they would consider the allegations of informers and summon the accused to appear before them to present their defence. In a paper which was offered to dissenting ministers they related that many hundreds had been convicted 'which hath produced a visible Reformation as to some scandalous crimes in many parts of the City and Suburbs' but thousands more were daily breaking the law. Accordingly they proposed that the nonconformist ministers should ask members of their congregations to act as informers.[39] In May 1697 John Woodhouse, who had recently closed his academy at Sheriff Hales, preached a sermon at Salters Hall in the presence of members of the London and Westminster societies for the re-formation of manners. As he reminded his listeners the business of the day was 'to stir up a Spirit for Reformation of the Lives and Manners of the Generation wherein we live'.[40]

In Parliament the moral reformers achieved only limited success in their efforts to secure the passage of new legislation. In February 1695 a Commons committee which included Edward Harley, Hugh Boscawen, Sir Francis Masham and Sir Henry Ashurst took on responsibility for processing a bill for the more effectual suppressing of profane cursing and swearing and an amended version received the royal assent on 23 April. The act introduced a two-tier fining system: for a first offence the magistrates were to impose a fine of one shilling on servants, day labourers and common seamen while all other persons were required to pay two shillings.[41] Subsequently, in February 1698, the Commons agreed that Sir John Philipps, one of the most fanatical of the moral reformers, and Edward Harley should prepare legislation for the suppression of profaneness, immorality and debauchery. On 12 March Harley informed his father that the bill for suppressing blasphemy and profaneness (as it was now called) had been given a second reading despite the attempts of many MPs to put off the debate for a week. Some three weeks later Sarah Foley, his future wife, was writing to Sir Edward that she was very glad to hear that 'the bill against prophanes is past your House, the Lord make it of use'. Sir Edward himself became more directly involved when he was added to a committee which had been given the task of drawing up reasons for rejecting certain amendments proposed by the Lords. The act which finally emerged contained no reference to immorality or debauchery. Its specific object was the punishment of any persons who by writing, printing, teaching or 'advised' speaking 'deny any of the persons in the Holy Trinity to be God or shal assert or maintain there are more Gods than One or shal deny the Christian Religion to be true or the Holy Scriptures of the Old and New Testaments to be of Divine Authority'.[42]

New thinking, whether atheistic in nature or within the general framework of Christian theology, had very little impact on upper-class men and women who had been given a strict Calvinistic upbringing. Although John Hampden went through a freethinking phase in the 1680s[43] this was a highly unusual episode for a person of his background. The emphasis which Lady Damaris Masham placed on the importance of reason in matters of religion was a product of special factors. Lady Masham was a highly intelligent woman with an inquiring mind and catholic tastes in literature. More significantly, she was a daughter of Ralph Cudworth the Cambridge Platonist and a friend of John Locke who lived for some years with the Mashams at Otes Hall in Essex. 'I Assure you', she told Locke, 'the Vehicles of the Platonists (whatever the Vortices of Des Cartes were) were Always much more my Favourites than the Muses.' Her preference for 'rational religion' led her to reject scepticism, which she described as 'the proper Disease of our Age', and uphold the claims of Protestantism. In a work published anonymously in 1696 she wrote that

> I fear all Mankind (before this present Age) lived and died Idolaters, and the greatest part for the future will do so . . . Can any Rational Man, not bred up in the bigotry of Popery, ever perswade himself that such a Religion can be from God?'[44]

Advances in scientific knowledge were not regarded as a threat to fundamental Christian beliefs but as a means of reinforcing them. Chewning Blackmore the nonconformist divine assured his pupil Thomas Foley that 'knowledge it self is not to be despised, I mean all usefull knowledg that is attainable in this Life'. Learning and piety were 'not contrary and inconsistent, but subordinate'.[45] Many dissenting ministers who earned a living as tutors or schoolmasters taught mathematics and other scientific subjects and Charles Morton's academy at Newington Green was particularly well equipped for experimental work.[46] Sir John Hartopp had a taste for universal knowledge, applied his mind to many different branches of science and engaged in 'mathematical speculations and practices'. Much of his time, however, was spent in studying his Bible which 'lay before him Night and Day'.[47] In 1662 Sir Edward Harley's library contained works on chemistry, scientific method and experimental philosophy as well as many books on religion. On the other hand, his accounts for the years 1696 to 1698 indicate that his purchases from booksellers mainly consisted of religious works by nonconformist divines and authors of an earlier generation together with publications listed as 'Holwell's Prophecies', 'Partridge's Prophecies' and 'Mother Shipton's Prophecy'.[48]

According to a contemporary Sir Edward's studies were largely concerned with the kind of knowledge 'which this Generation despises'. His research into the mysteries of the Christian religion was 'strict and impartiall'; but his faith was 'the faith of God's elect and of the operation of God'.[49] In 1695 he published *A Scriptural and Rational Account of the Christian Religion* in which he revealed the strength of his Puritan convictions. His model was a pure undefiled Christian religion which was free from 'all Profaneness, Superstition and Will-Worship'. Election, vocation, justification and sanctification were inseparable; and God was all-sufficient. In a spirited response to what he regarded as the gravest threats to true religion he condemned false teachers who were 'privily introducing damnable heresies, even denying the Lord that bought them'; the 'Epicurean sensualists' who 'corrupt themselves to be like natural Brute Beasts'; and the profane who 'take up a scoffing Name of Deist to act the Atheist'. In correspondence with members of his family Harley had frequently referred to the workings of divine providence and he made it clear to his readers that for him at least it was a concept which represented an immutable truth:

the Providence of God doth actually, effectually, continually govern and over-rule all the Actions and Operations of all

Beings to his Glory, according to his determinate Counsels.
For known unto God are all his Works from the beginning of
the World; so that all contingent Effects and Actions of all
created Beings are not only futurely turned and disposed
but primarily decreed and ordered to be infallibly sub-
servient to the Glory of God's eternal Truth, Justice and
Goodness.[50]

Sir Edward sent a copy of the book to his friend Francis Tallents.
In acknowledging the gift Tallents told him that he had bought a
copy some weeks earlier and had read it over twice 'with delight
and profit'. 'I bless the Lord', he added, 'that in this Atheisticall
age you are not ashamed to own the Gospel of Christ but do write
for it, and count it your great honour.'[51]

Another friend who received a copy of the book was Erasmus
Saunders of Jesus College, Oxford, a man who favoured ecclesiastical reform. Writing to Harley in December 1696 he observed,
in expressing his gratitude, that he praised God not only for the
book itself 'but also for the good and pious example of the Author
who hath vouchsafed to contribute so eminently to the advance-
ment of truth and piety'. It was rare for persons of quality to
engage in such enterprises and he feared that St Paul's complaint
that there were 'not many rich or noble that have thus approved
and practised virtue and truth' offered a partial explanation for
'the decay of Christian piety in our days'.[52] His perception was
shared by others, including Lady Masham who considered that
most gentlemen had little understanding of religion.[53] By the last
decade of the century there were some 70 county families which
men like Baxter and Tallents would have felt justified in describing
as godly, even though few of them were prepared to throw in
their lot completely with the nonconformists. Their numbers had
declined significantly since the outbreak of the Civil War[54] but
moderate nonconformists could take comfort from the fact that
upper-class patronage still survived in an age when zealous
Christians were 'ridicul'd and contemn'd by the men of reason'.[55]

The last word may be left to Sir Henry Ashurst, wealthy
London merchant, squire of Waterstock in Oxfordshire and friend
of Richard Baxter. In his will, which was drawn up in December
1710, he told his only son that it was his dying request that

since he cometh to a house he never built, to Gardens he
never planted and to Land he never purchased ... he

will incourage serious Religion there and set his blessed Grandfather's example before him and . . . keep such a pious Minister in his house that his blessed Grandfather would choose to instruct his ffamily at Waterstock and give him twenty pounds a year and his dyet.[56]

APPENDIX

DOMESTIC CHAPLAINS

This Appendix contains a list of Puritan county families which had domestic chaplains during the period 1650 to 1700. Those individuals marked * were deprived of their livings or fellowships in the early years of Charles II's reign.

ALSTON OF ODELL, BEDFORDSHIRE

At the time of his death in 1678 Sir Thomas Alston was employing *John Fenwick as his chaplain. In addition, *John Maidwell often preached at his house.
(PRO, Chancery Proceedings, Six Clerks Series, C.8/302/119. *NM*, ii, p. 225)

ARMYNE OF OSGODBY HALL, LINCOLNSHIRE AND ORTON LONGVILLE, HUNTINGDONSHIRE

Lady Mary Armyne (1594–1674), who lived at Westminster during her widowhood, took in *Thomas Cawton in 1665 as her chaplain. He was succeeded by another Presbyterian minister, John Dan. In a codicil to her will (20 June 1674) Lady Armyne left Dan a legacy of £30.
(*CR*, p. 106. *NM*, i, p. 196. *Al. Cant.*, ii, p. 6. PRO, Wills, PROB11/347/22)

ASHURST OF HACKNEY, MIDDLESEX AND WATERSTOCK, OXFORDSHIRE

In 1672 Henry Ashurst (d.1680) had his residence in Hackney licensed as a place for nonconformist worship. The following year it was reported that conventicles were held in his house. In the sermon preached at his funeral Richard Baxter related that 'his house was as a school of piety, meekness, and as a Church' and that distressed ministers often resorted to him. Among those who witnessed his will (10 July 1678) were *John Starkey, who had been licensed as a Presbyterian preacher in 1672, and *Roger Baldwin.

To judge from his will (9 December 1710) his son Sir Henry (1645–1711) usually kept a 'pious Minister' in his house.

Another son, Sir William (1661–1754), employed Peter Finch and John Thornley, both Presbyterians, as his chaplains.
(*CSPDom.*, 1671–2, pp. 313, 449. Guildhall Library, London, Diocese of London, Episcopal Visitation Books, MS 9537/20, 69. Richard Baxter, *Faithful Souls Shall Be With Christ*, pp. 39, 45, 52. PRO, Wills, PROB11/364/159 and PROB11/521/97. Gordon, pp. 4, 202, 263, 367)

ASSHETON OF WHALLEY ABBEY, LANCASHIRE

In 1668 the Bishop of Chester complained in a letter to the Archbishop of Canterbury that Sir Ralph Assheton (*c*.1603–80) had given his chaplain a small salary which should have been paid to 'an old curate'.
(Bodleian Library, Oxford, MS ADD C305, fo. 64)

AYSCOUGH OF OSGODBY GRANGE, YORKSHIRE

In 1672 *John Denton was living at Osgodby Grange, the seat of Sir William Ayscough (1614–95), when he obtained a licence as a Presbyterian preacher. Denton, who was a friend of John Tillotson, subsequently conformed: in 1690 he was reordained by the Bishop of Lincoln and became rector of Stonegrave, Yorkshire.

In 1689 it was reported that Thomas Coulton, a nonconformist minister, preached at Sir William's house.
(*CR*, p. 163. *DNB* (Denton). J. C. Atkinson (ed.), *North Riding Quarter Sessions Records*, *North Riding Record Society*, vii, p. 102)

BARNARDISTON OF BRIGHTWELL, SUFFOLK

The chaplains employed by Sir Samuel Barnardiston (1620–1707) included *Robert Franklyn and Robert Mercer (d.1667). Both men were Presbyterians. During the 1650s Franklyn had enjoyed the patronage of Lady Elizabeth Brooke of Cockfield Hall.
(*CR*, pp. 212, 349. *NM*, ii, pp. 439–42)

BARNARDISTON OF KEDINGTON, SUFFOLK

Sir Thomas Barnardiston (*c.*1646–98) had a nonconformist chaplain, Elias Travers.
(West Suffolk Record Office, Barnardiston Family Archive, 871. Joseph Boyse, *A Sermon on the Occasion of the Death of the Reverend Mr Elias Travers*, p. 15. *Al.Cant.*, iv, p. 261)

BARRINGTON OF HATFIELD BROAD OAK, ESSEX

*James Small, a Presbyterian divine, served as chaplain to Sir John Barrington (*c.*1615–83) and his wife Lady Dorothy (d.1703). *John Warren, a Congregational minister who had once held the living of Hatfield Broad Oak, also performed chaplaincy duties from time to time.
(*CR*, pp. 445, 511. Gordon, p. 50. *NM*, i, pp. 506–8. BL, Additional MSS 27352, fo. 213 and Additional MSS 27353, fo. 222)

BARWICK OF TOULSTON, YORKSHIRE

Lady Ursula Barwick (1601–82), the widow of Sir Robert Barwick (1589–1660), employed *Thomas Hardcastle and *Thomas Calvert, both Presbyterians, as her chaplains. Hardcastle wrote of her that she was a person 'to whom I must own myself to be much obliged'.

Ralph Thoresby refers to William Corlas as her chaplain in 1680. Corlas had been episcopally ordained in 1677 and was rector of Newton Kyme (a neighbouring village) during the years 1677 to 1682. The living of Newton Kyme was in the gift of Henry Lord Fairfax who was Lady Barwick's son-in-law.
(*CR*, pp. 99–100, 247. B. Dale, *Yorkshire Puritanism and Early Nonconformity*, pp. 37–8, 67. Ralph Thoresby, *The Diary of Ralph Thoresby* (ed. J. Hunter), i, p. 53. *Al.Cant.*, i, p. 398)

BICKLEY OF ATTLEBOROUGH, NORFOLK

Robert Billio, the nonconformist son of an ejected minister, served Sir Francis Bickley (1644–87) both as chaplain and as tutor to his children.
(*CR*, p. 55. *NM*, i, p. 528)

BOSCAWEN OF TREGOTHNAN, ST MICHAEL PENKEVIL, CORNWALL

Hugh Boscawen (1625–1701) employed *John Cowbridge as his chaplain. In addition, *Joseph Halsey (who had formerly served as his chaplain) regularly preached in his house for many years. Both men were Presbyterians. In his will (27 July 1700) Boscawen left £100 to Halsey and £20 to *John Knight, who had been ejected in Devon, or his widow if he was no longer alive.
(*CR*, pp. 139, 244. PRO, Wills, PROB11/462/151. *NM*, i, p. 372)

BOWYER OF KNYPERSLEY HALL, BIDDULPH, STAFFORDSHIRE

Sir John Bowyer (1623–66) gave shelter to *Joseph Cope, a Presbyterian divine, who probably served as his chaplain. To judge from the will (16 February 1688) of his son Sir John (1653–91) the vicar of Biddulph, whose living was in the gift of the Bowyer family, also had chaplaincy functions.
(*CR*, p. 135. PRO, Wills, PROB11/425/44)

BRIGHT OF BADSWORTH, YORKSHIRE

After the Restoration Sir John Bright had at least two nonconformist chaplains: *Matthew Sylvester who was to become a close friend of Richard Baxter, and Jeremy Wheat who was prevented by the Act of Uniformity from seeking ecclesiastical preferment.
(*CR*, pp. 473, 522)

BROOKE OF COCKFIELD HALL, YOXFORD, SUFFOLK

Lady Elizabeth Brooke (1601–83), the widow of Sir Robert Brooke (d.1646), had a number of chaplains, including *John Fenwick who remained a nonconformist, Samuel Chapman who was a partial conformist and Nathaniel Parkhurst who continued to perform this role after she presented him to the living of Yoxford in 1665. Thirty years later it was reported that Parkhurst refused to use the sign of the cross in baptism.

According to the sermon which Parkhurst delivered at her

funeral Lady Brooke had introduced an arrangement whereby 'a grave divine' visited Cockfield Hall every fortnight to expound the principles of religion and catechise the servants.
(*CR*, pp. 110, 193. *Al.Cant.*, iii, p. 310. *DNB* (Parkhurst). PRO, Wills, PROB11/376/69. Lambeth Palace Library, Gibson Papers, MS 942, 108. Nathaniel Parkhurst, *The Faithful and Diligent Christian Described and Exemplified*, pp. 49, 53–4, 72)

BURGOYNE OF SUTTON, BEDFORDSHIRE AND WROXALL, WARWICKSHIRE

In a letter written in July 1666 Sir Roger Burgoyne (1618–77) referred to William Randolph who had formerly been his chaplain and was now a physician. Randolph, who was the son of a physician, had graduated at St John's College, Cambridge in 1656.

At Wroxall the church was exempt from normal diocesan jurisdiction and the stipendiary curate also acted as chaplain when the family was in residence. The curates included *Luke Milbourne, who was ejected in 1662, John Stones, *Thomas Fownes and Humphrey Whyle. Sir Roger's wife, Lady Anne (d.1695), lived at Wroxall during her widowhood and it is clear from a sermon which he preached at her funeral that Whyle, who had been appointed in 1686, served as her household chaplain. Whyle was presented to the Warwickshire living of Wellesbourne in 1691 but in her will (4 February 1695) Lady Burgoyne described him as 'now of Wroxall'. She also left £5 to 'him that shall be Preacher at Wroxall at the time of my decease'.
(Buckinghamshire Record Office, Claydon House MSS (Letters), Sir Roger Burgoyne to Sir Ralph Verney, 23 July 1666. *Al. Cant.*, iii, p. 420. J. W. Ryland, *Records of Wroxall Abbey and Manor, Warwickshire*, p. lix. *CR*, pp. 210–11, 349–50. Humphrey Whyle, *A Sermon Preach'd at the Funeral of Anne Lady Burgoyne*. PRO, Institution Books, Series B, iv, p. 384 and Wills, PROB11/419/71)

COURTENAY OF POWDERHAM CASTLE, DEVON

*Francis Soreton lived for many years in the house of Sir William Courtenay (1628–1702) and was buried at Powderham. In 1672 he obtained a general licence as a Presbyterian preacher.
(*CR*, p. 452. *CSPDom.*, *1671–2*, pp. 314, 448)

CREWE OF UTKINTON HALL, TARPORLEY, CHESHIRE

In 1672 James Cokayne, a Congregational minister, secured a licence for Utkinton Hall, the seat of Sir John Crewe (1641–1711), as a nonconformist meeting house.

At the time of her death Sir John's mother, Mary Crewe (1604–90), had a nonconformist chaplain, John Wilson, who was said to have been 'very usefull'. Utkinton Hall was again licensed as a place for nonconformist worship in January 1690. In 1699 Sir John was employing a chaplain, Daniel Marks, who had been ordained as a deacon and would subsequently be presented to a Northamptonshire living.

(*CSPDom.*, 1672–3, p. 176. Gordon, pp. 17, 385. PRO, Registrar General, R.G.31/6, no pagination. BL, Additional MSS 70275, letter from Joseph Walferne to Robert Harley, 10 June 1699. *Al.Cant.*, iii, p. 142)

DAVIE OF CREEDY IN SANDFORD, DEVON

In his will (31 January 1678) Sir John Davie (1612–78) left £10 to *James Small 'my present Chaplin'. In 1672 Small had described himself as 'of Creedy' when seeking a general licence as a Presbyterian preacher.

Sir John's house was regarded as a 'chief place of resort' for Presbyterians.

(PRO, Wills, PROB11/358/109. *CR*, p. 445. *CSPDom.*, 1671–2, p. 309. Seth Ward, Bishop, 'Some Letters from Bishop Ward of Exeter, 1663–67', *Devon and Cornwall Notes and Queries*, xxi, p. 284)

DUCKENFIELD OF DUCKENFIELD, CHESHIRE

Samuel Angier enjoyed the patronage of the Duckenfield family from 1681 until his death in 1713. Although he soon formed his own nonconformist congregation he often conducted services in their domestic chapel and kept the register of baptisms, marriages and burials. In 1690 Sir Robert Duckenfield (1642–1729), who favoured the Presbyterians, was employing another nonconformist minister, William Buckley, as his chaplain. Five years later Sir Robert had his house and chapel licensed for nonconformist worship.

(*CR*, pp. 12–13. J. P. Earwaker, *East Cheshire: Past and Present*, ii, pp. 15, 26–38. PRO, Registrar General, R.G.4/1799, register of the chapel at Duckenfield Hall, 1676–1713)

DUNCH OF NORTH BADDESLEY, HAMPSHIRE AND PUSEY, BERKSHIRE

In his will (8 November 1667) Samuel Dunch of North Baddesley (1593–1668) left his chaplain *Samuel Blower an annuity of £20 for life. His son John Dunch of Pusey (1631–68) gave direction for the payment of £500 to his relative and chaplain *Humphrey Gunter in a nuncupative will (28 October 1668). Gunter acted as chaplain and tutor to his son Major (1653–79).

In 1669 it was reported that Major Dunch's house at Pusey was being used for conventicles and that the preachers involved were Gunter, John Wells and *Simon Barret. Three years later Major Dunch obtained licences permitting his houses at Pusey and Sandford in Oxfordshire to be used for Presbyterian worship. Gunter was named in Dunch's will (26 September 1679) as one of the trustees who were to be responsible for managing the estates. (PRO, Wills, PROB11/328/137 and 138, PROB11/362/37. *CR*, pp. 61–2, 238–9. Lyon Turner, iii, p. 345. *CSPDom.*, *1672*, pp. 577, 679)

ELLIS OF WYHAM AND NOCTON, LINCOLNSHIRE

In 1683 it was reported that 'Mr Hall' was serving as chaplain to Sir William Ellis (*c*.1654–1727). This may possibly have been Timothy Hall who had secured a general licence as a Presbyterian preacher in 1672.

During the years 1683 to 1692 Sir William employed Joseph Farrow as his chaplain. Farrow had been episcopally ordained but was not willing to conform. In 1686 *Matthew Bloom died at Sir William's house.

(*CSPDom.*, *1672*, p. 352. *CSP Dom.*, *1683*, p. 366. *NM*, ii, pp. 168–70. *CR*, p. 61).

FAGG OF WISTON, SUSSEX

Sir John Fagg (1627–1701) had at least two Presbyterian chaplains, *John Beaton and *Sampson Herne. Beaton, who was licensed as a Presbyterian preacher in 1672, was buried in Wiston parish church in 1680.

(*CR*, pp. 42, 255)

FOLEY OF GREAT WITLEY, WORCESTERSHIRE

Thomas Foley (1617–77) took on Edward Eccleston as his chaplain on the recommendation of his friend Richard Baxter. Eccleston subsequently decided to conform and in 1673 Foley presented him to the living of Old Swinford. He was succeeded by *Edward Brown, a Presbyterian divine.

In the 1680s Foley's son Thomas (1643–1702) had a Presbyterian chaplain, Nathaniel Oldfield.

(Dr Williams's Library, London, Baxter Letters, ii, ff. 187, 200–23. *Al. Cant.*, ii, p. 83. Henry Newcome, *The Autobiography of Henry Newcome, MA*, ed. R. Parkinson, *Chetham Society*, xxvii, pp. 209, 246. *CR*, p. 80. BL, Additional MSS 70014, ff. 21, 44; 70140, Thomas Foley to Edward Harley, 6 March 1688; and 70233, Sir Edward Harley to Robert Harley, 27 August 1687)

FOLEY OF PRESTWOOD, STAFFORDSHIRE

Philip Foley (1653–1716) employed a considerable number of nonconformist chaplains, including Richard Cook, *Richard Hilton, *James Illingworth, William Willets, John Warren, George Fowler and John Reynolds.

(*CR*, pp. 132, 267, 287–8. Dr Williams's Library, London, Baxter Letters, iii, fo. 237. J. Toulmin, *An Historical View of the State of the Protestant Dissenters in England*, pp. 559, 562. BL, Additional MSS 24484, fo. 153. Alexander Gordon (ed.), *Cheshire Classis Minutes, 1691–1745*, p. 200)

FOLEY OF STOKE EDITH, HEREFORDSHIRE

Paul Foley (*c*.1645–99) usually had a chaplain in his household. In 1675 it was reported from Herefordshire that 'Mr Hopkins, Mr Foley's chaplain' was in trouble with the authorities for allegedly criticising the bishops. This may possibly have been Samuel Hopkins, the son of a minister who had been ejected in Shropshire.

During the 1690s Foley employed Robert Comyn, an Oxford graduate, who was presented to the Harley living of Wigmore in 1699. Sir Edward Harley offered him another Oxford graduate, Silvanus Woodhill. In 1703 Woodhill was presented to the Foley living of Dormington.

(*CSPDom.*, 1675–6, p. 461. *CR*, p. 275. BL, Additional MSS 70114,

Paul Foley to Sir Edward Harley, 24 October 1698 and 24 July and 2 August 1699. *Al.Oxon.*, p. 1675)

GELL OF HOPTON HALL, DERBYSHIRE

During the 1650s Sir John Gell (1594–1671) had a Presbyterian chaplain, *Samuel Charles. His son Sir John (1613–89) employed a number of Presbyterian chaplains, including *Francis Tallents, Joshua Oldfield and Benjamin Robinson. In 1669 it was reported that conventicles were being held in his house. His son Sir Philip (*c.*1655–1719) had at least one Presbyterian chaplain, Timothy Manlove.

(*CR*, pp. 110–11, 474. *NM*, i, pp. 329–33. Derbyshire Record Office, Chandos-Pole-Gell MSS, 47/19(a), (Sir) John Gell to his son John, 6 July 1666, and 66/11(g), Elizabeth Gell to her brother John, *c.*1670. Walter Wilson, *The History and Antiquities of Dissenting Churches and Meeting Houses in London, Westminster, and Southwark*, i, pp. 373–4 and iv, p. 161. *DNB* (Joshua Oldfield). Lyon Turner, i, p. 54. BL Stowe MSS 746, fo. 112)

GRIMSTON OF GORHAMBURY, HERTFORDSHIRE

At an episcopal visitation undertaken in 1680 it was noted that Ambrose Rea, the rector of Wakes Colne in Essex, was 'Chaplaine to the Master of the Rolles'. Sir Harbottle Grimston (1603–85), the Master of the Rolls, was the patron of the living. In his will (23 May 1684) he left £20 to Gilbert Burnet who had been his chaplain at the Rolls chapel and £10 to James Blair his domestic chaplain. Blair had graduated at the University of Edinburgh in 1673 and was probably one of the Scottish Presbyterian divines whom Burnet recruited for wealthy English families which were in need of a chaplain.

When Sir Samuel (1643–1700), Grimston's only surviving son, drew up his will (22 May 1699) he also left £10 to his domestic chaplain.

(Guildhall Library, London, Diocese of London, Episcopal Visitation Books, MS 9537/23, fo. 23. *Al.Cant.*, iii, p. 432. Hertfordshire County Record Office, Verulam (Gorhambury) MSS, IX, A62, A75. *A Catalogue of the Graduates in the Faculties of Arts, Divinity, and Law, of the University of Edinburgh*, p. 103)

GURDON OF ASSINGTON, SUFFOLK

*John Hinde, a Presbyterian divine, served for some years as chaplain to John Gurdon (1595–1679) and remained at Assington Hall until his marriage in 1681. The Gurdons also maintained close contact with *Thomas Walker, the former vicar of Assington. In 1672 he obtained a licence authorising him to hold Presbyterian meetings in Assington Hall. In his will (25 June 1677) Gurdon left £3 to Hinde and £2 to Walker who was living at Assington in 1683. When Gurdon's son Philip (d.1690) drew up his will (20 June 1690) he bequeathed £10 to his 'old friend' Mrs Walker, the widow of Thomas Walker.
(*CR*, pp. 268, 507. PRO, Wills, PROB11/361/129 and PROB11/400/124)

HAMPDEN OF GREAT HAMPDEN, BUCKINGHAMSHIRE

Richard Hampden (1631–95) had several nonconformist chaplains, including *George Swinnock, a Presbyterian minister, and *John Nott. In addition, *George Crosse, *Richard Baxter and *Francis Tallents lived with him for a time. Nott left Great Hampden in 1689 when the Hampdens settled in London and was succeeded by 'Mr Barton' who was left £25 in Hampden's will (19 June 1695). This may possibly have been Samuel Barton of Corpus Christi, Oxford who in 1695 became chaplain to Paul Foley in his capacity as Speaker of the House of Commons. According to Thomas Hearne he was 'a little Puritanically inclin'd'.
(*CR*, pp. 149, 368, 473. Richard Baxter, *Reliquiae Baxterianae* (ed. Matthew Sylvester), part II, p. 448. Dr Williams's Library, London, Henry MSS, 90.5, Matthew Henry to his father, 8 June 1686. Gordon, pp. 1, 9, 10. PRO, Wills, PROB11/435/239. Thomas Hearne, *Remarks and Collections of Thomas Hearne*, Oxford Historical Society, ii, p. 221)

HARCOURT OF STANTON HARCOURT, OXFORDSHIRE

*Henry Cornish, a Presbyterian divine, served as chaplain to Sir Philip Harcourt (d.1688). In 1672 he and *William Gilbert, who was also described as 'of Stanton Harcourt', were granted general licences as Presbyterian preachers. Three years later *Thomas Clark joined the household. Sir Philip's will (10 August 1683) was witnessed by Cornish.

(*CR*, pp. 120, 137–8, 222. E. W. Harcourt, *The Harcourt Papers*, ii, pp. 2–3. PRO, Wills, PROB11/391/47)

HARLEY OF BRAMPTON BRYAN, HEREFORDSHIRE

For domestic worship Sir Edward Harley (1624–1700) and his family relied mainly on their own beneficed ministers (in particular the rector of Brampton Bryan) and visiting nonconformist ministers. Occasionally, however, he employed a resident chaplain: in the years 1685 to 1687, for example, Nathaniel Oldfield, a Presbyterian, was living with the Harleys.

(BL, Additional MSS 70128, Sir Edward Harley to his wife, 12 May 1685. Dr Williams's Library, London, Blackmore Papers, volume of correspondence, 18)

HARTOPP OF STOKE NEWINGTON, MIDDLESEX AND BUCKMINSTER, LEICESTERSHIRE

In 1673 and again in 1686 it was alleged that conventicles were held in the house at Stoke Newington which Sir John Hartopp (*c*.1637–1722) and his wife shared with their relatives the Fleetwoods. In 1684 *Edward Terry, a Congregational minister, was reported to be serving as Hartopp's chaplain; and in 1690 he witnessed the will of Sir John's father-in-law, Charles Fleetwood.

(Guildhall Library, London, Diocese of London, Episcopal Visitation Books, MS 9537/20, 17. Dr Williams's Library, London, Morrice MSS, P, 444, 570 and Q, 34. *CR*, p. 480. PRO, Wills, PROB11/412/201)

HESILRIGE OF NOSELEY, LEICESTERSHIRE

In 1676 *Samuel Muston was serving as chaplain to Sir Thomas Hesilrige (*c*.1625–80). The same year he was presented to the living of Hallaton which was in the gift of the Hesilrige family.

The curate of Noseley appears to have had chaplaincy functions.

(Anne Whiteman and Mary Clapinson (eds), *The Compton Census of 1676. A Critical Edition*, p. 334. *CR*, p. 360)

HOBART OF BLICKLING, NORFOLK

*John Collinges, a Presbyterian divine, served as chaplain to Sir John Hobart (1593–1647) and his widow Lady Frances (d.1664) and was also closely associated with subsequent generations of the family. In 1688 he was described as chaplain to Sir Henry Hobart (c.1658–98).

(John Collinges, *Par Nobile. Two Treatises. CR*, p. 128. HMC, *Marquess of Lothian MSS*, p. 131. Sir George Duckett (ed.), *Penal Laws and Test Act*, ii, p. 223)

HOGHTON OF HOGHTON TOWER, LANCASHIRE

Sir Richard Hoghton (1616–78) employed *Josiah Holdsworth,a Presbyterian divine, and Timothy Hill as his chaplains. In addition, other nonconformist ministers such as Thomas Key and *John Harvey sometimes resided at Hoghton Tower. Sir Richard's widow, Lady Sarah, also had nonconformist chaplains, among them Thomas Cotton and John Ashe.

In 1703 Sir Charles Hoghton (1651–1710) had his house licensed for meetings of Protestant dissenters.

(*CR*, pp. 251, 272, 303. BL, Additional MSS 4460, fo. 23; and 24484, fo. 132. Adam Martindale, *The Life of Adam Martindale*, ed. R. Parkinson, *Chetham Society*, iv, p. 210. PRO, Registrar General, R.G. 31/6, no pagination)

HONYWOOD OF MARKS HALL, ESSEX

Lady Hester Honywood (d.1681), the widow of Sir Thomas Honywood, appointed *Matthew Elliston, a Presbyterian minister, as one of the executors of her will (5 May 1674). Elliston was buried at Markshall in 1693. When John Lemot Honywood (d.1694), the last surviving son of Sir Thomas, drew up his will (21 October 1693) he left £10 to *Lewis Calandrine, a Presbyterian divine, who may possibly have been serving as his chaplain.

(PRO, Wills, PROB11/368/163 and PROB11/425/52. *CR*, pp. 98, 183)

HUNGERFORD OF CORSHAM, WILTSHIRE

*Thomas Rosewell was employed as chaplain and tutor in the household of Lady Margaret Hungerford (d.1673), the widow of

Sir Edward Hungerford (1596–1648). In her will (23 January 1673) she left £20 to the chaplain who would be serving her at the time of her death.

(*NM*, ii, pp. 512–16. *CR*, p. 418. PRO, Wills, PROB11/342/58)

HUTTON OF POPPLETON, YORKSHIRE

*Thomas Birdsall, a Presbyterian divine, served for many years as chaplain to Dorothy Hutton (1617–87) and her son Thomas (1638–1704). He was buried at Poppleton in 1687.

(*CR*, p. 57)

IRBY OF BOSTON AND WHAPLODE, LINCOLNSHIRE

Sir Anthony Irby (1605–82) had employed domestic chaplains before the Civil War and he continued the practice after the Restoration. During the years 1662 to 1682 he had three Presbyterian chaplains, *Thomas Cawton, *Thomas Clark and *William Bruce. His widow, Lady Katherine (d.1695), who lived in Westminster after his death, also had Presbyterian chaplains, Samuel Lawrence and Joseph Hill (who also appears to have acted as tutor to her grandson Sir Edward Irby). In her will (12 June 1695) she left Hill a legacy of £20.

(*CR*, pp. 82, 106–7, 120. Alexander Gordon (ed.), *Cheshire Classis Minutes, 1691–1745*, p. 187. James Wood, *The Believer's Committing of his Soul to Christ Considered*, p. 30. *DNB* (Joseph Hill). PRO, Wills, PROB11/429/238)

JACKSON OF HICKLETON, YORKSHIRE

After his ejection *Hugh Everard, the curate of Hickleton, was taken in by Sir John Jackson (1631–70) as his chaplain. In his will (1 March 1667) Everard left £20 to his patron.

Another of Sir John's ministers, *Nathan Denton, preached in Hickleton parish church for a year after his ejection from the living of Bolton upon Dearne. During a visitation carried out in 1664 Sir John was presented for neglecting to find a new minister for the living of Hickleton.

In 1669 it was reported that conventicles had formerly been held in Jackson's house.

(*CR*, pp. 163, 186. Dr Williams's Library, London, A. G. Matthews's collection of abstracts of wills of ejected ministers. Borthwick Institute of Historical Research, York Diocesan Records, YV/CB3, fo. 43. Lyon Turner, i, p. 163)

JERVOISE OF HERRIARD, HAMPSHIRE

In 1690 Thomas Jervoise (1616–93) was employing a chaplain. This may have been Thomas Austin who corresponded with Richard Burd, an Anglican divine who was resident in London, and Thomas Bayley, the Principal of New Inn Hall, Oxford, and who acted as one of the witnesses of Jervoise's will (6 February 1693). In 1688 Lady Honor St Barbe suggested to Jervoise's son Thomas that he should regard Austin as a friend as well as a servant. A man of the same name graduated at Sidney Sussex, Cambridge in 1679.

(Hampshire Record Office, Jervoise of Herriard Park MSS, 44M69/ E77, letters from Richard Burd, 31 May 1687 and 22 February 1690, Lady Honor St Barbe, 17 March 1688 and Thomas Bayley, 8 July 1689. PRO, Wills, PROB11/417/88. *Al.Cant.*, i, p. 58)

JOCELYN OF HYDE HALL, SAWBRIDGEWORTH, HERTFORDSHIRE

Sir Robert Jocelyn (1623–1712) employed *Andrew Cater, a Presbyterian divine, as his chaplain.
(Gordon, pp. 51, 232. *CR*, p. 105)

KEATE OF THE HOO, ST PAUL'S WALDEN, HERTFORDSHIRE

Sir Jonathan Keate (*c*.1633–1700) had at least two nonconformist chaplains, *John Peachy, a Presbyterian divine, and Joseph Hussey. In his will (21 April 1698) he left £5 to Mrs Cawthorne, 'the minister's wife': she was probably the wife of *Joseph Cawthorne.

(*CR*, p. 38. Gordon, p. 289. Walter Wilson, *The History and Antiquities of Dissenting Churches and Meeting Houses in London, Westminster, and Southwark*, iv, p. 411. PRO, Wills, PROB11/ 457/154. *NM*, ii, pp. 160–1)

LANGHAM OF COTTESBROOKE, NORTHAMPTONSHIRE

In his will (1 November 1670) Sir John Langham (1584–1671) left £100 to his chaplain, *Thomas Burroughs. Another nonconformist divine, Samuel May, also acted as his chaplain for a time.

Sir James Langham (c.1620–99), who was Sir John's eldest son, appears to have employed *Ralph Strettell as his chaplain when he was residing in London.

(PRO, Wills, PROB11/336/79. CR, pp. 91, 346, 466. BL, Additional MSS 70013, fo. 184 and 70124, Ralph Strettell to Sir Edward Harley, 28 November 1671, 6 January 1672, 5 May 1674 and 1 September 1677)

LUMLEY OF GREAT BARDFIELD, ESSEX

Lady Mary Lumley (d.1678), the widow of Sir Martin Lumley (c.1596–1651), referred to *Edward Whiston, a Presbyterian divine, in her will (17 July 1672).

Thomas Pritchard, who was vicar of Lindsell in the years 1678 to 1692, performed chaplaincy duties for Sir Martin Lumley (d.1702) and was also a close friend of his son, another Sir Martin (1662- 1711). When Pritchard drew up his will (29 October 1692) he described himself as 'of Great Bardfield'.

(PRO, Wills, PROB11/358/112 and PROB11/412/209. CR, pp. 523–4. Thomas Pritchard, *A Sermon Preached at the Funeral of Mrs Mary Dawes* and *A Sermon Preached at the Funeral of the Lady Lumley. Al.Cant.*, iii, p. 401)

MARWOOD OF LITTLE BUSBY, YORKSHIRE

Sir George Marwood (1601–80) employed *George Ewbank as his chaplain.

(George Ewbank, *The Pilgrim's Port. CR*, p. 186)

MASHAM OF OTES HALL, HIGH LAVER, ESSEX

Sir William Masham (1592–c.1656) had regularly kept a chaplain in his house before the Civil War. In his will (16 March 1656) he left £3 to the minister who would be living with him at the time of his death to enable him to buy books.

During the latter part of the century Henry Lukin, an Independent minister, received financial support from the Mashams and acted as their chaplain.
(PRO, Wills, PROB11/256/389. *CR*, p. 331. *DNB* (Henry Lukin). Gordon, p. 40)

MAYNARD OF TAVISTOCK, DEVON

Sir John Maynard (1604–90) had at least three nonconformist chaplains, *Richard Whiteway, *Edmund Moore and *Roger Morrice.
(*CR*, pp. 352, 355, 526–7)

MIDDLETON OF BELSAY CASTLE, NORTHUMBERLAND

Sir William Middleton (*c*.1636–90) employed *Nathaniel Baxter as his chaplain while living at Aldwark Hall in Yorkshire. In 1673 Belsay Castle was licensed as a Presbyterian meeting house. Sir William subsequently took in *James Calvert, a Presbyterian divine, who 'preached constantly in the chapel as chaplain, and educated his only son, to whom he was left tutor when his father died'. The son was Sir John (1678–1717) who continued the nonconformist tradition.
(*CR*, pp. 38–9, 99. *CSPDom.*, 1672–3, p. 427. *NM*, ii, p. 596. Dr Williams's Library, London, John Evans's list of dissenting congregations and ministers, 1715–1729, p. 90)

MORLEY OF GLYNDE PLACE, SUSSEX

*Nehemiah Beaton was taken into the family of Herbert Morley (1616–67) after his ejection but died in January 1663. In his will (24 September 1667) Morley left £5 to *Zachary Smith, late minister of Glynde, who subsequently became chaplain to his son William (1653–79).
(*CR*, pp. 42, 450. PRO, Wills, PROB11/325/141)

NORCLIFFE OF LANGTON, YORKSHIRE

*William Oliver, a Presbyterian divine, served as chaplain to Lady Dorothy Norcliffe (d.1686), the widow of Sir Thomas Norcliffe (1618–80).
(*CR*, p. 374)

NORTON OF SOUTHWICK, HAMPSHIRE

Richard Norton (1615–91) had a preference for Independent or Congregational ministers: *Urian Oakes was employed as his chaplain and *Giles Say preached in his house.
(*CR*, pp. 370, 427)

ONSLOW OF WEST CLANDON, SURREY

During the 1680s Edward Vernon, who was a half-conformist, was chaplain to Arthur Onslow (1622–88) and also held the living of Merrow which was in Onslow's gift.
(HMC, *Fourteenth Report*, Appendix, part IX, pp. 497–8. *Al.Oxon.*, p. 1542)

PELHAM OF LAUGHTON, SUSSEX

Sir John Pelham (*c*.1623–1703) employed *Edmund Thorpe, a Presbyterian divine, as his chaplain during the years 1662 to 1665. In his will (16 November 1702) he referred to his chaplain when alluding to the need for a sermon at his funeral.
(BL, Additional MSS 33148, ff. 121, 123, 125, 130, 142. *CR*, p. 485. PRO, Wills, PROB11/469/55)

PICKERING OF TITCHMARSH, NORTHAMPTONSHIRE

After his ejection *John Seaton sometimes preached at the house of Sir Gilbert Pickering (1613–68). In 1672 *Henry Searle was granted a licence authorising him to hold Presbyterian meetings in the mansion house of Sir Gilbert's widow, Lady Elizabeth (d.1679). He died almost immediately and in his place she nominated *Nathaniel Whiting, a Congregational minister.
(*CR*, pp. 430, 431, 527)

PRIDEAUX OF FORDE ABBEY, DEVON

In 1669 it was reported that Presbyterian conventicles were being held at the house of Edmund Prideaux (*c*.1634–1702) and that the ministers involved were *Nicholas Wakeley and *John Hodder. Prideaux had a Presbyterian chaplain, *Henry Backaller.
(Lyon Turner, i, p. 44. *CR*, pp. 20–1)

PUREFOY OF WADLEY, BERKSHIRE

According to the preacher at his funeral George Purefoy (1605–61) usually kept in his house 'a Chaplain in orders'.
(John Hinckley, *A Sermon Preached at the Funerals of that Worthy Personage George Purefoy the Elder of Wadley in Berkshire, Esquire*, p. 31)

PYE OF FARRINGDON, BERKSHIRE

In the early 1690s Sir Robert Pye (d.1701) was employing a nonconformist minister, William Brice, as his chaplain. He was the son of *William Brice. Sir Robert was said to be providing financial support for both Brice and *Humphrey Gunter who took it in turns to preach at Buckland.
(Gordon, p. 6)

ROBERTS OF GLASSENBURY, KENT

Thomas Brand, a Presbyterian divine, served as chaplain to Lady Bridget Roberts (d.1706), the widow of Sir Howland Roberts (*c*.1634–61), for sixteen years and was involved in the 'pious Education' of her children. In 1672 he sought a licence authorising him to minister to a nonconformist congregation in the domestic chapel.
   Another Presbyterian minister, Edmund Trench, was chaplain to Lady Roberts and her son Sir Thomas (1658–1706) during the years 1675 to 1684. In 1675 he married Bridget Roberts, a daughter of Lady Roberts.
(Samuel Annesley, *The Life and Funeral Sermon of the Reverend Mr Thomas Brand. CR*, pp. 71, 492. *CSPDom.*, 1671–2, pp. 337, 355, 396. *NM*, ii, pp. 174–8. Joseph Boyse, *Some Remarkable Passages in the Holy Life and Death of the late Reverend Mr Edmund Trench*)

RODES OF GREAT HOUGHTON, YORKSHIRE

The domestic chapel of the Rodes family was regularly used for nonconformist worship. Sir Edward Rodes (1600–66) employed Thomas Johnson, a Presbyterian, and Richard Taylor, an Independent, as his chaplains. In 1669 it was reported that conventicles were being held in the chapel and that these were attended by both Presbyterians and Independents. Three years later a licence was granted to *Jeremiah Milner, a Congregational minister, authorising him to hold meetings in the chapel and he continued to act as chaplain to Sir Edward's widow, Lady Mary (d.1681), and her son Godfrey (1631–81).

In 1689 William Rodes (1639–96) had the house and chapel licensed for the purposes of nonconformist worship.
(B. Dale, *Yorkshire Puritanism and Early Nonconformity*, p. 88. CR, pp. 350, 477. Lyon Turner, i, p. 163. BL, Stowe MSS 745, fo. 115. PRO, Registrar General, R.G.31/7, no pagination).

RUSSELL OF CHIPPENHAM, CAMBRIDGESHIRE

*Richard Parr, the late vicar of Chippenham, served as chaplain to Sir Francis Russell (c.1616–64).
(BL, Additional MSS 24485, fo. 32. CR, p. 381)

STANLEY OF BICKERSTAFFE HALL, ORMSKIRK, LANCASHIRE

In 1672 Lady Mary Stanley, the widow of Sir Thomas Stanley (1616–53), had Bickerstaffe Hall licensed for Presbyterian worship. Nonconformist ministers who preached in the chapel included *Nathaniel Heywood and *Zachary Taylor, both Presbyterians. In 1674 Heywood, who appears to have performed chaplaincy duties, was sentenced to six months' imprisonment for preaching at Bickerstaffe Hall.
(*CSPDom., 1671–2*, pp. 411, 502. *CSPDom., 1672–3*, p. 95. CR, pp. 259, 479–80. Nathaniel Heywood, *Christ Displayed, as the Choicest Gift and Best Master*, epistle dedicatory addressed to Henry Hoghton and his wife Lady Stanley. Sir Henry Ashurst, *Some Remarks upon the Life of that Painful Servant of God Mr Nathanael Heywood*)

STRICKLAND OF BOYNTON, YORKSHIRE

During the reign of Charles II, Stephen Hill, who had been a lecturer at Beverley, served as chaplain to Sir William Strickland (1596–1673). Shortly after his father's death Sir Thomas (1639–84) took in a Presbyterian minister, *James Calvert, who had once been vicar of Boynton. Calvert was employed both as chaplain and as tutor to his sons. In 1683 he was in trouble with the authorities for assisting Sir John Cochrane and his son in their escape to Holland. In his will (August 1683) Sir Thomas left £20 to Calvert 'whoe at present resides in my house'.

(*CR*, pp. 99, 266. *CSPDom., 1683*, pp. 168–70, 220, 227. Borthwick Institute of Historical Research, Wills in the York Registry, vol. 60, fo. 376)

STRODE OF BARRINGTON, SOMERSET

During the 1650s *John Bush, a Presbyterian divine, served as chaplain to William Strode (d.1666). In his will (10 June 1665) Strode left him an annuity of £2. His son William (d.1695) appears to have employed *Thomas Budd, a Presbyterian divine, as his chaplain. Budd had been ejected from the rectory of Kingsbury which had been leased to the Strodes for three lives. When Budd applied for a general licence in 1672 he described himself as 'of Barrington'.

(*CR*, pp. 92, 261. PRO, Wills, PROB11/323/2. Gordon, p. 224. *Al.Oxon.*, p. 206. Somerset Record Office, Phelips MSS, DD/PH 127. *CSPDom., 1672*, p. 293)

TRENCHARD OF WOLFETON HOUSE, CHARMINSTER, DORSET

The church at Charminster was a peculiar and the stipendiary curate acted as chaplain to the Trenchard family. In his will (25 April 1670) Thomas Trenchard (1640–71) left £100 to *Samuel Hardy of Poole who had served as his chaplain both before and after 1662. William Willes, who was curate of Charminster during the years 1673 to 1684, no doubt fulfilled this role for the household of Thomas Trenchard (1671–1702). This may have been the Presbyterian minister named as William Wills or Wallis who had secured a licence in 1672.

(*NM*, i, pp. 466–7. *CR*, p. 248. PRO, Wills, PROB11/344/3. John Hutchins, *The History and Antiquities of the County of Dorset*, ii, p. 556. *CSPDom., 1671–2*, pp. 500, 568)

VANE OF FAIRLAWNE, KENT

Lady Frances Vane (d.1680), the widow of Sir Henry Vane, employed *James Ayres, a Congregational minister, as her chaplain. In 1672 he obtained a licence authorising him to hold meetings at her house at Fairlawne. When she drew up her will (12 December 1679) Ayres was one of the witnesses. Among the legacies which she left was £50 to her 'good friend' *John Jackson, a Presbyterian minister.

(*CR*, pp. 4, 290–1. PRO, Wills, PROB11/361/168)

WALLER OF OSTERLEY PARK, MIDDLESEX

After the Restoration Sir William Waller (*c*.1597–1668) had three nonconformist chaplains, Samuel May, *Edward Veal and *John Sayer. Veal and Sayer were Presbyterians. Sayer was one of the witnesses to the codicils to Sir William's will (27 April 1668). In his own will (3 March 1675) he gave direction to his executor to pay back to Waller's son, another Sir William, the sum of £30 which he had received as a legacy 'but of late very doubtfull whither it were intended for mee by his father's Will'.

(*CR*, pp. 346, 428, 501. *NM*, i, p. 162. PRO, Wills, PROB11/330/78. Dr Williams's Library, London, A. G. Matthews's collection of abstracts of wills of ejected ministers)

WENTWORTH OF NORTH ELMSALL, YORKSHIRE

Noah Ward, a Presbyterian divine, served as chaplain to Sir John Wentworth (1645–71) during the latter part of his life. When Sir John's widow, Lady Catherine, married Heneage Finch, Earl of Winchilsea, he was immediately dismissed.

(*CR*, p. 509)

WHITELOCKE OF CHILTON FOLIAT, WILTSHIRE

In September 1661 James Pearson joined the household of Bulstrode Whitelocke (1605–75) and served as his chaplain and tutor to his sons. In 1672 he obtained a licence authorising him, as a Congregational minister, to hold meetings in Whitelocke's house, Chilton Lodge. From time to time other nonconformist ministers preached there.

(Bulstrode Whitelocke, *The Diary of Bulstrode Whitelocke, 1605–75* (ed. Ruth Spalding), pp. 636, 795. *CSPDom., 1671–2*, 585)

WILBRAHAM OF WOODHAY, CHESHIRE AND WESTON UNDER LIZARD, STAFFORDSHIRE

Lady Elizabeth Wilbraham (d.1679), the widow of Sir Thomas Wilbraham (1601–60), employed *John Cartwright as her chaplain at Woodhay Hall. In her will (19 December 1673) she left him £20. According to Oliver Heywood his son John, another nonconformist divine, also served as her chaplain.

During the 1650s her son Sir Thomas (1630–92), who lived at Weston, had a Presbyterian chaplain, *Francis Keeling. After the Restoration Sir Thomas and his wife, Lady Elizabeth (1631–1705), had a succession of nonconformist chaplains who were generally Presbyterians. These included John Rowney, *James Illingworth and *Samuel Beresford. Illingworth was one of the witnesses to Sir Thomas's will (16 July 1688).

In 1683 Gilbert Burnet supplied the Wilbrahams with a young Scottish chaplain.

(*CR*, pp. 50, 102–3, 288, 304. PRO, Wills, PROB11/363/71 and PROB11/412/233. Oliver Heywood and Thomas Dickenson, *The Nonconformist Register of Baptisms, Marriages, and Deaths, Compiled by the Revs. Oliver Heywood and T. Dickenson* (ed. J. Horsfall Turner), p. 61. BL, Additional MSS 70090, memorandum book of Sir Edward Harley, 1685, no pagination. *Al.Cant.*, iii, p. 494. Gordon, p. 88. Ralph Thoresby, *Letters of Eminent Men Addressed to Ralph Thoresby* (ed. J. Hunter), i, pp. 84–6, 179, 192–3, 261. HMC, *Bath MSS*, i, pp. 45–8)

WINWOOD OF DITTON PARK, BUCKINGHAMSHIRE

In 1669 Bulstrode Whitelocke presented Nathaniel Basenet to the Buckinghamshire living of Fawley at the request of his friend Richard Winwood (1609–88). Winwood apparently wanted to ensure that Basenet would be able to continue serving as his domestic chaplain. In his will (21 January 1687) Winwood left £50 to his present chaplain, Benjamin Archer. Although Archer was a fellow of Exeter College, Oxford and rector of Wexham, Buckinghamshire he normally resided with the Winwoods. Winwood had promised him the living of Quainton when it next fell vacant and in 1692 he was duly presented.

(Bulstrode Whitelocke, *The Diary of Bulstrode Whitelocke, 1605–75* (ed. Ruth Spalding), pp. 702, 714, 728, 737, 755, 756. *Al.Oxon.*, 29, 82. PRO, Wills, PROB11/390/43. Buckinghamshire Record Office, Claydon Hall MSS (Letters), John Verney to his father Sir Ralph, 27 June 1688. G. Lipscomb, *The History and Antiquities of the County of Buckingham*, i, 422)

WROTH OF PETHERTON PARK, SOMERSET

In his will (1 February 1672) Sir Thomas Wroth (1584–1672) left £10 to his household chaplain.
(PRO, Wills, PROB11/339/106)

YONGE OF COLYTON, DEVON

In his will (April 1661) Sir John Yonge referred to 'my chaplains' and the other Thursday lecturers at Colyton.
(PRO, Wills, PROB11/312/116)

NOTES

1 THE GODLY DIVIDED

1   Northamptonshire Record Office, Dryden MSS, D(CA)924.
2   J. T. Cliffe, *Puritans in Conflict*, pp. 171–3.
3   Sheffield Central Library, Strafford Letters, xvii, p. 66. J. T. Cliffe, *The Yorkshire Gentry from the Reformation to the Civil War*, pp. 293, 302, 303, 327, 350.
4   Lucy Hutchinson, *Memoirs of the Life of Colonel Hutchinson* (ed. James Sutherland), p. 190. Edward Hyde, Earl of Clarendon, *Calendar of the Clarendon State Papers in the Bodleian Library* (ed. O. Ogle, W. H. Bliss, W. D. Macray and F. J. Routledge), iv, p. 221.
5   Thomas Burton, *Diary of Thomas Burton* (ed. J. T. Rutt), iii, p. 174.
6   J. T. Cliffe, *Puritan Gentry*, pp. 208–9. *CSPDom.*, *1661–2*, p. 213.
7   Burton, *Diary of Thomas Burton*, iii, pp. 27, 96–7, 102.
8   *A Narrative of the Late Parliament* and *A Second Narrative of the Late Parliament*, *Harleian Miscellany*, iii, p. 477.
9   David Underdown, 'Parliamentary Diary of John Boys, 1647–8', *Bulletin of the Institute of Historical Research*, xxxix, p. 155. Burton, *Diary of Thomas Burton*, iii, pp. 414, 534.
10 *CSPDom.*, *1660–1*, p. 5. See below, p. 26.
11 Hutchinson, *Memoirs of the Life of Colonel Hutchinson*, p. 188.
12 *CJ*, vi, p. 141.
13 See below, pp. 22, 23, 25, 26, 30.
14 Hampshire Record Office, Jervoise of Herriard Park MSS, 44M69/F9, F10, 07. *CJ*, vi, pp. 269, 296.
15 Bulstrode Whitelocke, *Memorials of the English Affairs*, ii, pp. 277, 374, 484–5, 487. G. E. Aylmer, *The State's Servants: The Civil Service of the English Republic 1649–1660*, p. 253. BL, Additional MSS 37343, ff. 263–4. HMC, *Thirteenth Report*, Appendix, part I, p. 602. *A Narrative of the Late Parliament* and *A Second Narrative of the Late Parliament*, *Harleian Miscellany*, iii, p. 480.
16 *CJ*, vii, pp. 27, 29, 44, 123.
17 R. W. Ketton-Cremer, 'The Rhyming Wodehouses', *Norfolk Archaeology*, xxxiii, p. 38.

18 *CJ*, vii, pp. 220–1. *The English Revolution. III, Newsbooks I. Oxford Royalist*, i, p. 405. Thomas Carlyle, *The Letters and Speeches of Oliver Cromwell* (ed. S. C. Lomas), i, pp. 292–3, 298, 300–2, 412 and ii, p. 53. BL, Additional MSS 24861, fo. 17. HMC, *Thirteenth Report*, Appendix, part I, p. 582. *CSPDom., 1651*, pp. 200, 227.

19 Richard Baxter, *Reliquiae Baxterianae* (ed. Matthew Sylvester), p. 75.

20 Cliffe, *Puritans in Conflict*, p. 101. See also the Appendix below (pp. 206–28).

21 Burton, *Diary of Thomas Burton*, i, pp. 155, 169.

22 Clarendon, iv, p. 275.

23 See, for example, David Underdown, *Pride's Purge*, pp. 209–20.

24 Cliffe, *Puritans in Conflict*, pp. 110, 112, 114–17, 123, 126–8, 133, 153, 165–7, 170–4, 176.

25 HMC, *Leyborne-Popham MSS*, p. 51.

26 *The Dissenting Ministers' Vindication of Themselves from the Horrid and Detestable Murder of Charles I, Somers Tracts*, v, pp. 258–62.

27 Staffordshire Record Office, Leveson-Gower MSS, D593/P/8/2/2, letter of John Langley to Sir Richard Leveson, 7 May 1653.

28 Clarendon, v, p. 274.

29 Sir William Waller, *Vindication of the Character and Conduct of Sir William Waller*, p. 12.

30 BL, Sloane MSS 1519, fo. 188.

31 Edmund Ludlow, *Memoirs of Edmund Ludlow*, pp. 80–1.

32 Cliffe, *Puritans in Conflict*, pp. 27, 36, 37, 66, 72–4, 76, 166.

33 BL, Additional MSS 33084, fo. 64.

34 Cliffe, *Puritans in Conflict*, p. 78.

35 Ibid., pp. 67, 78, 80. Edmund Ludlow, *A Voyce from the Watch Tower* (ed. A. B. Worden), *Camden Fourth Series*, xxi, p. 108. BL, Harleian MSS 164, fo. 277.

36 *CSP Dom., 1648–9*, pp. 160, 291. *Calendar of the Proceedings of the Committee for the Advance of Money*, p. 1236–7. *Calendar of the Proceedings of the Committee for Compounding* p. 1837.

37 BL, Harleian MSS 164, fo. 277.

38 Cliffe, *Puritans in Conflict*, pp. 100–3. *A & O*, i, pp. 1188–1215.

39 *A & O*, ii, pp. 855–8. Baxter, *Reliquiae Baxterianae*, p. 72.

40 Northamptonshire Record Office, Dryden MSS, D(CA) 908, 914. *Al.Oxon.*, pp. 210, 1125. H. I. Longden, *Northamptonshire and Rutland Clergy from 1500*, ii, p. 295.

41 Baxter, *Reliquiae Baxterianae*, pp. 142, 144–6.

42 *NM*, i, pp. 448–9, 460–3.

43 Jane Houston, *Catalogue of Ecclesiastical Records of the Commonwealth 1643–1660 in the Lambeth Palace Library*, p. 23. *CR*, p. 226. *NM*, ii, p. 459.

44 Houston, p. 46. *CR*, p. 419. *NM*, ii, pp. 454–7.

45 BL, Additional MSS 70125, Sir William Waller to Edward Harley, 14 October 1651.

46 *DNB* (Thomas Cawton). Thomas Cawton the younger, *The Life and Death of that Holy and Reverend Man of God Mr Thomas Cawton*, epistle dedicatory. P. A. Irby, *The Irbys of Lincolnshire and the Irebys of Cumberland*, part I, p. 131. Cliffe, *Puritans in Conflict*, pp. 98, 113, 166.

47 Cawton, *Life and Death*, pp. 23–4. Thomas Case, *The Vanity of Vaine-Glory*, dedication to the reader.
48 HMC, *Thirteenth Report*, Appendix, part I, p. 582. HMC, *Fourteenth Report*, Appendix, part IX, p. 483.
49 John Nicholls (ed.), *Original Letters and Papers of State Addressed to Oliver Cromwell*, p. 66. Lady Brilliana Harley, *Letters of the Lady Brilliana Harley*, ed. T. T. Lewis, *Camden Society*, lviii, p. 247. Baxter, *Reliquiae Baxterianae*, p. 67. Staffordshire Record Office, Bradford Collection, P/1318, no pagination; and MS 100/1,19.
50 BL, Additional MSS 70005, ff. 79–80; 70007, ff. 2–3, 44–5; and 70130, Edward Harley's notes on the character and sayings of his father. *NM*, i, p. 119. HMC, *Seventh Report*, Appendix, p. 67. *CSPDom.*, *1650*, p. 24.
51 Edmund Calamy (1600–60), *A Patterne for All, Especially for Noble and Honourable Persons*. Houston, *Catalogue of Ecclesiastical Records*, p. 48.
52 Edmund Calamy (1600–60), *The Happinesse of Those who Sleep in Jesus*.

2   DISAFFECTION

1 J. T. Cliffe, *Puritans in Conflict*, pp. 27, 155, 160–3, 175. *CJ*, v, p. 264. Henry Cary, *Memorials of the Great Civil War in England*, i, pp. 325–6. H. G. Tibbutt (ed.), *The Letter Books 1644–45 of Sir Samuel Luke*, p. 202.
2 PRO, SPDom., Charles II, S.P.29/xi/141. For Sir Samuel's financial problems see below, pp. 162–3.
3 G. C. Moore Smith (ed.), *The Letters of Dorothy Osborne to William Temple*, p. 46.
4 *CSPDom.*, *1651–2*, p. 566. HMC, *Seventh Report*, Appendix, p. 458.
5 See, for example, the memorandum book of John Harrington, BL, Additional MSS 10114, ff. 29, 31–4.
6 HMC, *Leyborne-Popham MSS*, pp. 58–9. *CSPDom.*, *1650*, pp. 34, 380, 521.
7 Cliffe, *Puritans in Conflict*, pp. 183–4. BL, Additional MSS 70006, fo. 189.
8 HMC, *Ninth Report*, Appendix, part II, pp. 394–6. *CSPDom.*, *1650*, pp. 61, 75. *CJ.*, vi, p. 618 and vii, pp. 33, 78.
9 *CSPDom.*, *1651*, pp. 86, 99, 114, 132, 523.
10 BL, Additional MSS 70125, Sir William Waller to Sir Edward Harley, 14 October 1651. *CSPDom.*, *1651–2*, pp. 90, 91, 125. *CJ*, vii, pp. 119, 274.
11 Staffordshire Record Office, Leveson-Gower MSS, D593/P/8/2/2, letter of John Langley to Sir Richard Leveson, 30 April 1653. John Nicholls (ed.), *Original Letters and Papers of State Addressed to Oliver Cromwell*, p. 84. Thomas Burton, *Diary of Thomas Burton* (ed. J. T. Rutt), iii, pp. 173, 176–7, 179, 180, 318. Sir Henry Vane, *A Healing Question*, *Somers Tracts*, vi, pp. 306–7. Sir Henry Vane, *The Tryal of Sir Henry Vane, Knight*, p. 47. Edmund Ludlow, *A Voyce from The Watch Tower*, ed. A. B. Worden, *Camden Fourth Series*, xxi, pp. 310–12, 314.
12 Burton, *Diary of Thomas Burton*, iii, pp. 99, 100. Lucy Hutchinson, *Memoirs of the Life of Colonel Hutchinson* (ed. James Sutherland), p. 214.
13 Staffordshire Record Office, Leveson-Gower MSS, D593/P/8/2/2,

letter of John Langley to Sir Richard Leveson, 18 June 1653. *The Parliamentary or Constitutional History of England*, xx, pp. 152–3, 175–8, 183. Other wealthy Puritan squires who were selected included Robert Duckenfield, Samuel Dunch, John Pyne, Sir William Roberts and Anthony Stapley. For a detailed discussion of the social composition of the Parliament of Saints see Austin Woolrych, *Commonwealth to Protectorate*, pp. 165–93.

14 *Thurloe State Papers*, i, pp. 749–50. PRO, SPDom., Charles II, S.P.29/xi/ 141.

15 *CSPDom., 1655*, pp. 78, 93, 94. PRO, SPDom. (1655), S.P.25/lxxviA/ 45. Clarendon, vi, p. 112.

16 Essex County Record Office, Hatfield Broad Oak MSS, D/DBa/A4, book of expenses of Sir John Barrington, ff. 24–6 and D/DBa/025, 029/1 and 2.

17 *Parliamentary History*, xx, pp. 297–304.

18 *Thurloe State Papers*, v, p. 349.

19 Bulstrode Whitelocke, *Memorials of the English Affairs*, iv, p. 272.

20 John Bridges, *The History and Antiquities of Northamptonshire*, ii, p. 383.

21 BL, Additional MSS 70007, ff. 76–7, 80–1.

22 *Thurloe State Papers*, v, pp. 396–7.

23 Ibid., v, p. 313.

24 Ibid., iii, pp. 299–300, 302.

25 Vane, *A Healing Question*, vi, pp. 303–15. *Thurloe State Papers*, v, pp. 328–9, 349. *CSPDom., 1656–7*, pp. 98, 194.

26 Dr Williams's Library, London, Baxter Letters, i, fo. 226.

27 Burton, *Diary of Thomas Burton*, iii, pp. 100–1. *Parliamentary History*, xxi, pp. 2–7. Whitelocke, *Memorials of the English Affairs*, iv, pp. 274–80.

28 BL, Additional MSS 33148, ff. 78, 80–3, 85. Burton, *Diary of Thomas Burton*, i, pp. 283–7, 324 and ii, p. 30.

29 Burton, *Diary of Thomas Burton*, i, p. 356.

30 Ibid., i, pp. 379, 393 and ii, p. 5. *A Narrative* and *A Second Narrative*, pp. 453, 455, 457, 459, 463–4, 486. *Parliamentary History*, xxi, pp. 65, 89, 99–102.

31 Whitelocke, *Memorials of the English Affairs*, iv, pp. 313–14, 329. W. C. Abbott (ed.), *The Writings and Speeches of Oliver Cromwell*, iv, pp. 951–3. Burton, *Diary of Thomas Burton*, iii, p. 102.

32 *Thurloe State Papers*, v, pp. 220, 297. *A Narrative* and *A Second Narrative*, *Harleian Miscellany*, iii, pp. 486–7.

33 *Thurloe State Papers*, vii, p. 68.

34 *Thurloe State Papers*, vii, pp. 74–5, 80–1. Clarendon, vi, p. 58, 59.

35 Edward Hyde, Earl of Clarendon, *Calendar of the Clarendon State Papers in the Bodleian Library* (ed. O. Ogle, W. H. Bliss, W. D. Macray and F. J. Routledge), iii, pp. 408–9 and iv, pp. 8–9, 12, 15, 17, 18, 20, 24, 25, 28. Thomas Carlyle, *The Letters and Speeches of Oliver Cromwell*, ed. S. C. Lomas, i, pp. 292–3, 298, 300–2, 412, ii, p. 53 and iii, pp. 471–2.

36 *Thurloe State Papers*, vi, p. 896.

37 Hyde, *Clarendon State Papers*, iv, pp. 30, 31. *CSPDom., 1657–8*, p. 357. *CSPDom., 1658–9*, pp. 113, 119, 233, 561, 582.

38 Clarendon, vi, pp. 59–63. *Thurloe State Papers*, vii, pp. 25, 65–9, 74–5,

77–90, 99, 110, 165–6. *Clarendon State Papers*, iv, p. 103.

39 Clarendon, vi, p. 98.

40 *Thurloe State Papers*, vii, pp. 495–6.

41 Sir Edward Nicholas, *Correspondence of Sir Edward Nicholas*, ed. Sir George F. Warner, *Camden Third Series*, xxxi, pp. 122, 124–5, 130, 134–5, 148, 152.

42 *CSPDom., 1658–9*, p. 349. Clarendon, iv, p. 223. *Clarendon State Papers*, iv, pp. 186, 194, 204.

43 *CSPDom., 1658–9*, pp. 355, 583. Hyde, *Clarendon State Papers*, iv, p. 194. Edmund Ludlow, *A Voyce from the Watch Tower*, ed. A. B. Worden, *Camden Fourth Series*, xxi, p. 86 and *Memoirs of Edmund Ludlow*, p. 276.

3 BRINGING BACK THE KING

1 Edward Hyde, Earl of Clarendon, *Calendar of the Clarendon State Papers in the Bodleian Library* (ed. O. Ogle, W. H. Bliss, W. D. Macray and F. J. Routledge), iv, pp. 146, 168–9, 176, 194, 205, 209, 235–6.

2 Sir Edward Nicholas, *Correspondence of Sir Edward Nicholas*, ed. Sir George F. Warner, *Camden Third Series*, xxxi, pp. 97–8.

3 *Clarendon State Papers*, iv, p. 282.

4 *CSPDom., 1659–60*, pp. 50, 53, 68. Nicholas, *Correspondence, Camden Third Series*, xxxi, p. 179.

5 *Clarendon State Papers*, iv, p. 348. Clarendon, vi, pp. 120–1. Sir William Waller, *Recollections*, in *The Poetry of Anna Matilda*, pp. 105–6.

6 Somerset Record Office, Combe of Earnshill MSS, DD/CM 64/5.

7 Bulstrode Whitelocke, *Memorials of the English Affairs*, iv, pp. 378, 380. *Thurloe State Papers*, vii, p. 795.

8 Edmund Ludlow, *Memoirs of Edmund Ludlow*, pp. 302–3, 308–9, 312, 315–6.

9 Bulstrode Whitelocke, *The Diary of Bulstrode Whitelocke, 1605–1675*, pp. 552–3.

10 *The Parliamentary or Constitutional History of England*, xxii, pp. 29–33, 36. *CSPDom., 1659–60*, p. 338.

11 Bulstrode Whitelocke, *Memorials of the English Affairs*, iv, pp. 384, 386–8, 392, 396.

12 Ibid., iv, p. 387. Lady Eliott-Drake, *The Family and Heirs of Sir Francis Drake*, i, pp. 420–2. PRO, SPDom. (1660), S.P.18/ccxviii/27, 28, 30, 31, 36–41, 43, 50.

13 PRO, SPDom. (1660), S.P.18/ccxviii/49. *CSPDom., 1659–60*, pp. 293–5, 356. BL, Egerton MSS 2618, fo. 60.

14 Robert Latham and William Matthews (eds), *The Diary of Samuel Pepys*, i, pp. 57, 60, 62. Whitelocke, *Memorials of The English Affairs*, iv, p. 398.

15 *CJ*, vii, p. 849. Latham and Matthews (eds), *The Diary of Samuel Pepys*, i, p. 65.

16 BL, Additional MSS 70007, fo. 188.

17 Ronald Hutton, *The British Republic 1649–1660*, p. 129. BL, Additional MSS 70007, ff. 190–4, 200–1, 207. *CJ*, vii, pp. 855, 856, 858, 862, 866, 867, 873, 874, 877, 878, 880. *A & O*, ii, pp. 1459–62.

18 Frances P. and Margaret M. Verney, *Memoirs of the Verney Family During the Seventeenth Century*, ii, p. 160.

19 *Clarendon State Papers*, iv, p. 609. *CJ*, vii, p. 862. Nicholas, *Correspondence*, p. 199.

20 *Clarendon State Papers*, iv, pp. 156, 165, 573, 590, 592, 593, 595, 599, 604, 609, 614, 615, 634, 674.

21 Ibid., iv, pp. 671, 672.

22 Ibid., iv, pp. 639, 644, 671. BL, Additional MSS, 32679, fo. 9. *HMC, Fourteenth Report*, Appendix, part IX, p. 482. Sir John Bramston, *Autobiography*, ed. Lord Braybrooke, *Camden Society*, xxxii, pp. 114–5.

23 Clarendon, vi, p. 217. *CJ*, viii, p. 7. Edmund Ludlow, *A Voyce from the Watch Tower*, ed. A. B. Worden, *Camden Fourth Series*, xxi, p. 121.

24 BL, Additional MSS 70009, fo. 126 and Egerton MSS 2618, fo. 71.

25 Ludlow, *A Voyce from the Watch Tower*, p. 149.

26 Clarendon, vi, pp. 206–7, 217.

27 *CSPDom., 1660–1*, p. 8. Whitelocke, *Diary*, pp. 592–3.

28 Lucy Hutchinson, *Memoirs of the Life of Colonel Hutchinson* (ed. James Sutherland), pp. 228–30. *CSPDom., 1660–1*, p. 39. *CJ*, viii, p. 56.

29 Ludlow, *A Voyce from the Watch Tower*, pp. 126–7, 153–4. *CJ*, viii, pp. 59–60.

30 *CJ*, viii, pp. 60–1, 63–4. *LJ*, xi, pp. 143–4. Whitelocke, *Diary*, pp. 597, 606.

31 An Act of Free and General Pardon, Indemnity and Oblivion, 12 Charles II, cap. xi. Latham and Matthews, *The Diary of Samuel Pepys*, i, pp. 178, 277. *CSPDom., 1660–1*, p. 434.

32 HMC, *Ninth Report*, Appendix, part II, p. 494.

33 *CJ*, viii, pp. 60, 67.

34 *CJ*, viii, p. 286. *CSPDom., 1660–1*, p. 413. BL, Additional MSS 23206, ff. 30–1. *CSPDom., 1661–2*, pp. 114, 301, 346, 408. Sir James Harrington, *Horae Consecratae*, pp. 127, 218, 244–7, 259, 260, 324, 373 and some unnumbered pages. Harrington had inherited an estate worth £3,300 a year (*Horae Consecratae*, pp. 429, 431).

35 *CJ*, viii, pp. 139, 177–9. Act of Attainder, 12 Charles II, cap. xxx.

36 BL, Egerton MSS 2650, fo. 358. *CJ*, viii, p. 179. *CSPDom., 1660–1*, pp. 446, 557.

37 *Clarendon State Papers*, iv, p. 671. *CSPDom., 1660–1*, pp. 213, 500.

38 BL, Additional MSS 46500, ff. 92–4.

39 *CSPDom., 1661–2*, pp. 238, 242, 249, 293, 421, 479, 507. *CSPDom., 1663–4*, pp. 76, 127. *CSPDom., 1668–9*, pp. 553, 558–9. John Nichols, *The History and Antiquities of the County of Leicester*, ii, p. 748.

40 BL, Additional MSS 70009, fo. 198. Sir Henry Vane, *The Tryal of Sir Henry Vane, Knight*, p. 92.

41 Bramston, *Autobiography*, xxxii, p. 117.

42 G.E.C. (ed.), *The Complete Peerage*, iii, p. 533 and iv, p. 135. G.E.C. (ed.), *Complete Baronetage*, iii, pp. 120, 189, 231, 272.

43 HMC, *Eleventh Report*, Appendix, part V, p. 3. HMC, *Fourteenth Report*, Appendix, part IX, p. 482. Staffordshire Record Office, Swinfen MSS, D(W) 1738/A/2/5/1.

44 *CSPDom., 1660–1*, p. 457. Hoghton family papers, *A Calendar of the*

Deeds and Papers in the Possession of Sir James De Hoghton, Bart., ed. J. H. Lumby, *Record Society of Lancashire and Cheshire*, lxxxviii, p. 258.

45 *CSPDom., 1660–1*, pp. 470, 515.

46 Bristol Record Office, Ashton Court MSS, AC/02/13 and AC/C74/19. H. A. Helyar, 'The Arrest of Colonel William Strode of Barrington, in 1661', *Somersetshire Archaeological and Natural History Society*, xxxvii, pp. 16, 18, 19, 24, 26, 38. *CSPDom., 1661–2*, pp. 145, 437–8, 441. Somerset Record Office, Combe of Earnshill MSS, DD/CM65/3,6. *DNB* (William Strode). HMC, *Ninth Report*, Appendix, part II, p. 494.

47 Lucy Hutchinson, *Memoirs of the Life of Colonel Hutchinson*, pp. 234, 237–8, 243–77. *A Narrative of the Late Parliament* and *A Second Narrative of the Late Parliament*, *Harleian Miscellany*, iii, pp. 33–8.

48 BL, Additional MSS 22548, fo. 73. Lyon Turner, i, p. 49. Curzon had been described in 1662 as 'a great Presbiterian' (PRO, SPDom., Charles II, S.P.29/lxvi/35).

49 HMC, *Earl of Verulam MSS*, pp. 61–71.

4   BARTHOLOMEW DAY

1 Sir William Waller, *Vindication of the Character and Conduct of Sir William Waller*, pp. 226–9.

2 Dr Williams's Library, London, Baxter Letters, vi, fo. 223. Richard Baxter, *Reliquiae Baxterianae* (ed. Matthew Sylvester), pp. 90–1, 97, 103–4, 112, 148–51, 238.

3 Sir Edward Harley, *An Humble Essay Toward the Settlement of Peace and Truth in the Church*, pp. 25, 28, 36.

4 Gilbert Burnet, *History of his Own Time*, i, pp. 342–4 and ii, p. 70. Edward Stillingfleet, *Irenicum*, pp. 64, 66, 67, 413–6, and *Origines Sacrae*, epistle dedicatory. Baxter, *Reliquiae Baxterianae*, pp. 232, 234, 238. HMC, *Seventh Report*, Appendix, p. 463. Timothy Goodwin, *The Life and Character of That Eminent and Learned Prelate, the Late Dr Edward Stillingfleet*, pp. 10, 12–15, 19–20.

5 *Clarendon State Papers*, iv, p. 654.

6 BL, Additional MSS 70126, Hereford ministers to Edward Harley, 30 June 1660.

7 Sir John Bramston, *Autobiography*, ed. Lord Braybrooke, *Camden Society*, xxxii, p. 116. *The Parliamentary or Constitutional History of England*, xxii, pp. 385–7.

8 Baxter, *Reliquiae Baxterianae*, pp. 254, 265, 273.

9 *Parliamentary History*, xxii, pp. 374, 408–9, 414. In a contemporary account of the Staffordshire gentry Sir John Bowyer was described as a man who 'pretends Reformation and to be orth[odox]'. (PRO, SPDom., Charles II, S.P.29/ccxcv/118–19).

10 Statute 12 Charles II, cap. xvii. *Parliamentary History*, xxii, p. 415.

11 Baxter, *Reliquiae Baxterianae*, pp. 259–64.

12 *Parliamentary History*, xxiii, pp. 4–5, 16, 26, 29–31. *CJ*, viii, pp. 176, 185, 191, 194. John Collinges, *The History of Conformity*, p. 26.

13 Douglas R. Lacey, *Dissent and Parliamentary Politics in England, 1661–1689*, pp. 29–31. *CJ*, viii, pp. 288–9, 296, 402, 404–6, 408–13, 417, 424.

14 Statute 14 Charles II, cap. iv. Baxter, *Reliquiae Baxterianae*, p. 422.
15 BL, Additional MSS 70009, ff. 207–8, 274.
16 Bodleian Library, Oxford, Rawlinson Letters 52, fo. 357.
17 H. I. Longden, *Northamptonshire and Rutland Clergy from 1500*, viii, p. 137, xiii, p. 249 and xv, p. 131.
18 J. T. Cliffe, *Puritan Gentry* pp. 190–1.
19 *NM*, i, pp. 466–7. *CR*, p. 248. PRO, Wills, PROB11/344/3. *CSPDom., 1682*, p. 608.
20 Bodleian Library, Oxford, Rawlinson Letters 109, fo. 87.
21 Act for the Confirming and Restoring of Ministers (12 Charles II, cap. xvii).
22 These men were the patrons of the following ejected ministers: Thomas Cole of Brampton Bryan and Richard Hawes of Leintwardine, both in Herefordshire (*CR*, pp. 125, 253); Samuel Fairclough of Kedington, John Woods of Barnardiston and Mark Mott of Great Wratting, all in Suffolk (Samuel CLark, *The Lives of Sundry Eminent Persons*, part I, pp. 163–75. See also Cliffe, *Puritan Gentry*, pp. 176–7, *CR*, pp. 358, 541); Thomas Walker of Assington, Suffolk (*CR*, p. 507); Edward Bennet of East Morden and John Mitchell of Langton Matravers, both in Dorset (*CR*, pp. 47–8, 351); and Richard Symons of Southwick, Hampshire (*CR*, p. 443).
23 Clark, *The Lives of Sundry Eminent Persons*, part I, pp. 163–75. See also Cliffe, *Puritan Gentry*, pp. 176–7.
24 Clark, *The Lives of Sundry Eminent Persons*, part II, p. 202. Northamptonshire Record Office, Langham (Cottesbrooke) MSS, LC(C), 1623, 1624. PRO, Wills, PROB11/336/79. Thomas Burroughs, *A Soveraign Remedy for All Kinds of Grief* and *Directions About Preparing for Death*, preface addressed to the reader. *CR*, p. 91.
25 PRO, Institution Books, Series B, ii, fo. 307. BL, Additional MSS 70008, fo. 97. *DNB* (Pierce).
26 *CR*, p. 186. Dr Williams's Library, London, A. G. Matthews's collection of abstracts of wills of ejected ministers.
27 *CR*, pp. 139, 244. *NM*, i, pp. 285–6. BL, Additional MSS 15857, fo. 67.
28 Statute 17 Charles II, cap. ii. The formal title of this statute was 'An Act for Restraining Non-Conformists from inhabiting in Corporations'.
29 Lyon Turner, i, p. 191. *NM*, i, p. 285.
30 For further details about chaplains employed by the Puritan gentry see Chapter 10 and the Appendix.
31 See Chapter 12.
32 *NM*, i, p. 248. *Al.Cant.*, i, p. 258.
33 *NM*, i, pp. 324–7. Derbyshire Record Office, Chandos-Pole-Gell MSS, 54/16(c).
34 J. D. (John Dan), *Sermon at the Funeral of Lady Mary Armyne*, dedication to the reader by Richard Baxter. Clark, *The Lives of Sundry Eminent Persons*, part II, p. 194. PRO, Wills, PROB11/347/22. Bryan Dale, *Yorkshire Puritanism and Early Nonconformity*, p. 14. Ralph Thoresby, *Letters to Ralph Thoresby*, ed. W. T. Lancaster, *Thoresby Society*, xxi, p. 30.
35 Northamptonshire Record Office, Knightley MSS, K.LV.584.

36 PRO, Wills, PROB11/323/2. *CR*, pp. 47–8, 92. *NM*, ii, pp. 366–7. Similarly, Lady Amy Mildmay, the widow of Sir Henry Mildmay of Graces Hall in Essex, left money to thirteen ministers who were all named (PRO, Wills, PROB11/335/6, will dated 18 May 1669).

37 *CR*, p. 261. PRO, Chancery Proceedings, Six Clerks' Series, C.6/183/51.

38 Bodleian Library, Oxford, Rawlinson Letters 50, fo. 40. *NM*, ii, pp. 7–8. PRO, Wills, PROB11/328/137. *CR*, pp. 61–2, 313, 393.

39 See above, p. 38.

40 William Bridge, *Twenty One Several Books of Mr William Bridge*, ii, epistle dedicatory. Hertfordshire County Record Office, Lawes-Wittewronge of Rothamsted MSS, D/ELw F31.

41 Robert Latham and William Matthews (eds), *The Diary of Samuel Pepys*, iii, pp. 290–1.

42 Hertfordshire County Record Office, Lytton MSS 23451.

43 BL, Additional MSS 70140, copy of letter from Sir Edward Harley to his son Edward, 2 January 1692.

44 *Farewel Sermons*, pp. 369–70.

5 CHANGE AND DECAY

1 *The English Revolution. III, Newsbooks I. Oxford Royalist*, i, p. 216.

2 BL, Additional MSS 30013, fo. 59. George Lipscomb, *The History and Antiquities of the County of Buckingham*, ii, pp. 259–69.

3 *The English Revolution*, iii, p. 449. Christopher Shute, *Ars piè Moriendi: or the True Accomptant*, epistle dedicatory and pp. 25, 26, 29. PRO, Chancery Proceedings, Six Clerks' Series, C.9/43/107 and C.10/475/230. John Worthington, *The Diary and Correspondence of Dr John Worthington*, ed. R. C. Christie, *Chetham Society*, cxiv, p. 289. Samuel Clark, *The Lives of Sundry Eminent Persons*, part II, pp. 192–6.

4 Sir Joseph Williamson, 'Lincolnshire Families, Temp. Charles II', *Herald and Genealogist*, ii, p. 126. PRO, Chancery Proceedings, Six Clerks' Series, C.6/30/98, C.7/424/11, C.9/38/72 and C.10/71/106. BL, Harleian MSS 165, fo. 228. The following families also died out in the direct male line before 1700: Assheton of Whalley Abbey, Lancashire; Barrow of Barningham, Suffolk; Brereton of Handforth, Cheshire; Bright of Badsworth, Yorkshire; Brooke of Cockfield Hall, Yoxford, Suffolk; Cutts of Childerley, Cambridgeshire; Fowell of Fowelscombe, Devon; Honywood of Marks Hall, Essex; Mildmay of Graces Hall, Essex; Morley of Glynde, Sussex; Purefoy of Wadley, Berkshire; Rosewell of Forde Abbey, Devon, then of Limington, Somerset; Sleigh of Ashe, Derbyshire; Stoughton of Stoughton, Surrey; Wentworth of Somerleyton, Suffolk; Wilbraham of Weston under Lizard, Staffordshire; and Winwood of Ditton Park, Buckinghamshire. In some cases the estates passed to a kinsman with the same surname.

5 John Bridges, *The History and Antiquities of Northamptonshire*, i, pp. 66, 69–70. Edmund Ludlow, *A Voyce from The Watch Tower*, ed. A. B. Worden, *Camden Fourth Series*, xxi, p. 286. Northamptonshire Record

Office, Knightley MSS, K.XLV.509. George Ormerod, *The History of the County Palatine and County of Chester*, ii, p. 231. For the Knightley trusteeship arrangements see below, p. 106–8.

6 HMC, *Fourteenth Report*, Appendix, part II, pp. 240–1. BL, Additional MSS 70123, Peter Sainthill to Sir Edward Harley, 11 January 1661, and Egerton MSS 3330, ff. 14, 16. Edmund Calamy, *The Happinesse of Those who Sleep in Jesus*, p. 31. PRO, Wills, PROB11/330/78. B. D. Henning (ed.), *The History of Parliament: The House of Commons 1660–1690*, iii, p. 659. Despite the terms of his father's will Sir William Waller the younger was involved in the sale of the Osterley estate in 1670 (*VCH, Middlesex*, iii, p. 109).

7 BL, Additional MSS 53726, fo. 32.

8 Somerset Record Office, Combe of Earnshill MSS, DD/CM66/2, 6, 13. PRO, Chancery Proceedings, Six Clerks' Series, C.6/196/103.

9 PRO, Chancery Proceedings, Six Clerks' Series, C.6/35/110 and Wills, PROB11/357/67. Somerset Record Office, Combe of Earnshill MSS, DD/CM54, 71, 74, 79.

10 *Al.Cant.*, iii, p. 92. Hertfordshire County Record Office, Lytton MSS, 22891. BL, Stowe MSS 744, fo. 118.

11 Hertfordshire County Record Office, Lytton MSS 22896, 23453. R. Clutterbuck, *The History and Antiquities of the County of Hertford*, ii, pp. 376–8.

12 Essex County Record Office, Hatfield Broad Oak MSS, D/DBa/A4, ff. 22–4; F25; L26, 32, 34, 35, 49, 51. BL, Egerton MSS 2648, ff. 205, 225; 2649, fo. 173; 2650, fo. 153; 2651, fo. 183; and Additional MSS 27357, ff. 28, 32, 37.

13 Essex County Record Office, Hatfield Broad Oak MSS, D/DBa/E30/1 and F27. BL, Additional MSS 27355, fo. 25; and Egerton MSS 2650, ff. 112, 113, 115, 126.

14 BL, Egerton MSS 2650, ff. 111, 134.

15 BL, Additional MSS 27352, ff. 20, 22, 98, 195; 27353, ff. 52, 257; 27354, fo. 68; and 27355, ff. 30–1, 85–6, 141, 152, 175, 205, 220. fo. S Moller (ed.), *Alumni Felstedienses*, p. 6.

16 William Dillingham, *A Sermon at the Funeral of the Lady Elizabeth Alston*, pp. 40, 44.

17 PRO, Chancery Proceedings, Six Clerks' Series, C.8/302/119 and Wills, PROB11/445/92. Hertfordshire County Record Office, Lawes-Wittewronge of Rothamsted MSS, D/ELw/F29.

18 BL, Additional MSS 70112, Lady Elizabeth Alston to Sir Edward Harley, 4 July, 29 July and —— August 1697, Harley to Sir Rowland Alston, 13 August 1697; Sir Rowland Alston to Harley, 22 August 1697; and 70120, Harley to Anne Jollife, 12 August 1697, Anne Jollife to Harley, 11 March 1698 and undated letter. PRO, Wills, PROB11/442/279.

19 Thomas Manton, *A Practical Commentary, or an Exposition with Notes on the Epistle of Jude*, epistle dedicatory.

20 Bodleian Library, Oxford, Rawlinson Letters 53, fo. 30. *DNB* (Edmund Dunch).

21 Bodleian Library, Oxford, Rawlinson Letters 53, ff. 165, 256. PRO,

Wills, PROB 11/425/52. Anthony Wood, *The Life and Times of Anthony Wood*, iii, p. 441.

22 Robert Latham and William Matthews (eds), *The Diary of Samuel Pepys*, i, pp. 142, 161, 220, 295. PRO, Chancery Proceedings, Six Clerks' Series, C.10/175/118, and Institution Books, Series B, ii, fo. 323. Northamptonshire Record Office, Miscellaneous MSS, YZ 1351, 1352, 1354, 1355, 1356. BL, Additional Charter 45794.

23 Edward Reynolds, *A Sermon Touching the Use of Humane Learning*, epistle dedicatory. For the Yelverton family see also J. T. Cliffe, *The Puritan Gentry*, pp. 12, 26, 27, 48, 67, 95, 135, 206.

24 G. C. Moore Smith (ed.), *The Letters of Dorothy Osborne to William Temple*, pp. 106, 134. Anthony Wood, *Athenae Oxonienses*, ii, cols 340–1. PRO, Wills, PROB11/335/43. See also J. T. Cliffe, *Puritans in Conflict*, p. 193.

25 Wood, *The Life and Times of Anthony Wood*, ii, p. 13. A. G. Watson, *The Library of Sir Simonds D'Ewes*, pp. 56, 57, 60, 61, 91.

26 Richard Baxter, *Reliquiae Baxterianae* (ed. Matthew Sylvester), p. 448. BL, Additional MSS 70125, Francis Tallents to Sir Edward Harley, 31 December 1695.

27 BL, Additional MSS 70014, fo. 59 and 10114, John Hampden to Sir Edward Harley, 2 September 1690 and 10 December 1691; and Stowe MSS 747, fo. 16.

28 BL, Additional MSS 70125, Francis Tallents to Sir Edward Harley, 16 April, 2 July, 17 December and 31 December 1695 and 13 June 1696.

29 BL, Additional MSS 70018, fo. 158; 70125, Francis Tallents to Sir Edward Harley, 13 June 1696; and 70127, Harley to Richard Hampden, 24 February 1697.

6   A GODLY ELITE

1 PRO, Wills, PROB11/361/158.
2 BL, Additional MSS 29910, fo. 88. Bodleian Library, Oxford, Rawlinson Letters 50, fo. 22.
3 Folger Shakespeare Library; Newdigate Newsletters, L.c.1906. BL, Additional MSS 15857, fo. 67. PRO, Wills, PROB11/462/151.
4 Isaac Ambrose, *Redeeming the Time*, p. 14.
5 Seth Bushell, *The Believer's Groan for Heaven*, pp. 26, 27. BL, Additional MSS 4460, fo. 23. John Howe, *The Whole Works*, i, pp. 4, 8, 61.
6 Oliver Heywood, *His Autobiography, Diaries, Anecdote and Event Books* (ed. J. Horsfall Turner), i, p. 281 and ii, p. 44. *CR*, p. 57. *NM*, ii, p. 573.
7 BL, Stowe MSS 744, fo. 61.
8 J. T. Cliffe, *Puritans in Conflict*, pp. 59–60, 187.
9 Dr Williams's Library, London, Morrice MSS J, 44 and Baxter Letters, iv, ff. 142, 183–4, 208–9 and v, ff. 3, 9–11.
10 William Bagshaw, *De Spiritualibus Pecci*, pp. 56–9.
11 *CR*, p. 474. Lyon Turner, i, p. 54. Derbyshire Record Office, Chandos-Pole-Gell MSS, 47/15(c). *DNB* (Tallents).
12 *CR*, p. 373. *NM*, i, pp. 308–13. *DNB* (John Otefield). Walter Wilson, *The

History and Antiquities of Dissenting Churches and Meeting Houses in London, Westminster, and Southwark, iv, p. 161. Otefield's sons spelt their surname as 'Oldfield'.

13 Derbyshire Record Office, Chandos-Pole-Gell MSS, 41/31(bb), 66/11(s).
14 Derbyshire Record Office, Chandos-Pole-Gell MSS, 66/11(ga).
15 Derbyshire Record Office, Chandos-Pole-Gell MSS, 66/11(q).
16 Derbyshire Record Office, Chandos-Pole-Gell MSS, 66/11(t), 67/11(v).
17 HMC, *Ninth Report*, Appendix, part II, p. 398. BL, Stowe MSS 746, fo. 112.
18 Derbyshire Record Office, Chandos-Pole-Gell MSS, 66/11(ja). Bagshaw, *De Spiritualibus Pecci*, p. 60.
19 Richard Baxter, *Reliquiae Baxterianae* (ed. Matthew Sylvester), part III, p. 93. PRO, Wills, PROB11/351/57. B. D. Henning (ed.), *The History of Parliament: The House of Commons 1660–1690*, ii, pp. 336–40.
20 BL, Additional MSS 4460, fo. 62; 70114, Paul Foley to Sir Edward Harley, 23 March 1685 and 3 October 1687; and 70118, Elizabeth Harley to Sir Edward Harley, 8 October 1687. Gilbert Burnet, *History of his Own Time*, iv, p. 197.
21 Northamptonshire Record Office, Knightley MSS, K.LV.584.
22 *CSPDom., 1680–1*, p. 86. PRO, Wills, PROB11/435/239. John Bridges, *The History and Antiquities of Northamptonshire*, i, pp. 66, 70. BL, Additional MSS 70014, ff. 62, 85.
23 Staffordshire Record Office, Paget MSS, D603/k/2/2/28, 38, 42, 51, 55, 58 and D603/k/2/4/17. BL, Additional MSS 29910, fo. 20. John Wilford, *Memorials and Characters, Together with the Lives of Divers Eminent and Worthy Persons*, pp. 365–7.
24 Staffordshire Record Office, MS 100/1, p. 23 and Paget MSS, D603/k/2/2/60 and D603/k/3/2/120. BL, Additional MSS 29910, ff. 12–13, 164. Howe, *The Whole Works*, i, pp. 79–80.
25 BL, Additional MSS 29910, ff. 124, 296; 30013, fo. 58; and 70116, Abigail Harley to Sir Edward Harley, 16 August 1692.
26 BL, Additional MSS 29910, fo. 275. Sir Joseph Williamson, 'Lincolnshire Families, Temp. Charles II', *Herald and Genealogist*, ii, p. 121. *NM*, ii, pp. 168–70.
27 Bedfordshire County Record Office, Lucas MSS, L30/20/17.
28 Dr Williams's Library, London, Morrice MSS, P, 242. BL, Additional MSS 30013, ff. 52–3.
29 BL, Additional MSS 70012, fo. 62; 70013, fo. 77; 70016, Sir Edward Harley to Abigail Harley, 8 November 1692; 70017, fo. 230; 70018, ff. 14, 31; 70019, ff. 68, 110; and 70,138 B and C, accounts, no pagination.
30 BL, Additional MSS 29910, ff. 114–16, 119, 123, 132, 134–5, 139, 175–6, 278.
31 The contemporary spelling of Booth's title varied between 'Delamer' and 'Delamere'.
32 BL, Additional MSS 70006, ff. 285–6; and 70128, Sir Edward Harley to his wife, 2 July 1664.
33 Bodleian Library, Oxford, Rawlinson Letters 50, ff. 144, 146, 152, 197.
34 Buckinghamshire Record Office, Claydon House MSS (Letters), Sir

Roger Burgoyne to Sir Ralph Verney, 9 March 1672.

35 Derbyshire Record Office, Chandos-Pole-Gell MSS, 56/16.
36 BL, Additional MSS 30013, fo. 42.
37 Hampshire Record Office, Jervoise of Herriard Park MSS, 44M69/ E77, Lady Honor St Barbe to Thomas Jervoise the younger, 28 June 1687 and 1 July 1688. Lady St Barbe was a daughter of Richard Norton the Hampshire parliamentarian.
38 BL, Additional MSS 70114, Thomas Foley to Sir Edward Harley, undated letter [1688].
39 BL, Additional MSS 70124, Ralph Strettell to Sir Edward Harley, undated letter, 28 November 1671, 6 January 1672, 5 May, 4 August and 19 September 1674 and 1 September 1677. *CR*, p. 466.
40 BL, Additional MSS 70123, Erasmus Saunders to Sir Edward Harley, 18 December 1696.

7 IN COMMUNION

1 Bodleian Library, Oxford, Carte MSS 79, fo. 22. Anne Whiteman and Mary Clapinson (eds), *The Compton Census of 1676: A Critical Edition.*
2 BL, Stowe MSS 185, fo. 172.
3 Seth Bushell, *The Believer's Groan for Heaven*, pp. 26, 27.
4 William Dillingham, *A Sermon at the Funeral of the Lady Elizabeth Alston*, pp. 41–2. Whiteman and Clapinson, *Compton Census*, p. 325.
5 Zachary Cawdrey, *The Certainty of Salvation*, p. 27. M. H. Lee (ed,), *Diaries and Letters of Philip Henry*, p. 303. Henry Newcombe, *Diary of Rev. Henry Newcome from Sept. 30, 1661 to Sept. 29, 1663*, ed. T. Heywood, *Chetham Society*, xviii, pp. 140, 182. Bodleian Library, Oxford, Tanner MSS 35, fo. 117.
6 Thomas Pritchard, *A Sermon Preached at the Funeral of the Lady Lumley*, p. 23.
7 Harley was not, of course, referring here to the Church of Rome but to the Catholic Church in the general sense in which this term was used in the Apostles' Creed.
8 Lady Brilliana Harley, *Letters of the Lady Brilliana Harley*, ed. T. T. Lewis, *Camden Society*, lviii, pp. 240–2.
9 HMC, *Duke of Portland MSS*, v, p. 643.
10 For Harley's relations with nonconformist divines see above, pp. 11, 65, 81 and below, pp. 88, 99, 119, 130, 151–2, 159, 196–7.
11 Guildhall Library, London, Diocese of London Records, Episcopal Visitation Books, MS 9537/20, 17 and MS 9583/2, part VI, fo. 69.
12 *CSPDom., 1660–1*, p. 234. Northamptonshire Record Office, Miscellaneous MSS, ZB 73/30/1. BL, Lansdowne MSS 1027, fo. 56; and 1028, ff. 57, 260.
13 Bulstrode Whitelocke, *The Diary of Bulstrode Whitelocke, 1605–1675* (ed. Ruth Spalding), pp. 668, 670, 671, 675, 686, 689, 694, 703, 706, 708, 711, 717, 744, 783, 793, 808.
14 W. A. Shaw, *A History of the English Church, 1640–1660*, ii, p. 421. Bristol Record Office, Ashton Court MSS, AC/02/13. Somerset

Record Office, Combe of Earnshill MSS, DD/CM66/5. PRO, Wills, PROB11/357, 67.

15 PRO, Wills, PROB11/339/106.

16 J. T. Cliffe, *Puritan Gentry*, p. 161. PRO, Wills, PROB11/333/94.

17 BL, Additional MSS 70062, undated note by Sir Edward Harley about the ceremonial requirements; and 70233, Sir Edward Harley to Robert Harley, 13 August 1680. Sir Edward Harley, *An Humble Essay Toward the Settlement of Peace and Truth in the Church*, pp. 6, 7, 11, 14, 16, 18, 19, 24.

18 See, for example, Cliffe, *Puritan Gentry*, pp. 27–9, 224–5.

19 M. H. Lee (ed.), *Diaries and Letters of Philip Henry*, p. 87. *CJ*, viii, pp. 247, 258, 289. BL, Egerton MSS 2043, fo. 10. Edmund Ludlow, *A Voyce from the Watch Tower*, ed. A. B. Worden, *Camden Fourth Series*, xxi, p. 288.

20 Statute 25 Charles II, cap. ii. BL, Additional MSS 70012, ff. 51, 53; and Stowe MSS 185, ff. 177–8. PRO, Wills, PROB11/336/79. Richard Kidder, *The Life of Richard Kidder, D. D., Bishop of Bath and Wells Written by Himself*, ed. Amy Edith Robinson, *Somerset Record Society*, xxxvii, pp. 18–20. It is clear from Sir Roger Burgoyne's reactions that he rarely took communion and that for him the sacramental test was a matter of great consequence (Buckinghamshire Record Office, Claydon House MSS (Letters), Sir Roger Burgoyne to Sir Ralph Verney, 19 and 26 May and 2 and 9 June 1673).

21 Lyon Turner, i, p. 54. William Bagshaw, *De Spiritualibus Pecci*, pp. 57–9.

22 Richard Mayo, *A Sermon Preach'd in the Parish-Church of St James – Clerken-well on Occasion of the Much Lamented Death of the Honourable the Lady Diana Asshurst*, pp. 17–18. Lady Ashurst was one of the daughters of William Lord Paget (1609–78).

23 Borthwick Institute of Historical Research, Diocese of York, Archdeacon's Visitations, Y.V/CB3, 1680, City of York, ff. 498–9. I am grateful to Dr David Scott for providing me with this and other material from the York Diocesan Records.

24 J. W. Ryland, *Records of Wroxall Abbey and Manor, Warwickshire*, introduction, pp. xxxv, xxxvi, lvi, lviii–lxii, lxiv–lxv. Buckinghamshire Record Office, Claydon House MSS (Letters), Sir Roger Burgoyne to Sir Ralph Verney, 9 June 1673 and epitaph in verse on Burgoyne signed R. B. and received by Verney on 23 November 1677. Whiteman and Clapinson, *Compton Census*, pp. 175, 187. *NM*, ii, pp. 487, 492–3. Cliffe, *Puritan Gentry*, pp. 183–4.

25 Humphrey Whyle, *A Sermon Preach'd at the Funeral of Anne Lady Burgoyne*, pp. 7–9, 22–3.

26 Whyle, *A Sermon*, pp. 11, 12, 14. Bedfordshire County Record Office, Burgoyne MSS, DDX 143/1, no pagination. *DNB* (Comber and Addison). PRO, Wills, PROB11/419/71. Anthony Wood, *The Life and Times of Anthony Wood*, i, p. 359.

27 Wood, *The Life and Times of Anthony Wood*, i, pp. 363, 364. Dr Williams's Library, London, Morrice MSS, Q, 507. Adam Martindale, *The Life of Adam Martindale*, ed. R. Parkinson, *Chetham Society*, iv, p. 196. BL, Additional MSS 4236, ff. 95–6.

28 BL, Additional MSS 70235, Sir Edward Harley to Robert Harley, 7 July 1693. This was Bishop William Lloyd.
29 Dr Williams's Library, London, Morrice MSS, Q, 584. Thomas Hearne, *Remarks and Collections of Thomas Hearne, Oxford Historical Society*, vii, p. 343. Wood, *The Life and Times of Anthony Wood*, ii, pp. 26, 346, 422 and iii, p. 379. BL, Additional MSS 70015, ff. 55, 64, 94, 99.
30 *NM*, i, p. 220. *CR*, p. 16. Dr Williams's Library, Morrice MSS, J, 35.
31 *CR*, p. 381. PRO, Institution Books, Series B, ii, fo. 208. BL, Additional MSS 24485, ff. 32, 34.
32 *CSPDom., 1683*, pp. 187, 234.
33 Bodleian Library, Oxford, MS ADD C305, fo. 227.
34 Bodleian Library, Oxford, Rawlinson MSS, D1163, ff. 8–13, 16–18, 20.
35 Whiteman and Clapinson, *Compton Census*, pp. 382, 386, 387. Cliffe, *Puritan Gentry*, pp. 180–2. Bodleian Library, Oxford, Rawlinson MSS, D1163, fo. 12.
36 Northamptonshire Record Office, Peterborough Diocesan Records, Archdeaconry of Northampton, Correction Book 1682–3, Box X 638.7, no pagination.
37 Whiteman and Clapinson, *Compton Census*, pp. 52, 334, 447, 455, 600. C. V. Collier, *An Account of the Boynton Family*, pp. 24–6. Borthwick Institute of Historical Research, York Diocesan Records, Visitation Court Book, 1674/CB, fo. 283. The gentry families resident in the other parishes were the Curzons, Honywoods, Hesilriges and Wilbrahams.
38 Cliffe, *Puritan Gentry*, pp. 111, 164–5. John Nichols, *The History and Antiquities of the County of Leicester*, ii, pp. 748, 750, 754. *NM*, ii, p. 116.

8 GOSPEL PREACHING

1 Richard Baxter, *Faithful Souls Shall Be With Christ*, p. 42.
2 See, for example, J. T. Cliffe, *Puritans in Conflict*, pp. 142, 143.
3 Samuel Clark, *The Lives of Sundry Eminent Persons*, part I, p. 175. Gilbert Burnet, *History of his Own Time*, i, p. 343. PRO, Institution Books, Series B, ii, fo. 215. Thomas Birch, *The Life of the Most Reverend Dr John Tillotson*, pp. 24, 27. Charles Darby, *An Elegy on the Death of the Queen*.
4 BL, Additional MSS 70011, ff. 5, 103. PRO, Institution Books, Series B, i, fo. 179.
5 Staffordshire Record Office, Bradford Collection, 18/4/43. *Staffordshire Parish Registers Society: Weston-under-Lizard Parish Register*, introduction, p. v.
6 BL, Additional MSS 15857, fo. 67. For Halsey see above, pp. 45–60.
7 Dr Williams's Library, London, Baxter Letters, ii, ff. 187, 200–23. *Al.Cant.*, ii, p. 83. PRO, Institution Books, Series B, ii, fo. 200.
8 BL, Additional MSS 70019, fo. 321. Much of the phraseology in this passage was clearly borrowed from the sermon preached by Seth Wood at the funeral of Sir William Armyne in 1651: see J. T. Cliffe, *The Puritan Gentry*, p. 185.

9   BL, Additional MSS 70005, ff. 75–6, 91–2; 70006, fo. 13; 70008, fo. 221; 70010, ff. 25, 35, 37; and 70083, Thomas Cole to Sir Edward Harley, 17 January 1663. *CR*, p. 125. Bodleian Library, Oxford, Rawlinson Letters 52, fo. 340. *Al.Oxon.*, p. 978. A.T.Bannister (ed.), *Diocese of Hereford Institutions*, p. 34.

10 BL, Additional MSS 70012, fo. 39; and 70233, Sir Edward Harley to Robert Harley, 20 and 27 April 1685; and Lansdowne MSS 721, fo. 153. Bannister, *Diocese of Hereford Institutions*, pp. 42, 45.

11 BL, Additional MSS 70013, ff. 236, 252, 262, 264; 70128, Sir Edward Harley to his wife, 20 and 27 June 1685; 70143, fo. 24; and 70233, Sir Edward Harley to Robert Harley, 27 April, 21 July and 7 August 1685. *DNB* (Burgess).

12 BL, Additional MSS 70013, ff. 266, 268, 272, 275; 70128, Sir Edward Harley to Robert Harley, 27 October 1685; and 70233, same to same, 1 and 11 September and 1 and 16 October 1685. Bannister, *Diocese of Hereford Institutions*, p. 48.

13 BL, Additional MSS 70014, ff. 54, 56, 66; and 70112, William Beard, Mayor of Newcastle under Lyme, to Sir Edward Harley, 25 April 1688.

14 BL, Additional MSS 70014, ff. 58, 68, 82, 85, 89, 91, 95–6, 99, 101–3, 105; and 70233, Sir Edward Harley to Robert Harley, 14 June, 13 July and 18/19 July 1688. *NM*, ii, p. 618.

15 BL, Additional MSS 70120, Sir Edward Harley to Maurice Lloyd, 6 August 1688 and Lloyd to Harley, 8 August 1688; and 70233, Sir Edward Harley to Robert Harley, 3 August 1688.

16 Bannister, *Diocese of Hereford Institutions*, p. 50. BL, Additional MSS 70014, ff. 126, 171, 190, 201, 209, 213, 215, 219; and 70233, Sir Edward Harley to Robert Harley, 26 January, 16 March and 2 April 1689.

17 BL, Additional MSS 70116, Abigail Harley to Sir Edward Harley, 9 August 1692; and 70118, Edward Harley to Sir Edward Harley, 29 October 1689.

18 This may have been Walter Jackman or Jakeman who had graduated at Lincoln College, Oxford in 1675 (*Al.Oxon.*, p. 793).

19 BL, Additional MSS 70114, Paul Foley to Sir Edward Harley, 2, 5 and 17 April 1684. Bannister, *Diocese of Hereford Institutions*, p. 47.

20 BL, Additional MSS 70114, Thomas Foley to Sir Edward Harley, 23 November and 29 December 1685; and 70226, Foley to Robert Harley, 31 August, 7 and 16 November and 5 December 1685.

21 BL, Additional MSS 70014, fo. 41.

22 BL, Additional MSS 70014, fo. 350; 70016, ff. 148–9; 70120, George Nelson to Sir Edward Harley, 14 December 1696; and 70270, Robert Harley to his wife, 1 November 1690.

23 BL, Additional MSS 70017, fo. 237; 70117, Abigail Harley to Sir Edward Harley, 16 March 1695; 70118, Martha Harley to Sir Edward Harley, 14 March ——; 70120, George Nelson to Sir Edward Harley, 24 September 1694, 6 October 1695, 3 October 1696, 26 June and 19 July 1699; and 70234, Sir Edward Harley to Robert Harley, 7 November 1691.

24 BL, Additional MSS 70019, ff. 99, 103; 70120, George Nelson to Sir Edward Harley, 24 April 1699; and 70140, Thomas Foley to Edward

Harley, 7 March 1697. Thomas Hearne, *Remarks and Collections of Thomas Hearne, Oxford Historical Society*, ii, p. 221.

25 Northamptonshire Record Office, Knightley MSS, K.III.41.
26 BL, Additional MSS 29910, fo. 195 and 70114, Thomas Foley to Sir Edward Harley, 12 July 1697; and Lansdowne MSS 1029, fo. 41. Northamptonshire Record Office, Knightley MSS, K.LVI.594,600.
27 BL, Additional MSS 29910, fo. 296; and 70118, Edward Harley to Sir Edward Harley, 18 December 1697.
28 BL, Additional MSS 70019, fo. 56; and 70114, Thomas Foley to Sir Edward Harley, 4 February 1699.
29 BL, Lansdowne MSS 1029, ff. 41, 140; Additional MSS 70019, ff. 76, 78, 93, 94, 113 and 70275, Joseph Walferne to Robert Harley, 10 June 1699 and unsigned letter addressed to Robert Harley, 25 July 1699. Northamptonshire Record Office, Knightley MSS, K.LVI.607.
30 *NM*, i, pp. 451–2.
31 BL, Additional MSS 70114, Paul Foley to Sir Edward Harley, 24 October 1698. PRO, Wills, PROB11/453/189.
32 *NM*, i, pp. 222, 248. Nathaniel Parkhurst, *The Faithful and Diligent Christian Described and Exemplified*, p. 72.
33 Cliffe, *Puritan Gentry*, pp. 15, 21–2, 44, 135–6. BL, Egerton MSS 2649, ff. 195, 202, 217, 224.

9 CONVENTICLES AND MEETING HOUSES

1 *CSPDom., 1682*, pp. 608–9.
2 Robert Latham and William Matthews (eds), *The Diary of Samuel Pepys*, ix, pp. 30–1.
3 *CSPDom., 1682*, p. 382. *CSP Dom., 1683*, p. 78. PRO, Wills, PROB11/425/44.
4 *CSPDom., 1660–1*, p. 470.
5 PRO, SPDom., Charles II, S.P.29/cix/56.
6 PRO, SPDom., Charles II, S.P.29/xciii/6 and ci/102.
7 Seth Ward, Bishop, 'Some Letters from Bishop Ward of Exeter, 1663–1667', *Devon and Cornwall Notes and Queries*, xxi, pp. 285–6. *CSPDom., 1682*, pp. 37, 97–8. PRO, SPDom., Charles II, S.P.29/cvii/99.
8 Ward, 'Letters', pp. 226, 284–7, 330–1.
9 John Collinges, *Par Nobile. Two Treatises*, pp. 21–2, 30–1, 36–7. Bodleian Library, Oxford, Tanner MSS 115, ff. 49–51.
10 Collinges, *Par Nobile*, p. 37.
11 Statute 16 Charles II, cap. iv.
12 Richard Baxter, *Reliquiae Baxterianae* (ed. Matthew Sylvester), pp. 435–6.
13 Bulstrode Whitelocke, *The Diary of Bulstrode Whitelocke, 1605–1675* (ed. Ruth Spalding), pp. 636, 675, 684, 686, 689, 695, 696, 706–8, 711–14, 717–19, 723, 725, 726, 735, 736, 742, 748, 761, 770, 772, 778, 779, 781, 795, 796, 808, 815, 821, 836, 838.
14 Lyon Turner, i, pp. 44, 114, 163 and iii, p. 345.
15 J. T. Cliffe, *Puritan Gentry*, pp. 167–8. *NM*, i, pp. 407–8, 452.

16 Bodleian Library, Oxford, Rawlinson Letters 50, fo. 40. PRO, Wills, PROB11/328/138. *CR*, pp. 238–9. Whitelocke, *Diary*, p. 743.

17 Lyon Turner, i, p. 163 and iii, p. 761. Joseph Hunter, *South Yorkshire: The History and Topography of the Deanery of Doncaster*, ii, pp. 131–2. BL, Additional MSS 24484, fo. 48. Oliver Heywood, *His Autobiography, Diaries, Anecdote and Event Books* (ed. J. Horsfall Turner), i, pp. 234, 259, 265. *NM*, ii, pp. 143, 557, 572, 578–9.

18 *CJ*, ix, pp. 66, 71, 78, 87, 90. Anchitell Grey, *Debates of the House of Commons, 1667–1694*, i, pp. 104, 106, 111. *CSPDom., 1667–8*, p. 276.

19 Grey, *Debates of the House of Commons*, i, pp. 127, 129, 131.

20 *CSPDom., 1668–9*, p. 412. BL, Additional MSS 70128, Sir Edward Harley to his wife, 17 July 1669.

21 Statute 22 Charles II, cap. i. BL, Additional MSS 70011, ff. 226, 252.

22 Whitelocke, *Diary*, pp. 753, 754, 772.

23 Buckinghamshire Record Office, Claydon House MSS (Letters), Sir Roger Burgoyne to Sir Ralph Verney, 26 February 1672. *CSPDom., 1671–2*, pp. 305, 306, 308, 326, 337, 355, 376, 409, 411, 414, 434, 435, 437, 444, 500, 502, 586. *CSPDom., 1672*, pp. 33, 95. *CSPDom., 1672–3*, p. 260.

24 Lyon Turner, i, pp. 261, 268. *CR*, p. 350.

25 Lyon Turner, i, pp. 318, 353. *CR*, pp. 430, 527.

26 *NM*, ii, p. 636. Samuel Annesley, *The Life and Funeral Sermon of the Reverend Mr Thomas Brand*, pp. 18–19, 21. *CSPDom., 1671–2*, pp. 396–7.

27 *CSPDom., 1671–2*, p. 585. *CSPDom., 1672*, p. 33. Whitelocke, *Diary*, p. 795.

28 *CSPDom., 1671–2*, pp. 319, 410, 411, 414, 500, 568. *CSPDom., 1672*, pp. 577, 679. *CSPDom., 1672–3*, p. 261. Holman's elder brother (George Holman of Warkworth, Northamptonshire) was a Catholic who lived mainly in France (Anthony Wood, *The Life and Times of Anthony Wood*, i, p. 276. HMC, *Eleventh Report*, Appendix, part II, p. 228).

29 PRO, Institution Books, Series A, iii, fo. 251 and Wills, PROB11/361/129. Cliffe, *Puritan Gentry*, p. 178. *CR*, pp. 268, 507.

30 *CSPDom., 1671–2*, pp. 309, 337, 344 (James Small, chaplain to Sir John Davie, and Henry Cornish, chaplain to Sir Philip Harcourt). *CSPDom., 1672–3*, p. 176.

31 *CJ*, ix, pp. 264–6, 271, 279–81. BL, Additional MSS 70012, ff. 16, 18, 25, 33, 37.

32 Bodleian Library, Oxford, Rawlinson Letters 51, fo. 39.

33 Sir Henry Ashurst, *Some Remarks upon the Life of that Painful Servant of God Mr Nathanael Heywood*, pp. 30–5. *CR*, p. 259. Nathaniel Heywood, *Christ Displayed, as the Choicest Gift and Best Master*, epistle dedicatory written by Oliver Heywood.

34 William Harris, *Some Memoirs of the Life and Character of the Reverend and Learned Thomas Manton*, pp. 18, 40–1. HMC, *Duke of Buccleuch MSS*, i, p. 321. Baxter, *Reliquiae Baxterianae*, part III, p. 156.

35 Baxter, *Reliquiae Baxterianae*, part III, pp. 171–2.

36 J.D. (John Dan), *Sermon at the Funeral of Lady Mary Armyne*, dedication to the reader by Richard Baxter.

37 Baxter, *Reliquiae Baxterianae*, part III, p. 189 and *Faithful Souls Shall Be With Christ*, epistle dedicatory.

38 BL, Additional MSS 27352, fo. 196; 27354, ff. 14, 94–5, 106, 109, 115; and 27355, fo. 83.
39 Dr Williams's Library, London, Baxter Letters, ii, fo. 318.
40 BL Additional MSS 70015, ff. 267, 268; 70118, Edward Harley to Sir Edward Harley, 30 December 1691; 70119, Robert Harley to Sir Edward Harley, 12 December 1691; 70138B, account book, no pagination; 70233, Sir Edward Harley to Robert Harley, 20 August and 28 December 1680; and 70235, same to same, 11 December 1691. Baxter, *Reliquiae Baxterianae*, Appendix, pp. 130–2. *NM*, ii, p. 535.
41 BL, Egerton MSS 3330, ff. 14–16.
42 Harris, *Some Memoirs of the Life and Character of the Reverend and Learned Thomas Manton*, pp. 17, 35. William Bates, *A Funeral Sermon Preached Upon the Death of the Reverend and Excellent Divine Dr Thomas Manton*, pp. 51–2.
43 Walter Wilson, *The History and Antiquities of Dissenting Churches and Meeting Houses in London, Westminster, and Southwark*, i, pp. 331–2, 334–5, 339. BL, Additional MSS 29556, fo. 361.
44 BL, Stowe MSS 745, ff. 115–16; Stowe MSS 746, fo. 50; and Additional MSS 4460, fo. 20. Heywood, *His Autobiography, Diaries, Anecdote and Event Books*, ii, pp. 61, 67, 93, 98.
45 BL, Additional MSS 4460, ff. 81, 82; and 24484, fo. 48. Hunter, *South Yorkshire*, ii, p. 132. Ralph Thoresby, *The Diary of Ralph Thoresby* (ed. Joseph Hunter), i, p. 109.
46 Dr Williams's Library, London, Morrice MSS, P, 341, 355, 376, 409. BL, Additional MSS 70143, fo. 9. *CSPDom., 1683–4*, p. 229.
47 J. C. Jeaffreson (ed.), *Middlesex County Records*, iv, pp. 177–8. Dr Williams's Library, London, Morrice MSS, P, 377, 379, 380.
48 HMC, *Seventh Report*, Appendix, p. 680.
49 Dr Williams's Library, London, Morrice MSS, P, 530, 570 and Q, 34.
50 Isaac Watts, *Death and Heaven*, pp. 248–9, 251. Peter Toon (ed.), *The Correspondence of John Owen (1616–1683)*, pp. 157–61. For Edward Terry see the Appendix, p. 216.

10   KEEPING A CHAPLAIN

1 J. T. Cliffe, *The Puritan Gentry*, pp. 162–8.
2 See the Appendix below for a detailed list.
3 See, for example, Adam Martindale's reference in his diary to a number of Cheshire gentry who had domestic chaplains (Adam Martindale, *The Life of Adam Martindale*, ed. R. Parkinson, *Chetham Society*, iv, p. 203).
4 *CSPDom., 1671–2*, pp. 27, 326. *CR*, p. 293. Jacombe married a daughter of John Gurdon the Suffolk landowner.
5 BL, Additional MSS 33148, ff. 121, 123, 125, 130, 142. *CR*, p. 485.
6 *CR*, p. 193. PRO, Chancery Proceedings, Six Clerks' Series, C.8/302/119.
7 Martindale, *The Life of Adam Martindale*, pp. 197, 202, 203, 233. When Richard Norton was seeking a new chaplain in November 1672 he

offered a salary of £40 a year. This was considered to be a generous allowance for a young man who was just beginning his ministry (*The Autobiography of Henry Newcome, Chetham Society*, xxvii, pp. 202–3).

8 HMC, *Fourteenth Report*, Appendix, part IX, pp. 484, 497–8. *Al.Oxon.*, p. 1542.

9 PRO, Wills, PROB11/390/43. *Al. Oxon.*, p. 29. PRO, Institution Books, Series B, iv, p. 203.

10 See the Appendix below.

11 *CR*, pp. 82, 106–7, 120. E. W. Harcourt, *The Harcourt Papers*, ii, pp. 2–3.

12 *CR*, p. 99. *NM*, ii, p. 596. Dr Williams's Library, London, Morrice MSS, J, 14. *CSPDom., 1683*, pp. 168–70, 220, 227. Borthwick Institute of Historical Research, Wills in the York Registry, vol. 60, fo. 376.

13 *CR*, pp. 368, 473. George Swinnock, *The Works*, epistle dedicatory.

14 *CR*, p. 186. George Ewbank, *The Pilgrim's Port*, pp. 114, 116.

15 *NM*, ii, pp. 14–15, 21–3. *CR*, pp. 370, 427–8. BL, Additional MSS 39970, ff. 55, 66, 77. *CSPDom., 1672*, pp. 474, 476. Hampshire Record Office, Diocese of Winchester Records, Churchwardens' Presentments, 202 M85/3/1109–13. HMC, *Fourth Report*, Appendix, p. 231.

16 *NM*, i, pp. 529–30. *CR*, p. 331. *DNB* (Lukin). Gordon, p. 40. *CSPDom., 1671–2*, p. 304.

17 See below, pp. 156–61.

18 Lyon Turner, i, p. 54. *CR*, p. 474. Walter Wilson, *The History and Antiquities of Dissenting Churches and Meeting Houses in London, Westminster, and Southwark*, i, pp. 373–4 and iv, p. 161.

19 Joshua Toulmin, *An Historical View of the State of the Protestant Dissenters in England*, pp. 559, 562. BL, Additional MSS 24484, fo. 153. Dr Williams's Library, London, Baxter Letters, iii, fo. 237 and An Account of the Dissenting Academies from the Restoration of Charles the Second, p. 2.

20 PRO, Wills, PROB11/429/238. James Wood, *The Believer's Committing of his Soul to Christ Considered*, pp. 29, 30. Alexander Gordon, *Cheshire Classis Minutes, 1691–1745*, p. 187. Irene Parker, *Dissenting Academies in England*, pp. 60–1, 63.

21 BL, Additional MSS 70014, Paul Foley to Sir Edward Harley, 24 October 1698 and 24 July and 2 August 1699; 70019, ff. 43, 75, 76, 78; and 70091, Sir Edward Harley to the Bishop of Hereford, 24 March 1699. A. T. Bannister (ed.), *Diocese of Hereford Institutions, 1539–1900*, pp. 56, 58. *Al.Cant.*, i, p. 377. *Al. Oxon.*, p. 1675.

22 *CR*, pp. 445, 511. PRO, Wills, PROB11/358/109. Essex County Record Office, Hatfield Broad Oak MSS, D/DBa/A66/19. BL, Additional MSS 27352, fo. 213; and 27353, fo. 222. Bodleian Library, Oxford, Rawlinson Letters 104, fo. 84. Gordon, p. 50.

23 West Suffolk Record Office, Barnardiston Family Archive, 871. Joseph Boyse, *A Sermon on the Occasion of the Death of the Reverend Mr Elias Travers*, p. 15. *Al.Cant.*, iv, p. 261.

24 Wilson, *The History and Antiquities of Dissenting Churches and Meeting Houses in London, Westminster, and Southwark*, iv, p. 161. *DNB* (Joshua Oldfield). BL, Additional MSS 70014, ff. 21, 44, 324; 70128, Sir Edward Harley to his wife, 12 May 1685; 70140, Thomas Foley to Edward

Harley, 6 March 1688; 70226, Thomas Foley to Robert Harley, 10 November 1687; and 70233, Sir Edward Harley to Robert Harley, 27 August 1687. Dr Williams's Library, London, Blackmore Papers, volume of correspondence, 18.

25 See above, pp. 82–3.

26 John Howe, *The Whole Works*, i, p. 4.

27 Martindale, *The Life of Adam Martindale*, iv, pp. 177, 210, 223. *CR*, pp. 251, 272, 303. BL, Additional MSS 24484, fo. 132.

28 BL, Additional MSS 4460, fo. 23. *CR*, p. 423. Thomas Jolly, *The Notebook of the Rev. Thomas Jolly AD 1671–1693*, Chetham Society, New Series, xxxiii, p. 134.

29 *Chetham Society*, New Series, xxxiii, p. 133. *NM*, ii, p. 81. BL. Additional MSS 24484, fo. 132. Samuel Wright, *A Sermon Occasion'd by the Death of the late Reverend Mr Thomas Cotton, MA*, pp. 27, 30. Dr Williams's Library, London, An Account of the Dissenting Academies from the Restoration of Charles the Second, p. 12.

30 PRO, Wills, PROB11/363/71. *CR*, pp. 102–3.

31 HMC, *Bath MSS*, i, pp. 45–8. Hertfordshire County Record Office, Verulam (Gorhambury) MSS, IX, A62. *A Catalogue of the Graduates in the Faculties of Arts, Divinity, and Law, of the University of Edinburgh*, p. 103.

32 *CR*, p. 288. Joseph Hunter (ed.), *Letters of Eminent Men Addressed to Ralph Thoresby*, i, pp. 84–6, 179, 192–3, 261. PRO, Wills, PROB11/412/233.

33 *CR*, p. 50. M. H. Lee (ed.), *Diaries and Letters of Philip Henry*, p. 264.

34 *NM*, i, p. 316. *Staffordshire Parish Registers Society: Weston- under-Lizard Parish Register*, p. 22. Staffordshire Record Office, Bradford Collection, P/372 5/3.

35 *NM*, ii, p. 225.

36 Oliver Heywood, *His Autobiography, Diaries, Anecdote and Event Books* (ed. J. Horsfall Turner), i, pp. 223–4 and *A Narrative of the Holy Life and Happy Death of Mr John Angier*, pp. 62, 70.

37 Bulstrode Whitelocke, *The Diary of Bulstrode Whitelocke, 1605–1675*, (ed. Ruth Spalding), pp. 713, 719, 738. *NM*, i, p. 235.

38 BL, Additional MSS 29910, fo. 226.

11   THE GODLY HOUSEHOLD

1 Bodleian Library, Oxford, Rawlinson Letters 51, fo. 200. M. H. Lee (ed.), *Diaries and Letters of Philip Henry*, p. 314.

2 BL, Additional MSS 70011, fo. 152; 70012, ff. 5, 8; 70128, Sir Edward Harley to his wife, 6 February 1673; and 70144, Sir Edward Harley to Abigail Harley, 21 June 1690.

3 Thomas Pritchard, *A Sermon Preached at the Funeral of Mrs Mary Dawes*, pp. 20–1.

4 Thomas Pritchard, *A Sermon Preached at the Funeral of the Lady Lumley*, epistle dedicatory and pp. 16, 21–4.

5 PRO, Wills, PROB11/466/150. Henry Cooke, *A Sermon Preached at the*

Funeral of the Lady Lumley, pp. 18, 19. BL, Additional MSS 70140, Sir Edward Harley to Edward Harley, 3 March 1694.

6 Anthony Wood, *The Life and Times of Anthony Wood*, iii, p. 70.
7 Adam Martindale, *The Life of Adam Martindale*, ed. R. Parkinson, *Chetham Society*, iv, p. 197.
8 BL, Additional MSS 70019, fo. 322.
9 Samuel Annesley, *The Life and Funeral Sermon of the Reverend Mr Thomas Brand*, pp. 13–14. William Bagshaw, *De Spiritualibus Pecci*, pp. 57–9.
10 George Hughes, *Aphorisms or Select Propositions of the Scripture Shortly Determining the Doctrine of the Sabbath*, epistle dedicatory written by Obadiah Hughes, pp. 3, 4, 6.
11 BL, Additional MSS 70013, ff. 89, 250–1; 70017, fo. 188; 70233, Sir Edward Harley to Robert Harley, 16 December 1690; and 70235, same to same, 3 March 1694. Under the provisions of the statute 5 and 6 William and Mary, cap. xxii the commissioners for the licensing of hackney coaches in London had authority to allow up to 175 (out of a total of 700) coaches to ply for hire on the Lord's Day.
12 John Howe, *The Whole Works*, i, p. 64.
13 BL, Additional MSS 70012, fo. 10.
14 Joseph Hunter (ed.), *The Diary of Ralph Thoresby (1677–1724)*, i, p. 176 and ii, p. 432.
15 Isaac Watts, *Death and Heaven*, p. 250.
16 Samuel Clark, *The Lives of Sundry Eminent Persons*, part II, p. 203.
17 Pritchard, *A Sermon Preached at the Funeral of the Lady Lumley*, p. 22. Humphrey Whyle, *A Sermon Preach'd at the Funeral of Anne Lady Burgoyne*, pp. 8–9, 12–13.
18 Joseph Boyse, *Some Remarkable Passages in the Holy Life and Death of the late Reverend Mr Edmund Trench*, pp. 53, 58, 61.
19 In the autumn of 1687, for example, there was a special day of prayer at Witley Court, the Worcestershire seat of Thomas Foley, which was concerned with matters of both public and private concern (BL, Additional MSS 70014, fo. 41; and 70233, Sir Edward Harley to Robert Harley, 28 September 1687).
20 BL, Additional MSS 27356, ff. 34–5.
21 BL, Additional MSS 27351, ff. 51, 60–1, 70; 27352, fo. 185; 27353, fo. 32; 27354, fo. 67; 27355, fo. 16; 27356, fo. 104; and 27357, fo. 35. (References in the diary, Additional MSS 27351 to 27355, to her meetings with fellow Puritans are too frequent to be cited here.) Alan Macfarlane (ed.), *The Diary of Ralph Josselin 1616–1683*, p. 577.
22 Thomas Hervey (ed.), *Some Unpublished Papers Relating to the Family of Sir Francis Drake*, p. 50.
23 Gilbert Burnet, *History of his Own Time*, ii, p. 70. Zachary Cawdrey, *The Certainty of Salvation*, p. 27.
24 Whyle, *A Sermon Preach'd at the Funeral of Anne Lady Burgoyne*, p. 14.
25 PRO, Wills, PROB 11/323/2.
26 BL, Additional MSS 70009, ff. 260–2; 70013, fo. 204; 70060, catalogue of books, 9 October 1662 and bookseller's bill, 22 June 1675; and 70235, Sir Edward Harley to Robert Harley, 24 June 1684.

27 BL, Additional MSS 70013, fo. 50.
28 Bedfordshire County Record Office, Lucas MSS, L30/20/3.
29 Borthwick Institute of Historical Research, Wills in the York Registry, vol. 58A, fo. 271.
30 Thomas Burroughs, *A Soveraign Remedy for all Kinds of Grief*, p. 82.
31 Pritchard, *A Sermon Preached at the Funeral of the Lady Lumley*, p. 21.
32 John Wilford, *Memorials and Characters, Together with the Lives of Divers Eminent and Worthy Persons*, p. 326. Clark, *The Lives of Sundry Eminent Persons*, part II, p. 203. Richard Wroe, *A Sermon at the Funeral of the Right Honourable Henry, Earl of Warrington*, p. 20 and *A Sermon Preached at Bowden in Cheshire, April 6th 1691, at the Funeral of the Right Honourable Mary Countess of Warrington*, pp. 20–1.
33 HMC, *Duke of Portland MSS*, v, p. 645. BL Additional MSS 70019, fo. 323.
34 BL, Additional MSS 70130, Sir Edward Harley to Elizabeth Harley, 19 May 1696.
35 BL, Additional MSS 29910, fo. 225. Staffordshire Record Office, Swinfen MSS, D(W)1738/A/2/9.
36 BL, Additional MSS 70013, fo. 220.
37 HMC, *Bath MSS*, i, p. 44. Additional MSS 70015, fo. 103; 70233, Sir Edward Harley to Robert Harley, 30 November 1685; and 70234, same to same, 8 June 1691 and 12 July 1692.

12 EDUCATION IN AN UNGODLY WORLD

1 Adam Martindale, *The Life of Adam Martindale*, ed. R. Parkinson, *Chetham Society*, iv, p. 174.
2 See, for example, the reference to unlicensed teachers in and about London in *CSPDom., 1682*, p. 609.
3 See above, p. 46.
4 Bedfordshire County Record Office, Lucas MSS, L30/20/13.
5 J. T. Cliffe, *The Puritan Gentry*, pp. 80–1.
6 BL, Additional MSS 27351, ff. 12, 23, 275; and 27353, fo. 101. William Shelton, *A Sermon at the Funeral of Mr Christopher Glascock, the Late Eminent School-master of Felsted in Essex*, pp. 21, 24, 26–8.
7 Essex County Record Office, Hatfield Broad Oak MSS, D/DBa/A21, A66/36, A67/16, A70/6, F42. F. S. Moller (ed.), *Alumni Felstedienses*, pp. 6, 7, 10. *Al.Cant.*, ii, p. 401.
8 BL, Additional MSS 33148, ff. 124, 130, 135, 141, 149, 151–3, 160, 163, 165, 174; and 33149, ff. 135, 162, 177. *CSPDom., 1668–9*, p. 65. W. G. Hart (ed.), *The Register of Tonbridge School from 1553 to 1820*, pp. 35, 136. *DNB* (Wase and Littleton). *CR*, pp. 226, 494.
9 Martindale, *The Life of Adam Martindale*, iv, pp. 175, 177, 178, 196–7.
10 *NM*, i, pp. 224–5. Lord Russell, *The Speech of the Late Lord Russell to the Sheriffs at the Place of Execution*, 21 July 1683, p. 1.
11 Bulstrode Whitelocke, *The Diary of Bulstrode Whitelocke, 1605–1675* (ed. Ruth Spalding), pp. 615, 633–4, 636. For other chaplains who also acted as tutors see the Appendix (Bickley, Dunch of North Baddesley, Hungerford, Irby, Middleton, Roberts and Strickland).

12 Anthony Wood, *The Life and Times of Anthony Wood*, i, p. 465.
13 Bodleian Library, Oxford, Rawlinson Letters 49, *passim. NM*, i, p. 529. J. T. Cliffe, *Puritans in Conflict*, p. 196.
14 Staffordshire Record Office, Paget MSS, D603/k/2/2/28. *CSPDom., 1671*, p. 88. *NM*, ii, p. 333. *CSPDom., 1680–1*, p. 86. BL, Additional MSS 70018, fo. 175. Dr Williams's Library, London, Henry MSS, 90.5, Matthew Henry to Philip Henry, 8 June 1686.
15 William Tong, *Some Memoirs of the Life and Death of the Reverend Mr John Shower*, pp. 19–43. BL, Additional MSS 41818, ff. 289, 290; and 41819, ff. 116, 118, 206.
16 BL, Additional MSS 70011, ff. 91, 184, 194, 208, 212–13, 235, 237, 238, 252, 270; and 70115, Lady Abigail Harley to Sir Edward Harley, undated letter.
17 *NM*, ii, pp. 302–7. *CR*, p. 56.
18 BL, Additional MSS 70012, ff. 251, 266, 305, 307; 70231, Lady Abigail Harley to Robert Harley, 22 February 1677; and 70233, Sir Edward Harley to Robert Harley, 6 November 1675 and 6 August 1677.
19 Bodleian Library, Oxford, Rawlinson Letters 50, fo. 42 and 51, ff. 74–5. BL, Additional MSS 70012, ff. 202, 283; and 70014, fo. 5.
20 BL, Additional MSS 70013, ff. 28, 29.
21 Anthony Wood, *Athenae Oxonienses*, ii, col. 789. Cf. Wood, *The Life and Times of Anthony Wood*, ii, p. 477.
22 Bodleian Library, Oxford, Rawlinson Letters 51, fo. 244.
23 Cliffe, *Puritan Gentry*, Chapter 5.
24 Bodleian Library, Oxford, Rawlinson Letters 109, fo. 68. *CSPDom., 1660–1*, p. 510. *DNB* (Tuckney).
25 BL, Additional MSS 70114, Anthony Fido to Sir Edward Harley, 11 August 1660. F. J. Varley (ed.), *The Restoration Visitation of the University of Oxford and its Colleges, 1660*, Camden Third Series, lxxix.
26 Wood, *The Life and Times of Anthony Wood*, i, pp. 356–7, 359–60, 370, 423, 465 and ii, p. 56. See also HMC, *Fifth Report*, Appendix, pp. 374, 376.
27 Wood, *The Lives and Times of Anthony Wood*, i, p. 301.
28 BL, Additional MSS 70012, ff. 293, 309; 70013, ff. 39, 101, 104, 137; 70128, Sir Edward Harley to his wife, 1 January 1681; 70231, Lady Abigail Harley to Robert Harley, 27 July 1680 and 12 July 1681; and 70233, Sir Edward Harley to Robert Harley, 20 August 1680.
29 BL, Egerton MSS 2646, fo. 161; 2648, fo. 364; and 2649, ff. 31, 35–6, 43, 79, 290, 309, 315. Essex County Record Office, Hatfield Broad Oak MSS, D/DBa/C6. W. W. Rouse-Ball and J. A. Venn (eds), *Admissions to Trinity College Cambridge*, ii, pp. 338, 445, 465. HMC, *Seventh Report*, Appendix, p. 570.
30 *Al.Oxon.*, p. 1666. Hertfordshire County Record Office, Lawes-Wittewronge of Rothamsted MSS, D/ELw/F29.
31 *Al.Oxon.*, p. 1138. BL, Additional MSS 33146, ff. 17, 18, 20; and 33148, ff. 165, 168, 169, 193, 195, 200. Wood, *The Life and Times of Anthony Wood*, ii, p. 332.
32 Wood, *Athenae Oxonienses*, ii, col. 405. *Al.Oxon.*, p. 1517.
33 Derbyshire Record Office, Chandos-Pole-Gell MSS, 47/19(a). *Al. Oxon.*, p. 556.

NOTES

34 *Al.Oxon.*, pp. 20, 1090, 1607, 1620.
35 Whitelocke, *Diary*, pp. 731, 739, 743–5. Bodleian Library, Oxford, Rawlinson Letters 50, ff. 87, 93, 97.
36 Wood, *The Life and Times of Anthony Wood*, iii, p. 447.
37 Bodleian Library, Oxford, Rawlinson Letters 51, fo. 220.
38 *Al.Cant.*, i, p. 92. See Cliffe, *Puritan Gentry*, pp. 100–2.
39 For a general account of the dissenting academies see Irene Parker, *Dissenting Academies in England*.
40 Edmund Calamy (1671–1732), *A Continuation of the Account of the Ministers, Lecturers, Masters and Fellows of Colleges and Schoolmasters who were Ejected and Silenced after the Restoration in 1660*, i, pp. 177–97 and ii, pp. 731–45. Bodleian Library, Oxford, Rawlinson MSS, D208, ff. 1, 24. BL, Additional MSS 4236, fo. 57.
41 Daniel Williams, *A Funeral Sermon at the Decease of the Reverend Mr John Woodhouse*, pp. 104, 105. *NM*, ii, pp. 297–300.
42 Parker, *Dissenting Academies in England*, p. 71. Staffordshire Record Office, Paget MSS, D603/k/3/2/120. Bodleian Library, Oxford, Rawlinson Letters 51, fo. 347. BL, Additional MSS 70125, Francis Tallents to Sir Edward Harley, 13 June 1696; and 70226, Thomas Foley to Robert Harley, 30 March 1689. Dr Williams's Library, London, An Account of the Dissenting Academies from the Restoration of Charles the Second, p. 1.
43 Bodleian Library, Oxford, Rawlinson Letters 51, fo. 347.
44 BL, Additional MSS 70016, fo. 46; 70114, Thomas Foley to Sir Edward Harley, 25 July 1693; 70226, Thomas Foley to Robert Harley, 17 December 1687 and 26 February and 13 April 1689; 70227, Thomas Foley the younger to Robert Harley, 23 February, 1 May and 26 December 1689 and 6 November 1690; and 70270, Robert Harley to his wife, 19 May 1691.
45 Dr Williams's Library, London, letters to Bishop Stillingfleet, 201.38, Bishop Lloyd of Lichfield and Coventry, 13 November 1693. Parker, *Dissenting Academies in England*, p. 139.
46 Samuel Wesley, *A Letter from a Country Divine to his Friend in London, Concerning the Education of the Dissenters in their Private Academies*, pp. 5–7. Parker, *Dissenting Academies in England*, pp. 59–63. See also *CSPDom., 1682*, pp. 381–2, 551.
47 BL, Additional MSS 70013, fo. 81; and 70140, Sir Edward Harley to Edward Harley, 21 March 1682.
48 BL, Additional MSS 70141, Charles Morton to Edward Harley, 15 December 1683.
49 BL, Additional MSS 70013, fo. 262. Parker, *Dissenting Academies in England*, p. 138.
50 Bodleian Library, Oxford, Rawlinson Letters 51, ff. 87, 92, 102, 114. Narcissus Luttrell, *A Brief Historical Relation of State Affairs from September 1678 to April 1714*, i, p. 371. BL, Additional MSS 70013, ff. 264, 321.
51 Samuel Bury, *A Funeral Sermon Occasioned by the Death of the Late Reverend Mr Samuel Cradock BD*, p. 44. *CR*, pp. 140–1.
52 Joshua Toulmin, *An Historical View of the Protestant Dissenters in England*, p. 592.

53 Hertfordshire County Record Office, Lawes-Wittewronge of Rotham-sted MSS, D/ELw/F29. Sir William's son Henry was one of Cradock's pupils (Toulmin, *An Historical View*, p. 592).
54 Parker, *Dissenting Academies in England*, pp. 65–7, 139. *CR*, pp. 211–12. Oliver Heywood, *His Autobiography, Diaries, Anecdote and Event Books* (ed. J. Horsfall Turner), ii, pp. 10, 12, 15.
55 Staffordshire Record Office, Paget MSS, D603/k/3/2/120. BL, Additional MSS 70226, Thomas Foley the elder to Robert Harley, 26 February 1689.
56 *Al.Oxon.*, pp. 459, 513, 647. E. W. Harcourt, *The Harcourt Papers*, ii, p. 1. BL, Additional MSS 70114, Paul Foley to Sir Edward Harley, 9 December 1689.

13   GETTING AND SPENDING

1 J. T. Cliffe, *Puritans in Conflict*, pp. 81–92.
2 Dorset County Record Office, Roper MSS, D55/T60. PRO, Chancery Proceedings, Six Clerks' Series, C.6/166/117. Cliffe, *Puritans in Conflict*, p. 90. G. E. Aylmer, *The State's Servants: The Civil Service of the English Republic 1649–1660*, pp. 19–20, 167, 230, 272.
3 Cliffe, *Puritans in Conflict*, p. 87. East Devon Record Office, Drake of Buckland Abbey MSS, E59, F735, F736, F741, F769. Lady Eliott-Drake, *The Family and Heirs of Sir Francis Drake*, ii, pp. 4, 5, 28–30, 40–1, 65.
4 PRO, Chancery Proceedings, Six Clerks' Series, C.10/102/114. Clement Walker, *The Compleat History of Independency*, part I, p. 170. *VCH, Bedfordshire*, ii, pp. 340–3 and iii, p. 239. BL, Lansdowne MSS 887, fo. 39. In 1703 Nicholas Luke of Wood End was named as a trustee when Sir John Burgoyne settled his estate (J. W. Ryland, *Records of Wroxall Abbey and Manor, Warwickshire*, p. 194).
5 Lady Brilliana Harley, *Letters of the Lady Brilliana Harley*, ed. T. T. Lewis, *Camden Society*, lviii, p. 230. BL, Additional MSS 70091, notes on revenue and debts; and 70123, Samuel Shilton to Sir Edward Harley, 27 March 1651.
6 Hampshire Record Office, Jervoise of Herriard Park MSS, 44M69/F9, F10, F12, 07. PRO, Chancery Masters' Exhibits, C.103/36, Private Act, 1730. See also HMC, *Seventh Report*, Appendix, pp. 98, 117.
7 PRO, Chancery Proceedings, Six Clerks' Series, C.6/20/64 and C.7/141/47; and Wills, PROB11/290/212. Staffordshire Record Office, Cavenagh-Mainwaring MSS, D1743/T221h, T224; and MS 100/1, 21. J. G. Cavenagh-Mainwaring, 'The Mainwarings of Whitmore', *William Salt Archaeological Society, Collections for a History of Staffordshire* (1933), p. 66.
8 Hull University Library, Wickham-Boynton MSS, DDWB 20/56. PRO, Chancery Proceedings, Six Clerks' Series, C.5/31/12. Northamptonshire Record Office, Dryden MSS, D(CA) 305, 591, 661.
9 Statute 12 Charles II, cap. xi, section xlviii.
10 Lambeth Palace Library, London, MS 951/1, ff. 48–9. PRO, Exchequer, Land Revenue, Miscellaneous Books, L.R.2/cclxvi/fo.1. *CSPDom.*,

1661–2, p. 479. Leicestershire Record Office, MSS of Lord Hazlerigg of Noseley, DG21/78, 87, 90, 98, 106–7.

11 *CSPDom., 1661–2*, p. 409. Charles Dalton, *History of the Wrays of Glentworth, 1523–1852*, ii, pp. 114–15. BL, Additional MSS 27353, ff. 146, 148, 166, 176, 235–7.

12 Anthony Wood, *The Life and Times of Anthony Wood*, ii, p. 137. BL, Additional MSS 70125, Francis Tallents to Sir Edward Harley, 13 June 1696. PRO, Chancery, Entry Books of Decrees and Orders, C.33/cclx/ fo. 215. In the reign of Charles II Richard Hampden's estate was said to be worth £2,500 a year but in the last decade of the century the estate revenue amounted to only £1,355 a year. (Buckinghamshire Record Office, Notebook of Richard Grenville, D/X2/27, and Earl of Buckinghamshire MSS, 35/29).

13 Borthwick Institute of Historical Research, Wills in the York Registry, vol. 58A, fo. 11. Joseph Hunter, *South Yorkshire: The History and Topography of the Deanery of Doncaster*, ii, p. 136. G.E.C. (ed.), *Complete Baronetage*, iii, p. 150.

14 BL, Additional MSS 27355, fo. 25; 29910, fo. 119; and 33412, ff. 78, 89–91. Simeon Ashe, *The Efficiency of God's Grace in Bringing Gain-Saying Sinnes to Christ*, epistle dedicatory addressed to Lady Margaret Hungerford. *NM*, ii, pp. 513–14. PRO, Wills, PROB11/342/58. Narcissus Luttrell, *A Brief Historical Relation of State Affairs from September 1678 to April 1714*, i, p. 395.

15 Luttrell, *A Brief Historical Relation*, iv, pp. 583–4 and v, p. 14. BL, Additional MSS 30013, fo. 42. PRO, SPDom., Charles II, S.P.29/cdxxi/ 216. Staffordshire Record Office, MS 100/1, 19. Somerset Record Office, Popham MSS, DD/PO 32/2 and DD/POt 119. For the Boscawens, Barringtons, Grimstons and Pelhams see below, nn.16–19.

16 BL, Additional MSS 33144, ff. 210–15.

17 Essex County Record Office, Hatfield Broad Oak MSS, D/DBa/A73, A76/29, A77/8 and F27. Bodleian Library, Oxford, Rawlinson Letters 50, fo. 102. Northamptonshire Record Office, Langham (Cottesbrooke) MSS, L(C)918, letter from Sir Thomas Samwell to John Langham, 26 November 1691.

18 PRO, Chancery Masters' Exhibits, C.108/65, 66, 67. B. D. Henning (ed.), *The History of Parliament: The House of Commons 1660–1690*, i, p. 748. BL, Egerton MSS 2650, fo. 134.

19 BL, Harleian MSS 991, fo. 14. Hertfordshire County Record Office, Verulam (Gorhambury) MSS, I.A. 42, 45, 51, 66, 66A and IX.A., 23–4, 41, 47, 49. Dr Williams's Library, London, Morrice MSS, P, 452. Gilbert Burnet, *History of his Own Time*, ii, pp. 69–70.

20 *Royal Commission on Historical Monuments (England). An Inventory of Historical Monuments in Dorset*, vol. ii, *South-East*, part II, p. 163.

21 BL, Additional MSS 70008, ff. 91, 221; 70009, fo. 294; 70010, ff. 33, 37, 173; 70011, fo. 5; 70119, Thomas Harley to Sir Edward Harley, 7 June and 25 July 1661; 70123, Samuel Shilton to Sir Edward Harley, 14 December 1660; and 70128, same to same, 19 November 1661.

22 Buckinghamshire Record Office, Claydon House MSS (Letters), Burgoyne to Verney, 11, 18 and 25 January, 1 February, 31 May, 28

September 1675 and 20 November 1676. In 1673 the stables at Sutton had been destroyed by fire (Burgoyne to Verney, 11 and 15 November 1673).

23 BL, Additional MSS 30013, fo. 56. *Royal Commission on Historical Monuments (England). An Inventory of the Historical Monuments in Buckinghamshire*, i, pp. 162–3.

24 Hertfordshire County Record Office, Lawes-Wittewronge of Rothamsted MSS, D/ELw/E44, F18, F20, F22, F29.

25 BL, Additional MSS 29910, fo. 59. Wood, *The Life and Times of Anthony Wood*, ii, p. 137. PRO, Wills, PROB11/521/97.

26 BL, Additional MSS 70017, fo. 245. Luttrell, *A Brief Historical Relation*, iv, p. 583.

27 N. Pevsner and Enid Radcliffe, *The Buildings of England: Cornwall*, p. 224. HMC, *Duke of Buccleuch MSS*, i, p. 333. George Ormerod, *The History of the County Palatine and City of Chester*, ii, p. 251.

28 Bodleian Library, Oxford, Rawlinson Letters 51, fo. 200. E. S. De Beer (ed.), *The Correspondence of John Locke*, iii, pp. 99–100, 122, 197–8, 226, 462–3.

29 Sir Joseph Williamson, 'Lincolnshire Families, Temp. Charles II', *Herald and Genealogist*, ii, p. 121. BL, Additional MSS 70017, fo. 120.

30 Staffordshire Record Office, MS 100/1, 19. E. R. O. Bridgeman and C. G. O. Bridgeman, *History of the Manor and Parish of Weston-under-Lizard, in the County of Stafford, William Salt Archaeological Society, Collections for a History of Staffordshire*, New Series, ii, p. 142.

31 BL, Additional MSS 29910, ff. 272, 278, 288; and 30013, fo. 295.

32 Lady Brilliana Harley, *Letters of the Lady Brilliana Harley*, ed. T. T. Lewis, *Camden Society*, lviii, p. 134. BL, Additional MSS 70009, ff. 172, 298; 70010, fo. 223; 70115, Lady Abigail Harley to Sir Edward Harley, undated letters; 70128, Sir Edward Harley to his wife, 21 February 1665; and 70140, Sir Edward Harley to Edward Harley, 7 August 1694.

33 PRO, Wills, PROB11/355/113, 390/43 and 462/151.

34 J. G. Cavenagh-Mainwaring, 'The Mainwarings of Whitmore', *William Salt Archaeological Society, Collections for a History of Staffordshire* (1933), p. 72.

35 Buckinghamshire Record Office, Claydon House MSS (Letters), Burgoyne to Verney, 9 March 1674.

36 BL, Additional MSS 33084, fo. 154. Luttrell, *A Brief Historical Relation*, v, p. 261.

37 See Cliffe, *Puritan Gentry*, pp. 51, 54–9.

38 John Collinges, *Par Nobile. Two Treatises*, p. 35.

39 James Barker, *The Royal Robe*, epistle dedicatory addressed to Lady Grimston. Burnet, *History of his Own Time*, ii, p. 70.

40 Buckinghamshire Record Office, Claydon House MSS (Letters), Burgoyne to Verney, 18 June 1666. Humphrey Whyle, *A Sermon Preach'd at the Funeral of Anne Lady Burgoyne*, p. 19.

41 BL, Harleian MSS 7005, fo. 43.

42 Derbyshire Record Office, Chandos-Pole-Gell MSS, 66/11(g).

43 HMC, *Marquess of Lothian MSS*, p. 117.

44 BL, Additional MSS 33145, ff. 151, 163, 164, 166, 168, 201.

45 BL, Additional MSS 70115, Lady Abigail Harley to Sir Edward Harley, undated letter; 70138C, accounts, no pagination; and 70140, Sir Edward Harley to Edward Harley, 7 August 1694.
46 Bulstrode Whitelocke, *The Diary of Bulstrode Whitelocke, 1605–1675* (ed. Ruth Spalding), p. 790.
47 BL, Additional MSS 27352, fo. 195. See above, pp. 57–8.
48 Bodleian Library, Oxford, Tanner MSS 45, fo. 258.
49 Samuel Clark, *The Lives of Sundry Eminent Persons*, part II, p. 200.
50 BL, Additional MSS 70234, Sir Edward Harley to Robert Harley, 25 February 1690.
51 Richard Baxter, *Faithful Souls Shall Be With Christ*, pp. 51–2.
52 Thomas Manton, *A Practical Commentary, or an Exposition with Notes on the Epistle of James*, epistle dedicatory. Somerset Record Office, Popham MSS, DD/PO 32/2 and DD/POt 119.
53 Thomas Hervey (ed.), *Some Unpublished Papers Relating to the Family of Sir Francis Drake*, p. 51. PRO, Wills, PROB11/363/73 and 386/19.
54 PRO, Wills, PROB11/312/116, 323/47, 336/79, 342/58, 344/3, 347/22, 351/57, 358/109, 390/43. Clark, *The Lives of Sundry Eminent Persons*, part II, p. 194.
55 BL, Additional MSS 70019, fo. 320.

14 PARLIAMENT AND THE NONCONFORMIST INTEREST

1 J. T. Cliffe, *The Puritan Gentry*, Chapter 11. J. T. Cliffe, *Puritans in Conflict*, Chapter 1.
2 Bedfordshire County Record Office, Lucas MSS, L30/20/10.
3 Bodleian Library, Oxford, Tanner MSS 42, fo. 87.
4 BL, Additional MSS 70017, ff. 5, 28; 70126, Thomas Foley to Sir Edward Harley, 10 January 1693; 70234, Sir Edward Harley to Robert Harley, 25 February 1690; and 70235, same to same, 10 January 1693.
5 Buckinghamshire Record Office, Claydon House MSS (Letters), Burgoyne to Verney, 6 January 1661, 1 March 1663 and 25 January and 14 December 1674.
6 BL, Additional MSS 70114, Mary Foley to Sir Edward Harley, 10 May 1689.
7 See Douglas R. Lacey, *Dissent and Parliamentary Politics in England, 1661–1689*, pp. 30–1, 119, 476–9.
8 K. H. D. Haley, 'Shaftesbury's Lists of the Lay Peers and Members of the Commons, 1677–8', *Bulletin of the Institute of Historical Research*, xliii, pp. 95, 96, 99, 101, 102, 105.
9 Henry Booth, Earl of Warrington, *The Works of the Right Honourable Henry late Lord Delamere, and Earl of Warrington*, pp. 412, 495. Richard Wroe, *A Sermon at the Funeral of the Right Honourable Henry, Earl of Warrington*, p. 20.
10 See Andrew Browning, *Thomas Osborne Earl of Danby and Duke of Leeds, 1632–1712*, iii, p. 109.
11 *CSPDom., 1666–7*, pp. 445, 449–50, 458, 470.

12 B. D. Henning (ed.), *The History of Parliament: The House of Commons 1660–1690*, i, p. 219. PRO, Wills, PROB11/344/3. See above, p. 44.

13 *CSPDom., 1672–3*, pp. 572, 597, 608, 613. Henning, *The History of Parliament*, i, p. 393.

14 *CSPDom., 1675–6*, p. 461. For Hopkins see the Appendix (Foley of Stoke Edith).

15 BL, Additional MSS 70119, Thomas Harley to Sir Edward Harley, 21 March 1679.

16 William Salt Library, Stafford, Parker-Jervis Collection, 49/83/44, Philip Foley to John Swinfen, 4 February 1679.

17 Bodleian Library, Oxford, Rawlinson Letters 51, ff. 200, 213, 216, 234.

18 BL, Additional MSS 29910, ff. 108, 110; 37911, ff. 9, 12, 22; and 70120, William Michell to Sir Edward Harley, 26 December 1676 and Dorothy Michell to same, 19 July 1678. Bodleian Library, Oxford, Tanner MSS 38, ff. 55, 58. *NM*, ii, p. 209. HMC, *Marquess of Lothian MSS*, p. 131. *CSPDom., 1679–80*, p. 66. *CSPDom., 1682*, pp. 54–5. Humphrey Prideaux, *Letters of Humphrey Prideaux . . . to John Ellis*, ed. E. M. Thompson, *Camden Society*, New Series, xv, p. 124. Sir John Hobart and Lord Townshend subsequently fell out (HMC, *Eleventh Report*, Appendix, part IV, p. 29. Prideaux, *Letters*, pp. 120, 123).

19 BL, Additional MSS 29910, ff. 117, 120, 124, 137, 294; and 30013, ff. 291–3.

20 BL, Additional MSS 29910, ff. 143–4.

21 Narcissus Luttrell, *A Brief Historical Relation of State Affairs from September 1678 to April 1714*, i, pp. 31–2.

22 E. M. Thompson (ed.), *Correspondence of the Family of Hatton, Camden Society*, New Series, xxii, p. 220. Luttrell, *A Brief Historical Relation*, i, p. 32. Sir John Bramston, *Autobiography*, ed. Lord Braybrooke, *Camden Society*, xxxii, p. 377.

23 *CJ*, ix, pp. 645, 660, 664, 679, 681, 687, 694, 695. Roger Thomas, 'Comprehension and Indulgence', in G. F. Nuttall and Owen Chadwick, *From Uniformity to Unity 1662–1962*, pp. 224–6.

24 HMC, *Twelfth Report*, Appendix, part IX, p. 101. Thomas, 'Comprehension and Indulgence', pp. 226–7.

25 BL, Additional MSS 4236, fo. 227; and 70013, fo. 60. Dr Williams's Library, London, Morrice MSS, P, 288. Thomas, 'Comprehension and Indulgence', pp. 229–30.

26 *CJ*, ix, p. 711.

27 *CSPDom., 1680–1*, p. 473.

28 For the persecution of nonconformists see above, p. 121.

29 HMC, *Finch MSS*, ii, pp. 42, 43, 45. HMC, *Eleventh Report*, Appendix, part II, pp. 172–93. In 1692 Sir Edward Harley laid stress on the 'absolute Necessitie of Godly Majestrates' (BL, Additional MSS 70140, copy of letter written on 2 January 1692).

30 *CSPDom., 1683*, p. 300. PRO, SPDom., Charles II, S.P.29/cdxxi/216.

31 *CSPDom., 1682*, pp. 291–2, 425–6, 576.

32 *CSPDom., 1682*, pp. 389, 390, 407–8, 457. George Ormerod, *The History of the County Palatine and City of Chester*, i, general introduction, p. lxvii.

33 *CSPDom., 1683*, pp. 16, 77, 79, 80, 85, 90, 109, 114, 133–4, 180, 184, 187,

195, 332, 339. *CSPDom., 1683–4*, pp. 69, 142, 145, 146. Dr Williams's Library, London, Morrice MSS, P, 394, 434. HMC, *Third Report*, Appendix, pp. 245, 259.
34 HMC, *Seventh Report*, Appendix, p. 680. HMC, *Fourteenth Report*, Appendix, part IX, pp. 484–5.
35 *CSPDom., 1683*, pp. 78, 161. *CSPDom., 1683–4*, pp. 141–2. PRO, Wills, PROB11/425/44.
36 HMC, *Finch MSS*, ii, p. 43. Lady Eliott-Drake, *The Family and Heirs of Sir Francis Drake*, ii, pp. 38, 40–1, 43, 48. Luttrell, *A Brief Historical Relation*, i, p. 307. Dr Williams's Library, London, Morrice MSS, P, 421. *CSPDom., 1687–9*, p. 54.
37 T. B. Howell (ed.), *A Complete Collection of State Trials*, ix, cols. 1054, 1085, 1089, 1095–8.
38 *CSPDom., 1683–4*, pp. 230, 285–6.
39 Luttrell, *A Brief Historical Relation*, i, p. 341. HMC, *Fourteenth Report*, Appendix, part IX, p. 484. *CSPDom., 1685*, p. 23.
40 *CSPDom., 1685*, pp. 157, 228, 234, 242. Dr Williams's Library, London, Morrice MSS, P, 472, 477 and Q, 239(1). BL, Additional MSS 70013, ff. 239, 252, 269; and 70128, Sir Edward Harley to his wife, 30 June 1685.
41 BL, Additional MSS 41803, fo. 335.
42 HMC, *Marquess of Downshire MSS*, part I, pp. 73, 83–5, 109. Dr Williams's Library, London, Henry MSS, 90.5, Matthew Henry to Philip Henry, 10 November 1685; and Morrice MSS, P, 527.
43 HMC, *Marquess of Downshire MSS*, part I, p. 74. Thomas Jolly, *The Notebook of the Rev. Thomas Jolly AD 1671–1693*, Chetham Society, New Series, xxxiii, p. 74. Henry Newcome, *The Autobiography of Henry Newcome, MA*, ed. R. Parkinson, *Chetham Society*, xxvii, p. 261.
44 See Lacey, *Dissent and Parliamentary Politics in England, 1661–1689*, pp. 185–208.
45 BL, Additional MSS 70014, ff. 27, 28, 30. Dr Williams's Library, London, Morrice MSS, Q, 215.
46 BL, Additional MSS 70014, fo. 44.
47 Lacey, *Dissent and Parliamentary Politics in England*, pp. 202–6.
48 *CSPDom., 1687–9*, pp. 132, 141, 146, 148, 199, 200. Bramston, *Autobiography*, xxxii, p. 304. BL, Additional MSS 70118, Edward Harley to Sir Edward Harley, 15 February 1688.
49 Sir George Duckett (ed.), *Penal Laws and Test Act*, ii, p. 240.
50 Derbyshire Record Office, Chandos-Pole-Gell MSS, 41/31(fb).
51 *CSPDom., 1687–9*, pp. 353–4.
52 BL, Additional MSS 70014, fo. 118; and 70234, Sir Edward Harley to Robert Harley, 8 June 1691. Dr Williams's Library, London, Morrice MSS, Q, 343. Thompson, *Correspondence*, xxiii, p. 113.

15   FIN DE SIECLE

1 Thomas Jolly, *The Notebook of the Rev. Thomas Jolly AD 1671–1693*, *Chetham Society*, New Series, xxxiii, p. 92.
2 Dr Williams's Library, London, Morrice MSS, Q, 437. Derbyshire

Record Office, Chandos-Pole-Gell MSS, 48/50(ja) and (q).

3 BL, Additional MSS 70014, ff. 200, 203, 213.

4 Roger Thomas, 'Comprehension and Indulgence', in G. F. Nuttall and Owen Chadwick, *From Uniformity to Unity, 1662–1962*, pp. 231, 245–6.

5 *CJ*, x, pp. 74–5. Thomas, 'Comprehension and Indulgence', pp. 249–50.

6 *CJ*, x, p. 84. E. M. Thompson (ed.), *Correspondence of the Family of Hatton, Camden Society*, New Series, xxiii, p. 128.

7 Dr Williams's Library, London, Morrice MSS, Q, 505, 557, 558. *CJ*, x, pp. 133, 137, 143. Thomas, 'Comprehension and Indulgence', pp. 250–2.

8 Humphrey Prideaux, *Letters of Humphrey Prideaux . . . to John Ellis*, ed. E. M. Thompson, *Camden Society*, New Series, xv, p. 154. HMC, *Fifth Report*, Appendix, pp. 376, 377.

9 Hertfordshire County Record Office, Lawes-Wittewronge of Rothamsted MSS, D/ELw/F29.

10 BL, Additional MSS 70062, 'Specimina. December 3 1692'; and 70270, Robert Harley to his wife, 25 May 1689.

11 BL, Stowe MSS 747, fo. 16.

12 Statute 1 William and Mary, cap. xviii.

13 See above, pp. 115–17.

14 PRO, Registrar General, R.G.31, lists of places of worship registered under the provisions of the Toleration Act.

15 Adam Martindale, *The Life of Adam Martindale*, ed. R. Parkinson, *Chetham Society*, iv, p. 177. PRO, Registrar General, R.G.31/6, no pagination. Bodleian Library, Oxford, Rawlinson Letters 109, fo. 62.

16 PRO, Registrar General, R.G.31/6, no pagination. BL, Additional MSS 5836, fo. 185. George Ormerod, *The History of the County Palatine and City of Chester*, ii, pp. 230, 251. Alexander Gordon (ed.), *Cheshire Classis Minutes, 1691–1745*, p. 177.

17 J. P. Earwaker, *East Cheshire: Past and Present*, ii, pp. 26–38. Robert Halley, *Lancashire: Its Puritanism and Nonconformity*, p. 412. *NM*, i, p. 173. PRO, Registrar General, R.G.31/6, no pagination. The register of the chapel belonging to Duckenfield Hall has survived (R.G.4/1799). This was kept by Samuel Angier who also recorded such events as the deaths of Richard Baxter and other nonconformist divines.

18 Lyon Turner, i, p. 163 and iii, p. 761. PRO, Registrar General, R.G.31/7, no pagination. Borthwick Institute of Historical Research, Wills in the York Registry, Doncaster Deanery, will of William Rodes, 28 July 1694. Joseph Hunter, *South Yorkshire: The History and Topography of the Deanery of Doncaster*, ii, pp. 130–2.

19 Dr Williams's Library, London, John Evans's list of dissenting congregations and ministers 1715–1729, pp. 12, 48, 61, 90.

20 Samuel Annesley, *The Life and Funeral Sermon of the Reverend Mr Thomas Brand*, epistle dedicatory.

21 Gordon, pp. 1, 2, 4, 6–7, 40, 50, 164–5, 167.

22 PRO, Wills, PROB11/429/238. BL, Egerton MSS 3359, fo. 51.

23 BL, Additional MSS 70016, fo. 14; and 70125, correspondence of Francis Tallents with the Harleys (unbound). Tallents was also on

close terms with the Boscawens, Foleys of Staffordshire, Gells, Hampdens and Wilbrahams.

24 Dr Williams's Library, London, Blackmore Papers, volume of correspondence, 131. BL, Additional MSS 70112, Sir Edward Harley to Chewning Blackmore, 28 October 1692 and Blackmore to Harley, 15 November 1692; and 70234, Harley to his son Robert, 23 July 1692.

25 BL, Additional MSS 70917, fo. 194; 70116, Abigail Harley to Sir Edward Harley, 10 March and 12 April 1694; 70117, same to same, 12 and 16 March 1695, 8 July 1696, 3 June and 13 July 1697, and 21 and 25 April 1698; 70118, Edward Harley to Sir Edward Harley, 13 March and 10 April 1694; 70127, note signed by Bishop Croft of Hereford, 16 May 1665; 70234, Sir Edward Harley to Robert Harley, 17 October 1691; and 70235, same to same, 30 August 1693 and 10 April 1694. Dr Williams's Library, London, Blackmore Papers, 130, 132(a) and (b).

26 Hampshire Record Office, Jervoise of Herriard Park MSS, 44M69/ E77, Richard Burd, 22 February 1690. Gilbert Burnet, *History of his Own Time*, iv, p. 21.

27 BL, Additional MSS 70014, ff. 291, 294, 301, 305.

28 Dr Williams's Library, London, Morrice MSS, R, 123. *The Tryall of Skill Performed in Essex* (single-page broadsheet). John Bramston, *Autobiography*, ed. Lord Braybrooke, *Camden Society*, xxxii, p. 375. HMC, *Seventh Report*, Appendix, p. 502.

29 Prideaux, *Letters*, xv, p. 156.

30 BL, Additional MSS 70018, fo. 82.

31 Richard Kidder, *The Charge of Richard, Lord Bishop of Bath and Wells to the Clergy of his Diocese, at his Primary Visitation Begun at Axebridge, June 2, 1692*, pp. 14, 19. Kidder also criticised non-resident clergy (pp. 28–9).

32 John Howe, *A Funeral-Sermon for that Excellent Minister of Christ, the Truly Reverend William Bates, D. D.*, pp. 110–12.

33 Sir Henry Ashurst, *Some Remarks upon the Life of that Painful Servant of God Mr Nathanael Heywood*, epistle dedicatory addressed to Hugh Lord Willoughby of Parham.

34 BL, Additional MSS 70014, fo. 291; 70140, Sir Edward Harley to Robert Harley, 13 March 1694; and 70235, same to same, 18 July 1693 and 31 July 1694.

35 Northamptonshire Record Office, Langham (Cottesbrooke) MSS, L(C)918, Sir James Langham to John Langham, 6 March 1695.

36 Lady Damaris Masham, *Occasional Thoughts in Reference to a Vertuous or Christian Life*, pp. 4–6, 28–9, 151.

37 See David Hayton, 'Moral Reform and Country Politics in the Late Seventeenth-Century House of Commons', *Past and Present*, no. 128, pp. 48–91.

38 BL, Additional MSS 70015, ff. 131, 254, 274; 70016, ff. 19, 225, 233; and 70140, Sir Edward Harley to Edward Harley, 10 December 1692.

39 Hayton, 'Moral Reform and Country Politics', p. 63. Bodleian Library, Oxford, Rawlinson MSS, D129, ff. 1–15.

40 John Woodhouse, *A Sermon Preach'd at Salters-Hall, to the Societies for a Reformation of Manners*, p. 2.

41 *CJ*, xi, pp. 221, 235, 281, 283. Statute 6/7 William and Mary, cap. xi.
42 *CJ*, xii, pp. 132, 147, 155, 168–9, 177, 258, 276, 295. BL, Additional MSS 70019, ff. 25, 32; and 70114, Sarah Foley to Sir Edward Harley, 5 April 1698. Statute 9 William and Mary, cap. xxxv.
43 See above, pp. 64–5.
44 E. S. de Beer (ed.), *The Correspondence of John Locke*, ii, pp. 735, 759, 792; iii, pp. 80, 82, 105 and vi, p. 149. Lady Damaris Masham, *A Discourse Concerning the Love of God*, pp. 68, 122.
45 Dr Williams's Library, London, Blackmore Papers, volume of correspondence, 130.
46 See above, pp. 158–9.
47 Isaac Watts, *Death and Heaven*, pp. 241–3.
48 BL, Additional MSS 70060, catalogue of books, 9 October 1662; and 70137, account book, no regular pagination. The latter purchases may be identified as *Strange and Wonderful Prophecies* (1696), a work based on John Holwell's *Catastrophe Mundi* (1682); one of the almanacs regularly published by John Partridge; and *The Strange and Wonderful History of Mother Shipton* (1686).
49 BL, Additional MSS 70019, fo. 319.
50 Sir Edward Harley, *A Scriptural and Rational Account of the Christian Religion*, pp. 35, 39, 68, 83, 109.
51 BL, Additional MSS 70125, Francis Tallents to Sir Edward Harley, 29 July 1695.
52 BL, Additional MSS 70123, Erasmus Saunders to Sir Edward Harley, 18 December 1696. *DNB* (Saunders).
53 Masham, *Occasional Thoughts in Reference to a Vertuous or Christian Life*, pp. 173–4.
54 See J. T. Cliffe, *Puritans in Conflict*, p. 45.
55 BL, Additional MSS 70125, Stanley West to Sir Edward Harley, 22 August 1700.
56 PRO, Wills, PROB11/521/97.

BIBLIOGRAPHY

PRIMARY SOURCES

MANUSCRIPT

British Library

Additional MSS

4236	Thomas Birch's Tillotson collections.
4460	Thoresby MSS.
5836	Cole's collections for Cheshire.
10114	Memorandum book of John Harrington.
15857	Correspondence of Sir Richard Browne and the Evelyns.
22548	Miscellaneous original letters.
23206	Miscellaneous original letters.
24484	Hunter MSS.
24485	Hunter MSS.
24861	Papers of Richard Major.
27351–5	Diary of Mary Countess of Warwick.
27356	Occasional meditations of Mary Countess of Warwick.
27357	Autobiography of Mary Countess of Warwick.
29556	Correspondence of Hatton family.
29910	Papers of Swinfen and Jervis families.
30013	Copies of correspondence of Swinfen, Ricketts and Jervis families.
32679	Papers of the Holles Family.
33084	Pelham MSS.
33144	Pelham MSS.
33145	Pelham MSS.
33146	Pelham MSS.
33148	Pelham MSS.
33149	Pelham MSS.
33412	History of Hungerford family.
37343	Autobiography of Bulstrode Whitelocke.

37911	Windham papers.
39970	Baigent collections for Hampshire.
41803	Middleton papers.
41818	Middleton papers.
41819	Middleton papers.
46500	Papers of Roger Hill.
53726	Autobiography of Bulstrode Whitelocke.
53728	Sermons of Bulstrode Whitelocke.
70005 *et seq.*	Harley family papers.

Additional Charter

| 45794 | Will of Henry Lee of Titchmarsh, clerk. |

Egerton MSS

2043	Commons diary of Colonel Bullen Reymes.
2618	Leyborne-Popham MSS.
2646	Barrington correspondence.
2648–51	Barrington correspondence.
3330	Papers of first Duke of Leeds.
3359	Papers of first Duke of Leeds.

Harleian MSS

164	D'Ewes MSS.
165	D'Ewes MSS.
991	Notebook of Richard Symonds.
7005	Freschville MSS.

Lansdowne MSS

721	Account of ministers of Brampton Bryan, Herefordshire.
887	Warburton's collections for Bedfordshire.
1027–9	Kennet's collections for Diocese of Peterborough.

Sloane MSS

| 1519 | Fairfax correspondence. |

Stowe MSS

| 185 | Miscellaneous historical papers. |
| 744–7 | Miscellaneous original letters. |

BIBLIOGRAPHY

Public Record Office

Chancery

Proceedings, Six Clerks' Series (C.5–10).
Entry Books of Decrees and Orders (C.33).
Chancery Masters' Exhibits (C.103, 108).

Exchequer

Land Revenue, Miscellaneous Books (L.R.2).

Institution Books

Series A, 1556–1660; and Series B, 1660–1721.

Registrar General

Register of the chapel at Duckenfield Hall, 1676–1713 (R.G.4/1799).
Licences for places of nonconformist worship (R.G.31).

State Paper Office

State Papers Domestic Series, Commonwealth (S.P.18,25), Charles II
(S.P.29).

Wills

Wills proved in the Prerogative Court of Canterbury (PROB11).

Dr Williams's Library, London

A. G. Matthews's collection of abstracts of wills of ejected ministers.
An Account of the Dissenting Academies from the Restoration of Charles
the Second.
Baxter Letters.
Blackmore Papers.
John Evans's list of dissenting congregations and ministers, 1715–1729.
Henry MSS.
Letters to Bishop Stillingfleet (transcripts).
Lyon Turner collection.
Morrice MSS.

Greater London Record Office

Diocese of Winchester records, Archdeaconry of Surrey.

265

Guildhall Library, London

Diocese of London records.

Lambeth Palace Library

Gibson Papers.
MS 951/1.

Bedfordshire County Record Office

Burgoyne MSS.
Lucas MSS (Crewe-Swinfen correspondence).

Bodleian Library, Oxford

Carte MSS.
Letters to Archbishop Sheldon (MS ADD C305).
Rawlinson MSS and Letters.
Tanner MSS.

Borthwick Institute of Historical Research
(University of York)

York Diocesan Records.
Wills in the York Registry.

Bristol Record Office

Ashton Court MSS.

Buckinghamshire Record Office

Claydon House MSS (Letters) (on microfilm).
Earl of Buckinghamshire MSS (Hampden family papers).
Notebook of Richard Grenville.

Derbyshire Record Office

Chandos-Pole-Gell MSS.

Dorset County Record Office

MSS deposited by Mrs J. M. Lane (Trenchard family papers).
MSS deposited by Mr G. D. Roper (Forde Abbey estate).

BIBLIOGRAPHY

East Devon Record Office

Drake of Buckland Abbey MSS.

Essex County Record Office

Hatfield Broad Oak MSS (Barrington family papers).

Hampshire Record Office

Daly MSS (Norton family papers).
Diocese of Winchester records.
Jervoise of Herriard Park MSS.

Hertfordshire County Record Office

Lawes-Wittewronge of Rothamsted MSS.
Lytton MSS.
Verulam (Gorhambury) MSS (Grimston family papers).

Hull University Library

Wickham-Boynton MSS.

Leicestershire Record Office

MSS of Lord Hazlerigg of Noseley.

Northamptonshire Record Office

Peterborough Diocesan Records.
Dryden (Canons Ashby) MSS.
Knightley MSS.
Langham (Cottesbrooke) MSS.
Miscellaneous MSS.

North Yorkshire Record Office

Darley MSS.
Marwood MSS.

Sheffield Central Library

Crewe MSS (Rodes family papers).
Wentworth Woodhouse Collection, Strafford Letters and Bright MSS.

Somerset Record Office

Combe of Earnshill MSS (Pyne family papers).
Harrington of Kelston MSS.
Phelips MSS.
Popham MSS.

Staffordshire Record Office

Account of Staffordshire gentry (MS 100/1).
Bradford Collection (Wilbraham family papers).
Cavenagh-Mainwaring MSS.
Leveson-Gower MSS.
Paget MSS.
Swinfen MSS.

West Suffolk Record Office

Barnardiston Family Archive.

William Salt Library, Stafford

Parker-Jervis Collection (Swinfen family papers).

Folger Shakespeare Library, Washington, DC

Newdigate Newsletters.

PRINTED

A Narrative of the Late Parliament and *A Second Narrative of the Late Parliament, Harleian Miscellany*, iii (1809).
Ambrose, Isaac, *Redeeming the Time* (1674).
Annesley, Samuel, *The Life and Funeral Sermon of the Reverend Mr Thomas Brand* (1692).
Ashe, Simeon, *The Efficiency of God's Grace in Bringing Gain-Saying Sinnes to Christ* (1654).
Ashurst, Sir Henry, *Some Remarks upon the Life of that Painful Servant of God Mr Nathanael Heywood* (1695).
Atkinson, J. C. (ed.), *North Riding Quarter Sessions Records, North Riding Record Society*, 9 vols (1884–92).
Bagshaw, William, *De Spiritualibus Pecci* (1702).
Bannister, A. T. (ed.), *Diocese of Herefordshire Institutions, 1539–1900* (Hereford: 1923).
Barker, James, *The Royal Robe* (1660).

Bates, William, *A Funeral Sermon Preached Upon the Death of the Reverend and Excellent Divine Dr Thomas Manton* (1678).

Baxter, Richard, *A Treatise of Knowledge and Love Compared* (1689).

—— *Faithful Souls Shall Be With Christ* (1681).

—— *Reliquiae Baxterianae*, ed. Matthew Sylvester (1696).

Booth, Henry, Earl of Warrington, *The Works of the Right Honourable Henry late Lord Delamere, and Earl of Warrington* (1694).

Boyse, Joseph, *A Sermon on the Occasion of the Death of the Reverend Mr Elias Travers* (1705).

—— *Some Remarkable Passages in the Holy Life and Death of the late Reverend Mr Edmund Trench* (1693).

Bramston, Sir John, *Autobiography*, ed. Lord Braybrooke, *Camden Society*, xxxii (1845).

Bridge, William, *Twenty One Several Books of Mr William Bridge*, 2 vols (1657).

Burnet, Gilbert, *History of his Own Time*, 6 vols (1833).

Burroughs, Thomas, *A Soveraign Remedy for All Kinds of Grief*, 3rd edn (1675).

—— *Directions About Preparing for Death*, 2nd edn (1675).

Burton, Thomas, *Diary of Thomas Burton*, ed. J. T. Rutt, 4 vols (1828).

Bury, Samuel, *A Funeral Sermon Occasioned by the Death of the Late Reverend Mr Samuel Cradock, BD* (1707).

Bushell, Seth, *The Believer's Groan for Heaven* (1678).

Calamy, Edmund (1600–66), *A Patterne for All, Especially for Noble and Honourable Persons* (1658).

—— *The Happinesse of Those who Sleep in Jesus* (1662).

Calamy, Edmund (1671–1732), *A Continuation of the Account of the Ministers, Lecturers, Masters and Fellows of Colleges and Schoolmasters who were Ejected and Silenced after the Restoration in 1660*, 2 vols (1727).

—— *The Nonconformist's Memorial*, ed. Samuel Palmer, 2 vols (1775).

Calendar of State Papers, Domestic.

Calendar of the Proceedings of the Committee for Compounding.

Calendar of the Proceedings of the Committee for the Advance of Money.

Cary, Henry, *Memorials of the Great Civil War in England*, 2 vols (1842).

Case, Thomas, *The Vanity of Vaine-Glory* (1655).

Cawdrey, Zachary, *The Certainty of Salvation* (1684).

Cawton, Thomas, the younger, *The Life and Death of that Holy and Reverend Man of God Mr Thomas Cawton* (1662).

Clark, Samuel, *The Lives of Sundry Eminent Persons* (1683).

Collinges, John, *Par Nobile. Two Treatises* (1669).

—— *The History of Conformity* (1689).

Commons Journals.

Cooke, Henry, *A Sermon Preached at the Funeral of the Lady Lumley* (1704).

Cromwell, Oliver, *The Letters and Speeches of Oliver Cromwell*, ed. Thomas Carlyle and S. C. Lomas, 3 vols (1904).

—— *The Writings and Speeches of Oliver Cromwell*, ed. W. C. Abbott, 4 vols (Cambridge, MA: 1937–47).

Darby, Charles, *An Elegy on the Death of the Queen* (1695).

Dillingham, William, *A Sermon at the Funeral of the Lady Elizabeth Alston* (1678).

Duckett, Sir George (ed.), *Penal Laws and Test Act*, 2 vols (1882–3).
Ewbank, George, *The Pilgrim's Port* (1660).
Farewel Sermons (1663).
Firth, Sir Charles and Rait, R. S. (eds), *The Acts and Ordinances of the Interregnum, 1642–1660*, 3 vols (1911).
Goodwin, Timothy, *The Life and Character of That Eminent and Learned Prelate, the Late Dr Edward Stillingfleet* (1710).
Gordon, Alexander (ed.), *Cheshire Classis Minutes, 1691–1745* (1919).
—— (ed.), *Freedom After Ejection* (Manchester: 1917).
Grey, Anchitell, *Debates of the House of Commons, 1667–94*, 10 vols (1769).
Haley, K. H. D., 'Shaftesbury's Lists of the Lay Peers and Members of the Commons, 1677–8', *Bulletin of the Institute of Historical Research*, xliii (1970).
Harley, Lady Brilliana, *Letters of the Lady Brilliana Harley*, ed. T. T. Lewis, *Camden Society*, lviii (1854).
Harley, Sir Edward, *An Humble Essay Toward the Settlement of Peace and Truth in the Church* (1681).
—— *A Scriptural and Rational Account of the Christian Religion* (1695).
Harrington, Sir James, *Horae Consecratae* (1682).
Harris, William, *Some Memoirs of the Life and Character of the Reverend and Learned Thomas Manton* (1725).
Hearne, Thomas, *Remarks and Collections of Thomas Hearne*, Oxford Historical Society, ii and vii (1884, 1886).
Henry, Philip, *Diaries and Letters of Philip Henry*, ed. M. H. Lee (1882).
Hervey, Thomas (ed.), *Some Unpublished Papers Relating to the Family of Sir Francis Drake* (1887).
Heywood, Nathaniel, *Christ Displayed, as the Choicest Gift and Best Master* (1679).
Heywood, Oliver, *A Narrative of the Holy Life and Happy Death of Mr John Angier* (1685).
—— *His Autobiography, Diaries, Anecdote and Event Books*, ed. J. Horsfall Turner, 4 vols (Brighouse and Bingley: 1882–5).
Heywood, Oliver, and Dickenson, Thomas, *The Nonconformist Register of Baptisms, Marriages and Deaths, Compiled by the Revs. Oliver Heywood and T. Dickenson*, ed. J.Horsfall Turner (1881).
Hinckley, John, *A Sermon Preached at the Funerals of that Worthy Personage George Purefoy the Elder of Wadley in Berkshire, Esquire* (1661).
Historical Manuscripts Commission: *Third, Fourth, Fifth, Seventh, Ninth, Eleventh, Twelfth, Thirteenth* and *Fourteenth Reports*.
—— *Bath MSS.*
—— *Duke of Buccleuch MSS.*
—— *Duke of Portland MSS.*
—— *Earl of Verulam MSS.*
—— *Finch MSS.*
—— *Leyborne-Popham MSS.*
—— *Marquess of Downshire MSS.*
—— *Marquess of Lothian MSS.*
Hoghton family papers, *A Calendar of the Deeds and Papers in the Possession of Sir James De Hoghton, Bart.*, ed. J. H. Lumby, *Record Society*

of Lancashire and Cheshire, lxxxviii (1936).

Houston, Jane, *Catalogue of Ecclesiastical Records of the Commonwealth 1643–1660 in the Lambeth Palace Library* (Farnborough: 1968).

Howe, John, *A Funeral-Sermon for that Excellent Minister of Christ, the Truly Reverend William Bates, D. D.* (1699).

—— *The Whole Works*, 8 vols (1810–22).

Howell, T. B. (ed.), *A Complete Collection of State Trials*, 21 vols (1816).

Hughes, George, *Aphorisms or Select Propositions of the Scripture Shortly Determining the Doctrine of the Sabbath* (1670).

Hutchinson, Lucy, *Memoirs of the Life of Colonel Hutchinson*, ed. James Sutherland (1973).

Hyde, Edward, Earl of Clarendon, *Calendar of the Clarendon State Papers in the Bodleian Library*, ed. O. Ogle, W. H. Bliss, W. D. Macray and F. J. Routledge, 5 vols (Oxford: 1892–1970).

—— *The History of the Rebellion and Civil Wars in England . . . by Edward, Earl of Clarendon*, ed. W. D. Macray, 6 vols (1888).

J. D. (John Dan), *Sermon at the Funeral of Lady Mary Armyne* (1676).

Jeaffreson, J. C. (ed.), *Middlesex County Records*, 4 vols (1886–92).

Jolly, Thomas, *The Notebook of the Rev. Thomas Jolly AD 1671–1693*, Chetham Society, New Series, xxxiii (1894).

Josselin, Ralph, *The Diary of Ralph Josselin 1616–1683*, ed. Alan Macfarlane (1976).

Kidder, Richard, *The Charge of Richard, Lord Bishop of Bath and Wells to the Clergy of his Diocese, at his Primary Visitation Begun at Axebridge, June 2 1692* (1693).

—— *The Life of Richard Kidder, D. D., Bishop of Bath and Wells Written by Himself*, ed. Amy Edith Robinson, *Somerset Record Society*, xxxvii (1922).

Locke, John, *The Correspondence of John Locke*, ed. E. S. de Beer, 8 vols (Oxford: 1976–89).

Lords Journals.

Ludlow, Edmund, *A Voyce from the Watch Tower*, ed. A. B. Worden, Camden Fourth Series, xxi (1978).

—— *Memoirs of Edmund Ludlow* (1771).

Luke, Sir Samuel, *The Letter Books 1644–45 of Sir Samuel Luke*, ed. H. G. Tibbutt (Bedford: 1963).

Lukin, Henry, *The Chief Interest of Man*, 3rd edn (1718).

Luttrell, Narcissus, *A Brief Historical Relation of State Affairs from September 1678 to April 1714*, 6 vols (1857).

—— *The Parliamentary Diary of Narcissus Luttrell 1691–1693*, ed. Henry Horwitz (Oxford: 1972).

Manton, Thomas, *A Practical Commentary or an Exposition with Notes on the Epistle of James* (1651).

—— *A Practical Commentary or an Exposition with Notes on the Epistle of Jude* (1658).

Martindale, Adam, *The Life of Adam Martindale*, ed. R. Parkinson, *Chetham Society*, iv (1845).

Masham, Lady Damaris, *A Discourse Concerning the Love of God* (1696).

—— *Occasional Thoughts in Reference to a Vertuous or Christian Life* (1705).

Mayo, Richard, *A Sermon Preach'd in the Parish-Church of St James – Clerkenwell on Occasion of the Much Lamented Death of the Honourable the Lady Diana Asshurst* (1708).

Newcome, Henry, *The Autobiography of Henry Newcome, MA*, ed. R. Parkinson, *Chetham Society*, xxvi and xxvii (1852).

—— *The Diary of Rev. Henry Newcome from Sept. 30, 1661 to Sept. 29, 1663*, ed. T. Heywood, *Chetham Society*, xviii (1849).

Nicholas, Sir Edward, *Correspondence of Sir Edward Nicholas*, ed. Sir George F. Warner, *Camden Third Series*, xxxi (1920).

Nicholls, John (ed.), *Original Letters and Papers of State Addressed to Oliver Cromwell* (1743).

Osborne, Dorothy, *The Letters of Dorothy Osborne to William Temple*, ed. G. C. Moore Smith (Oxford: 1928).

Owen, John, *The Correspondence of John Owen (1616–1683)*, ed. Peter Toon (1970).

Parkhurst, Nathaniel, *The Faithful and Diligent Christian Described and Exemplified* (1684).

Pepys, Samuel, *The Diary of Samuel Pepys*, ed. Robert Latham and William Matthews, 11 vols (1970).

Pierce, Edward, *The Conformist's Plea for the Non-Conformist* (1681).

Prideaux, Humphrey, *Letters of Humphrey Prideaux . . . to John Ellis*, ed. E. M. Thompson, *Camden Society*, New Series, xv (1875).

Pritchard, Thomas, *A Sermon Preached at the Funeral of Mrs Mary Dawes* (1694).

—— *A Sermon Preached at the Funeral of the Lady Lumley* (1693).

Reynolds, Edward, *A Sermon Touching the Use of Humane Learning* (1658).

Russell, William, Lord Russell, *The Speech of the Late Lord Russell to the Sheriffs at the Place of Execution, 21 July 1683* (1683).

Shelton, William, *A Sermon at the Funeral of Mr Christopher Glascock, the Late Eminent School-master of Felsted in Essex* (1690).

Shute, Christopher, *Are piè Moriendi: or the True Accomptant* (1658).

Staffordshire Parish Registers Society: Weston-under-Lizard Parish Register (1933).

Stillingfleet, Edward, *Irenicum*, 2nd edn (1662).

—— *Origines Sacrae* (1663).

Swinnock, George, *The Works* (1665).

The Dissenting Ministers' Vindication of Themselves from the Horrid and Detestable Murder of Charles I, *Somers Tracts*, v (1811).

The English Revolution. III, Newsbooks I. Oxford Royalist, 4 vols (1971).

The Parliamentary or Constitutional History of England, 24 vols (1762–3).

The Tryall of Skill Performed in Essex (1690).

Thompson, E. M. (ed.), *Correspondence of the Family of Hatton*, *Camden Society*, New Series, xxii and xxiii (1878).

Thoresby, Ralph, *Letters Addressed to Ralph Thoresby*, ed. W. T. Lancaster, *Thoresby Society*, xxi (1912).

—— *Letters of Eminent Men Addressed to Ralph Thoresby*, ed. Joseph Hunter, 2 vols (1832).

—— *The Diary of Ralph Thoresby (1677–1724)*, ed. Joseph Hunter, 2 vols (1830).

Thurloe, John, *A Collection of the State Papers of John Thurloe*, 7 vols (1725).

Tong, William, *Some Memoirs of the Life and Death of the Reverend Mr John Shower* (1716).

Turner, G. Lyon (ed.), *Original Records of Early Nonconformity under Persecution and Indulgence*, 3 vols (1911–14).

Underdown, David, 'Parliamentary Diary of John Boys, 1647–8', *Bulletin of the Institute of Historical Research*, xxxix (1966).

Vane, Sir Henry, *A Healing Question, Somers Tracts*, vi (1811).

—— *The Tryal of Sir Henry Vane, Knight* (1662).

Varley, F. J. (ed.), *The Restoration Visitation of the University of Oxford and its Colleges 1660, Camden Third Series*, lxxix (1948).

Walker, Clement, *The Compleat History of Independency* (1661).

Waller, Sir William, *Recollections* (in *The Poetry of Anna Matilda*, 1788).

—— *Vindication of the Character and Conduct of Sir William Waller* (1793).

Ward, Seth, Bishop, 'Some Letters from Bishop Ward of Exeter, 1663–1667', *Devon and Cornwall Notes and Queries*, xxi (1940–1).

Watts, Isaac, *Death and Heaven* (1722).

Wesley, Samuel, *A Letter from a Country Divine to his Friend in London, Concerning the Education of the Dissenters in their Private Academies*, 2nd edn (1704).

Whitelocke, Bulstrode, *Memorials of the English Affairs*, 4 vols (1853).

—— *The Diary of Bulstrode Whitelocke, 1605–1675*, ed. Ruth Spalding (Oxford: 1990).

Whiteman, Anne and Clapinson, Mary (eds), *The Compton Census of 1676: A Critical Edition* (1986).

Whyle, Humphrey, *A Sermon Preach'd at the Funeral of Anne Lady Burgoyne* (1694).

Wilford, John, *Memorials and Characters, Together with the Lives of Divers Eminent and Worthy Persons* (1741).

Williams, Daniel, *A Funeral Sermon at the Decease of the Reverend Mr John Woodhouse* (1701).

Williamson, Sir Joseph, 'Lincolnshire Families, Temp. Charles II', *Herald and Genealogist*, ii (1865).

Wood, Anthony, *Athenae Oxoniensis* (1691).

—— *The Life and Times of Anthony Wood*, 5 vols (1891–1900).

Wood, James, *The Believer's Committing of his Soul to Christ Considered* (1729).

Woodhouse, John, *A Sermon Preach'd at Salters-Hall, to the Societies for a Reformation of Manners* (1697).

Worthington, John, *The Diary and Correspondence of Dr John Worthington*, ed. R. C. Christie, *Chetham Society*, cxiv (1886).

Wright, Samuel, *A Sermon Occasion'd by the Death of the late Reverend Mr Thomas Cotton, MA* (1730).

Wroe, Richard, *A Sermon at the Funeral of the Right Honourable Henry, Earl of Warrington* (1694).

—— *A Sermon Preached at Bowden in Cheshire, April 6th 1691, at the Funeral of the Right Honourable Mary Countess of Warrington* (1691).

SECONDARY SOURCES

A Catalogue of the Graduates in the Faculties of Arts, Divinity, and Law, of the University of Edinburgh (1858).

Aylmer, G. E., *The State's Servants: The Civil Service of the English Republic 1649–1660* (1973).

Birch, Thomas, *The Life of the Most Reverend Dr John Tillotson* (1752).

Bolam, C. G., Goring, Jeremy, Short, H. L. and Thomas, Roger, *The English Presbyterians* (1968).

Bridgeman, E. R. O. and Bridgeman, C. G. O., *History of the Manor and Parish of Weston-under-Lizard, in the County of Stafford*, William Salt Archaeological Society, Collections for a History of Staffordshire, New Series, ii (1899).

Bridges, John, *The History and Antiquities of Northamptonshire*, 2 vols (1791).

Browning, Andrew, *Thomas Osborne Earl of Danby and Duke of Leeds, 1632–1712*, 3 vols (Glasgow: 1944–51).

Cavenagh-Mainwaring, J. G.,'The Mainwarings of Whitmore', *William Salt Archaeological Society, Collections for a History of Staffordshire* (1933).

Cliffe, J. T., *Puritans in Conflict* (1988).

—— *The Puritan Gentry* (1984).

—— *The Yorkshire Gentry from the Reformation to the Civil War* (1969).

Clutterbuck, R., *The History and Antiquities of the County of Hertford*, 3 vols (1815–27).

Collier, C. V., *An Account of the Boynton Family* (Middlesborough: 1914).

Cozens-Hardy, B., 'The Norwich Chapelfield House Estate since 1545 and Some of its Owners and Occupiers', *Norfolk Archaeology*, xxvii (1941).

Cragg, G. R., *Puritanism in the Period of the Great Persecution 1660–1688* (1957).

—— *The Church and the Age of Reason (1648–1789)* (1966).

Dale, Bryan, *Yorkshire Puritanism and Early Nonconformity* (Bradford: 1909).

Dalton, Charles, *History of the Wrays of Glentworth, 1523–1852*, 2 vols (1880).

Dictionary of National Biography.

Eales, Jacqueline, *Puritans and Roundheads* (Cambridge: 1990).

Earwaker, J. P., *East Cheshire: Past and Present*, 2 vols (1877, 1880).

Eliott-Drake, Lady, *The Family and Heirs of Sir Francis Drake*, 2 vols (1911).

Foster, J. (ed.), *Alumni Oxonienses: the Members of the University of Oxford, 1500–1714*, 4 vols (1892).

G. E. C. (ed.), *Complete Baronetage*, 6 vols (Exeter: 1900–9).

—— (ed.), *The Complete Peerage*, 13 vols (Exeter: 1910–59).

Green, I. M., *The Re-establishment of the Church of England, 1660–1663* (Oxford: 1978).

Halley, Robert, *Lancashire: Its Puritanism and Nonconformity* (1872).

Harcourt, E. W., *The Harcourt Papers*, 14 vols (1880–1905).

Harris, T., Seaward, P. and Goldie, M., *The Politics of Religion in Restoration England* (Oxford: 1990).

Hart, W. G. (ed.), *The Register of Tonbridge School from 1553 to 1820* (1935).

Hayton, David, 'Moral Reform and Country Politics in the Late Seventeenth-Century House of Commons', *Past and Present*, no. 128 (1990).

Helyar, H. A., 'The Arrest of Colonel William Strode of Barrington, in 1661', *Somersetshire Archaeological and Natural History Society*, xxxvii (1891).

Henning, B. D. (ed.), *The History of Parliament: The House of Commons 1660–1690*, 3 vols (1983).

Horwitz, Henry, *Parliament, Policy and Politics in the Reign of William III* (Manchester: 1977).

Hunter, Joseph, *South Yorkshire: The History and Topography of the Deanery of Doncaster*, 2 vols (1828).

Hutchins, John, *The History and Antiquities of the County of Dorset*, 4 vols (1861–73).

Hutton, Ronald, *The British Republic 1649–1660* (1990).

—— *The Restoration, A Political and Religious History of England and Wales 1658–1667* (1985).

Irby, P. A., *The Irbys of Lincolnshire and the Irebys of Cumberland*, 2 vols (1938).

Ketton-Cremer, R. W., 'The Rhyming Wodehouses', *Norfolk Archaelogy*, xxxiii (1965).

Lacey, Douglas R., *Dissent and Parliamentary Politics in England, 1661–1689* (New Brunswick, NJ: 1969).

Lipscomb, George, *The History and Antiquities of the County of Buckingham*, 4 vols (1847–51).

Longden, H. I., *Northamptonshire and Rutland Clergy from 1500*, 15 vols (Northampton: 1938–43).

McInnes, A., *Robert Harley, Puritan Politician* (1970).

Matthews, A. G., *Calamy Revised* (Oxford: 1934).

Moller, F. S. (ed.), *Alumni Felstedienses* (1931).

Nichols, John, *The History and Antiquities of the County of Leicester*, 4 vols (1795–1811).

Nuttall, G. F. and Chadwick, Owen, *From Uniformity to Unity, 1662–1962* (1962).

Ormerod, George, *The History of the County Palatine and City of Chester*, 3 vols (1875–82).

Parker, Irene, *Dissenting Academies in England* (Cambridge: 1914).

Pevsner, N. and Radcliffe, Enid, *The Buildings of England: Cornwall*, 2nd edn (1970).

Rouse-Ball, W. W. and Venn, J. A., *Admissions to Trinity College, Cambridge*, 5 vols (1913–16).

Royal Commission on Historical Monuments (England). An Inventory of the Historical Monuments in Buckinghamshire, 2 vols (1912).

Royal Commission on Historical Monuments (England). An Inventory of Historical Monuments in Dorset, vol. 2, *South East*, 3 parts (1970).

Rubini, D., *Court and Country, 1689–1702* (1968).

Ryland, J. W., *Records of Wroxall Abbey and Manor, Warwickshire* (1903).

Shaw, W. A., *A History of the English Church, 1640–1660*, 2 vols (1900).

Spalding, Ruth, *The Improbable Puritan. A Life of Bulstrode Whitelocke, 1605–1675* (1975).

Spurr, John, *The Restoration Church of England, 1646–1689* (New Haven, CT: 1991).

Toulmin, Joshua, *An Historical View of the State of the Protestant Dissenters in England* (1814).

Underdown, David, *Pride's Purge* (Oxford: 1971).

—— *Royalist Conspiracy in England, 1649–1660* (New Haven, CT: 1960).

—— *Somerset in the Civil War and Interregnum* (Newton Abbot: 1973).

Ven, J. and J. A. (eds), *Alumni Cantabrigienses. A Biographical List of all Known Students, Graduates and Holders of Office at the University of Cambridge, from the Earliest Times to 1751*, 4 vols (Cambridge: 1922–7).

Verney, Frances P. and Margaret M., *Memoirs of the Verney Family During the Seventeenth Century*, 2 vols (1907).

Victoria County History, various counties.

Vulliamy, C. E., *The Onslow Family 1528–1874* (1953).

Watson, A. G., *The Library of Sir Simonds D'Ewes* (1966).

Watts, M. R., *The Dissenters from the Reformation to the French Revolution* (Oxford: 1978).

Wilson, Walter, *The History and Antiquities of Dissenting Churches and Meeting Houses in London, Westminster, and Southwark*, 4 vols (1808–14).

Woolrych, Austin, *Commonwealth to Protectorate* (Oxford: 1982).

Worden, Blair, *The Rump Parliament 1648–1653* (Cambridge: 1974).

INDEX

Abdy, Sir Anthony 198
Addison, Joseph 91
Addison, Lancelot, Dean of Lichfield 91
Ainsworth, – 132
Alderley, Cheshire 134
Aldwark Hall, Yorkshire 221
Aleppo 106
Alsop, Vincent 196
Alston: Lady Elizabeth 59, 83, 134; Lady Temperance 59–60; Sir Rowland 59–60, 124; Sir Thomas 16, 17, 59, 83, 124, 134, 155, 206; Thomas 155
Amsterdam 150, 159
Anabaptists 6, 185, 186
Angier, John 134–5
Angier, Samuel 160, 194–5, 211, 260
Anglesey, Countess of see Annesley, Elizabeth
Anne, Queen of England 64
Annesley, Elizabeth, Countess of Anglesey 110
Annesley, Samuel 196
Archer, Benjamin 124, 227
Archer, Isaac 92–3
Arches, Court of 47
Arlesey, Bedfordshire 92
Arminianism 153
Armyne: Eure 52; Lady Anne 110; Lady Mary 47, 52, 110, 118, 175, 206; Sir Michael 51¬2; Sir William (1953–1651) 3, 47, 51–2, 243; Sir William (1622–58) 51–2; Theophilus 51
Ashburnham, John 37
Ashe, Derbyshire 237
Ashe, John 132, 217

Ashe, Mary 180
Ashe, Simeon 5, 12, 90
Ashley Cooper, Sir Anthony, Earl of Shaftesbury 127, 177, 182
Ashurst (or Ashhurst): family of 75, 76; Henry 96, 118, 174, 204, 206–7; Joseph 160; Judith 118; Lady Diana 89, 118, 242; Sir Henry (1645–1711) 76, 89, 105, 117–19, 157, 160, 169, 191, 196, 199, 201, 204–5, 207; Sir Henry (d. 1732) 157, 158, 204–5; Sir William 160, 196, 207
Ashurst, James 92
Assheton of Middleton, Lancashire: family of 149; Ralph 14; Richard 149
Assheton of Whalley Abbey, Lancashire: family of 237; Sir Ralph 88, 143, 207
Assington, Suffolk 116, 215, 236; Hall 116, 215
Attleborough, Norfolk 208
Aubrey, Herbert 179
Aungier, Francis, Lord Aungier 31
Austin, Thomas 219
Ayres, James 225–6
Ayscough, Sir William 207

Backaller, Henry 222
Bacon, Francis 166
Badsworth, Yorkshire 209, 237
Bagshaw, William 71, 74, 88–9
Baldwin, Roger 207
Balls Park, Hertfordshire 55
Bampton, Oxfordshire 151
Baptists 86
Barker, James 171–2
Barlow, Thomas, Bishop of Lincoln 91–2, 207

277

Ormonde, Marquess of *see* Butler, James
Ormskirk, Lancashire 224
Orton Longville, Huntingdonshire, 206
Osborne, Dorothy 13–14, 63
Osborne, Sir Thomas, Earl of Danby 119
Osgodby Grange, Yorkshire 207
Osgodby Hall, Lincolnshire 51, 206
Osterley, Middlesex 54, 238; Park 84, 226
Otefield, John 71, 72
Otes Hall, Essex 220
Oulton, Thomas 101
Owen, John 112, 121, 122
Owthorpe Hall, Nottinghamshire 37
Oxford 183
Oxford, Earl of *see* De Vere, Aubrey
Oxford, treaty of 30
Oxford, University of 8, 9, 64, 91, 99, 113, 127–9, 150, 152–6, 161, 213; colleges and halls: Brasenose 152; Christ Church 155; Corpus Christi 215; Exeter 152, 227; Jesus 204; Lincoln 138, 152, 244; Magdalen College 48, 154; Magdalen Hall 152; New Inn Hall 219; Pembroke 92, 103, 161; St Edmund Hall 155–6; St John's 148; St Mary Hall 99
Oxfordshire 75, 105, 125, 138, 148, 151, 169, 178, 204, 206, 212, 215; deputy lieutenants of 151

Packer, John 70
Paget: Lords Paget, family of 76–8; Henry 157, 161; Lady Frances 76; William, Lord Paget (1609–78) 76, 150, 242; William, Lord Paget (1637–1713) 76, 157, 161, 186; William 157, 161
Palladio, Andrea 170
Paris 64
Parkhurst, Nathaniel 108, 209
Parkinson, James 138
Parliament, of 3 November 1640 (Long) 2, 5, 9, 10, 29–30, 47, 51, 53, 66, 76, 113, 125, 162, 165, 176; Rump 3, 4, 15, 16, 19, 22, 24, 27, 31, 32, 35, 187; of 4 July 1653 (Parliament of Saints) 16; of 3 September 1654 5, 17, 19; of 17 September 1656 17–18, 20; of 25 April 1660 (Convention Parliament) 31–5, 41–3, 179; of 8 May 1661 (Cavalier Parliament) 43, 114–15, 177–9; of 6 March 1679 180; of 7 October 1679 180, 182–3; of 21 March 1681 183, 184; of 19 May

1685 187; of 22 January 1689 192–3; of 20 March 1690 201; of 22 November 1695 201–2; *see also* Elections, parliamentary
Parliamentary statutes: Act of Indemnity and Oblivion, 1660 33, 35, 36, 46; Act of Attainder, 1660 34; Act for confirming and restoring of ministers, 1660 41–2; Act of Uniformity, 1662 43, 44, 49, 52, 62, 70, 87, 90, 93, 99, 106, 113, 123, 127, 142, 147, 209; Five Mile Act, 1665 46, 134, 147, 148; Conventicle Acts, 1664 and 1670 111–12, 114, 115; Test Acts, 1673 and 1678 88, 188, 189; Toleration Act, 1689 158, 192–3, 195–7; Act for licensing and regulating hackney coaches, 1694 250; Act for suppressing profane cursing and swearing, 1695 201; Act for suppressing blasphemy and profaneness, 1698 201–2
Parr, Richard 92, 224
Partridge, John 203, 262
Pasmore, John 8
Paston, Robert, Viscount Yarmouth 180
Peachy, John 219
Pearson, James 112, 116, 149, 226
Peculiars 8, 44, 94, 225
Pedmore, Worcestershire 104, 106
Pelham: family of 148, 165; John 148; Sir John 9, 20, 23, 123, 148, 155, 165, 171, 173, 177, 183, 191, 222; Sir Thomas 7, 16; Thomas 148, 183, 186, 191
Pembrokeshire 130
Pepys, Samuel 28, 29, 33, 49, 62, 109
Percy, Algernon, Earl of Northumberland 16
periwigs 153, 173
Peterborough, Bishop of *see* Henshaw, Joseph and Lloyd, William
Peterborough, Countess of *see* Mordaunt, Elizabeth
Peterborough, Diocese of 93–4; Consistory Court 94
Petherton Park, Somerset 228
Petworth, Sussex 183
Philipps, Sir John 201
Philleigh, Cornwall 46
Pickering: Christopher 85; Lady Elizabeth 33, 62–3, 84–5, 115, 222; Sir Gilbert 3, 5, 16, 18, 21, 24, 33, 34,

Archbishop of Canterbury 91, 97, 157, 183, 207
Titchmarsh, Northamptonshire 62, 63, 84–5, 115, 222; Hall 222
Tollemache, Sir Lionel, Lord Huntingtower and later Earl of Dysart 179
Tomkins, Thomas 142
Tompson, John 43–4
Tonbridge School, Kent 148
Topcliffe, Yorkshire 125
Tories 188, 189, 192, 197
Toulston, Yorkshire 208
Townshend: Mary, Lady Townshend 180; Sir Horatio, Lord Townshend 24, 111, 180
Travers, Elias 130, 208
Tregony, Cornwall 182, 191
Tregothnan, Cornwall 45, 46, 169, 209
Trelawney, Sir Jonathan, Bishop of Exeter 198
Trench, Edmund 140, 223
Trenchard: family of 9, 108; Philippa 121; Sir John 44, 121, 185–7; Thomas (1640–71) 44, 175, 178, 225; Thomas (1671–1702) 225
Trevor, Sir John 8
Tripoli corsairs 73
Troughton, John 148
Tuckney, Anthony 12, 153
Tully, Thomas 155–6
Turner, Francis, Bishop of Ely 104
Tryconnel, Countess of see Fitzwilliam, Eleanor

Usher, James, Archbishop of Armagh 40, 142
Utkinton Hall, Cheshire 117, 134, 169, 193, 194, 211
Utrecht, University of 158, 159
Uxbrige, treaty of 30

Vane: Christopher, Lord Barnard 164; Lady Frances 115, 225–6; Sir Henry 2, 4, 15–16, 19, 24, 27, 33, 35, 115, 164, 225; Thomas 164
Veal, Edward 226
Verney: Sir Ralph 79, 168, 171, 172, 177; Thomas 79
Vernon, Edward 124, 222
Villiers, George, Duke of Buckingham 70
Visitations, ecclesiastical 84, 89, 92–5, 105, 127, 214, 218

Wadley, Berkshire 223, 237
Wakefield, Yorkshire 114
Wakeley, Nicholas 113, 222
Wakes Colne, Essex 214
Wales 102
Walferne, Joseph 107
Walford, Herefordshire 100
Walker: Anna 215; Thomas 116, 215, 236
Walkington, Yorkshire 108
Waller: Lady Anne 12, 54; Lady Catherine 54; Sir William (c. 1597–1668) 6, 9, 12, 15, 16, 18, 22–7, 29–31, 39, 54, 76, 84, 110, 125, 226, 238; Sir William (c. 1639–99) 54, 159, 182, 226, 238; Thomas 54
Wallis, John 161
Walrond, William 111
Walton, Valentine 26
Walton Hall, Lancashire 132, 194
Ward, Noah 226
Ward, Seth, Bishop of Exeter 46, 110–11
Warkworth, Northamptonshire 246
Warren, John, ejected minister 130, 208
Warren, John, nonconformist chaplain 128, 213
Warwick, Countess of see Rich, Mary
Warwick, Earl of see Rich, Charles and Robert
Warwickshire 53, 89, 172, 210
Wase, Christopher 148
Waterstock, Oxfordshire 169, 204, 206; Hall 169
Watson, Thomas 120
Watts, Isaac 122
Weaver, John 196, 197
Wellesbourne, Warwickshire 210
Wells, John 212
Wendover, Buckinghamshire 181, 182
Wentworth, Thomas, Earl of Strafford 2
Wentworth of North Elmsall, Yorkshire: Lady Catherine 226; Sir John 226
Wentworth of Somerleyton, Suffolk, family of 237
Weobley, Herefordshire 198
Werrington, Devon 162
Wesley, Samuel 158–9
West, William 107
West Clandon, Surrey 222; Hall 124
West Drayton, Middlesex 76
Westfaling, Herbert 179
Westhyde, Herefordshire 128
Westminster Assembly of Divines 7, 99